The Life and Times of Little Turtle

THE LIFE AND TIMES OF LITTLE TURTLE

First Sagamore of the Wabash

Harvey Lewis Carter

UNIVERSITY OF ILLINOIS PRESS
Urbana and Chicago

© 1987 by the Board of Trustees of the University of Illinois
Manufactured in the United States of America
C 5 4 3 2 1

This book is printed on acid-free paper.

Library of Congress Cataloging-in-Publication Data

Carter, Harvey Lewis, 1904–
    The life and times of Little Turtle.

        Bibliography: p.
        Includes index.
        1. Little Turtle, 1747?–1812.   2. Miami Indians—
Biography.   3. Miami Indians—Wars.   4. Indians of North
America—Northwest, Old—Wars.   I. Title.
E99.M48L483   1987   973'.0497 [B]   85-28907
ISBN 0-252-01318-2

Frontispiece. *MISHIKINAKWA, The Little Turtle.*
Provenance concerning this portrait is completely lacking. It
is obviously an oil painting based upon the well-known lithograph (Figure 4). It may well convey the most truthful
impression of Little Turtle of any likeness that we have because it agrees more closely with written descriptions than
any other work. Reproduced by permission of the Indiana Historical Society.

Contents

List of Maps and Figures

Frontispiece. Little Turtle (oil painting)

Preface

I SUPPOSE THAT THE NOTION of writing something on Little Turtle must have been somewhere in the back of my head for well over fifty years. It was not until 1978, however, that I began to study the subject with any definite purpose in mind.

Meanwhile, a number of able works had been published by competent historians which greatly illuminated the subject that had long interested me. Bert Anson's well-written and much-needed tribal history, *The Miami Indians*, was published in 1970. In 1971 appeared Paul Woehrmann's thorough and well-documented study of Fort Wayne's early years, entitled *At the Headwaters of the Maumee*. Paul Hutton's admirable article on William Wells in 1978 not only presented new and accurate information but also did full justice to the character of Wells for the first time. Anson, however, deliberately minimized the attention that he gave to Little Turtle in order to avoid overshadowing the history of his tribe, while both Woehrmann and Hutton centered their attention upon Wells rather than upon Little Turtle. It seemed to me, therefore, that a book which focused upon this remarkable Indian chief would be facilitated rather than discouraged by the sterling works of these authors.

The sound and valuable editorial work of Gayle Thornbrough in this phase of frontier history, added to the earlier work of Clarence E. Carter and of Logan Esarey, has provided a solid basis for the extension I have made of the Family Compact existing between Turtle and Wells to cover the years of peace as well as the years of war.

My notes on the documents edited by Esarey and by Carter were made long ago. After the records of the Office of the Secretary of War (Record Group 107) were made generally available from the National Archives, I found nothing in them on Little Turtle that was not already in print. Nor was anything found therein that caused me to modify my conclusions concerning the long controversy waged by Little Turtle and William Wells with the administrators of Jeffersonian policy. I have preferred to cite these documents in their edited and published form, in all but a few instances, because print is more easily read than handwriting; and furthermore, edited, collated, and indexed material is a valuable aid to scholarship. My ancient notes on the Draper Manuscripts, made when they were accessible to me as a graduate student, have been checked against the microfilm copies now available. I have cited the original documents rather than the microfilm, but I have also listed the published versions of several manuscripts.

Although the sources for any work dealing with Indian-white relations are, of necessity, largely white, I have endeavored to write from an objective point of view. Inasmuch as the perspective of Little Turtle and William Wells represents a reasoned position, a middle ground, between white and Indian extremists, it is not surprising to find that their perspective is often substantiated by the verdict of historical investigation.

White territorial advance at the expense of Indians was something the Indians understood, to some degree, for their tribes had been encroaching on each other's territory for centuries. The differences lay mainly in the greater number of whites and in the addition of the concept of individual landownership. Of all the northern chiefs, Little Turtle most clearly comprehended these differences, and only he was fully prepared to make the necessary adjustment. However, he failed to be able to control the adjustment because of the lack of understanding by both his own people and the whites. More particularly, however, this lack of understanding characterized the American government.

Although this book contains all that I have been able to ascertain about Little Turtle, it is not, in the usual sense of the word, a biography. I have called it a "life and times," which I think to be permissible, but it is unavoidable that the emphasis more often falls upon the times than upon the man. For the first half of Little Turtle's life there is virtually no solid information at all. For the years of his military leadership the sources of information are chiefly those of the American government against which he fought. Finally, the correspondence of William Wells with the territorial governor and the secretary of war provide information about Little Turtle from 1795 until his death in 1812. This correspondence represents both white and Indian viewpoints, but it brings Wells to the center of the stage and leaves Little Turtle lurking in the wings. Obviously, in no period of his life can Turtle be made to dominate the scene. It is only at the Treaty of Greeneville and on his second trip to Philadelphia that he can come close to being the focal point of attention. Although I have sought to lessen these difficulties they cannot be completely overcome, and this may be the reason that no one has tried to write a book of this kind. Yet it has seemed to me that such a book is needed in order to do justice to one of the most unusual of Indian leaders.

Part 1, *The Background,* sets the stage for action. The fact that such action is slow to develop renders the stage setting all the more important. After introducing Little Turtle at the height of his fame, the anthropological and historical background of his tribe is sketched. An analysis follows of the historical problems to be solved with reference to his early life, in which conclusions are reached which are often at variance with traditional views. Finally, the advance of the American frontier into the Heartland is outlined so that the reader may understand the external conditions that Little Turtle, equipped only by his native background, had to confront.

Part 2, *The Warrior,* narrates Little Turtle's military career as much from the Miami standpoint as the fact that sources are mainly white permits. Care has been taken to include other Miami chiefs and the chiefs of allied tribes, while at the same time making it clear that Little Turtle was the only leader with a full grasp of the situation.

Part 3, *The Statesman,* begins with the Greeneville Treaty, where Little Turtle shares the limelight only with Anthony Wayne. The remainder of his life is seen largely through the correspondence of William Wells, and I have stressed that Turtle and Wells were of the same mind and worked closely together. Wells was the active partner, Turtle the silent one. Turtle himself was responsible for this because he needed a "front man" he could trust to represent him. Since Wells alone was responsible for the details of his letters, I have tried to avoid a too great attention to these and have endeavored to emphasize the larger issues concerning both men which were of historical significance.

The deaths of Little Turtle and of Wells are dealt with in Part 4, *The Tragedy.* I have compressed the account of the Fort Dearborn massacre in an effort to present it as a climax to the narrative. The appendixes summarize the effect of subsequent events upon the later history of the Miami and give information about the descendants of Little Turtle and of William Wells. Although ancillary to the main theme, this material has an intrinsic interest of its own. It is my hope that the reader will find that this arrangement of materials on Little Turtle and his times sets forth not only the biographical facts but also narrates and analyzes an important segment of early American history.

"First Sagamore of the Wabash," the subtitle which I selected for my book, may require some explanation. Sagamore is an Algonquian word signifying "war chief" or "lesser chief," as distinguished from sachem, meaning "head chief." Little Turtle, who lived on a tributary of the Wabash, was thus a sagamore, Miami speech being an Algonquian language.

In 1946 Indiana Governor Ralph F. Gates created the Council of the Sagamores of the Wabash in response to a suggestion made by Samuel R. Harrell, who had been named a Kentucky Colonel and felt that Indiana needed a similar reciprocal honorary organization. Kurt Panzer joined with Harrell in devising the details. They may have been influenced by the fact that a late nineteenth-century Hoosier senator, Daniel W. Voorhees, had been known as the "tall sycamore of the Wabash." It is more likely that the fact that Governor Gates was from Columbia City, in Whitley County, where Little Turtle was born and resided for most of his life, was a determining factor in their thinking. Whatever its origin, the practice of designating sagamores of the Wabash has been continued by all subsequent Indiana governors (SAGAMORE, 78–79).

My use of the phrase is intended to emphasize not only that Little Turtle was a genuine and original sagamore of the Wabash in the literal sense of the term but also to emphasize his preeminence in both war and peace. His intelligent leadership in waging war and his equally sagacious statesmanship in the maintenance of peace are deserving of more general recognition.

It remains for me to offer some explanation of my interest in Little Turtle, when most of my writing has been concerned with the mountain men of the far western frontier. The earliest of my forebears to settle in Indiana were Thomas Wyatt (1753–1829) and his wife, Nancy Cunningham (1757–1848). These contemporaries of Little Turtle were my mother's great-great-grandparents. Natives of Halifax County, Virginia, they moved to Greene County, Tennessee, after the American Revolution; in 1811, the year of the battle of Tippecanoe, they settled in Wayne County, Indiana. Their son, William Wyatt (1778–1841), settled nearby in 1814; his son, William Merrill Wyatt (1815–77), was the first of my ancestors to be born a Hoosier in the year before Indiana became a state. The land on which the Wyatts settled was a part of "the Gore," a wedge of land ceded by the Miami in 1795 at Greeneville, which was not incorporated into the state of Ohio.

After his father's death, William Wyatt moved to Carroll County in 1831 and bought land along Wild Cat Creek, formerly a favorite hunting ground of the Wea and Eel River Miami. Here, Merrill Wyatt married Martha Dowden (1819–1905). Alston T. Wyatt (1851–93) married Mary Elizabeth James (1852–84), daughter of James C. James (1818–79) and Marcella Wickard (1822–88). The Dowdens, Jameses, and Wickards had migrated from Butler County, Ohio, north of Cincinnati, wherein lay the hunting grounds of the Miami proper, which Little Turtle had tried vainly to keep at the Treaty of Greeneville.

My father's maternal grandfather, John Dow (1812–65), was born in Pennsylvania; when he was twenty-one he bought land in northeastern Clinton County, Indiana. The eastern boundary of his farm was the western line of the Big Miami Reserve. A year later, in 1834, the Miami sold a seven-mile strip on the west side and thereby opened the rest of Clinton County to settlement. By 1839 John Dow had felled trees, built a cabin, and cleared enough land to persuade Lucinda Gordon (1818–97) to marry him. Here, my grandmother, Margaret Elizabeth Dow (1840–1923), was born and in 1862 married Lewis Minnewether Carter (1836–1912).

The Carters, like the Wyatts, were native to Halifax County, Virginia, but had migrated by way of Monroe and Greenbriar counties (now West Virginia) and Highland County, Ohio, having arrived in Ohio about 1839 and in Indiana about 1856. They settled near Forest, in Clinton County, within what had been the Big Miami Reserve and where there was still much land to be cleared. I can well remember a wheat bin in my grandfather Carter's barn constructed from a huge tree trunk that he had cut and hollowed out by burning, much as the Miami had made their dugout canoes.

My grandmother often talked to her grandchildren, and I was probably her most attentive listener. One of her stories concerned her grandmother's family, the Troutmans. Two of her mother's sisters were captured by Indians when they were children; a younger brother had managed to escape: an Indian threw a tomahawk at him as he was running off, and the boy picked it up and threw it back at the Indians; admiring his spirit they let him go. The girls, in time, married Indians. Years later, when they visited Lucinda Gordon Dow, they gave her some baskets they had made and which she kept all her life. My grandmother did not mention the name of the tribe, but the later visit renders it probable that it was the Miami. She only said it was in "the early days," but it must have been between 1784 and 1794, at the time when Little Turtle and his allies were raiding along the Ohio River.

My father, Harry Holmes Carter (1873–1956), and my mother, Martha Frances Wyatt (1882–1933), were married at Forest, Indiana, in 1902 and migrated to Grove, Oklahoma, then known as the "Indian Territory." The death of an infant daughter led to their return to Indiana in 1904. It was owing to this circumstance that I was born a Hoosier on December 2, 1904. When I was nine my parents moved northeast about 100 miles to Whitley County, Indiana. I grew up on an onion farm near Collins, located between the two places that claim to have been the birthplace of Little Turtle. The muck land that I crawled over weeding onions was a swamp in Little Turtle's time, where he doubtless shot arrows at wild fowl, picked huckleberries, or captured turtles. In school I first learned something about the great Miami chief; indeed, several of my schoolmates were of mixed Miami and white blood.

Thus, I once knew very well the geography and topography of the area of which I presently write. Since undertaking this work, my wife and I have visited all of the old Miami village sites and all of the sites of battles in which Little Turtle participated, as well as some in which he did not take part.

In this account I have tried to be factual; where speculation has been necessary I give reasons for my conclusions. All historians are conditioned, to some extent, by race, sex, nationality, religion, class, heredity, environment, and character, as well as other influences. Although historians are obligated by training and by the nature of their profession to ascertain and present the truth, it is always the truth as they see it. I see Little Turtle as a remarkable man, the greatest of his race, and as such I have endeavored to depict him.

ACKNOWLEDGMENTS

For favors voluntarily conferred or cheerfully rendered in response to requests, but too varied to be enumerated or even classified here, I wish to express my gratitude to the following persons: D'Ann Campbell, Stephen Carter, Wyatt and Fern Carter, Lynn Dearman, Ruth Dorrel, Julie Eddy, George Fagan, Mary Eva Hardy, Walter Havighurst, Eugene Holycross, Richard Hufford, Paul Hutton, Donald Jackson, Katherine Kaufman, Mildred Luse, Marianna McJimsey, Kathleen Morris, Garl and Julia Mort, John Murphy, Gordon Palmer, Shirley Pearce, Jacqueline Peterson, Norma Peterson, Helen Pounds, Gerald Rahrer, Ananias Robbins, Franklin Schultz, Luke Sheer, William Sholty, Dwight Smith, Bill Swagerty, Helen Tanner, and Louis Wyatt. For defraying the cost of the first typewritten copy of my longhand manuscript, I wish to express my thanks to Colorado College. And a special thanks to Bruce Buck for the line drawings of the turtle and the crossed tomahawk and calumet which decorate the book.

A NOTE ON EDITORIAL PROCEDURES

It has been my intention to use the spellings Ouiatenon, Kenapakomoko, Pacan, and Mishikinakwa throughout, except where alternative spellings are listed as a matter of information. The historical spelling Greeneville has been used uniformly instead of the modern Greenville; St. Marys, without the apostrophe, in accord with modern geographical usage; Auglaize for the river of that name and Au Glaize to designate the place where the Auglaize River joins the Maumee River. The singular form is used to designate Indian tribes, including the Delaware, even though this is not the Indian name of that tribe. A deliberate decision also has been made to capitalize Heartland, Legion, Family Compact, Harmar's Defeat, St. Clair's Defeat, and Braddock's Defeat.

I have adopted the note system used by Donald Jackson in his distinguished editorial and historical work on the American frontier. Names of authors or key words in SMALL CAPITALS are citations to sources listed in the bibliography; in the case of two or more works by authors with the same surname, numbers have been assigned, as in SMITH (1). When a published work is being discussed, not merely cited, I list it fully by author and title in the notes. A conscious decision was made to omit place and publisher from the bibliography.

Harvey L. Carter
Colorado Springs, Colorado

PART ONE

THE BACKGROUND

1
"The Gentleman of His Race," 1797–98

THE YEAR 1797 was drawing to a close when a party of six weary travelers on horseback made their way slowly into Philadelphia from Pittsburgh. They wore the ordinary garb of the time—round hats, blue coats, and pantaloons—but on their feet were Indian moccasins. Their leader was twenty-seven-year-old William Wells, the white son-in-law of Mishikinakwa, or the Little Turtle, who was himself a member of the party. Turtle was the war chief of the Miami tribe, of which Wells was a member by adoption; their four companions cannot be identified, but they were also members of the tribe. They had left their homes near Fort Wayne in the Northwest Territory in late October and expected to reach Philadelphia a month later. However, they had gone first to Detroit to see James Wilkinson, recently appointed general-in-chief of the armies of the United States. Finding that General Wilkinson was just setting out with his military entourage for Pittsburgh, they decided to travel in his company. Wilkinson, a man who did things in a style that suited his own convenience and pleasure, took over six weeks to cover the 400 miles from Detroit to Pittsburgh. It was cold and often there was snow. Sometimes the encampment did not move at all. They arrived in Pittsburgh in mid-December and from that point the Miami traveled the remaining 300 miles at a considerably faster pace. Little Turtle, at the age of fifty, was troubled by gout and rheumatism, and was in need of medical attention by the time they arrived.[1]

Philadelphia, a city of close to 40,000 people, was at that time the metropolis of the United States. It was not only the scientific and cultural capital of the country but its political capital as well. A matter of unfinished political business brought the small Miami party to Philadelphia. Turtle had come to see John Adams, president of the United States, and he carried

3

with him a letter of introduction furnished by General Wilkinson. Soon after their arrival William Wells delivered the letter to the president, with the result that the Miami delegation was comfortably lodged on Market Street at government expense. It was further arranged that Little Turtle receive medical treatment at once; his interview with the president was to take place after the chief had improved in health.[2]

Who was Mishikinakwa, the Little Turtle, that he should be treated with such consideration? His name had been a familiar one to the American public since the November day over six years earlier when he had administered an overwhelming defeat to the army of General Arthur St. Clair, governor of the Northwest Territory. The defeat is still considered one of the most crushing blows ever suffered by an American army in the field; in actuality, perhaps, it was *the* most severe military reversal American arms has ever endured. To be sure, General Anthony Wayne had restored American prestige in 1794, and peace had been made with the allied Indian tribes. Little Turtle's reputation, however, was enhanced by the fact that he had advocated peace before it came and had made a good settlement, under the circumstances, at the Treaty of Greeneville in 1795. The government recognized, if the public did not, that Turtle's influence was all-important in maintaining the peace which had been achieved. The government also knew that Turtle was the only chief who had shown a desire to cooperate with its plans for converting the Indians from an existence by hunting to one by agriculture. For these reasons Little Turtle was treated as a "Very Important Personage" on the occasion of his visit.[3]

Little Turtle had visited Philadelphia before and had, in fact, been entertained by President Washington, in November 1796. At that time, however, he had shared the limelight with at least a dozen other chiefs of various tribes. Now, little more than a year later, he was a celebrity. For the first three months of 1798 he was lionized by both the public and the government. He had the good fortune to arrive after the excitement of inaugurating a new president had worn off but before the bitter political fight occasioned by the XYZ Affair with France and the passage of the Alien and Sedition Acts had broken out. His was a personal triumph, however, not a political one, for the rest of his life was to be spent in trying to gain the cooperation of the government in his plans to persuade his tribe to learn to become farmers.

President Adams acknowledged General Wilkinson's letter of introduction in a brief note to him, dated February 4, 1798. "I received your favor of the —— of December, by the Miami chief, the Little Turtle, and have received and observed him with attention. He is certainly a remarkable man. He is recovered of the small pox and what is worse, a severe fit of the gout. We shall endeavor to make him happy here, and contented after

4

his return. I thank you for introducing him to me and for the information you have given me concerning him."[4]

It would be of interest to know in what ways John Adams found Little Turtle remarkable, but one must be content with the knowledge that he did so judge him. Our curiosity must also remain unsatisfied about the information concerning Little Turtle furnished by General Wilkinson. The president was mistaken about the smallpox, for Turtle did not have that dread disease. Soon after his arrival in Philadelphia he had been vaccinated by the eminent Dr. Benjamin Rush, at the suggestion of Rush's good friend, Vice-President Thomas Jefferson.[5] One might surmise that Turtle may have discussed the smallpox epidemics, so frequent and fatal in the Miami villages, with General Wilkinson. On December 24, 1797, Wilkinson had written from Pittsburgh to his brother-in-law Owen Biddle, in Philadelphia, suggesting that Little Turtle be introduced to the American Philosophical Society, of which both Rush and Jefferson were members. Apparently Biddle promptly followed this suggestion.[6]

Thaddeus Kosciusko, the Polish patriot and one of several distinguished foreign officers who volunteered their services in the American Revolution, had subsequently put up a gallant fight to preserve the independence of his native country. Wounded, captured, and imprisoned in Russia in 1795, when Poland was partitioned for the third time, he returned to the United States in 1797. His visit coincided with Little Turtle's second sojourn in Philadelphia, and Kosciusko called upon the celebrated Indian chief and presented him with a brace of handsomely mounted pistols, advising him to use them against "the first man who ever comes to subjugate you." But the fighting days of both Turtle and Kosciusko were over.[7]

Gilbert Stuart, the noted American portrait painter, arranged with Wells to have the chief sit for a portrait. It is probable that the government commissioned Stuart, for the painting was to adorn the office of the secretary of war for several years. Unfortunately, it went up in flames when the British burned the capitol on August 24, 1814. A lithograph and a woodcut, reputed to have been made from the painting, are so different that it is unlikely that both were copied from Stuart's original. Although it is a poor piece of work, the lithograph has the best claim to being a copy. No written description of the original painting by Stuart seems ever to have been penned.

While Turtle was sitting for Stuart, an Irish gentleman was also having his portrait painted, and being fond of joking, he exchanged pleasantries, through Wells, with Turtle, who also was a witty conversationalist. One morning when Turtle seemed preoccupied and did not respond to the Irishman's raillery, the latter boasted to Wells that he had won a victory over his opponent. When Turtle was told this, he responded, "He mistakes;

5

I was just thinking of proposing to this man [Stuart], to paint us both on one board, and there I would stand face to face with him, and blackguard him to all eternity."[8]

Still another visitor in Philadelphia during the winter of 1797 and 1798 was Constantin Volney, whose real name was Boisgirais and who was later known as Count Volney. A successful writer on a variety of subjects, he had attained a reputation by his attacks on Jean-Jacques Rousseau. He came to the United States in 1795 with the intention of settling and thus made a tour of the Wabash country, where he was the object of what proved to be groundless suspicion by Anthony Wayne. He had seen 500 Indians in Vincennes, "Weeaws, Payories, Sawkies, Pyankashaws, and Miamis," and had noted chiefly their drunkenness.[9]

In Philadelphia, Volney called upon the famous chief of the Miami and was impressed by his astute observations, his powers of reason, and the quickness of his mind. During January and February 1798 he interviewed Turtle and Wells perhaps ten times. With the exception of his moccasins, Turtle wore conventional clothing, which Wells noted he could not have done at home without arousing the criticism and mistrust of his tribe. Volney commented on Turtle's light skin color, which he said was no darker than his own. With Wells acting as interpreter he learned of the chief's determination to keep the peace and to try to persuade his former warriors to turn to agriculture. Volney related to Turtle the theory that the Indians had crossed the Bering Strait from Asia to America. He was surprised that this did not impress Turtle, who rather wanted to know why the Asians could not have come from Indians who crossed the strait. Volney also asked Turtle whether he thought of remaining in Philadelphia. Turtle responded by asking how he would make a living. Who would buy the bows and arrows that he could make? Volney found it easier to talk with Wells and subsequently seems then to have left Turtle to pull hairs out of his chin and watch the passersby on the street.[10]

With the help of Wells, Volney compiled a short vocabulary of Miami words. Wells drew a rather stark picture of the limitations of Indian life and society, but at the same time he insisted that the Miami were capable of being civilized and had made as much progress as the Cherokee and other southern tribes. He believed that the Indians had become too dependent on the whites for survival. Wells's natural optimism broke through at various points, however, and it is clear that he had cast his lot with the Miami and was hopeful of success in altering their habits.[11]

About April 1, 1798, the Miami delegation departed from Philadelphia, apparently with the belief that complete agreement had been reached concerning the "civilization program" that Little Turtle wished to begin among his tribe. The essential feature was that Wells should have charge of it as

6

Indian agent at a salary of $300 per year. This was never carried out, and it is impossible to determine the reason. Just when the delegation arrived in Pittsburgh from Philadelphia is not known, but once there the group undertook a lengthy stay and did not leave until about May 24. They made certain purchases which were authorized by James McHenry, secretary of war, and facilitated by General Wilkinson. Some of these were personal, such as seven shirts and a pair of boots, a bridle, two pots, and some firearms, plus twelve and one-half yards of calico and two pairs of gloves, which were no doubt presents for the wives of Turtle and Wells.[12] The rest consisted of farming tools which were to be shipped to Cincinnati.

Upon arrival at Cincinnati on May 28, Wells continued on to Louisville for a quick visit to his brother Samuel Wells, returning about June 11. Turtle and his companions found lodging at a tavern and awaited Well's return and the arrival of the shipment from Pittsburgh. Meanwhile, General Wilkinson and his family left Pittsburgh on June 14 and came to Fort Washington, near Cincinnati, on June 18. On the same day there was a delivery at Fort Washington which was marked for "Little Turtle, Miami." It contained "one corn mill and sundries, one box, one small box, one barrel, six horse collars, six pair of chains, six blind bridles, six back bands, six belly bands, two pair plow lines, three pair swingle trees, two ploughs, and one harrow."[13] This list of articles, attested by Captain William Henry Harrison, who commanded at Fort Washington, is evidence that at least as early as 1798, and probably well before, Turtle was earnest in his desire that his warriors learn to become farmers. We do not know what use was made of the equipment, but do know that from this time on Wells and Turtle were unceasing in their efforts to persuade the government to finance "a civilization project" in their charge.

Apparently the group set out for Fort Wayne on June 25, for on that date the tavern keeper rendered his bill for board at $4.00 per week for four weeks for five Indians, or a total of $80.00. The charge for one Indian (Wells) for two weeks was $8.00. The liquor bill amounted to $86.62½ for the twenty-eight days, the daily consumption by the five Indians and Wells being one quart of wine, one pint of brandy, one-half gill of gin, and one-half pint and one-half gill of "bounce."[14] Turtle, Wells, and their companions drank quite moderately, and certainly no more than many army officers and other gentlemen of business and politics of the time, even when the bill was paid by the government.[15] At the same time, it was a sufficient amount of alcoholic consumption not to have done Turtle's gout any good. On a later occasion, when Little Turtle was told that the gout was a disease which afflicted gentlemen, he immediately replied, "I have always believed that I was a gentleman."[16]

The glimpses given of Little Turtle by Volney represent him at the height of his fame and mental powers, though somewhat beyond that point in physical health and prowess. However, Philadelphia was not his usual environment, so the view that Volney gives of Turtle is neither typical nor complete. That Little Turtle was a brave man requires no proof, but perhaps it would not be amiss to mention some other traits or attributes of his character.

Little Turtle was an intelligent man, for he planned carefully and executed ably the strategy and tactics whereby he so signally defeated General St. Clair. He was a humane man, however, for on that same occasion he called off the pursuit of the fleeing enemy, believing that enough men had been killed.

He was an eloquent man, skilled in oratory and debate in the Indian fashion and thus able to dominate the other chiefs assembled at Greeneville to fashion a treaty of peace. He was also an honorable man, for having signed the treaty he never wavered in his support of what had been agreed upon. As this was by no means true of all the chiefs who signed, his position earned for him, at the time of his death, the tribute of many whites.

Turtle was adaptable and readily learned to wear the clothing and to eat the food of white men; furthermore, he learned their manners so well that his behavior was much admired. Yet he was also determined once he had made up his mind to a course of action, as seen in his steadfast adherence to the plan for civilizing his tribe.

He was a subtle man, as when he craftily resigned his command before the battle of Fallen Timbers in favor of his chief critic and rival, Blue Jacket. His shrewdness gained an annuity for the Eel River Miami, as well as for the Miami proper, the Wea Miami, and the Piankashaw Miami, when more populous tribes had to be content with a single annuity.

The chief was a sociable man, fond of good conversation, good food, good wine, and affable and witty companionship. On the other hand, he was independent and did not fear to champion unpopular opinion, even if it isolated him and deprived him of followers. If convinced he was right he was a solitary tower of strength.

In his relations with others, with whom he might differ, Turtle was tolerant and did not seek to supplant established authority. The record of his friendship with Wells reveals no instances of fault finding or reproach that either man made toward the other. Yet he could be arbitrary, as, for example, his efforts to prohibit the sale of liquor to Indians though a moderate drinker himself.

The plan of Little Turtle to finance the civilization of his tribe through the gradual sale of their great landed possessions underscored his practicality. These possessions had been confirmed to the Miami through his own foresight in asserting a broad claim of tribal ownership. Yet below the surface he was a sentimental man, or perhaps it would be more accurate to say he had a sense of history, for he wished to retain, restore, or rebuild for his tribe the former glory of Kekionga. On behalf of his grandchildren, the children of William Wells and Sweet Breeze, he planned the ownership of Pickawillany, the spot where he had passed his earliest years.[17]

John Johnston, the inveterate enemy of Wells, was no great friend or admirer of Little Turtle during his lifetime. Years after Turtle's death, however, Johnston paid him a supreme compliment when he referred to him as "the gentleman of his race."[18] Even today, though proud of him as a war chief, the Miami sometimes speak of Little Turtle as "the gentle chief," remembering his plans for coexistence with the whites rather than his military leadership.

NOTES

1. JACOBS (1), 166.

2. VOLNEY, 357–58.

3. These matters and others in this chapter that are treated fully later in this work will not be footnoted here.

4. WILKINSON, II, 154.

5. SHEEHAN (1), 230.

6. JACOBS (1), 166–67. Wilkinson had been proposed for membership in the American Philosophical Society and was elected on January 18, 1798.

7. DRAKE (2), Book 5, 57.

8. Ibid., 57–58. Harrison's biographer, Moses Dawson, seems to have been the ultimate source of this anecdote and was responsible for the rather stilted language in which it was told. The Miami vocabulary compiled by Bussard does not lack for scatalogical terms, the use of which is probably meant by the term "blackguard."

9. VOLNEY, 354. Volney wrote, after visiting Vincennes, "They will hold the cup with both hands like monkies [*sic*], burst into unmeaning laughter, and gargle their beloved cup to enjoy the taste of it the longer; hand about the liquor with clamorous invitations, bawl aloud at each other, though close together, seize their wives and pour the liquor down their throats, and, in short, display all the freaks of vulgar drunkenness. Sometimes tragical scenes ensue: they become mad or stupid, and falling in the dust or mud, lie a senseless log till next day. We found them in the streets by dozens in the morning, wallowing in the filth with the pigs. It was rare to pass a day without a quarrel, by which about ten men lose their lives yearly."

10. Ibid., 357, 365, 375–76. Turtle told Volney that he had seen Spaniards in Louisiana and saw no difference between their skin color and his own. By this it should not be concluded that Turtle had been to New Orleans; he had been in the portion of Louisiana near St. Louis only.

11. Ibid., 373–74, 381. Volney had met Wells in Detroit and believed that he was the only man in America who could be trusted to help him compile an Indian

language vocabulary. Having had to leave Detroit before the compilation could proceed, Volney was delighted to have a second opportunity in Philadelphia, where Turtle could verify Wells's information. Many of their meetings were devoted to this task.

12. JACOBS (1), 171. Jacobs draws the unwarranted conclusion from the purchase of the calico and gloves that Little Turtle's wife was a member of the party.

13. NORTHWEST. This interesting document is quoted with permission of the Indiana Historical Society Library.

14. JACOBS (1), 170. Certain dates have been inferred from the date of this bill and the fact that it covers twenty-eight days. The bill itself states both the total amount and the equivalent amount per day for the whole party.

15. ESAREY, I, 29. Harrison to Dearborn, July 15, 1801. See also DAWSON, 10–11. Harrison estimated that each of 600 "Wabash Indians" consumed 100 gallons of liquor annually, or 8⅓ gallons per month. The per capita consumption of Little Turtle's party for twenty-eight days was 2⅓ gallons, half of which was wine.

16. HOPKINS, 53–54.

17. These observations have not been documented here because they are more fully treated and documented later in this work.

18. KNAPP, 361.

2

Some Miami Customs and Traditions, 1658–1790

THE FIRST WRITTEN MENTION of the Miami was in 1658 by Gabriel Druillettes, who called them Oumamik, which is usually said to be a Chippewa term meaning "the peninsula dwellers." The explanation does not make sense, for the Miami did not dwell on any peninsula but rather in a crescent at the lower end of Lake Michigan. It is also said to have meant "the pigeon people" from the Miami word *memiah,* meaning "pigeon." This suggestion also makes no sense, because the pigeon was not the totem of any of the divisions of the Miami tribe, nor of the tribe as a whole. The French were writing the word as Miamiouek by 1670 and Miamis by 1681. Altogether there are thirty-four variants of the name.[1]

Thomas Forsyth, an early American trader and agent to the Sauk and Fox, referred to the fact that the Miami and the Illinois were formerly one people, which he called "the great Ninneway Nation." This suggests the possibility that Miami and Illinois are different versions of the same word, *ninneway,* or some variant thereof. If so, the true meaning would seem to have been "the people," a common designation of primitive tribes for themselves in all parts of the world.[2]

Gabriel Druillettes in 1658 also designated the Miami as Outitchakouk, meaning "the crane people." This is the name of the leading division of the Miami, rendered by other French writers as Tchiduakouingoues or Atchatchakangouen, and is derived from the Miami word for crane, which is written as *tshetshahkuoh* or *atchitchak.*[3] The crane (Latin, *grus;* French, *grue*) was probably the slate-colored sandhill crane, not the somewhat larger white whooping crane. The sandhill crane, however, is about three feet, eight inches in height, a stately bird that often engages in an eccentric dance, bowing with elaborate courtesy, leaping exuberantly into the air, half spreading its wings, and generally comporting itself in a manner at odds with its habitual dignity. It spent the warmer months in the marshy meadows of northwestern Indiana and flew off to Florida for the colder portions of the year.[4] In the middle of the eighteenth century some French writers referred to the Atchatchakangouen Miami as "la Nation de la Grue."[5]

The first reference to the Miami by the English was made in 1728 in the records of the colony of Pennsylvania, where they were called "the Naked Indians." The Miami were not more naked than their neighboring tribes, and this designation probably merely reflected the fact that French traders had less clothing and cloth available for use in the Indian fur trade than was supplied by British merchants to their colonies. After 1748 Pennsylvania records refer to the Miami as the Twightwees, a name apparently introduced by the Pennsylvania Dutch trader Conrad Weiser, who may have learned it from the Iroquois. The term is said to have been derived from the alarm cry of the sandhill crane, or alternatively from an Algonquian word, *tawa*, meaning "naked."[6] These explanations have about equal plausibility. Whatever the origin of the various names, readers as well as writers may consider it fortunate that the name Miami survived rather than Twightwee or Atchatchakangouen. English and American usage adopted the French spelling of Miami but altered the pronunciation from Me-aw'-me to Mi-am'-e.

Only the Atchatchakangouen Miami were "the crane people"; each of the other five Miami divisions or bands had its own totem. When Little Turtle signed an agreement among the various tribes opposing the Americans, which had been drawn up by the British at Au Glaize in 1793, he made a drawing of a turtle. In other words, he used his clan totem, as signatories of other tribes did.[7]

The earliest French writers were so impressed by the deference shown to the Atchatchakangouen head chief by the head chiefs of the other Miami divisions that some scholars have speculated that "the crane people" derived some of their ceremonial powers from the Mound Builders, whom they replaced. All opportunity to substantiate the truth of such speculation disappeared in 1790, when the Harmar expedition destroyed Kekionga and with it two large chests of historical reminders the Miami used when they wished to recite their past.[8] It is unlikely that the Miami possessed any record comparable to that of the Walam Olum or Red Score of the Delaware tribe.[9]

The six divisions of the Miami were further divided into a number of clans, each with a separate totem indicating that all members of a given clan were related. Although knowledge on this subject is far from complete, it is probable that there were originally three clans in each of the six divisions, or a total of eighteen clans, and each clan had its own chief.

Large villages might have all three clans represented in considerable numbers; small villages probably were composed of but one clan. There were village chiefs as well as clan chiefs. A clan member could not marry within his or her own clan, and all children belonged to the clan of their father. The wife in a Miami family was thus always an outsider, retaining membership in the clan into which she had been born. Definite bilateral tendencies existed in the Miami kinship system, however, despite its marked patrilineal character.

Chieftainships were hereditary, though a chief's successor was not his own son but the son of his sister. If several sisters of a chief had sons, then his successor might be the one who was put forward for public acknowledgment by his mother at the proper time. Once the successor was so acknowledged he served as a sort of deputy chief, until such time as the old chief died. This system had the advantage of preventing young children from becoming chiefs. It also passed the chieftainship of a village or of one of the six Miami bands from one clan to another since the successor was a member of his own father's clan and not that of his uncle, whom he succeeded.[10]

The Miami system of kinship terminology was further complicated, however, by the fact that it took no account of generations. All patrilineally related women of whatever generation were referred to by the same term, and this usage was extended to their children as well. An eighteenth-century French account stated, "I have seen men of 80 claim that young girls were their mothers." Henry Hay, in 1790, reported that Chief Le Gris referred to his grown son as "my brother and old play fellow" and to his deceased only daughter as "my very great friend."[11]

The head chief of a Miami band possessed the authority to make decisions for the good of the band. He was also the village chief of the largest village. Lesser village chiefs had the same civil and administrative powers for their villages that the head chief held for the band as a whole. The civil chiefs were given meat and furs and spoils of war by members of the tribe, but they did not gain much by this personally for their property was available to any needy tribal member. The head chief was not permitted to join war parties. A small group of young men attended him when he traveled, which might be frequently or for extended periods of time, for it was his function not only to maintain good relations with the other Miami bands but also to provide alternatives during war against the possibility that the war was unsuccessful. On occasion a head chief might establish a village near a tribe or white trading or military post with which he might be conducting negotiations. In short, diplomacy was largely in the hands of the Miami head chiefs.

13

The war chiefs had ritual functions as well as military ones. They were responsible for the waging of war, but they did not have the power to initiate war or to make peace without a vote of the tribal council. This council was composed of all chiefs, who gathered for meetings and public occasions at the large council house in the head chief's village.

Miami female chiefs functioned among the women as organizers and supervisors of feminine affairs. They could not prevent a war, but they had the power to stop one which they no longer wished to support. Occasionally women had visions which directed them to accompany war parties, and this was usually permitted by the war chiefs.

The Miami, unlike many tribes, did not carry on protracted wars with their nearest neighbors. In the eighteenth century they warred habitually with more distant foes such as the Sioux, the Pawnee, the Chickasaw, the Choctaw, the Cherokee, and the Iroquois. These wars were more in the nature of raiding parties than full-scale wars. Secrecy and surprise were essential to success in such operations. Ritual war dances formed a part of their preparation; feasts and dances were held to celebrate victories.

Despite the existence of these various governmental functions the Miami were a highly individualistic people. Individuals were seldom prevented by force from doing anything they wished. What someone might chose to do was not the result of deliberate planning to any great extent but rather was a matter of impulse or of obedience to some communication with the spirit world, in which he or she had implicit faith. It is in this respect that Little Turtle was exceptional, for he was accustomed to planning ahead far more than most of his tribe, including those who were in positions of responsibility. He may have been impelled in this direction by his observation of white society.

The Miami religion was filled with the practice of magic to such an extent that the tribe appeared to some whites to be more superstitious and less susceptible to conversion to Christianity than other tribes. There was a Medicine Society which practiced ritual cannibalism. Little Turtle was credited by Lewis Cass and Henry Schoolcraft with having been the greatest influence toward bringing this practice to an end.[12] The Miami do not seem to have utilized religious ritual very much to ensure good harvests or a favorable outcome to their hunting. However, they did use ritual in connection with warfare, insofar as the tribe was concerned.

Their control of the portage and other key locations along the Maumee-Wabash line accounts for the ability of the Miami to maintain an ascendancy over their more numerous neighbors for so long. News traveled along this line and frequent meetings were convened at Ouiatenon and Kekionga. The Miami did all they could to enhance the image of natural superiority they enjoyed as a result of their superior location.[13]

14

Some Miami Customs and Traditions, 1658–1790

In common with other primitive peoples, the Miami prepared their children for becoming men and women and marked this event with elaborate ceremony. A Miami boy knew exactly when he became a man, and he was henceforth expected to act like one. For a woman, adult life meant motherhood; to be a man meant being a hunter and a warrior. Men cleared land, made tools, weapons, and dugout canoes, hunted, fought, and engaged in politics and religion. Women were not excluded from the latter two activities but were less concerned with them than were the men. Women planted and worked the fields, transported burdens, made clothing and wove cloth of buffalo hair, wove baskets and fashioned pots, cooked and cared for children. The division of labor was fairly rigid but not absolute; for example, trade was engaged in by both sexes.[14]

Men and women both engaged in the skinning of animals. Men did their own cooking on war expeditions. Children joined men and women to dig roots, pick berries, or catch fish. Both sexes participated in amusements such as dancing, ball games, and games of chance. In mixed ball games women were permitted to do things that were prohibited tó men. In some activities, such as ritual dances, the sexes were segregated.[15]

The Miami did not make birch bark canoes but occasionally used the clumsier dugout canoe, especially for transporting goods. Their usual mode of travel was on foot. When women and children traveled the pace was a slow walk; when war parties moved they did so at a dog trot, usually in single file. Warriors paired off and shared the labor normally done by the women, since the latter did not usually go to war.

Members of a war party slept without posting guards but close enough to one another so that anyone hearing a suspicious noise could alert the next man by touching him. The war chief dispatched scouts, posted his men, and directed and encouraged them up to the time of attack. Once the attack was underway, every man was to fight as if the outcome rested upon him alone. The usual practice was to attack from more than one direction at once. Since the members of a party were usually few in number, an attack was never attempted unless it was believed that victory could be obtained without heavy loss.[16]

Little Turtle's partner in war parties was Makwah, who lived a few miles up the St. Marys River from the head of the Maumee. (Turtle, whose first wife was a sister of Makwah, later married Makwah's daughter, that is, his first wife's niece.) Little Turtle was a master of the type of warfare practiced by his tribe. He alone, among his fellow war chiefs, possessed the ability to command large forces as well as small ones and to extend his military skill to the successful planning and execution of campaigns against the white men. More than most military leaders, even among whites, he had an interest in and an understanding of the problems of peace and a well-conceived plan for dealing with those problems. He was also a skillful and wily diplomat and an orator of first rank among his people.

The Miami seem to have been immune to malaria and other fevers common to the river bottom and swamplands among which they located their villages. These bottomlands along the Wabash and the Maumee were among the most fertile in the world. The Miami women raised beans, pumpkins, squashes, and melons. They were especially famous for their extensive cornfields, which yielded a white ear of corn with softer kernels than the flinty grains of other tribes. They made maple sugar in the early spring and sassafras tea from both the roots and bark of that tree. Hazel nuts, walnuts, hickory nuts, and pecans were gathered in the fall; wild strawberries, raspberries, blackberries, dewberries, and huckleberries were plentiful in early summer. The women also collected many roots for use in cooking, such as the wild potato, the wild onion, and the root of the pond lily.

The Wabash and its tributaries abounded with bass, pike, catfish, red-horse, and many other kinds of fish. The small lakes of northern Indiana teemed with the small but delectable bluegill. Swamplands were filled with turtles; marsh-dwelling birds and all kinds of waterfowl were found there also in great numbers. The Miami were well nigh omnivorous and seem to have eaten all birds except the crow, the raven, and the loon. Having no regular meals, they ate when they were hungry, if food was available; if not, they scrounged for it or did without eating for a while.[17]

It is a mistake to think of the homeland of the Miami as either a trackless wilderness or an impenetrable thicket. Although all of Ohio and Indiana, up to and in places beyond the Wabash River, and the southern third of Illinois was forested land, it was interlaced with a network of well-trodden paths that would rival the network of improved highways by which automobiles traverse the region today. Furthermore, there were small natural prairies within the woodland. The upper two-thirds of Illinois, except for the land bordering the Illinois and Rock rivers, was a vast prairie, which began in northwestern Indiana and continued across the Mississippi River to embrace all of Iowa and small strips of northern Missouri and southern Minnesota. The Grand Prairie was filled in summer with waving grass and blooming flowers as far as the eye could see. Just as the forested land had its small prairies, called oak openings, so the Grand Prairie had its occasional groves of oak, beech, or walnut trees.[18]

The Miami built their villages in the woodlands on freshwater lakes and rivers, where they dwelt for eight months of every year. There were paths following along the rivers on both sides; paths connecting the villages by the most direct possible route; great war paths leading to distant tribes; and paths to white trading posts and other natural meeting places, such

16

as the Falls of the Ohio, and Chicago, Kekionga, and Detroit. The forested land was their summer hunting preserve, extending from the Wabash to the Ohio, with no villages in between until the Miami allowed the Delaware to settle at Muncie Town and Anderson Town. There was big game in the form of deer, elk, and bear, and small game such as raccoons, opossums, woodchucks, rabbits, and squirrels.

When the winter approached, however, the Miami did not simply tighten their belts and prepare for a period of scarcity. Instead, they migrated to the Grand Prairie where the buffalo spent the winter and, camping among the animals, slaughtered all they needed for food and clothing. They emerged from the winter better fed than at any other time of the year. They had to share the buffalo hunt with other tribes who had moved into the Grand Prairie, but they were able to keep their ancient hunting rights intact by their annual pilgrimage. The nearest spot for the Atchatchakangouen Miami to maintain their winter hunting grounds was sixty miles from Kekionga, west by northwest on the Yellow River. If need be they could go further away, even into Illinois. The Ouiatenon and the Piankashaw bands were much nearer a good buffalo supply. The Miami hunted buffalo by setting fire to the prairie grass on all sides of a herd and killing the animals as they stampeded toward a narrow line of escape that had been left unfired.[19]

Like all Indians, in time the Miami made use of horses, but none of the woodland tribes were as changed by this as were the tribes of the Great Plains. Neither in hunting nor in warfare was the availability of horses able to alter a people's habits greatly in heavily forested country. The forests between the Wabash and the Ohio were composed of hardwood trees, the most common being the oak, the elm, the beech, the ash, the walnut, the hickory, the maple, the poplar, and along the streams, the sycamore. Many of these trees reached great age and enormous size. The Miami found ash the best wood for bows and spears, and the hickory was superior for arrows.

By the close of the eighteenth century the Miami had adopted, to some degree, the single-room log cabin for use as dwellings in their villages. However, probably more than half of them clung to the traditional form of shelter, the matted-grass or bark-covered wigwam. It is hard to conclude whether or not the Miami women were good housekeepers; some French travelers were impressed by their cleanliness while others commented on their slovenly habits.[20]

Although the Miami learned about brandy from the French, they do not appear to have been demoralized to any great degree by the use of liquor provided by French traders. At the Carlisle Conference of 1753, the Delaware, the Shawnee, and the Iroquois, who had long been acquainted with and traded with the Dutch and the English, were reported to have been drunk most of the time. The Miami, on the other hand, who had only recently begun trade with the English, were said to have been sober in their behavior and to have displayed a martial spirit.[21] It was not long before the English traders corrupted the Miami with the use of liquor, but the American traders were the most unscrupulous of all in this respect, and the Miami declined rapidly as a result.

Into this society and this environment Little Turtle was born. There is but one certain piece of information concerning his early years: in 1797 he told Count Volney that he knew how to make a bow and arrows, something he surely learned as a boy. Miami men married at about age twenty-four or twenty-five, and women at about age eighteen, so it may be assumed that Little Turtle had been married for eight or ten years by the time he first came to prominence in 1780. He also probably had fathered all his children by that time.[22] He was thirty-three years old in 1780 and half of his life had passed before anything definite is known about it. Ten additional years, from 1780 to 1790, provide but little specific information of a personal nature. It is only from 1790 until his death that information is available such as a biographer might expect to use in writing the life story of the Miami chief. Thus, Miami tribal history and social organization is examined in the hope that some occasional light might be shed upon Little Turtle.

NOTES

1. HODGE, I, 852–55.
2. BLAIR, II, 199–202.
3. HODGE, I, 852–55.
4. The sandhill crane is described in HORNADAY, 256–57.
5. BLAIR. La Potherie used this phrase, meaning "the crane people," in 1753. SABREVOIS (1718) mentioned a division of the Miami called *les gros*. A photocopy of this memoir, furnished by courtesy of the Public Archives of Canada, confirms that it is indeed written *les gros* and not *les grues*. It is thought, however, that Sabrevois compiled his memoir from the reports of others; and if so, it seems probable that he miscopied the word, for no other writer ever mentioned such a division.
6. HODGE, I, 854–55. Forty variant spellings are listed by Hodge for Twightwee. After the name came into general use in the English colonies writers seem to have ceased using the term "the Naked Indians." In the period of the American Revolution, Twightwee gradually was replaced by Miami.
7. Ibid. Some writers have considered this a personal signature, but the identity of his clan totem with his own name was coincidental. Signing with the clan totem was a standard practice.
8. The dependence of the Miami upon such souvenirs as an aid to memory cannot be overstressed. At the Carlisle Conference in 1753, an Oneida chief, Scaroyady, said, "The Twightwees intended to say something to you; but they have mislaid some strings which has put their Speeches into Disorder; these they will rectify

and speak to you in the afternoon." See SHEEHAN (1), 109. The statement that the two chests of belts and pipes were destroyed in 1790 is found in TROWBRIDGE, 10.

9. The Walam Olum of the Delaware Indians was preserved by Constantine Rafinesque, who obtained a copy in 1820 that had originally come from Anderson Town, where the Delaware had been allowed to settle by the Miami. See WALAM OLUM, 243–65. It was in 1820 that the head chief, William Anderson, moved his people beyond the Mississippi. The Miami historical materials were by no means so well organized as the Walam Olum and probably covered a much shorter span of time.

10. See MIAMI, 684, which states that the Miami system of kinship terminology was "of standard Omaha type," a patrilineal system. QUIMBY, 136, is puzzling and confusing in his description of the Miami kinship system. CALLENDER, 610–21, is lucid and authoritative on this subject. Examples of succession to the chieftainship, citing the cases of Pacan and Richardville, will be discussed later in this work.

11. HAY, 222. The quotation from the French writer is in QUIMBY, but the identity of the writer is not given.

12. ANSON, 25. Cass and Schoolcraft visited Fort Wayne in 1821.

13. The position of Ouiatenon and Kekionga with respect to news was similar to that of New York and Washington, D.C., today.

14. QUIMBY, 138; MIAMI, 681–89.

15. TROWBRIDGE, 59–64, gives detailed information on Miami amusements.

16. GUTHMAN, 123–29.

17. TROWBRIDGE, 64–66. See also BARCE, 34–43.

18. DUNBAR, I, 14–23. Indian trails, like animal trails, usually followed the path of least resistance.

19. HAY, 223, 228, 246, 256, indicates that in 1789–90 Pacan was making his winter hunt in Illinois but that Le Gris, Little Turtle, and Tacumwah were making theirs near enough to return occasionally to the Miami villages. It is notable that Tacumwah, Pacan's sister, conducted her own separate hunt.

20. SAVREVOIS (1718) was very favorable in his description of living conditions at Ouiatenon. CHARLEVOIX (1721) was most unfavorable on the same subject.

21. JACOBS (3), 54.

22. TROWBRIDGE, 41–42, describes marriage customs. A man did not marry until he had been on a war party.

3

Some Early Miami History, 1658–1747

To THE LAND lying east of the Mississippi, north of the Ohio, south of the Great Lakes, and west of Pennsylvania, the Congress of the Confederation gave the name Northwest Territory and enacted an ordinance in 1787 to provide a government for it. At that time the Mississippi River was the western boundary of the United States, hence the name was appropriate. The expansion of the United States to the Pacific Ocean and the creation of new states from the Northwest Territory rendered the name obsolete. What had been the Northwest now became the Midwest. Historians, however, used the designation Old Northwest, an excellent term which, although not accurate for the present, still retains historical validity.

More recently, a popular regional historical writer has bestowed upon the lower portion of the Old Northwest the apt name Heartland, a term which recognizes not only its central and strategic placement but also the vital importance that the region bears to the great national body of which it is a part. It is a term deserving of use and one I have adopted here.[1]

The Heartland had been inhabited by the Mound Builders, who made it their home for over 1,000 years. Archaeologists have been able to determine the Adena-Hopewell culture by examination of the artifacts unearthed from the huge mounds left by this Indian people as lasting monuments to their once flourishing, but now vanished way of life. Following the Adena-Hopewell culture, that portion of the Heartland lying in a semicircle about the southern extremity of Lake Michigan was occupied, for perhaps half a millennium, by people of the so-called Fisher culture. This period ended at the close of the fifteenth century, just as the transatlantic voyage of the Mediterranean mariner Christopher Columbus brought the first permanent Europeans to the New World.[2]

20

At about that time an Algonquian-speaking tribe of Indians, known as the Miami, established itself in the location where the Fisher culture had been. By language the Miami were most closely related to the Illinois, whose several tribes dwelt on the river of that name. Culturally they appear to have been similar to the Sauk and the Fox tribes, who resided farther north in present-day Wisconsin. They were certainly less numerous than their more distant relatives, the Ottawa, the Chippewa, and the Potawatomi, who lived still farther north.[3]

In this prehistoric time, before any contact with white people, most anthropologists believe that the Miami were confined to the west, south, and east of lower Lake Michigan. However, others suggest that the Miami spread from this location to the Wabash valley and to the three rivers in western Ohio which bear their name to this day. There are several excellent reasons for believing that they occupied the larger area in addition to the more restricted one near Lake Michigan. Unless the Miami had villages on the three rivers of western Ohio for a considerable length of time, it is hard to explain why these rivers are not called something else. The five-year sojourn of La Demoiselle's people at Pickawillany, to be detailed in the next chapter, is insufficient to account for the permanence of the Miami name in southwestern Ohio.

Even in the seventeenth century, and still more in the eighteenth, the Miami extended permission to certain other tribes to occupy land which they claimed was anciently theirs and which they still claimed to own and hunt over but upon which they no longer resided. At the Treaty of Greeneville, Little Turtle claimed that the Miami owned all of western Ohio, all of Indiana, a strip of eastern Illinois including Chicago, and a strip of southern Michigan. None of the other tribes at Greeneville disputed this extensive claim. In the smaller area around southern Lake Michigan, the Miami controlled three portages, the St. Joseph–Kankakee portage on the east, the Chicago portage at the center, and the Fox-Wisconsin portage to the west. The Miami did not use birch bark canoes; they were walkers who seem to have had a settled policy of controlling portages for the purpose of collecting a toll from the canoe peoples and asserting their tribal claims to lands drained by certain rivers whose portages they held. It is probable that they controlled, in addition, the all-important Maumee-Wabash portage and the useful St. Marys–Great Miami portage, which also commanded the headwaters of the Wabash.[4]

It is, therefore, asserted with some certainty that the Miami occupied the whole of the area until the westward onslaught of the Confederated Iroquois, well armed with Dutch guns, began to be felt about 1653, inaugurating a half century of bitter warfare. The Five Nations of the Iroquois Confederacy did not fight with each other or with the Dutch, who supplied their weapons, but they did fight successfully with everyone else, even holding their own against the French in Canada. In 1645 they made peace with the French, then proceeded to attack their relatives, the non-Confederated Iroquois, including the Neutral Nation, the Tobacco Nation, the Huron, and the Erie, tribes living both north and south of Lake Erie. Between 1649 and 1653 they killed a majority of the members of these tribes and drove the remnant westward, where it survived under the name of the Wyandot.[5] The Miami were the first of the Algonquian tribes to meet the furious onslaught of the Iroquois. Lacking guns, the Miami were driven to Chicago, where their kinsmen, the Illinois, attacked them and drove them into the northwest corner of their territory at the Fox-Wisconsin portage.[6]

Three things enabled the Miami to survive. First, they adopted a policy of mobility. Their Illinois cousins attempted to defend their own palisaded villages but were slaughtered in the absence of La Salle. By the time the Iroquois came against the Fox villages, that tribe had firearms from the French, and the Iroquois were unable to conquer them. The Miami were twice forced beyond the Mississippi, only to be thrown back by the Sioux. Their ability to stick together and move about enabled them to last long enough to resume the fight on more equal terms.

A second factor in the survival of the Miami was the Mohican tribe. The Iroquois seem never to have considered the peaceful gathering of furs, as the Mohican did. The Miami absorbed a considerable number of Mohican hunters into their tribe during the Iroquois wars. The Mohican had been fighting the Iroquois for years and helped the Miami by teaching them to know their enemies.[7]

The third and greatest aid to Miami survival was their contact with the French, who provided them with the firearms necessary to fight the Iroquois on equal terms. Eventually they were able not only to reoccupy their former territory but also to carry the war to New York, where the Miami attacked the Seneca, the western and most numerous of the Confederated Iroquois.[8]

The French first heard of the Miami in 1658, but it was not until 1670 that a French missionary, Father Claude Allouez, visited them at their palisaded village at the Fox-Wisconsin portage. Nicholas Perrot, the trader, came in 1671.[9] Father Jacques Marquette and the trader Louis Joliet hired two Miami guides at the portage as they began their great exploration down the Wisconsin and the Mississippi in 1673. Father Marquette found the Miami to be "the most civil, the most liberal and the most shapely" of the Indians he had seen and was impressed by the respectful attention their warriors accorded his sermons. He observed that the Mascouten and Kickapoo allies of the Miami seemed "like peasants" in the rudeness of their behavior, compared with the well-mannered Miami.[10] Nicholas Perrot remarked upon their keen appreciation of metal and found the women as favorably impressed by iron and copper kettles as the men were by guns and gunpowder. On one occasion he noted that the Miami created a sensation among other tribes by claiming that they knew how to make gunpowder.[11]

Both Father Allouez and Nicholas Perrot reported that there were six divisions of the Miami and that all six bands were in Wisconsin during the earliest years of French contact. Each of these bands had its own chief, but the head chief of the Atchatchakangouen Miami (The Crane People) was deferred to by the chiefs of the other divisions. According to Perrot, on one occasion, when all six divisions traveled from different localities to trade with him in southwestern Wisconsin, the other bands would have starved had not the Atchatchakangouen come in with enough food to feed all of them. The Ouiatenon Miami were second in population and seemed at times to challenge the supremacy of the Crane People. Antoine de la Mothe, Sieur de Cadillac, who admired the Miami, warned that they were threatened with destruction because of the jealousy between the chiefs of the various bands. The Piankashaw Miami and the Pepikokia Miami appeared to have been somewhat more disposed to warfare than the other divisions and, as a consequence, were usually reported to have fewer warriors. The Kilatika Miami and the Mengakonkia Miami are mentioned less frequently by French sources than the other four divisions. All spoke the Miami tongue and could also converse with the Illinois tribes, whose language was very similar.[12]

Naturally, the Miami formed the spearhead of the movement that drove the Iroquois back, for they wished to recover their homeland. In this they were successful, and when Cadillac founded Detroit in 1701 he wanted the Miami to settle nearby. Wary of becoming too dependent upon the French, they declined his offer. A portion of the Fox tribe accepted and moved near Detroit, but only with the intention of killing the French in order to seize their goods. In the war that followed the Miami aided the French and saved Detroit. This was done at the cost of losing the Fox-Wisconsin portage permanently and exposing the Chicago portage and the St. Joseph–Kankakee portage to frequent attack by the Fox. And it was one of the reasons that, early in the eighteenth century, the Miami decided to abandon these two locations, though not giving up their claims to them. The second reason was that New York had passed from Dutch to English control and the English governor at Albany in 1701 had sent overtures to the Miami inviting them to trade there. Although they did send several canoes to Albany loaded with furs in 1708, the Miami refused the governor's offer, as they had Cadillac's proposal for a closer French connection.[13]

What the Miami did was to complete the reoccupation of their former domain by establishing themselves on the strategic Maumee-Wabash line. Having undertaken this maneuver, which forced the French to establish trading and military posts in their two largest villages, Kekionga and Ouiatenon, the Miami sent a delegation to Albany in 1723, inviting the English to send traders to their villages as well. This bold diplomatic move did not work out as they had hoped. Instead of preserving their independence on an equal footing with the French and the English, it opened a rivalry for the control of the Heartland on the part of the two European nations and forced the Miami into an increasingly uncomfortable position. Furthermore, it aggravated the rivalry among the various divisions of the Miami themselves.

The Ouiatenon Miami seem to have initiated the movement, gradually abandoning Chicago and the Kankakee River hunting grounds between 1704 and 1717 and turning a deaf ear to efforts by the French to persuade them to return. Their new location was on the left bank of the Wabash, about six miles below present-day Lafayette, Indiana. In 1717 the French acquiesced and built Fort Ouiatenon on the right bank of the river, opposite Ouiatenon village. This fort was soon garrisoned with ten or twelve men under an officer holding the rank of captain. No doubt the move of the Ouiatenon Miami was regarded as a challenge to their leadership by the Atchatchakangouen Miami in their village at present-day Niles, Michigan, on the St. Joseph River.[14]

The Atchatchakangouen already had a resident French trader at their village in the person of Jean Baptiste Bissot, Sieur de Vincennes. This trader, known as the elder Vincennes, was very popular and consented to move with them to the headwaters of the Maumee, formed by the junction of the St. Marys River with another St. Joseph River at present-day Fort Wayne. Vincennes made the move in 1712 or 1713 with the knowledge and approval of the French authorities at Detroit, but he died in 1719 before a fort and trading post had been erected. In 1721 Fort St. Philippe was built at the junction of the St. Marys and the Maumee and was garrisoned by a small force.

The Atchatchakangouen village known as Kekionga (The Blackberry Patch) was located on the right bank of the St. Joseph River about a quarter of a mile above the junction. In the 1750s another village, that of the younger Le Gris, was established nearly opposite to Kekionga, in the angle between the St. Joseph and the Maumee, and it was here that the French traders lived in later times during the English and American periods of Miami history. The portage to the Little River, a tributary of the Wabash, was only six or eight miles in length, depending on the time of year. Goods from Detroit were brought up the Maumee from Lake Erie.[15]

The Piankashaw Miami moved from Peoria on the Illinois River to the confluence of the Vermilion River with the Wabash, about sixty miles below Ouiatenon. The Kickapoo and the Mascouten, two non-Miami tribes who had long consorted with the Miami, also moved to the Vermilion. About 1732 François Marie Bissot, the son of the elder Vincennes, established a trading post on the lower Wabash at what is now Vincennes, Indiana.[16] The younger Vincennes persuaded a portion of the Piankashaw Miami, including the head chief, La Demoiselle, to move to this location, and eventually most of the Piankashaw moved there as well.

The Pepikokia Miami moved from the Kalamazoo River in Michigan to the Tippecanoe River in Indiana. Their principal village, called Kithtippecanuck, was located on the right bank of the Tippecanoe River, just above its junction with the Wabash. This was about eighteen miles above Ouiatenon. The village was also called Petit Piconne by the French, and the Pepikokia were sometimes referred to as the Tepicon Miami, a name derived from the Tippecanoe River. They also had a considerable village on the upper river, at the west end of Lake Tippecanoe (Bone Prairie). The Potawatomi, who were much more numerous than the Miami, possessed themselves of the Chicago and St. Joseph locations abandoned by the Miami and pressed gradually to the middle course of the Tippecanoe River, dividing the Pepikokia. The Miami at Kekionga did not resist the Potawatomi encroachment but endeavored to retain their claim to the land by maintaining their winter hunt on the Kankakee.[17]

It is not known where the Kilatika Miami and the Mengakonkia Miami were living at the time of the Miami reoccupation of the Maumee-Wabash line. Since there were no French trading posts among them, all references to them in French documents ceased about the time the move was made. This has led to the assumption that they were absorbed by the Atchatchakangouen, often referred to as the Miami proper, an assumption that seems questionable because two well-established divisions would not suddenly disappear, nor would they be absorbed quickly by other bands.

There were two concentrations of Miami on tributaries of the Wabash that have not been mentioned, and it is only common sense to believe that one of these was the Kilatika and the other the Mengakonkia, although it is not certain which was one and which was the other. Because the Kilatika were somewhat more numerous and more frequently mentioned in earlier references, it is more probable that they were the band on the Eel River who were later called the Eel River Miami, but it may have been the other way around. It is known that there was a large village called Kenapakomoko (Snake-fish Town) located on the Eel River, six miles above present-day Logansport, Indiana. The village was spread out for two or three miles along the right bank of the river.[18] The head chief, Kaweahatta (The Porcupine), was a contemporary of Coldfoot and of La Demoiselle, but he outlived them by many years, dying about 1794.

The Mengakonkia Miami were probably those living on the Mississinewa River who had no large village but many small ones. They were an independent band, having once refused their annuities from the American government prior to the War of 1812. This band, the most traditional and the least subject to white influence, was the one into which the famous white captive Frances Slocum married and among which she lived out her days as an Indian.[19]

The trading post at Vincennes was considered to be within the jurisdiction of Louisiana rather than Canada. In 1736 the French authorities in both provinces planned an attack on the Chickasaw tribe, who had disrupted their trade near modern-day Memphis on the Mississippi. French forces from New Orleans did not arrive in time, and the younger Vincennes, with 200 Miami warriors, who formed a part of the Canadian force, suffered a disastrous defeat by the Chickasaw. Vincennes was among those captured, tortured, and killed, as was Denis Drouet de Richerville, grandfather of the later Miami chief Jean Baptiste Richardville (1761–1841), one of several Richervilles who participated in this campaign.[20]

In addition to their heavy loss of lives in the battle, the disaster had important consequences for the Miami. They were now more open to English traders, at first from the Carolinas and later from Pennsylvania. These traders charged only half as much for better goods than the French could supply. The loss of Vincennes, a popular and energetic leader, put the French at a disadvantage in the trade war and led directly to the Pickawillany adventure, as we shall see.

Nearly all American historians dealing with the period of English and American control of the Miami homeland make frequent use of the term Miami Confederacy. It should be apparent by this time that the term is a misnomer, as there was no Miami Confederacy. The term is used because the English traders and colonial officials used it. They were familiar with the Iroquois Confederacy, which banded together five (later six) of the Iroquois-speaking tribes, and assumed that the Miami had a similar arrangement. As the French were well aware this was not the case.

The fact was that the Miami had no governmental union at all. They were united only by a common language, common customs, and, in earlier times, a common deference on the part of the head chiefs of five divisions for the head chief of the Atchatchakangouen division. In later times this deference was preserved only as a diplomatic device to avoid giving a definite answer. In other words, it was a way of passing the buck when dealing with the whites. The Ouiatenon (Wea Miami) and the Piankashaw were eventually recognized as separate tribes by the American government. It is true that the Miami divisions never fought one another, although they sometimes threatened to do so. It is also true that they did not support one another well in war: some divisions might only send a token force of warriors; and, if it was of a mind to do so, each division acted independently of the others.[21]

There is much disagreement over population figures for the Miami. If La Salle's figures for warriors as given on the Franquelin map of 1682 (published in 1684) are approximately correct, there were, in the neighborhood of Starved Rock on the Illinois River, 2,400 warriors representing all divisions of the Miami except the Mengakonkia, compared to 1,200 Illinois warriors.[22] Calculating on the basis of one woman and two children for each warrior, there could have been a Miami population of at least 10,000, but this figure may be too large. Still, the Miami population was larger in earlier times, although since they subsisted more by hunting than by agriculture, as indicated by the large area over which they held sway, they were not as numerous as current revisionists of Indian population figures would have us believe. Their constant wars in the period under study lessened their population, as did the great smallpox epidemics of 1715, 1733, and 1752, which reduced their numbers until there were probably no more than 2,000 in the 1750s when Little Turtle was a youth. By the time he became a war chief there may have been no more than 1,500.[23]

Considering their heavy loss of population, it was an achievement for the Miami to have held the Maumee-Wabash line against the pressure of more populous tribes, and an even more remarkable achievement to have held it against the advancing frontier of white civilization for a long time. That they were able to do so was mainly the work of their great leader Mishikinakwa, the Little Turtle.

NOTES

1. HAVIGHURST.

2. QUIMBY, 72–83, 99–102, map, 109.

3. Ibid., passim. See also HYDE, 57.

4. ASPIA, I, 570–71. Little Turtle's uncontradicted assertion occurred on July 21, 1795. He also stressed the importance of the Maumee-Wabash portage. In addition, to anyone who, like me, was born and raised a Hoosier, who tends to fondly regard his native state through the rose-tinted glasses of James Whitcomb Riley's homespun verse, it is simply unthinkable that there could ever have been a time when the heart of the Heartland could have been uninhabited.

5. The Wyandot were the remnant of the Huron, but there is general agreement that they absorbed survivors from the other non-Confederated Iroquois, especially the Erie. See HYDE, passim.

6. Ibid., 184–85. The Miami struck back at the Iroquois in 1670, immediately after obtaining French weapons. They also aided the Fox in maintaining their location. There is, however, no doubt that the Miami controlled the Fox-Wisconsin portage in these early years.

7. MOHICAN, 205. The Miami appear to have crossed the Mississippi into Iowa about 1661 and again about 1691. See HYDE, 179.

8. HUNT, passim. Hunt demonstrated that the fur trade was the important cause of the Iroquois wars. In my opinion, later explanations that have been offered are less satisfactory. Miami retaliation is treated in GOODMAN, 8–12.

9. THWAITES (2), 204, reports the visit of Father Allouez. For Perrot, see BLAIR, I, 221–23, 231–72.

10. KELLOGG, 323–26. See also KENTON, 340–41.

11. THWAITES (1), XVI, 166–67.

12. Perrot's enumeration of the six Miami divisions occurs in Ibid., XVI, 152. HODGE, I, 852–55, lists 113 variant spellings for Ouiatenon, 45 for Piankashaw, 16 for Pepikokia, 12 for Atchatchakangouen, 5 for Kilatika, and 4 for Mengakonkia. There are fewer variants in the last three divisions because in later times these divisions were grouped together as the Miami (sometimes called the Miami proper). After 1752 the term Miami embraced a part of the Pepikokia band. The Ouiatenon and Piankashaw bands were referred to as if they were separate tribes, which eventually they became.

13. THWAITES (1), XVI, 211–12, indicates that the French were fully aware of English efforts to detach the Miami from their French connection. GOODMAN, 10–11, notes the English overtures from Albany.

14. The Ouiatenon Miami were reported at their Wabash River location as early as 1700, but some were still at Chicago as late as 1718. See THWAITES (1), XVI, 361. They continued to hunt buffalo in winter on their former location even after it was occupied by the Potawatomi. The Ouiatenon villages were south of the Wabash, immediately west of Wea Creek's junction with the river; Fort Ouiatenon was on the north side of the Wabash, about a mile below the villages. See KRAUSKOPF, passim; also OUIATENON, 123–33. The latter is a report on recent excavations on the site of the French fort and trading post. SHEER presents an excellent summary of the available knowledge concerning this tribe in earlier times.

15. WOERHMANN, 1–6. Le Gris's Village has sometimes been mistaken for Kekionga, but the facts stated here are substantiated by Miami legend as reported by TROWBRIDGE, 12. Neither Kinietz in 1938 nor Trowbridge in 1824 recognized Le Gros's reference to The Gray as being the younger Le Gris. ROY, 31–75, is an account of the elder Vincennes.

16. On the younger Vincennes and the founding of Post Vincennes, see PHILLIPS, 311–18. In 1982 the Indiana State Historical Society Library, Indianapolis, acquired a document written and signed by the younger Vincennes "at the post of the Wabash" on October 15, 1732.

17. The Pepikokia at Kithtippecanuck traded at Ouiatenon; those on the upper Tippecanoe traded at Fort Miamis at the headwaters of the Maumee. See BARNHART and RIKER, 122. See also KRAUSKOPF, 220–21.

18. WHITSETT, 72–82, contains some reliable information on Kenapakomoko, despite the erroneous supposition that it was connected in some way with Little Turtle. WINGER (2) deals with the band on the Mississinewa but must be read with caution. It is reasonably certain that these two bands were the Kilatika and the Mengakonkia Miami; it is much less certain which was which.

19. WINTER, 163–80, gives an interesting account of the artist's visit to Frances Slocum at her home in 1839, when he painted a portrait of her with her two daughters.

20. The best account of the Chickasaw campaign is BARNHART and RIKER, 81–90. See also CHAPUT, 112–13.

21. Cadillac referred to the Miami in 1718 as "a numerous nation but much divided by the jealousy of their chiefs" and predicted that "unless they unite they will likely be exterminated, which would be a pity as they are a worthy people." There is no doubt that his observation was correct, but it should be added that the French establishment of trading posts at Ouiatenon and Vincennes, in addition to the one at Kekionga, greatly aided the Ouiatenon and Piankashaw Miami in becoming independent of control by their traditional leading band, the Atchatchakangouen Miami. For Cadillac's prediction, see THWAITES (1), XVI, 213, 361–62.

22. A reproduction of Franquelin's map is found in PARKMAN, 314–15. It may be noted that René-Robert Cavelier, Sieur de La Salle, had found the Miami in Michigan on the St. Joseph River in 1679 and that he also referred to this river as the river of the Miami.

23. GOODMAN, 69–81, reproduces certain letters of Governor Robert Dinwiddie to the Board of Trade in London in 1752 in which he estimated the tribes of "the Miami Confederacy" to number 10,000 warriors. This was a gross exaggeration. Dinwiddie was correct, however, in pointing out that the Miami had the power "to stop, and prevent the French having any intercourse between the Mississippi and Canada." This power derived from their strategic location on the Maumee-Wabash line, not from their numbers.

4

The Pickawillany Adventure, 1747–52

By VIRTUE OF THE FACT that they discovered and controlled the mouths of two great rivers, the French were able to lay claim to all the land that those river systems drained. This was a good-sized chunk of the most valuable land in North America. They sailed their ocean-going vessels up the broad St. Lawrence as far as Montreal and soon learned from the Indians how to get to the four upper Great Lakes by paddling up the Ottawa River and portaging to Nipissing Bay. Once on the Great Lakes it was easy to find various portages which set them upon streams that contributed to the mighty Mississippi, which they followed to the Gulf of Mexico. Thus, they were possessed of a vast territory, scantily populated by Indian tribes eager to trade furs for cloth and metal goods. The result was they were able for a long while to control a vast inland empire from a few trading and military posts with a very small number of traders and soldiers and a minimum of goods and supplies. In the early eighteenth century, however, it became increasingly apparent that the French had spread themselves too thin.

The connecting link between Canada, governed from Quebec, and Louisiana, governed from New Orleans, was the Maumee-Wabash line from Lake Erie to the lower Ohio River, on which the French maintained three trading and military posts among the Miami Indians. The posts were Fort Miamis, located at the portage from the Maumee to the Wabash (present-day Fort Wayne), Fort Ouiatenon, on the Wabash, where the river turns southward and where the Grand Prairie opens to the west (near present-day Lafayette), and Fort Vincennes, on the lower Wabash, where the great buffalo path crossed the river (present-day Vincennes). Because of their great distance from both Montreal and New Orleans, the Miami were less well provided with goods by the French than most of the other Indian tribes, but the fact that the French maintained three posts among them attests to their importance and to their strategic location. The attachment of Fort Vincennes to Louisiana, with the dividing line at Terre Haute, is indicative of the concern of the French authorities for this remote post.[1]

The Miami were aware of the competitive nature of English-French relations and sought to take advantage of it. The French knew of traders from the English colonies on the lower Wabash as early as 1715. There was a more definite report of Carolina traders on the Wabash in 1725, and by 1731 Pennsylvania traders were on the river, with those from Virginia not far behind. There was sufficient penetration of the Wabash country by the time that Fort Vincennes was established in 1732 to warrant the conclusion that it had been founded largely as a counter-stroke to the threat posed by English colonial traders. The French strategy was unsuccessful because the Miami had no difficulty in discerning that English goods were better in quality, greater in quantity, and cheaper in price than French goods. With these three economic factors operating in their favor, the English would have had no trouble persuading the Miami to sever their French connection were it not for the governmental and military presence of the French in their principal villages.[2]

Despite the foregoing facts, a Wyandot chief called Nicholas is commonly credited with having begun the pro-English movement in 1738. His band lived near Detroit, but in 1742 he joined the Wyandot band at Sandusky Bay, where he traded with the English merchants who came there. In 1747 he planned to strike a decisive blow at French control by capturing the fort at Detroit. However, his conspiracy was revealed by a Wyandot woman and the plan was thwarted. Nicholas then joined the Seneca on the Cuyahoga (near modern-day Cleveland), where he died suddenly in late 1747.[3]

Nicholas was, without doubt, a central figure in the pro-English movement, but it may be questioned whether he was the originator of it because his residence near Detroit surely meant that his band was better supplied by the French than the Piankashaw Miami at Fort Vincennes. Their head chief was Memeskia (The Dragonfly), who was called La Demoiselle by the French. This name was no reflection on the virility of "the old Piankashaw King," as the English called him, but a fairly exact translation of his Miami name. La Demoiselle's pro-English leanings surfaced in 1736 when the death of the younger Sieur de Vincennes deprived the Piankashaw Miami of a strong and popular leader. La Demoiselle, known also to the English as Old Briton, was in contact with Nicholas, and their plans were similar and concerted to some extent.

In 1745 La Demoiselle removed his village from the Embarras River near Fort Vincennes and established it somewhere near Kekionga. His purpose was to persuade Wisekaukautshe, or Coldfoot (Le Pied Froid), head chief of the Atchatchakangouen Miami, to revolt against the French and join with him in establishing a village nearer the Ohio River, at some location more accessible to the English colonial traders. This was in accordance with the diplomatic protocol of the Miami head chiefs.[4]

Whether La Demoiselle would have succeeded is uncertain. His diplomacy was cut short by an action taken by the Wyandot chief, Nicholas, who killed five French traders and confiscated their goods on the Sandusky River. Nicholas now had no alternative but to move against Detroit. This move was aborted, as we have seen, but acting on reports received from the Wyandot that Detroit had been captured, the Miami at Kekionga seized eight French traders and burned a portion of Fort Miamis. No doubt the Miami were encouraged by the fact that La Demoiselle had received a belt from the Seneca urging him to kill Sieur Douville, commandant at Fort Miamis. Coldfoot, angered by the false reports from Nicholas and fearful of French retribution from Detroit, refused to break the French connection. La Demoiselle, probably in the late summer of 1747, moved his village to Pickawillany (near present-day Piqua), on the Great Miami River, about ninety miles southeast of Kekionga.[5]

The location of Pickawillany was an admirable one, about 100 yards below the confluence of Loramie's Creek with the Great Miami River. To the west lay a prairie of moderate extent. Trails led up the creek to a portage to the St. Marys River, down which Kekionga could be reached, and up the river to a portage to the Scioto River. This trail continued north to Sandusky Bay, whereas the Scioto led southward to the Ohio River. Twenty miles northwest lay the headwaters of the Wabash. Down the Great Miami but crossing to the Little Miami River (in the vicinity of present-day Dayton) lay the Miami war trail to the Ohio River and beyond the Ohio to Cherokee country. English traders approached by land over this trail.[6]

Prominent among those who joined La Demoiselle in his venture was the Atchatchakangouen Miami war chief Mishikinakwa (The Turtle), together with his wife, a Mohican woman, and their small son, who was less than a year old. This baby bore the same name as his father but was called Little Turtle, to distinguish him from his father. The family had formerly lived in a small village at the west end of Blue Lake, some eighteen miles from Kekionga.[7]

In the following year, 1748, Assepansa (The Raccoon), nephew of La Demoiselle, and Mishikinakwa made a long journey eastward to Lancaster in the colony of Pennsylvania. For five days they met with representatives of the colonial government of Pennsylvania and negotiated a treaty that called for friendship and alliance as well as trade between that colony and "the Miamis of the Wabash." The Treaty of Lancaster was signed by both these chiefs on July 23, 1748. It is interesting to note that they claimed to represent twelve villages of their tribe, although, as we now know, they represented only Pickawillany and its rebellious population, which was not located on the Wabash River.[8]

Nevertheless, it is fair to say that they did not really misrepresent the state of affairs among the Miami villages on the Wabash. French authorities reported that La Demoiselle's move to Pickawillany had thrown the Miami at Kekionga into great disorder. Seeking to counteract the confusion, Coldfoot and Kaweahatta (The Porcupine), head chief of the Kilatika Miami at Kenapakomoko (Snake-fish Town) on the Eel River, journeyed to Detroit in August 1747 with the intention of going on to Montreal. They were forced to abandon their plans for a conference with French governmental leaders, however, by reports that a Mohawk war party was at Niagara. Their prompt action thus came to naught, and the weakness of the French was rather glaringly revealed by their alarm at the Mohawk threat. In 1749, when the news of the Treaty of Lancaster reached the Miami towns along the Wabash, the Piankashaw Miami still near Fort Vincennes moved in a body to the White River, reducing the distance between them and Pickawillany by half. From Ouiatenon and from Kekionga itself a steady stream of Miami came to Pickawillany in 1750 and 1751. In the latter year Christopher Gist visited Pickawillany, in the company of George Croghan, and reported that over 400 families had settled there. Reckoning 5 members per family, it is clear that La Demoiselle's village, with a population of at least 2,000, was the metropolis of Miami country. Trade with English colonial merchants was flourishing. The names of 60 traders are known, and doubtless many of these came to Pickawillany more than once in the years from 1747 to 1752.[9]

French authorities at Detroit, Montreal, and Quebec, well aware of English encroachment, were frantic but powerless. In 1749 they dispatched Céloron de Blainville on his well-known journey to strengthen French claims to the Ohio valley by depositing leaden plates, suitably inscribed, at selected points where tributary streams merged with "the beautiful river." His journey was a diplomatic mission and a military intelligence operation undertaken because the French were not sufficiently strong to send a war party with any hope of success (Céloron himself had declined to lead such a forlorn venture). Céloron visited Pickawillany in mid-September of 1749 but had so little in the way of gifts that La Demoiselle scornfully refused to accept what was offered. Although not positively refusing to return to the Wabash, La Demoiselle would give no firm promise to do so.[10]

Céloron's visit alerted La Demoiselle to the possibility of a French military expedition, however, and in 1750 The Turtle constructed a fort and stockade at Pickawillany. It was a fortuitous move, for in 1751 a party of

Nipissing Indians, led by French officers, made their appearance but judged the fort too strong to risk an attack. They did kill two Miami warriors, however, and in revenge the Miami waylaid two French traders near Kekionga. By early 1752 it was reported that, except for Coldfoot and his immediate family, Kekionga was nearly deserted.[11]

It is hard to say whether Coldfoot was loyal to the French out of principle or whether he was exercising a cautious diplomacy. The Miami seldom committed themselves beyond the point of no return. They had always dominated more populous tribes by their skill at diplomacy as much as by their military prowess. Possibly Coldfoot was simply waiting to see whether the English or the French were the stronger party, which he considered to be his duty to his people. As head chief of the Atchatchakangouen Miami he was first among equals. If the French won his position would be strengthened; La Demoiselle and all the others would come back to the fold. If the English won La Demoiselle and the Piankashaw Miami might become *primus inter pares*. None of this was certain, however, for Coldfoot might simply join his war chief, The Turtle, and claim that he had been with them in spirit all along and was simply doing his duty in providing an alternative in case the anti-French movement failed.[12]

Speculation ended suddenly on June 21, 1752, when Charles de Langlade, a French-Ottawa of mixed-blood, attacked Pickawillany with 30 Frenchmen, 30 Ottawa, and 180 Chippewa from Michilimackinac. His expedition was probably ordered from Detroit, although he seems to have been allowed full discretion as to its conduct. His force passed through Wyandot territory south of Sandusky Bay without being detected, but it is not clear whether he took Pickawillany by surprise or whether he practiced a deception on La Demoiselle. The latter seems more probable, for the Miami claimed later that the full force of 240 appeared suddenly after having sent a small party with wampum belts and a fine French coat as tokens of peace. After receiving the peace tokens the Miami warriors had left on their hunt, according to plan. When the attack came at mid-morning, only La Demoiselle and a few men were at the fort, eight English traders were in the stockade, and the women and children were in the cornfields. Not all the women and children were able to reach the stockade; some hid out along the river. The Miami in the fort held out for several hours, but Langlade persuaded them to surrender the traders in return for which he would break the siege and leave. One trader had been killed, five were surrendered, and the women hid two who later escaped. Fourteen Indians were killed, including La Demoiselle, who, in the words of Thomas Burney, one of the escaped traders, "for his attachment to the English, they boiled, and eat him all up." Over 3,000 pounds worth of goods were found. Langlade's men carried off all they could and destroyed the rest. Because they were so heavily laden with booty and so far from home, they took no women and children as prisoners.[13]

Captain William Trent left Logstown, on the Ohio, a few miles beyond the Forks, on June 21, 1752, the very day of the fall of Pickawillany. On July 20 he arrived at Pickawillany, found it deserted, and took down two French flags, replacing them with the British flag. He had known what to expect upon his arrival for he had picked up Thomas Burney and Andrew McBryer at the lower Shawnee town on the Scioto on July 6. When, on July 29, he arrived back at the mouth of the Scioto, he found La Demoiselle's widow and her young son, Assepansa, La Demoiselle's nephew and successor, and The Turtle, as well as two additional men and a dozen women and children. Doubtless among the latter were Turtle's wife and his five-year-old son, Little Turtle.[14]

Captain Trent made them some handsome presents, urging them to hold fast to their "chain of friendship" with the British. This they endeavored to do, for Assepansa and Turtle were among the Miami who attended meetings at Carlisle, Pennsylvania, and Winchester, Virginia, in 1753. The legislatures of those colonies voted 200 pounds each to the Miami to assuage their feelings over the Pickawillany disaster. Pennsylvania also voted 600 pounds for "necessities," the Quaker euphemism for military supplies. Governor Dinwiddie wrote a letter to the Board of Trade in London stressing that the Miami were in a position to sever communications between Canada and Louisiana along the Wabash line. It was all to no avail. The French were able to prevent Captain Trent's attempt to build a fort at the Forks of the Ohio. They built Fort Duquesne there instead and garrisoned it in the spring of 1754.[15]

For the Miami the lesson of Pickawillany was clear: the French connection was stronger than the British "chain of friendship." At the close of 1752 the Miami sent a present of two English scalps to the governor of Canada as a token of their repentance; however, they continued also to trade with the English. When in the spring of 1753 the French appeared on Lake Erie with several *batteaux* filled with troops, the Miami, along with other tribes, sent representatives to Montreal and made formal apology and submission to the French. When the British sent a strong force under General Braddock to retrieve the Forks of the Ohio, he was defeated within seven miles of Fort Duquesne by a small French force and a large assemblage of Indians. Langlade commanded the northern Indians and De Ligneris, who had been transferred from Fort Ouiatenon to Fort Duquesne, was joined by a tremendous number of the Wabash Indians. At Braddock's Defeat there were Indians present even from beyond the Mississippi.[16]

Less well known but equally impressive was the raid into Virginia made in June 1756 by the Sieur de Bellestre, commandant at Fort Miamis. With

25 French and over 200 Miami, Bellestre spread terror throughout the Old Dominion. The force killed or captured nearly 300 Virginians at the headwaters of the James River, slaughtered hundreds of cattle, and carried off untold booty on 120 pack horses.[17]

Although Assepansa and The Turtle returned to their respective homes in 1752, there is evidence that it was not until 1763 that the Miami completely abandoned Pickawillany. The Shawnee chief Black Hoof recalled a battle which took place at Pickawillany in 1763 between the Miami and the Wyandot, who favored the French, and the Delaware and the Shawnee, who were partisans of the British. The former fortified themselves and the latter could not take their fort after a siege of seven days. It seems probable that it was the remains of Fort Pickawillany that was defended.[18]

NOTES

1. The establishment of the three French posts along the Maumee-Wabash line is detailed in BARNHART and RIKER, 71–85. The description of location given here is an approximation only.

2. For a comparison of English and French trade goods, see JACOBS (3), 90–114.

3. GOODMAN, 15–22; GIPSON, 173–76. Both Goodman and Gipson present good accounts of the conspiracy of Nicholas. The basic documents are in THWAITES (1), XVII, passim.

4. TROWBRIDGE, 8. Head chief Jean B. Richardville told Trowbridge in 1824 that he could remember "the time when difficulties were settled, in consequence of one of the war chiefs having spent winter among the Cherokees, Shawnees, or Creeks, with a view to arranging the preliminaries." Everything points to the conclusion that La Demoiselle's residence near Kekionga was an example of this type of direct diplomacy. Some historians have been so puzzled to explain the presence of "the old Piankashaw King" near the Miami proper that they have chosen to refer to La Demoiselle simply as a Miami, ignoring clear evidence that he was a Piankashaw Miami, not a Miami proper. The English traders also called him Old Britain or Old Briton because of his preference for British goods. See also EDMUNDS (1), 1–20, which places the Piankashaw head chief's village near Fort Wayne.

While there is no hard evidence to support it, it is possible that La Demoiselle may have established his village on the Eel River, where Turtletown was later located, during his diplomatic overtures to Coldfoot. One reason for this belief is that there were clearly two locations of what is called Turtletown within a short distance of one another. A second reason is that this location controlled the Eel River portage, giving the Piankashaw head chief some sort of equal footing with Coldfoot, who controlled the Maumee-Wabash portage. It was the prerogative of a head chief and his family to locate on a portage and collect the fees that were charged for its use by travelers.

5. GIPSON, 176.

6. My wife and I visited the site of Pickawillany in the spring of 1982. It is now private land and there are no historical markers. See MCFARLAND, 479–88.

7. The various problems in connection with the birth of Little Turtle will be discussed in the next chapter.

8. PENNSYLVANIA, 316–19. The name Mishikinakwa is spelled in this document as Ciquenackqua, which is further discussed in the next chapter. The Miami are referred to as the Twightwees, an English usage discussed elsewhere in this work. They are described as "situate on or about the River Ouabache [Wabash]." Pickawillany drew most of its population from that general region.

9. THWAITES (1), XVII, 480–85, documents the confusion at Kekionga and Coldfoot's trip to Detroit. DARLINGTON estimates the population of Pickawillany, and GOODMAN, 40, lists the names of the English traders. The subject of Indian population is highly conjectural.

10. THWAITES (1), XVIII, 36–58, reproduces a portion of Céloron's journal.

11. Ibid., 94–98, reproduces the report of De Raymond, French resident at Kekionga, in 1751.

12. The French believed that they had persuaded Coldfoot not to join La Demoiselle, and they reported the names of other Miami chiefs loyal to the French. Nevertheless, international diplomacy was no less subtle among the Indians than among the whites. The question of who deceived whom in this instance must be left unsettled.

13. See Ibid., 128–31. French sources for the actual destruction of Pickawillany are almost nonexistent. Langlade kept a journal which disappeared in the nineteenth century before scholars had made use of it. Trent's *Journal* in GOODMAN, 83–105, is the best contemporary source. His information was based on the story of Thomas Burney, one of the escaped traders, verified by his own subsequent visit to the scene. Of secondary accounts, that of HANNA, II, 257–59, and GIPSON, 186–224, are the best. EDMUNDS (2), 169–84, makes no mention of the elder Mishikinakwa (Turtle), whose position at Pickawillany was second only to that of La Demoiselle himself.

14. GOODMAN, 100–105.

15. GIPSON, 224; JACOBS (3), 115–35. Governor Dinwiddie's letter is in GOODMAN, 69–81.

16. BARNHART and RIKER, 116–20.

17. Ibid., 120-21.

18. HILL, 4–5. TROWBRIDGE, 27, gives a garbled account of a battle at Pickawillany that appears to be a mixture of the 1752 and 1763 battles, as dimly recalled by the Miami chief Le Gros in 1824.

5

Enter, Little Turtle, 1747

DURING THE NEGOTIATION of the peace treaty between the Indians and the Americans at Greeneville in midsummer of 1795, there was a faint echo of events at Pickawillany, which has so far passed unnoticed. The principal spokesman for the Indians was the Miami war chief Mishikinakwa (Little Turtle), who had defeated the American frontier armies in 1790 and 1791, after which he had vainly counseled the other tribes to seek peace. The United States had entrusted the negotiation to Major General Anthony Wayne, who had decisively defeated the Indians nearly a year earlier; by doing so he forced even the most reluctant to come to Greeneville for peace talks. In the course of their discussions, Little Turtle boldly asserted the Miami claim to the western half of Ohio, all of Indiana, and a slice of eastern Illinois, from the mouth of the Wabash up to and including Chicago, and sought to preserve the Ohio River as the southern boundary of the land of the Miami.[1]

On July 24 General Wayne made an able reply in which he noted the broad extent of the Miami claim but did not dispute it in behalf of other tribes. Instead, he pointed out traces of old French or British forts at certain locations and demanded that land be ceded to the United States, for military purposes, at each of these locations. Little Turtle stated that the French and British, as tenants, had been allowed to build forts in all of these places except one, but he pointed out that the Indians had never sold or ceded to either nation the land on which the forts had stood. Concerning the one exception, on July 30 he spoke as follows: "Elder Brother, listen to me with attention. You told us that you discovered on the Great Miami traces of an old fort. It was not a French fort, brother, it was a fort built by me."[2]

Wayne had said that "prints very conspicuous, are on the Great Miami, which were possessed by the French forty-five years ago."[3] This would have been in 1750 when Fort Pickawillany, located just below the junction of Loramie's Creek and the Great Miami, three miles north of the present-day city of Piqua, actually was built. This fort, as we have already seen, was erected by the pro-English Miami followers of La Demoiselle for the purpose of defying the French by trading with the British, and it was partially destroyed by the French leader Charles de Langlade in 1752.

It is remarkable that, until now, no one has questioned Little Turtle's statement, as reported by the interpreter, that it was a fort built by himself. In 1750 Little Turtle was about four years of age, so it is clearly impossible that he could have been the builder of Fort Pickawillany. What Little Turtle must have said was, "It was a fort built by Mishikinakwa." Since that was Little Turtle's Indian name, it was naturally rendered by the interpreter as "me." But Mishikinakwa was also the name of the earlier Miami war chief who signed the Treaty of Lancaster in 1748 and actually did construct Fort Pickawillany in 1750.[4] This chief is generally believed to have been the father of Little Turtle, and here we have uncovered the most important single clue that exists in proof of his parentage.

The interpreter at Greeneville was Captain William Wells, Little Turtle's white son-in-law, who had at this time, it must be concluded, no knowledge concerning his father-in-law's birth and parentage. By 1805, however, Wells apparently did have such knowledge, for in that year, while he was Indian agent at Fort Wayne, he acquired title from the Federal Land Office to the section of land where the ruins of Fort Pickawillany were located. Soon afterward he obtained two adjoining fractional sections, which brought his holdings at this location to a total of 1,161 acres in one piece.[5] As land was plentiful at the time, there seems to be no reason that Wells should have chosen this particular spot, about ninety miles from his residence at Fort Wayne, except that he wished to pass on to his children by Sweet Breeze, Little Turtle's daughter, who died in 1805, an inheritance closely associated with the history of their Miami ancestors.

If modern psychologists are correct in the belief that a child's essential character is formed by the time he is five years old, or thereabouts, the Pickawillany adventure must have had a decisive influence in shaping the character of Little Turtle. Perhaps his later perception of the necessity for the Miami to adapt themselves to civilized life as represented by the Americans was sharpened by the familiarity gained as a child with colonial traders and their material goods. He may also have learned very early the harmful effect of liquor upon the Indians. Above all, he may have grasped from traders like Croghan, Trent, and Gist the colonial American interest in the acquisition of land and later determined to make use of that interest for the benefit of his tribe. On these matters we can only speculate. There are, however, more immediate problems which have to do not only with the question of his parentage but also with his divisional affiliation within the Miami tribe, with the time and place of his birth, and with the origin and meaning of his name. While these problems may not be solved, enough light can be shed upon each of them to render our knowledge more accurate than the contradictory information that has hitherto prevailed.

Little Turtle is not the only historical figure concerning whose origins conflicting reports abound. History is filled with great men of obscure origins that invite the invention and perpetuation of mythical accounts. One may note the similar case of Thayendanegea, better known as Joseph Brant, a renowned Mohawk chief and a close contemporary of Little Turtle. Brant's biographer has written: "By some authors, Thayendanegea has been called a half breed. By others he has been pronounced a Shawanese by parentage and only a Mohawk by adoption. Some historians have spoken of him as a son of Sir William Johnson; while others again have allowed him the honor of Mohawk blood but denied that he was descended from a chief."[6]

Although maternity is nearly always easier to establish than paternity, the reverse is true in the case of Little Turtle. His mother's name is unknown, but there was a very early and strongly persistent tradition that she was a Mohican. This eastern Algonquian tribe had its homeland between the Connecticut and the Hudson rivers, where its members fought long and bitter wars against the Iroquois Confederacy in the seventeenth century. Their numbers were greatly reduced, in consequence, but bands of Mohican penetrated the land of the Miami simultaneously with the Iroquois to gather furs. Unlike the Iroquois they did so peaceably. As early as 1720, at the invitation of the Miami, a village was established by a Mohican band on the Kankakee River.[7] The elder Mishikinakwa rose to prominence as a war chief through his victories over the Iroquois, aided by the Mohican, and he may well have taken a wife from their village. The fact that Little Turtle's granddaughter Kilsoquah (Mrs. Rivarre) denied the truth of this tradition has not prevented its universal acceptance by historians.

Kilsoquah's account was given to Samuel P. Kaler and three companions on August 3, 1906, when she was ninety-six years old. She had no personal recollection of her grandfather, for she was only two years old when he died in 1812. As she spoke no English, her son, Anthony Rivarre, Jr., acted as her interpreter in their home at Roanoke, Indiana. Her statement, as reported by Kaler, was as follows:

> Turtle's grandfather was a chief in the Eel river country. His father was a Frenchman about half-blood, so that Turtle was but three quarters Indian. Before my father died someone read to him in a history that his grandmother, that is, Little Turtle's mother was a Mohican Indian. Father was much pained

to hear this mistake, for he said he knew his mother was a pure Miami, as was his grandfather's first wife. . . . Turtle had two wives, the first, my grandmother was the sister of Mak-wah, who lived on St. Mary's river near Fort Wayne. Turtle then lived at Turtle Village [Turtletown] at the bend in Eel river, where he was born and his father before him. She died, leaving two sons and one daughter, and he could not stay there after that, so he moved up on the trail to the Fort, and then married Mak-wah's daughter, niece of his first wife. I do not know of any children by the last wife, nor do I know of any by the first wife except my father Mak-e-shen-e-quah, and Coesse's father Kat-e-mong-wah, and one daughter, Ma-cute-mon-quah, who married great White Loon.[8]

Although this statement appears to be a straightforward one, it does not stand up well under close examination. Some years earlier Kilsoquah had told Jacob P. Dunn that both of Little Turtle's parents were Miami. In 1906 she informed Kaler that Little Turtle's father was half French. None of Little Turtle's contemporaries regarded him as having white blood, despite the fact that, according to Volney, he was of very light color. Furthermore, if Little Turtle's father had been a half-blood Frenchman, he would have borne his father's name, as did Richardville, La Fontaine, Godfroy, and other Miami chiefs of known French blood. There were no resident French traders at Turtletown where his father is said to have been born.

Kilsoquah also stated that Little Turtle's grandfather was chief of Turtletown and that he was born there. This would not only have been before the Miami are known to have had a village there, but it also implies that the chief was the father of a half-blood Frenchman. This is practically an impossibility because few French women were ever in the Miami country and none are known to have married Indians.

For all these reasons Kilsoquah's statement has never won much credibility. Other portions of her statement concerning Little Turtle's second marriage and her denial of the existence of his daughter who married William Wells run counter to the testimony of contemporaries. If Kilsoquah knew so little concerning her grandfather, it is not unreasonable to question whether her father could have known with any certainty that his grandmother was not a Mohican.[9]

In 1812 Lewis Cass, territorial governor of Michigan, sent C. C. Trowbridge to Fort Wayne to gather information on the customs of the Miami. Trowbridge, a Yankee from upper New York State, spent the winter of 1824–25 talking with a Miami chief called Le Gros, who was paid for his information. Among other things, he told Trowbridge that Little Turtle was not a Miami at all.

The Little Turtle is not considered a Miami. A frenchman who traded from the Mississippi to the Lakes, purchased in the west an Iowau girl and adopted her as his daughter. In one of his subsequent visits from Montreal he employed a Mohiccan Indian, partly civilized to accompany him in capacity of a servant. In the Kickapoo country [Illinois] the master and man became engaged in a battle and the former was wounded in the thigh. The Mohiccan carried him with incredible labour & fatigue to the Miami village [Fort Wayne] and when he reached there the grateful frenchman poured out his lamentations because he had lost all his goods and had no means to reward him. The Mohiccan offered to accept of the Iowau girl & the other consented. They were married, settled among the Miamis, and had a great many children, of whom the eldest was Little Turtle.[10]

Whereas Kilsoquah's story was so specific that her errors are easily demonstrated, the story of Le Gros was so vague and so devoid of detail on essential matters that it must be outright dismissed as an idle tale. The total absence of names, dates, and places, except in the most generalized form, renders it worthless to historians. At best it may be a tale spread by unsubstantiated gossip among the Miami; at worst it may be a malicious fabrication by Le Gros, arising from the long smoldering envy of a lesser chief directed toward the great Miami war chief, who was dead and unable to contradict the tale. Despite the fact that it was told only a dozen years after the death of Little Turtle, no historian has ever given it any credence. The only point of interest is that Little Turtle's father, not his mother, is said to have been a Mohican, which may possibly be taken as a reversed image of the fact.

Many variations are found in the spelling of the Miami name of Little Turtle because the Miami language was a spoken language, not a written one. Indians made use of pictographs but not of phonetic symbols. Phonetic sounds were set down in writing by Frenchmen or Englishmen as they seemed to the ear of the listener. The spelling of all Indian words varied, therefore, with the individual who wrote them down on paper. The name Mishikinakwa, as employed in this work, represents the most common or standard French transliteration of the Miami spoken word. Since Little Turtle was born within the period of French domination of the land of the Miami, it would seem to be the most appropriate form.[11]

Other French forms need not concern us here, but variant English forms may be of some interest. The earliest English spelling recorded is Ci-quenackqua (The Turtle) in the Treaty of Lancaster in 1748.[12] The interpreter was Conrad Weiser, a Pennsylvania Dutch trader who knew more German and Iroquois than English and Miami. It is obvious that the first syllable of the name is omitted in this version, and this may indicate that the pronunciation heard by Weiser's German ear used a mere compression of the lips for the initial sound, forcing the second syllable to be more heavily accented. In 1752 William Trent, an English colonial trader, wrote the name of the same chief, whom we have shown to have been the father of Little Turtle, as Mushaguanockque, giving definite expression to the first syllable, although with a different vowel sound than that usually heard by English ears.[13]

Because of the close association of Little Turtle and William Wells, it would have been appropriate to have adopted the spelling favored by Wells were it not for the fact that he followed no consistent pattern. On each of three occasions when Wells was the official interpreter he produced slightly different spellings. In 1795, at the Treaty of Greeneville, Wells wrote Meshekunnoghquoh; in 1805, at the Treaty of Vincennes, he wrote Mashekanochquah; in 1809, at the Treaty of Fort Wayne, he wrote Meshakenoghqua.[14] Another early form was that used by Moses Dawson, the first biographer of William Henry Harrison, who wrote Meshecunnaqua.[15]

Later forms exhibit still more variant spellings, but it is not necessary to list them here. It is of some importance, however, that Jacob Piatt Dunn, a reliable amateur scholar of the Miami tongue, preferred to write Meshekinnoquah and that both Calvin Young and Otho Winger followed Dunn's usage in their writings on Little Turtle.[16] Less familiar is Mechekaunohqua, used by John Wentworth in 1881–82 at the Chicago centennial observances of the Fort Dearborn massacre.[17] A map prepared for public use by the state of Indiana in 1932 used Mishikinoqkwa (or sometimes Mishikinooqkwa).[18] A marker designating the site of the house built by the federal government on the Eel River in Whitley County, Indiana, near the Allen County line, for Little Turtle in his later years reads Meshemenocquah, and the caption on the lithograph reputed to represent Little Turtle reads Mishekiniqua. It seems probable that the third syllable in the former and the antepenult in the latter are in error.[19]

It is clear that the first two syllables, *mishi* (or variants thereof), constitute the word for "great" or "big" in the Miami and other Algonquian languages. The last syllable, *kwa* (or variants thereof), is the Algonquian word for "woman" and is the feminine ending attached to many words. Jacob Piatt Dunn was undoubtedly correct in saying that the literal meaning of the word was "the wife of the great turtle," and also that the Miami used the word to designate the painted turtle alone and no other species of turtle.[20] The entire word must be used, for no portion of the word means "turtle," except in combination with all other portions. One must conclude that the word meant simply "turtle," as did several other Miami words. The Miami knew from the word used *which* turtle was meant. Little Turtle was so-called to distinguish him from his father of the same name, and after his father's death he was often called Turtle himself.

Since none of the turtles for which the Miami had specific names bears a name that could be construed as meaning "the great turtle," nor would such a name be appropriate for any of them, it seems probable that this term had only a mythical significance, perhaps referring to the earth itself. Among the Algonquian tribes, including the Miami, the turtle symbolized the earth and was addressed as "mother." This may account for the feminine ending *kwa*, or *quah*, in their name for the painted turtle, which was probably thought to have had the function of perpetuating the likeness of the mythic or symbolic "great turtle." The turtle, like the Indian women, transported its housing when it traveled. It may be of interest that the Chippewa word Michilimackinac, for the island at the strait of that name, located between Lakes Michigan and Huron, meant "great turtle."[21]

The Miami had separate and distinct designations for each of the five most common and numerous species of turtles found along the Wabash and its tributaries, as well as among the many small lakes of northern Indiana, which constituted the heart of the Miami homeland. The smallest and most familiar of the turtles was the painted turtle *(Chrysemys picta)*, sometimes called the painted terrapin or the pond tortoise, whose shape is rather flat, with a shell measuring from six to eight inches. The plates of its carapace, or upper shell, are of a greenish-black color with yellow edges; the plastron, or undershell, is yellow with brown markings; and upon its legs and tail the markings are bright red. This was the turtle known in the Miami language as *mishikinakwa*.[22] In the Hoosier vulgate it is pronounced me'-she-kin-aw'-quaw.

Little Turtle's parentage is of some assistance in the determination of the year of his birth. Their Pickawillany sojourn embraced the five-year period from the late summer of 1747 to June 21, 1752. Since no one has ever contended that he was born at Pickawillany, we may assume that he was born either in early 1747, before his parents embarked on that ill-fated adventure, or in late 1752, after their return to their former home in the vicinity of Kekionga.

The year 1751 was favored by Jacob Piatt Dunn on the basis of a statement reputed to have been made by Little Turtle regarding his age in 1804. Dunn did not give his source, which has been found to be a statement made by the Baltimore Quaker Gerard T. Hopkins, who visited Fort Wayne in 1804 and said that Little Turtle told him "he had seen fifty-three winters." There are three ways that this statement could plausibly have been inaccurate, however, although Hopkins made it in good faith. Hopkins may have inquired how long Little Turtle had resided in the vicinity of Fort Wayne, and the reply given would have been correct, for the chief would have excluded the winters spent at Pickawillany. Or Hopkins may have asked Turtle's age and been given the answer by sign language, that is, by showing the fingers of both hands five times, making fifty. Then, if the chief held up one hand, and then bent over two fingers, Hopkins may have

44

counted only fifty-three, when fifty-eight was intended. Most plausibly, Hopkins may have written fifty-eight, but many years later either Martha Tyson, his editor, or the printer may have read it as fifty-three. Probably the statement is in error for one of these reasons. If Turtle was born in 1751 he would have been born at Pickawillany, for which neither tradition nor evidence exists. It is also contrary to a statement made by Volney based on his interview with Turtle in 1791. Finally, it conflicts with his age as given in newspapers at the time of his death. For all of these reasons, then, 1751 must be excluded as a date for his birth.[23]

Samuel G. Drake stated in the 1834 edition of his *Book of the Indians* that contemporary newspaper accounts of the death of Little Turtle in 1812 reported his age as sixty-five years. Drake reproduced the following notice of the chief's death, identified only as "from the public prints": "Fort Wayne, 21 July, 1812. On the 14 inst. the celebrated Miami chief, the Little Turtle, died at this place, at the age of 65 years. . . ." Furthermore, Volney, who conversed with Little Turtle in Philadelphia in 1798, referred to him as "a man who has spent fifty years in the management of public affairs."[24] This statement cannot, of course, be taken literally, but it can be used as an indication of Little Turtle's age in 1798 and was received from the chief himself. It should be noted that Volney wrote "fifty years," not "over" or "about" fifty years. These two statements of age, made several years apart, are both precise in indicating 1747 as the year of birth. Since the most probable time of his parents' move to Pickawillany was the late summer of 1747, his birth likely took place in the late winter or early spring of that year.

Calvin M. Young published a biography of Little Turtle in 1917 in which he cited 1752 as the probable year of birth and the likely place of birth as a small Miami village located at Devil's Lake, at the west end of Blue Lake, in Whitley County, Indiana.[25] Since then most writers have accepted the date but rejected the place favored by Young. The evidence is much stronger for the opposite conclusion. Young was not explicit about his reasons for preferring 1752 over 1747 as the year of birth. Apparently he was aware of the Pickawillany sojourn of Little Turtle's parents but did not investigate the matter and simply made the wrong choice. There seems to be no evidence pointing to 1752, whereas that pointing to 1747 is fairly definite and reasonably satisfactory.

The two rival locations for the honor of having been the birthplace of Little Turtle are, as the crow flies, only about six miles apart. Turtletown, or Turtle Village, was located in Section Nine, Union Township, Whitley County, Indiana; Devil's Lake is situated in Section Nine of Smith Township in the same county. Turtletown was at the point where the Miami trail leading to their winter hunting grounds on Yellow River, about sixty-five miles west by northwest from Kekionga, crossed the Eel River, at a point about sixteen miles from Kekionga. Devil's Lake is located between the inlet and the outlet of Blue Lake, both of which are known as Blue River, a small tributary of the Eel River, which it joins about five miles below Turtletown. Devil's Lake contains only about two acres and is a mere 100 yards or so west of Blue Lake, which in contrast is between 500 and 600 acres in extent. The village was on high ground north of Devil's Lake and about equally distant from Blue Lake, Blue River at the inlet, and Devil's Lake, with a fine spring for a water supply. Kekionga was eighteen miles away and could be reached either by a trail joining the Yellow River trail east of Turtletown, about eleven miles from Kekionga, or by the Miami trail from Kekionga to Chicago. The Miami trail passed about a mile and a half north of the inlet of Blue Lake and was the longer route by two miles. Indian artifacts abound at and near both locations, so that neither has an advantage in this respect.[26]

Turtletown was undoubtedly the village of Little Turtle's father after his return from Pickawillany, and it was also the village of Little Turtle himself after his father's death. He continued to reside there until the government built a house for him about two miles upstream, nearer to Fort Wayne and close to the place where he had first come to prominence by defeating Colonel La Balme in 1780.[27] It is not surprising, therefore, that Turtletown has long been assumed to have been his birthplace. The fact that most of his life was spent there, however, does not justify the assumption that he was born there. Wallace Brice wrote in 1868 that Turtle "was the son of a chief, born at his village on Eel River," but Brice also wrote that "he was born on the upper reaches of Eel river," which is so much less definite as to raise a question as to the accuracy of this information.[28] In neither case does Brice give any source. Samuel Kaler, in his 1906 interview with Kilsoquah, sought to bolster the assumption by her testimony, but we have seen that her story was so inaccurate that no confidence can be placed in it.

Calvin Young's belief that Devil's Lake was the true birthplace of Little Turtle was based upon a tradition that was current among old settlers near that location in the early 1860s, when he had lived there as a youth. When he published his biography of Little Turtle in 1917, the assumption that Turtletown was the birthplace was well established and could not be over-turned because the old settlers from whom Young had heard the alternative tradition were all dead. Nevertheless, Young's conviction was based on an actual tradition which appears to have been a more solid basis for choice than the plausible assumption that formed the basis for the belief that Turtletown was the birthplace.

46

A close scrutiny of the matter reveals two indications, neither of which is conclusive, that Young may have been right in his preference for Devil's Lake. The Devil's Lake location is more appropriate to the earlier part of the eighteenth century, when the elder Mishikinakwa was engaged in warfare against the Iroquois and other Indian tribes, because it is secluded and not directly on a main trail or water course. At the same time, it had access to Kekionga by two routes and was well situated as the village of a war chief, who might have liked to ensure that his family was safe from molestation while he was on a campaign. Calvin Young reported that Devil's Lake received its name as a result of some unspecified supernatural occurrence which so frightened the residents that they abandoned the village and ran all the way to Kekionga.[29]

It is a speculation, of course, but one worth considering, that the village may have been deserted as a result of the great smallpox epidemic of 1752, which was such a supernatural event to the Miami. A reconstruction of events might be that upon the elder Mishikinakwa's return from Pickawillany in 1752, his followers contracted smallpox in Kekionga, where Coldfoot and many more had recently died of that disease.[30] They then reoccupied their old village at Devil's Lake, where so many became ill and died that they abandoned it, giving rise to the name Devil's Lake. The survivors then established their village at Turtletown, on the Eel River. Such a reconstruction is rendered more plausible by the fact that Turtletown is known to have existed at two locations about one-half mile apart. The earlier one may have been the site occupied briefly by La Demoiselle from 1745 to 1747, before the Pickawillany adventure began. The elder Mishikinakwa lived at Turtletown until his death, and the village was named for him rather than for his famous son.

One of the unfortunate consequences of the belief that Little Turtle was born on the Eel River is the assumption by almost all historians that this made him an Eel River Miami; this is most emphatically not true. Little Turtle signed several treaties, beginning with that of Greeneville in 1795 and ending with that of Fort Wayne in 1809. The Eel River Miami, as well as the Wea and Piankashaw Miami, signed separately from the Miami proper. Little Turtle signed all treaties as a Miami, not as an Eel River Miami.[31] The Eel River Miami resided principally at their great village of Kenapakomoko (Snake-fish Town), six miles above present-day Logansport. They received their government annuities after 1795 separately from the Miami proper. The Miami annuities were shared by the Atchatchakangouen Miami of Kekionga and their other small villages nearby, of which Turtletown was probably one, and also by the Mengakonkia Miami on the Mississinewa River, and by Le Gris's Village, which represented a portion of the Pepikokia Miami. Le Gros told Trowbridge in 1824 that Le Gris was head of the Turtle clan, but this is probably an error. Little Turtle himself was more likely the head of that clan, for he signed one document by drawing a turtle as his mark. Le Gros, of course, was responsible for the story that Little Turtle was not a Miami at all. If Le Gris was head of the Turtle clan, it would indicate that Turtle was a Pepikokia.[32]

Henry Hay, who visited Le Gris's Village in 1790, said that Le Gris and Little Turtle were brothers-in-law. If this is true it is most unlikely that Little Turtle was a Pepikokia.[33] The most probable conclusion is that Little Turtle was an Atchatchakangouen Miami, the leading division of the six divisions of the Miami tribe. He was not the head chief of that division, however, as has been stated by many writers, but the war chief, as his father had been. A war chief might be chosen from among village chiefs on the basis of his success in war; the head chief's position was hereditary. Both Mishikinakwas, Turtle and his son, Little Turtle, attained the position of war chief of the Atchatchakangouen Miami as a result of signal victories, the father by defeating the Iroquois and the son by defeating La Balme.

Perhaps the best evidence in support of the belief that Little Turtle was an Atchatchakangouen Miami is to be found in his often quoted and pridefully stated remark at the Greeneville Treaty in 1795, when he referred to "the Miami village," meaning Kekionga, which was much older and more prestigious than Le Gris's Village, where the traders lived, as that "glorious gate, which your younger brothers had the happiness to own, and through which all the good words of our chiefs had to pass." It is hard to believe that anyone except an Atchatchakangouen could have spoken with such pride of the primacy of The Crane People among the various Miami divisions. It may also be taken as a statement of the central importance of the Miami among the tribes of the Heartland, who had learned to clear it with Kekionga before they acted.[34]

NOTES

1. ASPIA, I, 571–72.
2. Ibid., 576.
3. Ibid., 573.
4. GOODMAN, 105, specifically identifies Musheguanockque as one of three Miami chiefs who signed the Treaty of Lancaster in 1748. Trent spelled the name as given in this note. For the precise location and time of construction of Fort Pickawillany, see MCFARLAND, 479–88.
5. HILL, 159. In 1807 John Johnston acquired land adjacent to that acquired by Wells. He lived there while he was Indian agent at Piqua in a house that still stands and which I visited in 1982. The significance of the acquisition by Wells of this particular tract of land cannot be lightly dismissed.
6. STONE, I, 1–2.

7. MOHICAN, 205. DAWSON (1824) appears to be the earliest printed source of the statement that Little Turtle's mother was a Mohican. A reason for its general acceptance is that it accounts for Little Turtle's late rise to prominence, because inherited chieftainship among the Miami was in the female line. This would apply to Little Turtle as a clan chief or village chief but not necessarily to his status as a war chief.

8. KALER and MARING, 79–80. Samuel Kaler deserves credit for having sought to establish the facts concerning Little Turtle's birth by an interview with his granddaughter nine years before her death at the age of 105. On the other hand, he did not subject her statement to critical and impartial analysis. Kaler did not take her statement that Little Turtle was one-quarter white very seriously. However, he accepted her statement that Little Turtle was born on the Eel River at Turtletown without considering that her further assertion, that his father and grandfather were also born there, rendered it virtually untenable and directly undermined her belief that he was part white. Some of Kaler's associates in the interview were landowners along the Eel River and may have had a tendency to believe what they wished to believe, in spite of contradictions.

9. It should be remembered that Kaler's interview was conducted through Kilsoquah's son, who acted as interpreter. Her explanation of Miami practice with regard to names, however, is of considerable value. She said, "Anthony Rivarre [her son] is named after Great White Loon, but he is only White Loon. If it is desired to name a child after Full Moon, it must be changed to Old Moon or Half Moon." Ibid., 82. Thus, Mishikinakwa was the name of both her great-grandfather and her grandfather, but the former was called Turtle so the latter was referred to as Little Turtle. After his father's death the son was often called Turtle. Kilsoquah herself referred to her grandfather simply as Turtle, or so her son translated what she said into English.

10. TROWBRIDGE, 87–88. Although Le Gros provided some good material on Miami customs, his more strictly historical information is of little value. Trowbridge apparently made no effort to check his story of Little Turtle's origins. His insistence on spelling Miami as Meearmeear, although there was no "r" sound in the Miami language and he admitted that the "r" is "intrusive," may raise some question as to his qualities as a reporter.

11. VOLNEY, 356–86; DRAKE (2), Book 5, 52–58.

12. PENNSYLVANIA, 318. The name has usually been spelled Aquenackqua by writers using this source, including CARTER (2), 3–18. This is unfortunate because it leads to the mistaken conclusion that in the Miami language *mishi* meant "little" and *aquenackqua* meant "turtle," neither of which is true. The spelling at the Treaty of Lancaster was definitely Ciquenackqua, which is obviously a slurred and shortened form of Mishikinakwa. A parallel case is Shingomesia for Meshingomesia in the 1840 treaty with the Miami.

13. GOODMAN, 105. This spelling is interesting because Trent clearly does not omit the first syllable, although he was writing only four years after the Treaty of Lancaster. He had contact with The Turtle for a longer period than the negotiators of Lancaster. His evidence gives convincing proof that the whole name, not merely a portion of it, meant "turtle."

14. KAPPLER, II, 50, 81, 103. Wells was the interpreter, but someone else may have been responsible for the writing and spelling, which could account for the variations.

15. DAWSON, passim.

16. DUNN, passim.

17. WENTWORTH.

18. GUERNSEY. Both spellings appear on the same map.

19. A photograph of this marker appears in WHITLEY, August 1971. I last visited the site in May 1982.

20. DUNN, 282–83.

21. Cadillac wrote, "Missilimakinak means in our language Isle de la Tortue [Turtle Island]." THWAITES (1), XVI, 350. See also MACKINAC, 1–14.

22. See POPE, passim, for information on the various turtles commonly found in Indiana. There were four other turtles for which the Miami had names. The common snapping turtle *(Chelydra serpentina)*, known for its vicious bite, they called *atchepong.* One of their small reservations in the early nineteenth century was located on the Salamonie River in Jay County, Indiana, at the mouth of Atchepong Creek. The spiny soft-shelled turtle *(Trionyx spiniferous)*, they called *akotyah.* The Treaty of the Forks of the Wabash (Huntington, Indiana) in 1838 was signed by a Miami chief whose name was listed as Awkooteaw. The common box turtle *(Terrapene carolina)*, known as a land dweller and furnished with complete armor, was called *weeweetchak*, whereas the common map turtle *(Graptemys geographica)* was known as *kachkityot.*

The five Miami words for various turtles have been gleaned from the short vocabularies of VOLNEY and of THORNTON, both of which were compiled from information furnished by Little Turtle and William Wells and from a vocabulary of 236 words compiled by BUSSARD in the twentieth century from Miami still resident in Indiana. A copy of the Thornton manuscript was furnished courtesy of the American Philosophical Society, Philadelphia. A copy of the Bussard manuscript was obtained courtesy of the Indiana Historical Society, Indianapolis.

23. DUNN, 44; HOPKINS, 52–53.

24. DRAKE (2), Book 5, 57. Despite a considerable search Drake's newspaper source has not been located. VOLNEY, 386. Volney also said that Little Turtle's skin color was no darker than his own, but this does not necessarily indicate that he had some white ancestry. There were differences of coloration among Indians as among whites. Turtle remarked to Volney that he found both the great number of whites and the great differences of appearance among them hard to understand.

25. YOUNG (1), 125–26. Kilsoquah's confirmation of the assumption that Little Turtle had been born at Turtletown on the Eel River seems to have been accepted locally at a time when the Devil's Lake tradition had almost died out. For that reason Young's revival of the earlier tradition seems to have received little attention in Whitley County. Young's evidence is not conclusive, but it is more persuasive than Kilsoquah's statement of 1906. Both sites were very familiar to me, as I lived between the two during the years 1914–27.

26. See the photographs of artifacts published herein, which were selected from several hundred specimens plowed up within a radius of two miles of Devil's Lake

by my nephew, Stephen Carter, during the years 1948–82. Some are of the historical period; others are prehistoric.

27. WHITLEY, August 1971, has a map prepared by Eudolph Holycross, a local authority on Little Turtle, which locates accurately all of the historic spots along the Eel River.

28. BRICE, 201.

29. YOUNG (1), 126.

30. THWAITES (1), XVIII, 108.

31. KAPPLER, II, 39, 64, 80, 101.

32. TROWBRIDGE, 12.

33. HAY, 228. Probably Kilsoquah's statement that Little Turtle married first a sister and then a daughter of Makwah, who lived on the St. Marys River, is correct. Le Gris, however, may have married a sister of Little Turtle.

34. ASPIA, I, 5

6

The Miami Hold the Heartland, 1752–90

THE SEVEN YEARS' WAR, as the French and Indian War was known in Europe, did not begin until 1756, if we date it from the formal declaration of hostilities. It has often been remarked, however, that it began in 1754 with the contest between French and English colonial forces for military control of the Forks of the Ohio River. It would perhaps be somewhat more accurate to say that it began in 1752 with the destruction of the English trading post among the Miami at Pickawillany, thus converting the Seven Years' War to the Eleven Years' War.

The early clashes between the two colonial powers were won by the French and their Indian allies, but a number of brilliant victories on land and sea in 1759, culminating in the capture of Quebec, put all of Canada into British hands. The Treaty of Paris, signed on February 10, 1763, brought the French colonial empire in North America to an end by forcing France to cede Canada to Great Britain and Louisiana to Spain. Although official news of these enormous transfers of land and authority did not reach St. Louis until September 1763, the Indians of the Heartland had known since September 1760, when French authorities in Canada had officially surrendered to the British, that tremendous changes were impending.

Major Robert Rogers, of Rogers' Rangers, arrived in Detroit on November 29, 1760, received the surrender of Captain François de Bellestre, unfurled and ran up the Union Jack, and departed on December 23. Before leaving he dispatched Lieutenant Butler and Ensign Wait, with a few Rangers, to take charge of Fort Miamis at the headwaters of the Maumee and Fort Ouiatenon on the Wabash, respectively, and left Captain Donald Campbell in charge at Detroit. Major Henry Gladwin superseded Campbell at

Fort Detroit on September 1, 1761, and promptly sent Ensign Robert Holmes, with fifteen redcoats, to relieve Butler at Fort Miamis; Lieutenant Edward Jenkins was sent with twenty men to relieve Wait at Fort Ouiatenon. The British seem to have regarded Ouiatenon as the more important post because it was nearer Louisiana, which in 1761 was still in French hands. They also began the practice of referring to the Ouiatenon Miami as the Wea, although they did not alter the name of the fort.[1]

The shift to British control caused considerable unrest among the Indians. In 1761 wampum belts were sent by the Seneca to the tribes near Detroit and to those on the Maumee-Wabash line advocating a concerted attack upon Fort Detroit and Fort Niagara, but the western tribes did not trust the Seneca and made no response. In 1762 a speaker, known merely as the Delaware Prophet, began to preach a return to the Indian ways before the coming of the whites and to advocate a general war to drive out all whites or else exterminate them. This was in eastern Ohio, on the Tuscarawas River, but the message spread rapidly westward. The Indians were stirred by this emotional gospel because of the extraordinarily stupid orders of Sir Jeffrey Amherst, commander-in-chief of all British forces in North America, for the regulation of Indian trade. The new policy was to make no gifts to the Indians, distribute no free ammunition, and to give or sell them no liquor. Coupled with these arbitrary changes, now that the French competition was eliminated, the price of trade goods was doubled. Naturally enough the new policy was the cause of immense dissatisfaction, but Amherst refused to modify it despite the urgent warnings of British traders, including Sir William Johnson and George Croghan. Amherst held the Indians in great contempt and had gone on record as advocating that blankets infected with smallpox be distributed to them. The practice was not adopted, but Amherst's orders regarding trade, although doubtless not uniformly followed or enforced, could not be entirely ignored.[2]

Among the Ottawa living near Detroit was a war chief of impressive appearance and domineering personality named Pontiac. A powerful speaker, he cleverly turned the Delaware Prophet's crusade against all whites to one against the British and adopted the Seneca plan for an attack on Detroit. His attempt to get his warriors inside the fort was foiled by Major Gladwin, who was forewarned by other Indians. On May 7, 1763, Pontiac blocked the straits and settled down to a siege of the fort. Although reinforcements managed to get through in late July, they were defeated in an attempt to take the offensive, and the siege was finally given up by Pontiac on October 30, 1763. Meanwhile, the Indian uprising had become general and all the smaller British forts had been taken, though Fort Niagara and Fort Pitt, as well as Detroit, were able to hold out. The unprecedented siege of nearly six months, with the issue always in doubt, had thoroughly alarmed the British and their American colonies.[3]

A party, led by Jacques Godfroy, was sent by Pontiac to Kekionga to urge the capture of Fort Miamis. The Miami did not require much urging. Using the Miami mistress of Ensign Holmes as a decoy, they lured him from the fort, captured him, and forced him to surrender the fort. Godfroy and his party then proceeded down the Wabash to Fort Ouiatenon where the Wea allowed him to force the surrender of Lieutenant Jenkins and his men. Beyond these actions the Miami did not aid Pontiac. In October they sent 100 warriors to observe the progress of the siege of Detroit and concluded that the fort could not be taken.[4]

After Pontiac abandoned the siege of Detroit he established his village at Roche de Bout, near the mouth of the Maumee, on an island in the river. Here, in 1764, the British emissary Captain Thomas Morris met with Pontiac and learned that he had not changed his hostile feelings toward the British. In 1766 Pontiac traveled to New York, where Sir William Johnson persuaded him to adopt a more friendly attitude. Pontiac was overbearing and presumptuous toward other western tribes, however, and Johnson and Croghan made use of this fact to undermine Pontiac's influence so greatly that he never succeeded in becoming a peacetime leader. In 1769 he was murdered by a Peoria Indian in Cahokia, Illinois, to the relief of the British authorities.[5]

The death of Pontiac allowed the British to reverse General Amherst's policies without a loss of face. By the establishment of a line beyond which colonial settlement was prohibited by the Royal Proclamation of October 7, 1763, the British government endeavored to protect the western Indians from encroachment by the colonial population and to continue the valuable fur trade that had long been fostered by the French. The British now reverted to the French practice of gift giving to ensure Indian good will. In fact, they became far more generous in this respect than the French had been, and the Indians soon became reconciled. French traders still operated in the Miami villages, supplying British goods, and intermarried more freely with Miami women than they had before. In later times the Miami regarded the years from 1763 to 1775 as a kind of Golden Age. Had the British policy been along these lines from the outset, the great uprising under Pontiac might have been averted.[6]

The Proclamation line extended from Florida to Quebec along the Appalachian watershed. Although the line did not alter land grants by colonial charter, it forbade land acquisition or settlement in the western portions of such grants and so ran counter to the growing land hunger of the people in the colonies. This land hunger was manifested by two groups, the colonial land speculators and the individual families who had already settled in the

54

Appalachian mountain valleys near the line, or in some cases beyond it. The land speculators were small in number but nonetheless active and influential men who constantly formed companies and sought to have their land acquisition schemes legalized by the British government. They included traders like George Croghan and William Trent, government officials like Sir William Johnson and Lord Dunmore, and ambitious men with some money like Benjamin Franklin and Richard Henderson. The British government, though hard pressed by these companies, consistently refused them legalization.

The frontier movement of settlers was more difficult to control. They moved beyond the line, occupied such land as they chose, took their chances with the Indians, and in the long run prevailed by sheer numbers. South of the Ohio the Proclamation line was modified to bulge farther west. The 1768 Treaty of Fort Stanwix, with the Iroquois Confederacy, had the effect of legalizing some 30,000 squatters in western Pennsylvania and forcing the Delaware and the Shawnee to move entirely into what is now eastern Ohio. In only one instance did the speculators and settlers effectively combine. Richard Henderson's Transylvania Company bought land in Kentucky directly from the Cherokee and employed Daniel Boone in 1775 to cut a wilderness trail and lead settlers into the area. Since the purchase was illegal the settlers may as well have squatted on the land, as most of the frontier families did.[7]

The Miami were not directly affected by frontier expansion at this time. They regarded the Ohio River from the mouth of the Scioto to the mouth of the Wabash as their southern boundary. The land between the Wabash and the Ohio was their hunting ground, just as Kentucky was the hunting ground of the Cherokee and the Chickasaw tribes, who lived in what is now Tennessee. They were indirectly affected when the frontier movement caused the Shawnee to occupy land on the Great and Little Miami rivers, but they did not object to sharing this area, as they did not object to sharing the lower Maumee with the Ottawa or the prairie land north and west of the Wabash with the Potawatomi and the Kickapoo.

The Miami considered these Algonquian tribes as friendly squatters who were not objectionable because they made the same use of the land as the Miami themselves did. They did not cease to regard the land as theirs, and the tribes who squatted on it seem to have acknowledged the Miami right until the land cessions of the nineteenth century made the land valuable in cash annuities or goods. In addition, around 1770 the Miami extended an invitation to the Delaware to settle on the White River in Indiana, and by 1790 there were several Delaware villages established there. It is possible that the Miami may have regarded the Shawnee and the Delaware as forming a buffer between them and the white settlers of Kentucky, but this is uncertain.[8]

The transfer of land by the king of France to the king of England in 1763 was something that the Indians of the Heartland could not easily comprehend, for they were not familiar with the claims of European monarchs to ownership of land in North America by right of discovery and exploration. The Miami made their position a matter of explicit record following a conference held in Detroit in late August 1765, at which Pontiac and George Croghan were present. After the conference had officially ended the Miami chiefs withdrew, but they returned in a few days after deliberating among themselves. They told Croghan that they had never been conquered by the French, nor had they ever sold any land to them; therefore, under these circumstances, the French king had no right to give their land to the English king. The French had always treated them with respect and civility, and they expected the British to do likewise. Croghan did not argue the matter with them, although he was certainly aware that such an attitude of independence was contrary to the English legal view that landownership rested with the Crown.[9]

The British government itself was not entirely consistent in its land policy, as is well illustrated by certain events of 1774. Lord Dunmore, the last royal governor of Virginia, had seized control of Fort Pitt from the colony of Pennsylvania early in that year. Both colonies claimed the Forks of the Ohio under their charters or royal grants. On April 30 frontier settlers of Virginia murdered the relatives of the Mingo chief Logan, who was friendly to the whites. Logan went on the warpath, and Lord Dunmore's War ensued. The Virginians were narrowly victorious over the Shawnee chief Cornstalk at the battle of Point Pleasant on October 10, and Dunmore was able to move against the Shawnee villages of the Hocking valley in Ohio and dictate a peace which allowed the settlement of Kentucky to go forward for a short while.

On June 22, 1774, the British Parliament passed the Quebec Act, which attached the whole area north of the Ohio to Quebec, inaugurating a policy that not only contravened the royal charter of Virginia but rendered Dunmore's War a futile exercise. The Quebec Act was also unpopular with other colonies and became a contributory cause of the American Revolution.[10] It was popular with the Indians insofar as its practical aspects were concerned because it was for them a further restoration of what they had become accustomed to under the French regime. The theory that the English king owned their land and that his government could dispose of it still amounted to no more, in Indian eyes, than a hill of beans.

The American Revolution confused and divided the Indians. The Iroquois Confederacy was broken by it: the Oneida and Tuscarora supported the colonists, and the other four tribes aided the British. Among the latter, Brant and his Mohawk were the most active. Cornstalk, the Shawnee chief who had made peace as a result of Lord Dunmore's War, remained friendly to the colonists but was murdered by frontier militia in 1777, providing a typical example of the fact that American pioneers did not recognize or appreciate Indian friendship. The result was that the Shawnee once more went on the warpath.

The Delaware head chief White Eyes was a steadfast ally of the colonists, but their great war chief Buckongahelas was not. White Eyes was able to negotiate a treaty which held out the prospect that the Delaware, if they could persuade other tribes to join the American cause, might become the leaders of a fourteenth state under the Articles of Confederation. But he too was murdered while with an American military expedition, his death officially attributed to smallpox. In 1782 the Moravian mission at Gnadenhutten in eastern Ohio, on the Tuscarawas, was raided by Major David Williamson at the head of 160 Pennsylvania frontier militiamen. They murdered 90 Delaware Moravian Christians: 29 men, 27 women, and 34 children.[11] These atrocities help to explain the bitterness with which the Indians of the Heartland continued the Revolutionary War even after the peace treaty of 1783, about which they were not consulted. The Miami, though remote from these events, were nonetheless well aware of them.

When George Rogers Clark, a Kentucky frontier leader, conceived the plan of taking the offensive against the British and their Indian allies north of the Ohio in 1777, he brought the American Revolution directly to the Miami. His capture of Kaskaskia and Vincennes in 1778 strongly impressed the Piankashaw Miami who lived near Vincennes, and they became pro-American, whereas the remaining Miami bands were loyal to the British. Clark, a man of resourceful action and great daring, was able to accomplish much with only limited support from Virginia and none at all from the Congress of the Confederation. Although he had no gifts for the Indians, he behaved with such self-assurance and boldness that they admired him nonetheless. When he told them a highly colored version of the American Revolution in terms that they could understand, they wanted to be on his side. Said Clark, "... if we killed a Deer they [the English] would take the skin away and leave us only the meat." This left the Americans naked, so "at last we complained—the King got mad and made his Soldiers Kill some of our People and Burn some of our villages. Our Old Men then held a Great Council and made the tomahawk very sharp. ..." Thus, the Piankashaw Miami and the Illinois Indians were won over to the American cause. To all the Indians of the Heartland, Clark was the biggest of the Big Knives, as they called the Americans.[12]

The Miami at Kekionga followed a cautious course. Early in 1778 they had refused to follow their resident trader, Charles Beaubien, in a raid on Kentucky. Beaubien recruited a party of sixty Shawnee, under Chief Blackfish, who had the good fortune to capture Daniel Boone. They took Boone to Detroit but refused to turn him over to Colonel Henry Hamilton for a ransom of £100. Instead they adopted him into their tribe. However, Boone managed to make his escape about the time that Clark was marching on Kaskaskia.[13] When Hamilton came in force to Kekionga, on his way to recapture Vincennes, the Miami joined him. But after Clark took Vincennes once more, and Hamilton and his men as well, they resumed their policy of caution. It was not until the defeat of La Balme and the sudden rise of Little Turtle that they became definitely committed to the British. But not even Little Turtle's victory was enough to win the Piankashaw away from the American side.

Although Clark had not been strong enough to mount his cherished attack on Detroit, he had held Kaskaskia and Vincennes, and the British offensives against St. Louis and the Falls of the Ohio had failed. Clark had burned the Shawnee villages in southwestern Ohio in 1780. The Delaware and the Wyandot had defeated Colonel Crawford's campaign against upper Sandusky in 1782, and in revenge for Williamson's attack on Gnadenhutten, Crawford had been burned at the stake with horrible tortures. The Miami could hardly have anticipated that the Treaty of Paris in 1783 would transfer their land to the Americans, who had failed to conquer them and who had actually been aided by the Piankashaw Miami band. For them it was a repetition of what had occurred in 1763.

The British did not deal honestly with the Indians of the Heartland. They retained Detroit instead of surrendering it to the Americans, as provided by the treaty. They continued to supply the Indians with goods and to summon them to conference at Detroit. British agents among the Indians included Alexander McKee, Matthew Elliott, and the Girty brothers, Simon, James, and George, all of whom were regarded as renegades by the Americans. After 1783 these agents still urged the Indians to raid the Kentucky and Ohio settlements. Colonel Haldimand, as governor-general of Canada, assured the Indians they would not lose their lands.[14] Gifts were more plentiful than ever now that they served a political purpose. Finally, raids on frontier settlements were exactly the type of warfare at which the Indians excelled and which they thoroughly enjoyed. The new American government could not compete with the British in gifts, nor could it adequately protect its frontier settlers. Those settlers could only try to protect themselves by waging war in the same way that the Indians did, and they seldom had second thoughts about doing so.

Indians often took prisoners, usually women and children, but at times also grown men. What happened after capture was unpredictable. Men might be tortured, enslaved, and roughly treated; women were less likely to be physically tortured or killed. Children were not usually ill treated and often grew up to marry or be adopted into an Indian tribe. Frequently they were traded from one tribe to another for whiskey, and when whiskey was involved, no one could be sure what would happen. Frontiersmen were less likely to take captives, but such instances did occur, and there were cases where Indians were educated in white schools and treated as family members. Although more impulsive in their actions for both good and bad treatment of captives, the Indians were less given to racial prejudice and were more likely to develop affection for their prisoners.

The government of the United States, under the Articles of Confederation, had been strong enough to win independence from Great Britain, thus acquiring title to all Crown lands, including those that Britain had received from France in 1763, within the boundaries agreed upon. However, the Crown lands had two defects of title. First, they were claimed by individual states under their colonial charters. This defect was removed as, one by one, the states with such claims relinquished them to the United States. Second, and more significant, the Crown lands were occupied by Indian tribes whose right of occupation, though not of ownership, had always been recognized by both France and England.

The Articles of Confederation gave explicit control of Indian affairs to the United States. The Congress of the Confederation, acting under this power, began to make treaties with Indian tribes which provided compensation in return for such cessions of land as they might be induced to make. In this way the United States eventually acquired unclouded title to lands ceded by England, subject to Indian rights of occupation. By doing so the Indian rights of occupation acquired a status virtually tantamount to recognized rights of ownership, which was an advance over the theoretical rights of Indians, as previously defined. However, the rights were theoretical only, because the United States was committed to a policy of eliminating them through treaties that provided compensation.

The Indian tribes gradually came to understand and accept the theory and practice, as defined by the government, but the process was long, drawn out, and is still subject to some litigation. It was complicated by the fact that the Indians did not recognize the rights of their leaders to make such agreements, although if an individual Indian made his mark on a piece of paper and received something in compensation for doing so, he recognized it as a binding transaction.[15]

Some early treaties require brief notice at this point. In October 1784, at the second Treaty of Fort Stanwix, the Iroquois Confederacy relinquished to the United States any claim to land north of the Ohio. They had made a similar agreement with the British in 1768 at the first Treaty of Fort Stanwix. In January 1785, at Fort McIntosh, a treaty with the Ottawa, the Delaware, and the Wyandot limited those tribes to an area between the Cuyahoga and Maumee rivers. At Fort Finney, at the mouth of the Great Miami, in January 1786, a portion of the Shawnee agreed to the extension of the Fort McIntosh line from the head of the Great Miami to the mouth of the Wabash, but this was repudiated later by most of the Shawnee tribe and many of the signers.[16]

From the viewpoint of the United States these treaties opened southern Ohio to settlement. The Congress of the Confederation passed a land ordinance in 1785 under which land surveys were begun in eastern Ohio, and another ordinance in 1787 which provided for the possible admission of new states and, in the meantime, for territorial government. The government promptly negotiated sales of land to the Ohio Associates, who settled the Muskingum valley, and soon sold a tract between the Great and Little Miami rivers to John Cleves Symmes.

The Miami were not party to any of these treaties and did not admit their validity, for the terms led to encroachment upon land that they regarded as theirs. They took the lead in trying to unite the various tribes in repudiating the treaties and in maintaining the Ohio River as the boundary between Indian country and American settlements. In this they were aided and encouraged by the British at Detroit.

The British allowed Joseph Brant, the Mohawk chief, to play a leading part in the conferences that were held, even though Brant was not trusted by the Heartland Indians. He was unable to win them over to the doctrine he had espoused that all the land belonged to all the Indians and that, in this matter, no one tribe could act without the consent of all. Brant's doctrine was later to be revived by Tecumseh with no greater success. This was an alien concept, entirely theoretical, and had never been followed by any tribe, including Brant's Iroquois Confederacy. The Wyandot and the Delaware were willing to follow Brant, but the Miami and the Shawnee prevented any others from agreement. Although no united front was possible, Governor Arthur St. Clair persuaded some of the Wyandot and the Delaware to ratify the former treaties by a new treaty at Fort Harmar, near Marietta, in 1789. Most of these two tribes joined the majority and decided to fight for the Ohio River boundary.[17]

The United States government endeavored to be fair in its Indian policy. The army under General Josiah Harmar was authorized to evict squatters from Ohio, but the job was too big to be done effectively. The Ordinance of 1787 declared that no Indian lands would be taken without the Indians' consent. The Fort McIntosh and Fort Finney treaties gave Indians the right to deal with trespassers on their lands as they chose. In only one respect was the government inconsistent: it guaranteed Indian lands to them by treaty at the same time that it planned eventually to create new states out of the same land.

The government underwent an important change in 1789 when it chose General Washington as president under a new constitution that was much stronger than the Articles of Confederation. The frontier movement would have overwhelmed and probably exterminated the Indians in the long run. Sheer numbers would have triumphed in the end, but the end would have been long deferred. The new government was untried, but it was able to cope with the Indians in an organized and authoritative way and to give approval and direction to the frontier growth.

The war that the Heartland Indians undertook in defense of their homes and their way of life would not have amounted to much except for their two assets: the British at Detroit were able to supply the Indians with the wherewithal to fight, and the Miami had a military genius in the person of their war chief, Little Turtle.

NOTES

1. PECKHAM (2), 58–66, 90–91. KRAUSKOPF states that Lieutenant Jenkins was forced to make presents to the Indians before he was allowed to take charge at Fort Ouiatenon.

2. PECKHAM (2), 90–102.

3. Ibid., 112–55, 201–10, 237–38.

4. Ibid., 160–61; ANSON, 66.

5. PECKHAM (2), 243–318, passim. The affair involving Captain Thomas Morris will be fully treated in the next chapter.

6. ANSON, 58–94.

7. PHILBRICK, 1–52, presents a good summary of the frontier movement prior to the American Revolution from a legal point of view.

8. WESLAGER, 332–36. The Miami did not concede joint ownership rights to the Delaware until 1809 by the Treaty of Fort Wayne. Dissatisfied, the Delaware decided to move beyond the Mississippi, although they did not act on this decision until 1820. The Potawatomi and other Indians who entered Miami land without invitation were eventually regarded as co-owners by the Miami. Thus, squatter's rights proved to be capable of recognition among Indians as among whites.

9. PECKHAM (2), 285–86.

10. PAXSON, 51, states that the Quebec Act was regarded by the United States as an act of war and not a law.

11. WESLAGER, 304–9, 315–17.

12. Clark's exploits are too well known to require narration here. See SYMPOSIUM (1), 40. The quotations are from Chalou's article.

13. PECKHAM (1), 98–115. Hamilton's expedition to Vincennes will be treated in the next chapter.

14. The activities of the British agents are detailed in HORSMAN, passim. On Sir Frederick Haldimand, see PHILBRICK, 136–38, 143–45.

15. A fine survey of the subject of securing title to Indian lands is Dwight L. Smith, "The Land Cession Treaty: A Valid Instrument of Transfer of Indian Title," in SYMPOSIUM (2), especially 87, 102.

16. ANSON, 98–100. See also BILLINGTON, 2, map.

17. STONE, II, 264–70; PHILBRICK, 140–42; HORSMAN, 51–55.

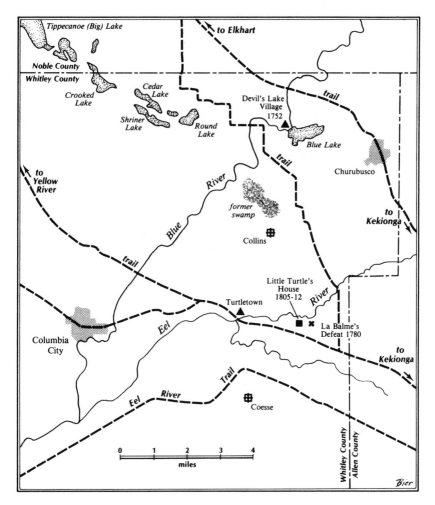

Map 1. *Little Turtle's Homeland.* Blue Lake, Turtletown, Kekionga, the streams, and some of the trails are shown. Little Turtle was strongly attached to his homeland.

Figure 1. *Miami Arrowheads.* Some are prehistoric; some are from the period covered by Little Turtle's life span. All were plowed up between 1950 and 1980. Courtesy of Stephen Carter.

Figure 2. *Other Miami Artifacts.* Like the arrowheads, these were found within a radius of two or three miles from the west end of Blue Lake. Courtesy of Stephen Carter.

Figure 3. *Little Turtle.* The source and authenticity of this woodcut cannot be established, but the decorations worn are compatible with Miami custom and the facial features are not incompatible with those of the lithograph (Figure 4). Reproduced by permission of the Indiana Historical Society.

Figure 4. *Little Turtle, or Mich-i-Kin-i-qua.* This lithograph of the Miami war chief, conqueror of Harmar and St. Clair, is reputed to have been made from the portrait painted in 1797 by Gilbert Stuart. The original painting was destroyed when the British burned Washington in 1814. Photograph courtesy of the Indiana Historical Society. Reproduced by permission of the Smithsonian Institution. B.A.E. negative no. 794.

Figure 5. *Pacanne (Pacan)*. This line drawing of the head chief of the Atchatchakangouen Miami was made by Henry Hamilton in 1778, during his expedition from Detroit to Vincennes. Pacan was head chief from 1764 to 1816. Reproduced by permission of the Houghton Library, Harvard University.

Figure 6. *Paccane (Pacan)*. A second drawing of Pacan was made in 1794 by Mrs. John G. Simcoe, wife of the British lieutenant-governor of Canada. The similarity of the two drawings, made sixteen years apart, is remarkable. Reproduced by permission of the Archives of Ontario, Canada.

Figure 7. *Colonel Augustin Mottin de La Balme.* La Balme was attacked and killed by Little Turtle near Turtletown in 1780. This success earned for Little Turtle the position of war chief of the Miami proper, which his father had also held. Reproduced by permission of the Whitley County (Indiana) Historical Society.

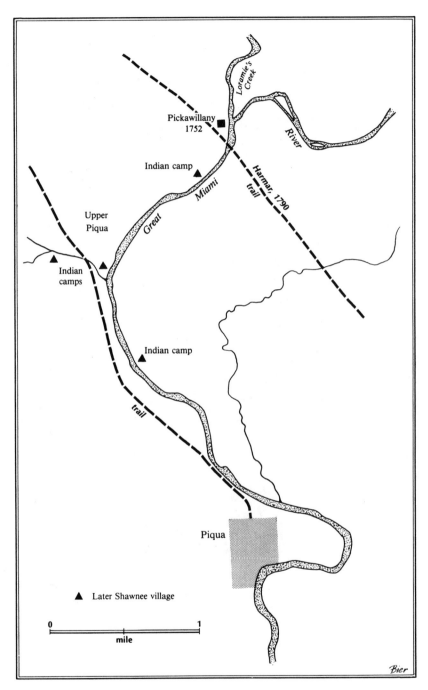

Map 2. *Pickawillany.* As a child (1747–52) Little Turtle lived at this fort and British trading post near Piqua, Ohio. The fort, built by his father, was attacked and partly destroyed by a French and Indian expedition in 1752.

PART TWO

THE WARRIOR

7

The Miami Triumvirate, 1752–90

ATTENTION MUST NOW BE GIVEN to the leadership of the Miami and to the rather considerable influence on events that this small but strategically located tribe was able to exert. There were three Miami chiefs who rose to power and directed the affairs of the tribe during this period: Le Gris, Pacan, and Little Turtle, to use the names by which they were most commonly known. Thus mentioned, they are certainly ranked in the order in which they achieved public recognition and in the order of ascending importance as well. The use of the term triumvirate is not intended to imply any formal division of power among them, in the fashion of the triumvirates of ancient Rome, but merely to indicate that, from the time of their first public recognition to the time of their deaths, they were powerful men in the direction of the affairs of their tribes.

On April 21, 1752, Charles le Moyne, Sieur de Longueil, reported to the minister of colonial affairs in France that a great smallpox epidemic had struck the Miami. This was two months before the fall of Fort Pickawillany, except for which event the remnant of the Miami might have removed to that location and entered permanently the orbit of English influence. Longueil wrote, "Coldfoot and his son have died of it, as well as a large portion of our most trusty Indians. Le Gris, Chief of the Tepicons, and his mother, are likewise dead; they are a loss because they were well disposed toward the French."[1]

In 1824 Chief Le Gros informed Trowbridge, "There was a village on the head of Tippecanoe river. About seventy or eighty years ago, small pox destroyed all the inhabitants but an old woman and her son who came to the Miami. The child was afterward the chief of the Turtle tribe and died not many years ago. He was called 'the Gray.'"[2] In this brief and

65

somewhat inaccurate report there is contained valuable historical evidence. The child referred to was probably the nephew of the elder Le Gris, whose death by smallpox occurred in 1752. He was a young relative of that chief and entitled to succeed him as chief of the remnant of the Pepikokia village located at the west end of Tippecanoe Lake, where the river of that name emerges and flows through Bone Prairie. Undoubtedly there were many more survivors than the child and his mother. When the remnant of the band "came to the Miami," they were not absorbed by the Atchatchak-angouen at Kekionga but founded their own village on the east side of the St. Joseph River, in the angle between it and the Maumee River. This probably occurred within a year or two after the smallpox epidemic of 1752, so the report of Le Gros as "seventy years ago" is approximately correct.

The new settlement became known before long as Le Gris's Village, and Le Petit Gris, as he was sometimes called, was clearly the recognized chief by 1764. Hence it may be concluded that he was born between 1740 and 1744. The elder Le Gris seems to have been both a village chief and a war chief, and the same was true of the younger Le Gris. Neither was head chief of the Pepikokia band, whose principal village was Kithtippe-canuck, or Petit Piconne, at the mouth of the Tippecanoe River. From this time the Pepikokia band was split, with the upper Tepicon at Le Gris's Village acting in concert with Kekionga, and the lower Tepicon band acting in concert with the Ouiatenon. The younger Le Gris was originally named Waspikingua, the meaning of which is unknown. He was also called Na-kakwanga, meaning "crooked legs," or more precisely, "crippled ankles." Most frequently he was referred to as Le Gris (The Dappled Fawn).[3]

Le Gris's Village was about the same size as Kekionga, which was located on the west side of the St. Joseph River about a quarter of a mile above the junction with the St. Marys. The Indian population of Kekionga was greater, however, because most of the traders lived at Le Gris's Village. The well-established trails came into Kekionga, which was the starting point for the portage to Little River. Kekionga also had a large council house where official meetings were held. Le Gris's Village often flooded in the spring, but Kekionga was located on higher ground.[4] A small stream called Spy Run parallels the St. Joseph at a distance of about a mile but flows into the St. Marys just below the junction. It was on this watershed that Kekionga was located.

The original French fort had been established in the angle formed by the Maumee and the St. Marys. The later French fort and the English fort were located in the angle formed by the St. Joseph and the Maumee. The St. Marys is somewhat larger in volume than the St. Joseph River, but the latter is somewhat more swiftly flowing. The Miami cornfields were to be found along all three streams, but especially along the Maumee. Some writers designated Kekionga in such a way as to include both Miami villages at the headwaters of the Maumee. Indians often referred to it by the name of the head chief, as they did in the case of smaller villages. Thus, in Coldfoot's time it was referred to by his name. The practice continued during Pacan's minority and even later, but it eventually became Pacan's Village. Indians also called it Kekionga, of course, and whites frequently used the term Miamistown.[5]

Pacan (The Nut) became head chief under rather dramatic circumstances in 1764, when he was "yet a minor."[6] He was probably a nephew of Coldfoot, certainly a relative on the female side and thus in line for the hereditary succession when he should reach a proper age, which normally would have been twenty-three or twenty-four. But there is reason to think that he may have been no older than seventeen in 1764 when he assumed the powers of head chief of the Atchatchakangouen Miami at Kekionga. He was thus more closely contemporary with Little Turtle than with Le Gris, for if he was seventeen in 1764 their births would have occurred in the same year. Like Little Turtle he was too young to have taken any part in events connected with Pontiac's uprising. Le Gris, on the other hand, may well have had some part in them.

After Pontiac gave up the siege of Detroit the British sent Colonel John Bradstreet westward to overawe the Indians with a force of 1,200 men. By August of 1764 he had reached Sandusky Bay and sent Captain Thomas Morris to Kekionga with instructions to proceed to Ouiatenon, Vincennes, and Kaskaskia. Morris was given an escort of only 50 Oneida Indians and Jacques Godfroy as guide and interpreter. Godfroy, it will be recalled, had incited the Miami to capture the British garrisons at Miamistown and Ouiatenon during Pontiac's uprising. He was now under sentence of death but was told he could earn his pardon by ensuring the safety of Captain Morris. The party started up the Maumee and reached Pontiac's Village on August 27, 1764.[7]

Here Morris found himself the center of hostile demonstrations by some 600 Indians, chiefly Ottawa but including many belonging to other tribes. Pontiac at first assumed a threatening posture, but he then moderated his attitude sufficiently to attach his nephew to the party and allow it to proceed to Kekionga. Morris was not able to set out until September 1; early on September 7 they arrived at Le Gris's Village. En route, on September 5, they had seen a Miami riding a handsome white horse that had been taken nine years earlier on the occasion of Braddock's Defeat. At Le Gris's Village a hostile demonstration, similar to the one he had already experienced, awaited Morris, and he was placed in the rather ruinous Fort Miamis, where he spoke with a member of the former English garrison who was chopping wood. Morris believed this treatment had been prompted by a delegation of Delaware and Shawnee Indians which had just departed. They had urged the Miami to kill Morris or give him to them as a prisoner. Godfroy gave him little reassurance. At Pontiac's Village, Atawang, a pro-British Ottawa chief, had given Morris a volume of Shakespeare. He endeavored now to compose his mind by reading *Antony and Cleopatra* but was unable to convince himself that he faced less than death by torture.[8]

Morris's worst fears were aggravated when he was roughly seized by two Miami warriors, armed with tomahawks, who dragged him across the fordable St. Joseph River to the edge of Kekionga. The villagers were in an uproar. They bound his arms and set him on a bench while a number of people spoke for and against him. Godfroy spoke on his behalf and was supported by Pontiac's nephew. Morris's two captors spoke against him, and one of them had tied him to a post "when young Pacanne (King of the village, but yet a minor) rode up and untied me saying, 'I give that man his life. If you want meat go to Detroit, or upon the lake, and you'll find enough; what business have you with this man who is come to speak to us?' "[9] Morris was returned to the fort, where he was visited by two of Pacan's sisters. After a day of deliberation the Miami council informed him that he must return to Colonel Bradstreet, who had now reached Detroit.[10]

Captain Morris was convinced that he had narrowly escaped death. This was possibly so, but probably not. It is hard to avoid the conclusion that the whole affair at Kekionga had been contrived in advance by the chiefs of the Miami council and that the events had been acted out exactly as they had planned them. They were fully informed of what had occurred at Pontiac's Village before Morris had left it, and they had plenty of time to perfect their plans. Pacan was not quite of an age to assume his position as hereditary head chief at Kekionga, an assumption which was always signaled by some public act of authority. Captain Morris's arrival, however, presented an opportunity too good to be missed, and young Pacan's minority was shortened by a few years.

The Miami accomplished several things beyond a dramatic induction to power for their young chief. They stopped Morris from proceeding on his mission and thereby asserted their independence of the British and their precedence over Ouiatenon and Vincennes within the Miami tribe. They allowed Pontiac's nephew to support the action of their head chief but denied him the leading role that his uncle had intended. They enacted their drama at Kekionga on the very day, September 7, 1764, that Colonel Bradstreet had forced the Indians, including a Miami delegation, to make peace at Detroit with the English. And Bradstreet was thus placed under obligation to the Miami for having saved the life of his ambassador, Captain Morris. The whole performance furnished a fine example of the way in which the Miami for so long exercised a leadership far beyond that to which their scanty numbers entitled them.[11]

Before he left Kekionga, Captain Morris gave Pacan a letter attesting the fact that he owed his life to the timely intervention of the Miami head chief. In 1765, when George Croghan visited Detroit by way of Kekionga, Pacan accompanied him. At that time Croghan gave Captain Morris a handsome present, which he in turn presented to Pacan in appreciation of his decisive action of the previous year.[12]

George Croghan's river voyage from Fort Pitt to the mouth of the Maumee in 1765 is remarkable for the fact that he kept two journals: in one of these he recorded the events of the trip, and in the other he wrote comments on the nature of the land through which he traveled. The second journal was for the benefit of land speculators with whom Croghan was closely associated. In describing the Wabash valley Croghan nearly exhausted his vocabulary of superlatives. He and his party left Fort Pitt on May 15, encamped at the Falls of the Ohio on June 1, and reached the mouth of the Wabash on June 6, where two days later they were attacked by eighty Kickapoo and Mascouten from near Fort Ouiatenon. Croghan lost two white and three Indian companions; he himself and nearly all of his surviving men were wounded. They were taken captive, but Croghan's Indians, who were Shawnee, Delaware, and Seneca, protested that a mistake had been made. On June 15, when the party reached Vincennes, the Piankashaw told them, "Our and your chiefs are gone to make peace and you have begun a war, for which our women and children will have reason to cry."[13]

Croghan and his party reached the Kickapoo and Mascouten villages near Ouiatenon on June 23, where their hostile action was likewise condemned. Conferences with the Indians now began. On July 13 the Miami chiefs from Kekionga came and smoked the peace pipe. Croghan set out for the Illinois villages on July 18 but met Pontiac on the way, and they all returned to Ouiatenon for further peace talks. Croghan resumed his journey on July 25. His captivity had resulted in ending the hostility of Pontiac, which might otherwise have been hard to achieve.

Instead of following the Wabash to its forks at Huntington, Croghan traveled the Eel River route and arrived at the portage to Kekionga, on August 1. On August 6 he left Kekionga, arriving at Detroit, by way of the Maumee, on August 17.[14] Although Croghan spent a month at Ouiatenon and several days at Kekionga, he does not mention by name a single chief, with the sole exception of Pontiac. He was a veteran trader, but it is clear that he was no longer interested in the Indians as customers; he was only interested in acquiring land. George Croghan's change of perspective presaged what was to be the American attitude. The British government, however, wanted to foster trade, so for the next decade good relations with the Miami prevailed at Detroit.

In August 1773 both Pacan and Le Gris attended a conference at Detroit where Sir William Johnson sought to unify the tribes by promoting the idea that the Indians were all one people, an appealing concept, true in a theoretical sense, but of little practical use. That the land belonged to all Indians in common was the artificial and illogical deduction that was made. The Miami chiefs responded politely to Sir William, although they took the occasion to remind him of their ancient wrongs at the hands of the Iroquois Confederacy.[15] Sir William died during the following year, on the eve of the American Revolution.

The settlement of Kentucky and the American Revolution developed simultaneously and merged when George Rogers Clark secured, from the state of Virginia, full sanction and limited backing for an offensive campaign north of the Ohio River. With volunteers recruited mainly on the Monongahela, he set out from Redstone Fort on May 12, 1778, pausing at the Falls of the Ohio and going overland from the lower Ohio to Kaskaskia, which he took by complete surprise on July 4, 1778. Colonel Clark brought news of the French alliance concluded with the United States earlier that year and was thus able to win the support of the French villagers at Kaskaskia and at Cahokia, sixty miles away. Vincennes had a British lieutenant governor, Edward Abbott, but there were no soldiers with him. Clark won the support of the French villagers by sending Father Pierre Gibault to them and then assigning Captain Leonard Helm to take over the fort. Near Vincennes was the Piankashaw village of Old Tobacco and his son, Young Tobacco, who were persuaded to the American cause by Captain Helm. Helm moved up the Wabash to Ouiatenon against a British force, which he found, however, had prudently withdrawn before his arrival. Land speculators were not far behind Clark. Thomas Bentley, a Kaskaskia trader acting for the Illinois Company and the Wabash Company, soon negotiated land purchase treaties with the Kaskaskia and the Piankashaw tribes.[16]

Within a very short time Lieutenant Governor Henry Hamilton, at Detroit, had news from the Indians of Clark's exploits. By August 6–8 Colonel Hamilton informed his superiors in London and Quebec, with a fair degree of accuracy, of what had occurred and indicated that he planned to take prompt military action. After two months of preparation, Hamilton set out on October 7 from Detroit with 162 white soldiers, of which 33 were British regulars, and 70 Indians; most of the volunteers were French. Hamilton was well supplied with food and took with him some light artillery. He also hoped to win support from the "Wabash Indians" along the way.[17]

It took three weeks to reach Kekionga (October 7–27); a full month (October 28–November 28) was required to travel to Ouiatenon, one-half of which was spent getting over the portage and down the Little River to the Forks of the Wabash; and the journey from Ouiatenon to Vincennes took nearly three more weeks (November 29–December 17). Upon his arrival at Vincennes, Hamilton met no resistance from Captain Helm, who surrendered at once. The Indians, who had joined him en route, had no opportunity to impress Hamilton with their prowess in war, but he had, on the other hand, impressed them very strongly by his demonstration of strength.

Both Pacan and Le Gris accompanied Hamilton's expedition to Vincennes. Little Turtle may have done so, but he was still an unknown, and there is no definite knowledge that he was in the party. Pacan took two other chiefs and on October 17 met Hamilton on the lower Maumee, on the prairie of the Mascouten. Pacan told Hamilton that the American rebels commonly referred to him as a dog and said they would treat him like one.[18] Hamilton spent four days at Miamistown, during which his men moved the boats and supplies over the portage. On November 8, while Hamilton's boats were still on the Little River waiting for the water to rise behind a dam, Pacan, with his special guard of eleven young warriors, joined the expedition.[19]

A fairly large number of Miami accompanied Hamilton. On November 15 Le Gris, as principal war chief, made a speech to them as they were encamped below the Forks of the Wabash. Individual warriors then spent some time in loud devotional singing to their *nattes,* or budgets, as Hamilton called them (from the fact that each warrior carried his sacred articles in a wallet or leather bag).[20] Pacan came to Hamilton's tent on November 24 to discuss with him certain belts being circulated by the Chickasaw. More warriors were added at Kenapakomoko and Kithtippecanuck and, of course, at Ouiatenon, where the Kickapoo, Mascouten, and Potawatomi joined, as well as the Wea. During a turkey hunt on November 9 at Terre Haute a Shawnee was accidentally blinded in one eye, and the next day Le Gris spoke to quiet any discontent that might have arisen from the incident.[21]

Following the occupation of Vincennes, Hamilton granted the Indians permission to leave, for they were of little use in repairing Fort Sackville, as Fort Vincennes was now called. Pacan, as became a head chief, did not ask permission but called upon Hamilton on January 20, 1779, to say that he was leaving and that he would return in the spring by way of the Falls of the Ohio. On February 5 Le Gris and two Ottawa chiefs informed Hamilton that they were sending messages to the Maumee. Many Ottawa, Wyandot, and Delaware, as well as Piankashaw, Ouiatenon, and Miami, assembled at Fort Sackville on February 21 to hear Young Tobacco declare his allegiance to the British and confess once more his foolishness in joining the Americans and in selling land to them.[22]

On February 22, after an incredible march across Illinois during a time of rising water that flooded the bottomlands, George Rogers Clark, at the head of about 170 men, arrived at Vincennes. Approximately half of Clark's volunteers were Frenchmen who ascertained that the French of Vincennes preferred them to the British. Hamilton, realizing that he could not count on any but his British regulars, held out for two days against Clark's demand for surrender. The Miami, under Le Gris, were doubtless in the woods during this time, waiting to see which of the white leaders would prove to be the stronger. When Hamilton and his regulars surrendered the Miami went home. The Piankashaw then resumed their friendly attitude toward the Americans, who were able to retain Vincennes.

It is possible that the Wea Miami, under Little Face, may have played some part in the outcome. During the time Hamilton was at Fort Sackville an Ottawa band went to Kaskaskia with the intention of killing Colonel Clark. The attempt failed. There is some evidence that Charles Beaubien, the French trader at Kekionga who accompanied the Wea to Kaskaskia, may have forewarned the American leader of the Ottawa's plot to assassinate him.[23]

In November of the following year, 1780, while Henry Hamilton was still a prisoner at Williamsburg, Virginia, the third member of the Miami triumvirate, Little Turtle, made his sudden leap to a position of power and influence among the Miami. The event that catapulted him to attention was one of the most obscure and peculiar happenings of the American Revolution. The campaign of George Rogers Clark was responsible for it in a way; and, curiously enough, Charles Beaubien played a crucial part in it as well.

Among those who accompanied La Fayette to America in 1777 was a cavalry officer named Augustin Mottin de La Balme. He was about forty years old and had attained the rank of colonel. The Continental Congress gave him a commission as inspector general of cavalry, but he seems to have been dissatisfied with the post and resigned after three months to engage in private business,[24] though it is not clear what the business enterprise was. He had formulated certain plans of his own by the summer of 1780 when he wrote from Pittsburgh to the French minister, Luzerne, at Philadelphia, "Three Frenchmen and I are about to start well armed to navigate the Ohio and reach the Illinois, being accompanied by a Shawnee princess somewhat old."[25] It would appear that he was acting in accordance with plans already discussed and probably approved by Luzerne. Other letters and speeches and the testimony of people who knew him, favorably or unfavorably, suggest that his plan was to accomplish what Clark had been unable to do, that is, to capture Detroit from the British.

A condition of the alliance between France and the United States, ratified in 1778, was that France would not attempt to recover Canada. La Balme had provided himself with letters from individuals who asserted that he had "always been a firm and steadfast friend to the interests of America." However, a letter from Thomas Bentley to George Rogers Clark, written from Vincennes on July 30, 1780, warned that La Balme was "pro-French and Anti-American."[26]

When La Balme reached Kaskaskia he claimed to be acting under instructions from Congress. This was not true. He was certainly anti-Virginian, for he was extremely critical of Clark and of Virginia. He realized that Clark and the Virginians were none too popular with the French, nor with the Indians, and felt that he could obtain support better by making it clear that he had no connection with them. He had sent Godfroy de Linctot to recruit from among the Indians of northern Illinois and southern Wisconsin. La Balme was extremely popular at Kaskaskia and succeeded in raising money, supplies, and some volunteers there. These he led to Vincennes, where he enlisted more volunteers.[27]

La Balme had originally planned an attack upon Detroit with 400 Frenchmen and 800 Indians. From his statement that he had to be at Ouiatenon by October 20, 1780, it may be inferred that Linctot was expected to join him there with his Indian forces. La Balme arrived there on time but with far fewer men than he expected to have, and Linctot did not arrive at all. It seems probable that La Balme may have reached Ouiatenon with about 100 men but that he experienced desertions at this point. With 60 men he traveled from Ouiatenon to Kekionga in only four days (October 20–24), which was so rapid a trip that it has been doubted whether he in fact did it.[28] Apparently the party went on horseback, and the Miami at Kekionga were aware of their approach only shortly before their arrival. Even so, a few of the traders had time to send some of their stores down the Maumee for safety.[29]

At this point La Balme acted in such a way as to cast doubt upon his intelligence and ability. Kekionga was of use to him only as a base for operations against Detroit. Such use could have been made of it if, following Clark's example at Kaskaskia and Vincennes, he had conciliated the inhabitants by any means in his power. Instead La Balme pursued an opposite course. He took possession of the village and remained there for twelve days, during which he allowed his men to plunder the stores of two very influential traders, Charles Beaubien and François La Fontaine.[30] Beaubien was the British agent, but he was also the husband of Tacumwah, the sister of Pacan and the mother of Jean Baptiste Richardville, soon to be recognized as Pacan's hereditary successor as head chief of the Atchatchakangouen Miami and associated with him as deputy chief. Tacumwah and her son controlled the portage to the Wabash and enjoyed its revenues. La Fontaine's son later married Richardville's daughter. La Balme's men helped themselves liberally to the liquor of the traders, after which they behaved toward the Indians in ways that were resented. Probably the available liquor had been consumed and all the cattle had been roasted and eaten by the end of the twelve days, when La Balme withdrew twelve miles west of Kekionga and encamped, after having quickly put up an earthwork.[31]

The site of the camp was along the Eel River, three miles directly east of Turtletown, the home of Little Turtle. This explains how Little Turtle came to be in charge of the Indian attack on La Balme's camp; the French officer had plundered Kekionga and was now just "a whoop and a holler" away from Turtletown. No doubt the Kekionga warriors were eager for revenge, but the command belonged to Little Turtle because the enemy was now in his territory.

The attack began just before dawn on November 5, 1780. The Frenchmen were able to fire one volley, killing five Miami, before they were overwhelmed. La Balme and thirty of his men were killed, some prisoners were taken, and a few of his force escaped into the woods. Eventually several survivors made their way to Vincennes and Kaskaskia. One of the prisoners, Rhè or Rhys, La Balme's aide-de-camp, was taken immediately by the Miami to Detroit and turned over, on November 13, to the commander, Major Arent De Peyster.[32] De Peyster, chagrined that La Balme's approach had been unknown to him, sent his prisoner to Niagara, along with La Balme's commission in the French army. Later his men recovered at Kekionga a book, a double-barreled rifle, a German flute, and some papers of La Balme relating to the expedition. De Peyster admitted that, had La Balme reached Detroit and been supported by the French villagers there, it would have caused him "a deal of trouble."[33]

La Balme's defeat is frequently referred to as a massacre, which it definitely was not—it was the first of Little Turtle's notable military victories. La Balme's party was fully armed and encamped with standard military precautions against attack. Half of his force was killed and the rest put to disorganized flight. The Miami loss was sufficient by Indian standards to have discouraged a leader less resolute than Little Turtle. His reputation in the eyes of his tribe was enhanced by the fact that the victory was won over a force that had terrorized Kekionga for twelve days. From this time forward he was a war chief whom the Miami followed with confidence. Nevertheless, ten years were to pass before much was widely known of his activities. It can only be said that from 1780 to 1790 he led many raids against frontier settlements along the Ohio and in Kentucky, which increased his fame and influence among the Miami and other tribes.

The effect of La Balme's expedition was unfortunate for the United States. Clark's conquest of Vincennes had brought the Piankashaw Miami definitely within American control. During the winter after La Balme's defeat the Piankashaw, joined by the French at Vincennes, sent a message to Ouiatenon and asked that it be delivered to Pacan at Kekionga. The Wea Miami complied, but it is not clear whether they endorsed the message, which urged Pacan to join the Piankashaw against the British. Pacan's response was to take the message to Detroit, where, on February 25, 1781, he publicly rejected it in strong terms and reaffirmed his loyalty to the British. Governor Haldimand was impressed by Pacan's speech and by the fact that he concluded it by singing the Miami war song and was, furthermore, joined in doing so by those Miami present.[34] From this time to 1787 the Piankashaw Miami were firmly on the American side, the Miami proper firmly on the British side, and the Wea Miami were as a weather vane on a gusty day.

Meanwhile, Congress created a regular army of 700 men, with Brigadier General Josiah Harmar in command. General Harmar's headquarters were at Fort Harmar, near Marietta, but he planned to station troops at Vincennes under Major John Francis Hamtramck. When this became known at Kekionga, Pacan was forced to consider whether it would be better policy for the Miami to continue their allegiance to the British at Detroit or whether the American concentration at Vincennes would provide a more dependable connection. Such a matter required investigation and deliberation before it could be decided.

Accordingly, Pacan established a village on the Embarras River, about twenty or thirty miles northwest of Vincennes, near the village of La Demoiselle, the son of the Piankashaw chief who had been killed at Pickawillany in 1752. The younger La Demoiselle had been a guide for John Filson, the Kentucky cartographer, in 1785.[35] When General Harmar arrived at Fort Vincennes in August 1787 he accepted Pacan's offer to serve as guide and hunter. General Harmar set out at once on "a good will tour" to Kaskaskia, a tour which extended from August 9 to September 3, by which time Major Hamtramck arrived at Vincennes.[36] Following a conference with the Indians, Harmar departed, leaving Hamtramck in charge of a garrison of ninety-five men. Pacan continued to perform various services for Hamtramck, who came to value his good qualities and employed him as an emissary to other Indian tribes.

A year later, in August 1788, Hamtramck sent Pacan to a council held by Alexander McKee, British commissioner for Indian affairs, at Roche du Bout on the Maumee. Upon his return Pacan was to report to Hamtramck on the proceedings of the meeting. As a result of their year-long acquaintance Pacan was trusted by Hamtramck.[37] On August 18, while Pacan was away on this mission, Major Patrick Brown, commanding sixty Kentucky militiamen, made his appearance at Vincennes. Hamtramck learned that Brown had just destroyed the villages of Pacan and La Demoiselle, had murdered a number of their people, and had stolen six of Pacan's horses, which the major refused to give up. Hamtramck was outnumbered at the time and had to submit to Brown's insolence. From Vincennes, Brown and his men returned to Kentucky instead of continuing their depredations. Those of Pacan's village who had been able to escape camped at Terre Haute awaiting their chief's return. When Pacan reached Terre Haute and heard their story he did not continue to Vincennes to render his report but conducted his people back to Kekionga.[38] From this time to 1795 the Miami proper were committed to the maintenance of the Ohio as the northern limit of American frontier settlement. Through no fault of his own, Pacan's diplomatic efforts toward an understanding between the Miami and the United States had ended in failure.

Late in 1789 a young man, half English and half French, journeyed from Detroit to Kekionga and spent ninety-nine days there from December 16, 1789, to March 24, 1790. This visitor was Henry Hay, the twenty-four-year-old son of Jehu Hay, who had been captured with Hamilton at Vincennes in 1779. The purpose of his visit to Kekionga is not known, but he left a most interesting diary which, in addition to giving a vivid picture of life in the Miami villages, sheds some further light upon Le Gris and Little Turtle. Pacan was absent during the entire time, as he and most of the inhabitants of Kekionga had gone on their winter hunt along the Kankakee River in Illinois.[39]

Pacan's sister, Tacumwah (The Other Side), was present during some of Hay's visit, and her son, Jean Baptiste Richardville, Pacan's heir-apparent according to Miami custom, was there as his deputy chief. Jean Baptiste was probably born in 1761. His father, Antoine Joseph Drouet de Richerville, a trader at Kekionga from about 1750 to 1770, had later moved to Three Rivers, Canada, where his son had been educated before returning to Kekionga.[40] Following Antoine de Richerville's departure, Tacumwah, a Miami female chief and also a trader, married Charles Beaubien. Young Henry Hay had some dealings with her and referred to her as having once been a beautiful woman.[41] Jean Baptiste Richardville had been a chief since about 1785, his mother having secured his right to succeed his uncle by the traditional Miami custom whereby authority was publicly asserted: the Miami had been about to burn a captive white man at the stake, and she had prompted her son to cut the captive loose and set him free.[42]

76

Hay recorded that Richardville was so bashful that his mother usually spoke for him in council, but this may have been an error of observation—Tacumwah may have been speaking for herself rather than for her son. Richardville was a member of a social club formed by Hay and other white traders during his visit. The young chief was fond of music, but he does not seem to have participated with Hay in drinking bouts and wenching, as other traders did.[43] Hay spent more time in Le Gris's Village than in Kekionga. The traders were mainly located there, and trade was dull because many of the Miami were away on the winter hunt. At times the St. Joseph River was frozen, so that people crossed on the ice from one village to the other.

On December 19, 1789, "Little Turtle, a chief of the Miamiae with his war party consisting of about fifteen or sixteen" arrived in Kekionga. They had taken two captives whom they subsequently lost to the Americans because the captives were left on the Little Miami while Little Turtle sought more.[44]

Hay became very friendly with Le Gris, who was fond of rum and not above begging for some; he promised on one occasion not to get drunk but failed to keep his word.[45] In contrast, neither Pacan nor Little Turtle are recorded by any writer to have drunk to excess. Le Gris was occupied with various matters of business with the Delaware, the Shawnee, the Miami towns of the Wabash, and with the British traders. Little Turtle and Le Gris came together on several occasions to breakfast with Hay.[46] Le Gris and his family gave presents to Hay, but Little Turtle does not seem to have done so. Hay did not give a physical description of either man.

On January 3 both Turtle and Le Gris "went off to their wintering camps." These camps were probably on Turkey Prairie (near Leesburg), about forty miles west by northwest of Kekionga. The chiefs returned in a short time to deal with a letter from chiefs Kaweahatta (The Porcupine) and Shamekunesah (The Soldier) at Kenapakomoko.[47] Again, on March 5, Hay recorded that Le Gris's "wife and brother arrived here with some other of their family from their wintering and hunting ground." That they were accompanied by Little Turtle gives some credence to Hay's statement that Le Gris and Little Turtle were brothers-in-law.[48]

Pacan's absence meant that Le Gris was unusually busy. Although Pacan was well represented by his sister and her son, his absence was nonetheless felt. Turtle was an active war chief, serving as right-hand man to the older war chief. Le Gris transacted little business that Turtle was not involved in helping to decide and carry out. Le Gris was talkative, sociable, even ingratiating; Turtle was reserved, available, and dependable. He had not yet reached the point of ascendancy that he was soon to attain. After 1790 the roles of Little Turtle and Le Gris were somewhat reversed.

A month after Hay's departure, Antoine Gamelin arrived from Vincennes with a final and very perfunctory peace offer from the American territorial governor, Arthur St. Clair. From Le Gris, whom he mistakenly believed to be the "great chief of the Miamis," he received an evasive and dissembling answer.[49] Pacan would have been more direct and defiant. Yet the message was clear. Kekionga was the center of the alliance of tribes that had been constructed mainly by the Miami triumvirate. The Shawnee had established two villages on the Maumee only a mile or two east of Le Gris's Village. Henry Hay reported that Blue Jacket and George and James Girty were there. The Delaware had two villages on the St. Marys River, about three miles below the junction. The British traders, George Ironside, John Kinzie, and others, were present in full force.[50] The raiding parties would continue unless the Americans could carry the war to the Maumee.

NOTES

1. THWAITES (1), XVIII, 108.

2. TROWBRIDGE, 12. This reference provides a good example of both the importance and the defects of oral history. "Gray" is one meaning of the French word *gris:* it might also be translated as "grizzled" or "dappled," as in the English term "dappled gray."

3. BARNHART (2), 228–29, uses all of these names. Other forms of Nakakwanga that have been noted are Nawuskounanda, Necaquangai, Nicaquongay, Naquakouande, and Nagohquangogh. HAY, 224, states that Le Gris's brother, The Deer, "had formerly been great chief of this village but chose to give it up to his Brother." From this it may be concluded that Le Gris was too young to become hereditary chief directly after the smallpox epidemic of 1752 and that for some years one of his uncles exercised the power until his nephew reached his majority.

4. HAY, 254, describes a thaw and consequent flooding on February 26, 1790. Most of the residents were away on their winter hunt at the time.

5. BARNHART (2), 47, 116–17, says that Hamilton was confused about where the portage path began because he wrote that he went to *pied froid* on the other side of the St. Joseph. On the contrary, Barnhart himself was confused, for he reversed the locations of Le Gris's Village and Pacan's Village (Kekionga), on p. 45, by placing the former on the west of the St. Joseph and the latter on the east. Hamilton is quite clear in saying that he crossed the St. Joseph to start the portage from *pied froid*, on the west, where the portage path naturally began at Kekionga. That village in Pacan's time was slightly upriver from where it had been in Coldfoot's time, that is, at the beginning of the portage path, which still retained Coldfoot's name.

6. MORRIS (2), 316, refers to Pacan as "just out of his minority." Thwaites edited the revised and published version of Morris's journal. MORRIS (1), 3–11, uses the

phrase "yet a minor." Other spellings of Pacan include Paccan, Paccane, Pacane, Pecon, Pikawn, and Pecahn. The word meant specifically the pecan nut but was applied to other varieties of nuts as well.

7. MORRIS (2), 301–4.

8. Ibid., 305–11. The detail about Braddock's horse is not in the original journal. It is impossible to say whether Morris later embellished his journal with imaginative or authentic details.

9. MORRIS (1), 8.

10. MORRIS (2), 316–17. One of his visitors must have been Tacumwah, mother of J. B. Richardville. The visit is not mentioned in the original journal.

11. ANSON, 71, suggests the possibility that the whole episode was carefully planned. In my opinion it is a probability.

12. MORRIS (2), 317.

13. CROGHAN, 126–39.

14. Ibid., 141-53. Thwaites used portions of both of Croghan's journals for his published version.

15. MICHIGAN, XIX, 308–10.

16. ABERNETHY, 202, 245–48.

17. BARNHART (2), 37–41.

18. Ibid., 112–13.

19. Ibid., 114–19.

20. Ibid., 121–22.

21. Ibid., 128, 133–36, 141. Hamilton picked up ten warriors at Kenapakomoko and twenty-two at Ouiatenon.

22. Ibid., 165, 173–74, 176.

23. Ibid., 188.

24. MICHIGAN, XIX, 699.

25. ALVORD, 163–67.

26. Ibid., 162, 169–70.

27. Ibid., 195–96. Richard Winston to John Todd, Kaskaskia, October 14, 1780. "There passed this way a Frenchman called himself Col. de la Balme, he says in the American Service. I look upon him to be a Mal Content much disgusted with the Virginian yet I must say he done some good, he Pacified the Indians, he was received by the inhabitants as the Hebrews would receive the messiah . . . he went from here against Detroit."

28. MICHIGAN, X, 448–49. Letter of Major Arent De Peyster to General F. Haldimand, Detroit, November 16, 1780. George Croghan made the trip from Ouiatenon to Kekionga in seven days, in 1765, by horseback, but he traveled the Eel River route and lost one day at Kenapakomoko. There is no basis for the supposition, WHITLEY (April 1970), that La Balme traveled by the Eel River route and never reached Kekionga at all. The distance from Kekionga to Ouiatenon was between 100 and 120 miles by trail but much longer by water, although at high water the river route was quicker.

29. BRUNO. Bruno's recollections were set down in 1830, fifty years after the event. In some respects he may have magnified what happened. On this point he was doubtless accurate, although he claimed not to have removed his own goods.

The fact that he said that La Balme and his men were there but three days may indicate that he returned after caching his goods on the Maumee and saw only the last three days of the sack of Kekionga.

30. Bruno said Antoine Beaubien, which was incorrect. The report made by De Peyster said they "entered the village, took the Horses, destroyed the Horned Cattle and plundered a store I allowed to be kept there for the convenience of the Indians. . . ." Major Arent De Peyster to Brigadier General H. Watson Powell, Detroit, November 13, 1780, in MICHIGAN, XIX, 582.

31. The Eel River site, in addition to the embankment, yielded many human bones found by Charles Moore, owner of the site in the late nineteenth century. This evidence seems to outweigh the belief of M. Rhè, La Balme's aide-de-camp, that they were on the Aboite River. The probability is that they mistook the Eel River for the Aboite, which is very small at the point where they would have crossed it and was probably not recognized. Although some believe that the embankment was an Indian fortification, the Indians did not construct earthworks for defensive purposes. La Balme, a professional soldier, probably felt safe after taking this precaution. KALER and MARING first gave recognition to the Eel River site, but Kaler's account of the La Balme expedition is not only unverified by any sources but is fanciful in placing the sack of Kekionga a week too early and the battle in February 1781. He was unaware of the materials cited herein, although they were published prior to his work. See George F. Schultz, "La Balme Bibliography," in WHITLEY (October 1980).

32. MICHIGAN, XIX, 582.

33. Ibid., 598–600. Captain A. Thompson to Major Arent De Peyster, Miamis[town], March 14, 1781.

34. Ibid., 595–96.

35. BUFFALO, 192.

36. THORNBROUGH (3), 47. General Josiah Harmar to the Secretary of War, Fort Harmar, November 24, 1787. "I was accompanied by two Indians (Pacahn, a Miami chief and his comrade), who hunted and supplied the party with meat (Buffalo and deer) both on the march and on our return." Hamtramck arrived on August 25, 1787. Ibid., 36.

37. Ibid., 108. Major Hamtramck to General Harmar, Poste Vincennes, August 12, 1788. "Pakane the Indian chief who went after the drumer the deserter last year and a good Indian, is going to the Miami and will know the result of this council." Pacan may have been keeping a foothold in both the American and the British camps, but the fact that he established his village near Vincennes is an indication that he expected to shift to the Americans, if all went well.

38. Ibid., 114–17. Hamtramck was extremely irritated at Brown's defiance. GUTHMAN, 158–60, says that Brown "was not a lawless man. His outrageous attacks upon the Indians represented release of emotion and revenge." Nevertheless, Brown and his men defied the United States government. They were also horse thieves, arsonists, and murderers, which are not exactly lawful occupations.

39. HAY, 223.

40. Ibid. See also CHAPUT, 112–17. Richardville was the spelling used by this chief, who was not a nephew of Little Turtle, as often stated, but of Pacan, at whose death he became head chief.

41. Ibid., 246.

42. BRICE, 314–15. Brice relates that later, on a journey to Washington, D.C., Richardville met in an Ohio town the man whom he freed from death.

43. HAY, 230, 246–47, 250.

44. Ibid., 219–20.

45. Ibid., 229–30.

46. Ibid., 229.

47. Ibid., 232, 236, 242.

48. Ibid., 256. If they were brothers-in-law it must have been that Le Gris had married a sister of Little Turtle.

49. ST. CLAIR, II, 155–60, has Antoine Gamelin's journal. Gamelin's error in believing Le Gris to have been "the great chief" rather than Pacan has caused a number of historians to make the same error. Governor Harrison habitually referred to Pacan as "principal chief of the Miami." See ESAREY, I, 375 and passim.

50. HAY, 225, 226, 232, 235–44, 247–49, 255, 258–60.

8

Enter, William Wells, 1784

THE EARLIEST TRANS-APPALACHIAN FRONTIER was along the Youghiogheny and Monongahela rivers in what is now southwestern Pennsylvania, where settlement began before the end of the French and Indian War, as early as 1758. At that time the region was claimed by Virginia as well as by Pennsylvania; the earliest settlers were largely from Virginia. There were about 2,000 people in the area by 1768 when the Treaty of Fort Stanwix was concluded, in which the Iroquois gave up their claim to the region south of the Ohio River. White settlements multiplied now by leaps and bounds: the region contained 5,000 families by the close of 1769 and 10,000 at the end of 1771.[1]

Into one of those families, that of Captain Hayden Wells, was born his youngest child, probably in early 1770 but possibly in the latter part of 1769, near Jacobs Creek, a settlement at the junction of that stream with the Youghiogheny, about twenty-five miles above the Forks of the Ohio. Just when Hayden Wells moved from his native Virginia to Jacobs Creek is unknown, although he may have been among the earlier settlers, for it is thought that he fought in the French and Indian War. He also participated in Lord Dunmore's War, in 1774, and was for a time in the Continental Army. He and his eldest son, Samuel, made a trip to the Falls of the Ohio in 1775, but the family did not remove to that location until 1779. Mrs. Hayden Wells died either shortly before or soon after the move down the Ohio. Two friends of Captain Wells, Colonel William Pope and Colonel William Oldham, both Virginians and both officers who had resigned their commissions in the Continental Army, joined him in making the migration. Captain Wells and his sons manned the lead flatboat as the party floated down the Ohio.[2]

Wells's party settled at or near Louisville, as the settlement located at the Falls of the Ohio was beginning to be called. Captain Wells established Wells Station about thirty miles directly east of Louisville, in the Bear Grass valley. Samuel Wells was a volunteer under George Rogers Clark in 1780 and again in 1782. In 1781 he helped to protect Kentucky from Indian attack.[3]

Clark had hoped to make his expedition against Detroit in 1781, but the Indians, led by Joseph Brant and Alexander McKee, ambushed Colonel Archibald Lochry on the Ohio below the mouth of the Great Miami, forcing Clark to give up the offensive and to try to defend Kentucky. Fortunately most of the Indians went home, but Brant and McKee, with some 200 men, crossed the Ohio, where they defeated and scattered a party under Squire Boone, who was moving his people and animals to the Bear Grass for safety. While the Indians were feasting, Colonel John Floyd, with a party of only 25 including Hayden and Samuel Wells, came upon them. Outnumbered, Floyd lost half his men, including Hayden Wells. Samuel Wells saved Floyd's life by giving him his own horse and running beside him.[4]

Thus, young William Wells was left without mother or father and was taken into the household of his father's friend, Colonel William Pope. Apparently he was able to get some schooling for his letters in later life show a command of language at least equal to Meriwether Lewis and considerably better than William Clark, both of whom were his close contemporaries.

In March 1784 William, now about fourteen and able to use a gun, went hunting with three boys, William and Azael Linn and Nicholas Breshears, at Robert's pond, six miles southwest of Louisville. They killed some game, among which was a bear cub. As they put their guns down in order to strap the bear cub onto the shoulders of William Linn, a party of Indians that had been watching them came from concealment and captured them. The Indians hurried with their prisoners across the Ohio and made their way to the Delaware towns on the White River, the largest of which were Anderson Town and Muncie Town, where the present-day cities bearing those names now stand.[5]

A letter from George Girty headed "Buckungehelas Town, September 5, 1784" and sent to Alexander McKee at Detroit reported, "I am likewise informed that the Kickapoos and Weas have taken several prisoners lately from about the Falls and Salt Creek. . . ."[6] This may be a reference to the capture of these boys six months earlier, although raids of this sort were frequent in 1784 and it could refer to some capture made later in the summer. The composition of the party that captured Wells is unknown, but it is assumed, from the fact that his three companions were left at the Delaware villages, that some of the captors were Delaware. However, this is not necessarily the case, for captives were often sold or traded by their captors to other tribes. The three boys left among the Delaware were later able to make their escape.[7]

William Wells was taken to the Kilatika Miami village of Kenapakomoko, which renders it certain that he was captured by warriors of this band of the Miami. It does not necessarily follow that, because he was placed in the home of the head chief of this band, Kaweahatta (The Porcupine), this chief was his actual captor. The Porcupine had been in power before Little Turtle and Pacan were born; he was a contemporary of Coldfoot and La Demoiselle and the elder Le Gris and was certainly more than sixty years of age at this time.[8] Although he had outlasted his contemporaries, his village was smaller than in former times, probably because it had been harder hit by smallpox than Kekionga or Ouiatenon. It was located on the Eel River, six miles above its junction with the Wabash, and was strung out along the north bank of the stream for nearly three miles. The French called it L'Anguille, but they had no trading post there. Although the Kilatika Miami traded at Ouiatenon, they were politically more closely associated with Kekionga. Shamekunesah (The Soldier) was war chief, and he may have led the party that captured William Wells.[9]

It is quite possible that Kaweahatta may have been given Wells or else purchased him from his actual captor. He and his wife may have regarded the fourteen-year-old boy as a replacement for a son they had lost. These are matters that are not known and only surmised from knowledge of similar cases. While there is no direct knowledge of his early years of adjustment to captivity, it seems probable that Wells told the chief that his parents were dead, his family scattered, and that he had no home of his own. What is definitely known is that The Porcupine and his wife adopted the boy into their own family and that Wells regarded them as his father and mother.[10] He was given the name Apekonit, a Miami word for several different plants such as the wild bean or ground nut, the wild potato, and the wild carrot. Wells was rather short in stature but very active, with a freckled face, a winning smile, and red hair. So perhaps his Indian name might be translated as "carrot top" or "red head."[11]

There can be no doubt that the boy was treated very well by his elderly adopted parents or that he was an apt learner of Indian ways. As the years passed his recollection of his natal family grew dim. He was just the right age to enjoy the outdoor life of an Indian hunter. Being intelligent, he absorbed what he was taught about plants and animals and readily learned the Miami language. He was observant of Indian customs and learned to act in all respects like an Indian, even to pride himself on being better at some things than the Indians themselves.[12] After a few years he was taken on war parties to the Ohio River, where he was taught to act as a decoy in luring flatboats to shore so the Indians might then attack the voyagers.[13]

84

William's brothers were apparently unable to learn anything of his whereabouts until 1788, after William had been four years in captivity. His brother Carty Wells lived at Coxe's Fort, southeast of Louisville. Carty operated a small boat in which he took supplies to Colonel Hamtramck at Vincennes and carried dispatches for him to points on the Ohio River.[14] After learning from Colonel Hamtramck that William was at Kenapakomoko, Carty went there, probably in January 1789. He talked with William but found that his brother was not very sure that he recognized him and showed no desire to return to Louisville.[15] William thought he might remember his brother Samuel, so later that year Samuel made the trip up the Wabash. William did recognize his oldest brother and agreed to pay him a visit at Louisville. When he did so, he brought some of his Miami friends and stayed a few days. William returned to live among the Miami rather than with Samuel, as the latter tried to persuade him to do.[16] Upon his return William married a Wea Miami woman, and a child was born to them in the following year. He married at an age more common among the whites than among the Miami.[17]

There are several reasons for believing that William's brothers did not locate him before 1789. Time must be allowed for William's memory of them to fade and for him to have developed a feeling of affection for his adopted parents. It is known that his brother Carty ascended the Wabash in January 1789. Samuel Wells went to see William later, and it is reasonable to assume that he must have done so at the earliest possible time. It is also likely that William would not have waited long to pay his visit to Louisville. Finally, it is probable that William was already courting his Wea Miami wife and that this was a powerful factor in his rejection of his brothers' pleas that he return to Kentucky. In any case, his brothers could not have visited him earlier than 1788, when Hamtramck first learned where William was living.[18]

There is no evidence to indicate that William Wells by this time had come to the notice of Little Turtle, as is so frequently stated, for Wells himself said that The Porcupine was his adopted father. Although it is commonly believed that he did, there seems to be no positive proof that Wells was engaged in aiding Little Turtle and his warriors to repel the invasion of General Harmar in 1790.[19] It is reasonable to assume that Kenapakomoko may have furnished a small contingent of warriors for that purpose, since Harmar's invasion was known well in advance to the Indians. It may be concluded that in this way Wells was noted by Little Turtle, who would have singled out anyone who distinguished himself as a fighter, as Wells, from all that is known of him, is certain to have done. It would not be surprising if, by such conduct, Wells earned not only the respect and friendship of Little Turtle but also was rewarded by marriage with that chief's eldest daughter. The fact that Wells had a wife and child in Ken-apakomoko was not, according to Miami custom, a barrier to a second marriage, but it is more probable that Wells married Sweet Breeze, Turtle's daughter, only after he knew that Kenapakomoko had been destroyed in 1791 and had learned that his Wea wife and their child were captives of the whites.[20] These matters will be reserved for later consideration.

Although William Wells was happy and contented with his life among the Miami prior to 1790, the battles that occurred between Indians and white men in 1790 and 1791 forced him to think about the future. He was intelligent enough to see very clearly that, despite Indian victories in those battles, the war would be won eventually by the whites. He was also concerned about his future and that of his children, for he had been troubled by the tendency of the Indians to live wholly in the present, with little appreciation of the past or consideration for the future.[21] Wells was a man of strong loyalties. His problem was that he could not forget his loyalty to his Indian friends anymore than he could ignore his loyalty to his white relatives. Little Turtle was able to devise a plan for enabling him to be true to both of his loyalties. (This, too, is a subject to be explored in more detail at the appropriate chronological time.) The difficulty was that Wells had voluntarily remained an Indian too long before Little Turtle's plan became operative, and his decision to do so was something white society never forgave.

NOTES

1. Billington, 155–56.
2. In general the present account follows that of Paul A. Hutton, "William Wells: Frontier Scout and Indian Agent," in *Indiana Magazine of History*, 74 (September 1978), 183–84. Lyman C. Draper's interview with Darius Heald, grandson of Samuel Wells, in Draper, 23S62–65, states that the father of Samuel and William Wells was named Hayden Wells.
3. Draper, 23S62–65.
4. Draper, 8J128. See also Roosevelt, II, 272–73, 284–86.
5. Butler, 104. A copy of this source was kindly furnished by Paul A. Hutton. The account preserved by the Wells family was that the boys were fishing at the pond, but Butler's account seems more reliable.
6. Butterfield, 382, Appendix R. Buckongahelas Town was one of the Delaware towns on the White River.
7. Butler, 104.
8. The name of The Porcupine was also spelled Gaviahatte. Dunn says that both these name for The Porcupine are Delaware words; the Miami term for hedgehog was *ahkahwit*. The French for hedgehog is *porcèpin*, from which the English word "porcupine" is derived. The Canadian porcupine is about twenty times bigger than

the European hedgehog. See THWAITES (1), XVII, 481–82, where The Porcupine is reported as traveling to Detroit in 1747 with Coldfoot. The French name is printed Porc-Epic by error in this reference.

9. WHITSETT, 72–82.

10. HECKEWELDER, XII, 45. Wells himself gave this information to Heckewelder.

11. DUNN, 115. See also the various Miami vocabularies. The name was used to designate still other plants besides those mentioned. DRAPER, 21S57, has a brief physical description of Wells by Colonel Thomas Hunt, who commanded at Fort Wayne, 1798–1802.

12. These statements are conclusions drawn from a wide variety of sources dealing with the later life of William Wells. There are no sources bearing directly on his early years of captivity.

13. LRSW, Reg. Ser., Record Group 107, John Johnston to William Eustis, November 6, 1810. Johnston was the inveterate enemy of Wells, but there is no reason to doubt that he had this information from Wells himself. It is possible, but unlikely, that Wells first became known to Little Turtle on one of these small war parties prior to 1790.

14. THORNBROUGH (3), 22, 40, 145, 160. Carty Wells was identified by Paul A. Hutton as the "Mr. Wells, of Coxe's Fort" mentioned several times by Colonel Hamtramck. William Pope was also a river merchant and dispatch bearer at this same time.

15. DRAPER, 23S62-65.

16. Ibid.

17. WENTWORTH, 45, Appendix A. The Wolcott grandchildren of William Wells stated that he had a wife among the Wea, as well as Sweet Breeze, Little Turtle's daughter, the wife from whom they were descended. It is probable that his first wife was not a Wea Miami but a Kilatika Miami from Kenapakomoko. This was often considered to be a Wea village due to its proximity to Ouiatenon. Wells may have been already married when he visited his brother Samuel, in Louisville, but there is no indication of it; he must have married soon after, however, to have had a child by the summer of 1791.

18. Precision is impossible here, but it is clear that all the factors mentioned were operational in the period 1788–90.

19. All early accounts say that Wells fought against both Harmar and St. Clair, but only the latter seems capable of absolute proof. It may be assumed safely, however, that he fought against Harmar, for otherwise there would have been no basis for the trust placed in him by Little Turtle in the St. Clair campaign.

20. Such a reconstruction would place the marriage of Wells and Sweet Breeze between mid-August and early November 1791. This is merely the best conjecture possible under the circumstances known.

21. VOLNEY, 372–74, 378–79. Volney displayed a skill in his interview with Wells which was unusual. No one else seems to have got below the surface of his thoughts.

9
Harmar's Defeat, 1790

THE TERM "MIAMI CONFEDERACY," as applied to the alliance of the Indian tribes of the Heartland that, supplied by the British, successfully opposed American military efforts in 1790 and 1791, is not quite such a misnomer as when used to indicate the six bands of the Miami tribe in earlier times. Certainly Kekionga was the central clearinghouse for the negotiations among the tribes that composed its membership, and these negotiations were never successful without the endeavors of Pacan, Le Gris, and Little Turtle, the Miami triumvirate. The original impetus for a western confederation had come from Joseph Brant. When his leadership was repudiated in 1786, the leadership, in fact but not in name, passed to Alexander McKee, British superintendent of Indian affairs, whose trading house at the Maumee Rapids became the central meeting place for grand councils held thereafter. That is to say, after the Indian tribes had come to preliminary agreement at Kekionga, they would meet at McKee's to be entertained with food and drink, to be assured by McKee that the British would back them against the Americans, and to agree on what immediate course of action should be undertaken. Although the Miami formed the keystone of the "Confederacy" because they controlled the Maumee-Wabash line, they were actively aided by the Shawnee and the Delaware, for in 1789 the Shawnee had established two villages on the Maumee within two miles of its head, and the Delaware had located two villages on the St. Marys within three miles of it.[1] The bustle of business noted but sketchily reported by Henry Hay in late 1789 and early 1790 involved the concerted preparations of the western tribes for dealing with an anticipated American military expedition.

Solidarity among the tribes was difficult to achieve. The Delaware were unhappy that they had no lands of their own and openly declared that they saw no reason to fight for lands where they lived as the guests of the Miami. They were investigating the possibility of moving beyond the Mississippi to Spanish Louisiana.[2] The Shawnee were inclined to want the military leadership of the "Confederacy," which the Wyandot felt was theirs by reason of their reputation as fighters. The Shawnee were also favored unduly by Alexander McKee and Matthew Elliott, who had married into their tribe.[3] The Miami were viewed by the Americans as the prime instigators of the "Confederacy," and they had never given up land as had the Delaware, the Shawnee, and the Wyandot. But they could no longer command much support from either the Piankashaw or the Wea Miami and could put fewer warriors in the field than any of the other tribes. The Potawatomi, the Ottawa, and the Chippewa were numerous but tended to side with Brant and the Canadian Indians. In addition, their lands were not directly threatened by the American frontier movement. Obviously the "Confederacy" had its problems, which were serious enough to handicap effective unified action in 1790.

The British wanted to have their cake and eat it too: they insisted on holding Detroit after they had officially ceded it to the United States in 1783. This was the key to the entire situation. If the British government had honorably carried out the terms of the Treaty of 1783, the Indians of the Heartland would have been forced to come to terms with the United States. But the certainty of British military supplies and the promise of actual British intervention enabled the Indians to prolong their resistance. The Indians did not yet know the full extent of British duplicity, but the Miami, especially Little Turtle, were beginning to suspect it.

The American government underwent a change in 1789 with the adoption of a new constitution and the election of George Washington as president. The most pressing of the new government's problems was the hostility of the western tribes. Even financial stability was closely tied to the ability of the government to sell western lands to prospective settlers, who would not buy unless the government could guarantee protection from Indian raids. The new government had the power, which the old one had lacked, to levy taxes to provide an army. This power was to be tested in 1790 against the Indians. The administration did not feel strong enough to test it against the Indians and the British at the same time, as it logically should have done. When it was ready to move against the Indians with General Harmar's expedition against Kekionga, the government took the precaution of notifying the British that the object of the expedition was merely to punish the Indians and not to oust the British from Detroit![4] Major Patrick Murray, who commanded at Detroit, must have smiled as he passed the information on to "the headquarters of iniquity," as Governor Arthur St. Clair called Kekionga.

According to the instructions furnished on September 14, 1790, by Secretary of War Henry Knox to Governor St. Clair and General Harmar, the latter was to undertake his expedition to demonstrate the power of the United States, punishing the Miami "by a sudden stroke, by which their towns and crops may be destroyed." They were to be punished "for their own positive depredations, for their conniving at the depredations of others, and for their refusing to treat with the United States when invited thereto."[5] Inasmuch as the response of the Americans to Indian depredations was always one of retaliation, it is difficult to see how they could have expected the Indians to respond to American depredations by seeking peace. Colonel Hamtramck, at Vincennes, declared that destroying crops and burning Indian villages was useless, for "they can make themselves perfectly comfortable on meat alone, and can build houses with as much facility as a bird does his nest."[6] Hamtramck was right. Restricted punitive action produces only greater resistance on the part of those who are being punished. No peace would be possible unless the Indians were defeated in the field or the British were ousted from Detroit.

Josiah Harmar, of Philadelphia, had been a colonel in the Revolutionary War. He was given command of the regular army and brevetted brigadier-general because more volunteers had enlisted from Pennsylvania than from any other state. Thirty-seven years old in 1790, his career had been in no way spectacular, although he was regarded as a dependable officer. The army he was to command in 1790, however, consisted of only 320 regulars. Volunteers numbering 1,133 were enrolled, chiefly from the Virginia and Pennsylvania frontiers, the former including the Kentucky counties of Fayette, Jefferson, Lincoln, Nelson, Bourbon, Madison, Mercer, Mason, and Woodford, created in the 1780s.[7] These troops were militiamen, some mounted and all enrolled for a limited time. They had been given almost no military training, although some had previous experience on similar expeditions. The best of them had an exaggerated idea of their prowess as compared to the regulars and were better at ignoring than following orders. The poorest of them had enlisted for the money, food, and liquor provided and were as likely to desert as to fight. General Harmar had no great opinion of his militia, but his disposition was to use them as much as possible, supported, if necessary, by small detachments of regulars.

The army was assembled at Fort Washington (Cincinnati) on September 15 and marched northward on September 30, 1790.[8] Harmar had great difficulty in dealing with the private contractors who furnished his supplies: they were unable to meet their contracts on time and unable to supply the full amounts specified. Thus, privates were entitled to only one ration per diem; officers drew more, depending upon their rank. A ration consisted of one and one-quarter pounds of beef or three-quarters pound of pork, eighteen ounces of bread or flour, and one gill of rum, brandy, or whiskey. For every 100 rations there were allocated two quarts of salt, four quarts of vinegar, four pounds of soap, and one and one-half pounds of candles. With slight variation this was the standard ration up to 1812.[9] Harmar's greatest shortage was forage for horses, as his campaign had been planned for summer when no forage should have been necessary.

The route followed to Kekionga was that of the old Miami war trail. The army ascended the west bank of the Little Miami River to present Xenia, crossed northward to Piqua, on the Great Miami, then up Loramie's Creek, northwest to the St. Marys River and along the right or north bank of that river to its junction with the St. Joseph, which was the destination of the expedition. Harmar and the infantry arrived around noon on October 17, having averaged about ten miles per day. Colonel John Hardin and some of the mounted militia had arrived at 4 P.M. on October 15.[10] Harmar had expected to be harassed by Indians during the march, but this had not occurred. Furthermore, the seven villages located at the headwaters of the Maumee were found to be deserted when the army arrived.

The Indians had apparently expected a larger invading force. There were rumors that Harmar had 6,000 or 8,000 men at his disposal. The three tribes with villages in the vicinity had not followed a unified course of action: the Delaware had withdrawn south to their White River villages; the Shawnee had withdrawn down the Maumee to the Au Glaize River; and the Miami had evacuated their women and children to the northwest, to Flat Belly's Village or to the Potawatomi villages on the Elkhart River, although their warriors, under Little Turtle, were lurking within a few miles of Kekionga, awaiting an opportunity, or seeking to create one, for a fight under favorable conditions. The Miami warriors were posted between Harmar's army and the various points to which their women and children had been withdrawn.[11]

The Indians had not burned their villages, so Harmar's first action on October 17 was to order this done. Many of the Indians dwelt in log cabins, 185 of which were burned, together with a greater number of the more traditional Indian dwellings. The gardens near many of the houses were also demolished. The bottomlands between Le Gris's Village and the Shawnee and Delaware villages were filled with fields of corn, which had matured but had not been harvested. Harmar estimated that 20,000 bushels of corn in the ear were destroyed.[12] Anything of value was, of course, appropriated by the soldiers before the destruction began.

A conflict had arisen during the march between Colonel Hardin and Colonel Trotter of the militia. Hardin was senior to Trotter, but Trotter was the more popular with the men, who refused to obey Hardin. General Harmar did not attempt to settle the dispute. On October 18 he gave Colonel Trotter 200 militia and ordered him to scour the country to the west of Kekionga in an effort to find any Indian force that might still be in the area. Trotter and his men spent several hours at this task, and in the evening returned to report they had killed two Indians. They had seen a third Indian who was well mounted, and Colonel Trotter and some of his officers had dashed off in pursuit but had been unable to catch him.[13] Trotter's irresponsible conduct induced the general to give Hardin a similar force for further scouting the next day.

As a matter of fact, Trotter's action in leaving his men to chase a single Indian was probably a circumstance as fortunate as it was stupid. The single Indian was undoubtedly trying to lead Trotter's whole command into an ambush that Little Turtle had prepared in the marshland around Lake Everett, north of the trail to Turtletown and south of the great trail to Chicago. It appears that Little Turtle designed to attempt an ambush along either trail and had probably expected the main trail to be explored first, instead of the other way around. This conclusion is buttressed by the fact that Colonel Hardin found the overnight camp of the Miami warriors along the trail to Chicago, which he scouted the next day. The Indians had camped on the watershed between the Eel River and the St. Joseph about five miles from Kekionga.[14] Overnight they had decided to post their ambush in a different location, and Hardin, a better leader than Trotter, led his men into the trap.

Colonel John Hardin was a Virginian who had been on the frontier most of his life. He had seen service in Lord Dunmore's War and had been an officer of Daniel Morgan's famous riflemen during the Revolution. He was a brave and capable officer with one defect: despite his experience as an Indian fighter, he had never acquired the least understanding of or respect for the Indians and held them always in contempt. Hardin was given 180 militia, including a troop of cavalry under Major Fontaine; in addition, he had 30 regulars under Captain Armstrong.[15] That the overnight camp he discovered was only five miles out of Kekionga should have warned Colonel Hardin. Actually, it caused him to press forward in such haste that he forgot to give orders to one company to move. When they had gone three miles along the Kekionga-Chicago trail (present-day U.S. 33), an Indian on horseback came into view and fled before the approaching troops, taking a trail which branched to the right at an angle to the main trail.[16]

At this point Hardin noted the absence of one company and sent Major Fontaine's cavalry troop back to bring it up. Meanwhile, the rest of his command followed rapidly on the trail taken by the lone Indian, sent as a decoy by Little Turtle, who himself waited with his warriors posted in

92

ambush among the trees on both sides of a narrow prairie that the trail traversed. The Indians were also posted on the other side of the Eel River, which the trail crossed. The trail followed slightly higher ground with boggy mucklands on either side, joining another main trail after about three miles at a point long known as Heller's Corner, from which it was only two miles to the place where the Chicago trail crossed the Eel River, now called Heller's Corner.[17]

This situation had been admirably chosen in all respects. Hardin, if victorious, would have been unable to prevent the Miami from retreating safely by means of the other trail, and they would still have been able to interpose themselves between the American forces and their women and children. On the other hand, if the Indians were the victors, Hardin's men would have had either to retreat by the narrow trail down which they had advanced or break up and take to the swamps.

Hardin and his men were in high spirits, following a trail of trinkets that Little Turtle had ordered to be strewn along the path to give the impression that the Indians were in flight. As they reached the Eel River and crossed the stream, however, the Miami attacked from three sides. Major Fontaine had found the laggard company and was hurrying them forward with the assurance that "the Indians was retreating as fast as possible," but as they neared the fight they were met by militiamen in full flight, who called out, "For God's Sake retreat—you will Be all killed—there is Indians enough to Eat you all up."[18] Most of the stragglers did not need a second invitation to join their fleeing comrades.

The regulars stood and fought, but only eight of the thirty survived, including Captain Armstrong, who was forced to hide in a marsh, up to his shoulders in a slimy mire, in order to escape. The militia lost about forty men as Little Turtle's warriors pursued and picked off the stragglers. Hardin's attempts to rally the militia were futile. According to Captain Armstrong only nine militiamen stayed to fight alongside the regulars.[19]

Armstrong blamed Hardin for overconfidence and the militia for its panic. According to Armstrong, who was an eyewitness and would have had every reason to magnify the numbers of the enemy, the defeat was accomplished by only about 100 Indians. This is the number that Kekionga and Le Gris's Village were able to field, with a few Indians from nearby villages, so it is probable that the victory was gained by the Miami alone. Other later accounts represent the Indians to have been of many tribes and to have numbered as many as 800.[20] Reports of this nature should be discounted because such a number is not compatible with the strategy employed. With a larger force, even if an ambush were used a portion of the Indians would surely have been stationed along the main trail to close the trap or cut off retreat. The fact that this was not done argues powerfully for a small force.

Nevertheless, the plan was a clever one and well executed. Little Turtle's sagacity contributed at least as much to the result as the mistakes of his opponents.

The outcome was sufficient to convince General Harmar to order his entire force to head for home two days later. No doubt the militia had greatly magnified the number of Indians that had ambushed Colonel Hardin, although Hardin himself wanted to stay and fight. Harmar pointed out the scarcity of their provisions and the total lack of forage for the horses. The army spent a day destroying the Shawnee villages and marched up the St. Marys about eight miles before nightfall on October 21. Colonel Hardin was persistent in his desire to try to redeem his reputation, and by dusk he had persuaded Harmar that he should be allowed to return to Kekionga with a force to engage the Indians, if they had already returned to their villages, as he believed they were likely to have done.

This time Harmar entrusted the command to Major John P. Wyllys, of the United States Army, who had at his disposal, 60 regulars under Captain Joseph Asheton and 340 militia under Colonel Hardin.[21] A plan of action was devised to be put into effect when they reached the three rivers at dawn on October 22. Major Hall was to cross the St. Marys and hide his men in the trees on the west bank of the St. Joseph River; Colonel Hardin, with the rest of the militia, including the mounted militia under Major Fontaine, and Major Wyllys, with his 60 regulars, were to cross the Maumee and drive the Indians from Le Gris's Village into the St. Joseph, where they would be caught in a cross fire.[22]

The Miami warriors were in both Le Gris's Village and Kekionga inspecting the ruins of their homes. They had been joined by some Ottawa and Shawnee from the Maumee, for the news that Harmar had retreated had traveled down the river. Major Hall succeeded in posting his men unobserved, but the larger force was seen by Little Turtle before it crossed the Maumee. He instructed a few well-mounted Indians to expose themselves to the mounted militia, which crossed the Maumee first. Then he collected as many warriors as he could and crossed the St. Joseph, at the usual ford, to the west bank just below Kekionga, where they hid behind trees above where Major Hall was stationed.[23] When the mounted militia crossed the Maumee and spied the decoy Indians they rode off in pursuit, which took them out of the battle. The regulars crossed the Maumee and were subjected to a merciless fire from across the St. Joseph. Colonel Hardin got some but not all of the remaining militia to cross the Maumee to support the regulars.

The fighting was close and fierce, and Major Wyllys was killed. Some of the Indians were driven into the St. Joseph and were caught in a cross fire, as planned. Little Turtle directed the warriors, who raced down from the ruins of Kekionga, against Major Hall's men and against any who pursued the Indians into the river. When Harmar, eight miles up the St. Marys, received news of the fight, he sent a relief force of only thirty volunteers, which met the remnants of Hardin's militia as they retreated up the St. Marys to rejoin the main army.[24]

In this fight fifty of the sixty regulars were killed, including two officers; the militia lost about seventy-five men.[25] The Indian loss was estimated by Harmar to have been equal to his own, but this, as usual, was an exaggeration. The Miami loss was greater, however, than the tribe could well afford, and it is known that a nephew of Little Turtle was killed.[26] Chief Richardville, who was a participant, recalled in later years that the St. Joseph was nearly clogged with the bodies of horses and men, both Indian and white. This could well be true because October was a time of very low water.[27] Although not so great as has been represented, the Indian loss was sufficient that no harassment of Harmar's retreat was attempted. This, of course, is an additional indication that no large numbers from other tribes aided the Miami in either of their engagements.

General Harmar had marched from Fort Washington to Kekionga and back in one month's time at the head of an army, but he had left an eighth of his men dead in the tamarack swamps and huckleberry marshes of northeastern Indiana. His report to the secretary of war indicated that he had accomplished his mission with entire success.[28] No one seems to have believed his report, however, and Congress authorized the addition of one full regiment to the regular army and the recruitment of 2,000 volunteers as soon as possible. The War Department authorized a military court of inquiry into the conduct of the campaign, and although Harmar was absolved of misconduct he resigned his command.[29] His campaign was soon known only as Harmar's Defeat, and justly so. The best that can be said is that he conducted a prudent campaign, risking little and accomplishing less.

Only three-eighths of Harmar's men took part in any fighting, and four-fifths of the regulars and one-fourth of the militia who saw action were killed. It cannot be claimed that the militia behaved very well in either of the battles. They did somewhat better in the second one, but not enough to merit Harmar's statement in his diary that "the militia behaved charmingly." He had recorded of the first fight that "Col. Hardin was worsted . . . by about 100 or 130 Indians, owing to the shameful conduct of the militia who threw away their arms and would not fight."[30] General Harmar was not an eyewitness on either occasion, but his information concerning the first battle appears to have been more reliable than that of the fight at the three rivers. Only thirty-one men were reported wounded, which indicates that many militiamen moved out of rifle range as rapidly as possible.

Little Turtle distinguished himself throughout the campaign. He had shown admirable good sense in not killing Colonel Trotter and his officers on October 17 when they separated themselves from their men to chase his decoy. To have done so would have alerted the invaders and rendered the successful ambush of Hardin the next day much more difficult. The ambush of October 18 was executed exactly as planned, and the planning had been perfect. Even more remarkable was Little Turtle's ability to quickly improvise a plan on October 22, with the enemy just across the river, before the Indians were aware of their presence. The Miami fought desperately on this occasion because of the destruction of their villages but also because they had a leader to direct them in whom they had confidence.

The effect of these victories upon the Indian tribes of the Heartland was notable. Prior to Harmar's Defeat the tribes were allied loosely but not well enough for even the Delaware and the Shawnee to help the Miami defend their headquarters. Now they were impressed so favorably by the achievements of Little Turtle and the Miami in turning back, almost unaided, a formidable invasion that they all wanted to fight under such distinguished leadership and were willing to minimize their ancient distrust of one another.

Little Turtle and Le Gris went to Detroit soon after Harmar's Defeat, not only to display their trophies of war to the British, but also to ascertain what help they could get in making up their losses and to concert their plans for the future. They learned that Lord Dorchester, the governor-general of Canada, was expecting to play the role of mediator between the Indians and the Americans.[31]

A diversionary expedition against Ouiatenon had been planned by the Americans in order to give the main thrust under General Harmar a better chance of success. This expedition had set out from Vincennes under Major Hamtramck on September 30 and was timed to coincide with Harmar's march to Kekionga. Hamtramck, however, had a force of only 330 men, composed of the regulars available from Fort Knox at Vincennes, French volunteers from the town, and some recently arrived militiamen from Kentucky. Although his force was less than a quarter that of Harmar, it moved more slowly and required eleven days to reach the Piankashaw Miami village on the Vermilion River, only to find it entirely deserted. Hamtramck had insufficient rations for a long campaign, Kentucky volunteers were deserting, and he feared that the Wea were awaiting him at Ouiatenon with a force greater than his own. Thus, after burning the village he returned to Vincennes. Later, when he heard that 600 Piankashaw, Wea, and Kickapoo had assembled to resist him at Ouiatenon, he concluded that his course of action had been justified.[32] Hamtramck was prudent, and probably justified, except that he overestimated the number of Indians that he might have encountered. It cannot be said, however, that his expedition had any bearing on Harmar's success or failure. From the outset his force was inadequate to the task assigned him, and no one realized the fact better than he.

The winter of 1790–91 was one of such severity that the great herd of buffalo on the Illinois prairie was decimated in the blizzards. This natural disaster did more to weaken the Miami and other Indian tribes than the military campaign of 1790 had done. Indian morale was elevated by Little Turtle's victories over an American army that had announced its intention to punish the western tribes, but the loss of the buffalo meant that the tribes were more than ever dependent on British supplies.[33] Furthermore, the British authorities were now desirous of mediating between the Indians and the United States, thereby forcing the Indians to forego any advantage they might have gained by undertaking a unified offensive in 1791. Plans were made instead for a general council to be held at the Maumee Rapids in midsummer of that year. By then the United States had resumed the offensive, and the time of opportunity for Indian offensive action had passed.

NOTES

1. Major Ebenezer Denny's pictorial sketch map, entitled "A View of the Maumee Towns Destroyed by General Harmar," is reproduced in GUTHMAN, 198. Denny was General Harmar's aide-de-camp and later aide-de-camp to General St. Clair.

2. HAY, 226.

3. HORSMAN, 59.

4. ASPIA, I, 96. Governor Arthur St. Clair to the British officer in command at Detroit, September 19, 1791. Secretary Knox also wrote to Lord Dorchester, governor-general of Canada; and Alexander Hamilton, although it was none of his business to do so, gave assurances to the British minister to the United States.

5. ST. CLAIR, II, 181–83. Henry Knox, secretary of war, to Governor Arthur St. Clair, September 14, 1790.

6. Ibid., 197–98. Major Hamtramck to Governor St. Clair, December 2, 1790. It is not contended that the destruction was without effect, merely that it was not decisive.

7. GUTHMAN, 177.

8. There is a good account of Harmar's expedition in DILLON, 245–54, drawn from official documents. GUTHMAN, 188–94, is the best modern account.

9. WOEHRMANN, 70. Woehrmann presents a fine study of the army supply problems in this period.

10. The diaries or journals of Captain John Armstrong, Major Ebenezer Denny, and General Josiah Harmar are in agreement as to the time of arrival. Portions of these diaries are reprinted in MEEK, 74–108. Denny wrote that Hardin was sent

ahead with the mounted militia because of reports that the Indians were evacuating their towns.

11. For exaggerated estimates see WOEHRMANN, 30–31. For the evacuation see THORNBROUGH (3), 266. Major Hamtramck to General Harmar, November 28, 1790. Hamtramck reported that two Frenchmen from Ouiatenon had told him that "the Indians of the Miamie burnt their village and had retired on Elk River, where they lodged their women and children. . . ."

12. THORNBROUGH (3), 266. Harmar to Hamtramck, November 29, 1790. See also ASPIA, I, 106. Harmar to Knox, November 4, 1790.

13. MCMASTER, 598–99, discusses the Hardin-Trotter rivalry, but neither he nor any other writer seems to have understood that the lone Indian pursued for half an hour by the officers was trying to draw Trotter's whole command into an ambush, which seems obvious from the repetition of the tactic on the following day. The findings of the military court of inquiry are in ASPMA, I, 20–36. Several officers expressed the opinion that had Trotter located the Indians they would have been soundly defeated. On the contrary, there is every reason to believe that had he found them he would have been ambushed with the same results suffered by Hardin the next day.

14. ASPMA, I, 20–26. See also the journals reprinted in MEEK. It should be noted that Armstrong's journal is abbreviated by Meek but is reprinted in full in DILLON.

15. ASPMA, I, 34–35. Deposition of Colonel John Hardin. It appears that Hardin's force was largely composed of the men led by Trotter on the previous day, but the total was smaller by ninety men.

16. BARCE, 165–66, gives a perceptive account on this point. His is one of the few treatments of the subject to display an acquaintance with the terrain.

17. The place now known as Heller's Corner is the site of the Eel River church and cemetery. There is a small stone marker here identifying the location as that of a battle in 1790. It is clear, however, that Hardin's force was led off the main trail on a smaller trail to the right, eight miles out from Kekionga. This would be at what is today called Midway, where a road to the right crosses the Eel River after two miles and one mile further on reaches the former site of the Heller's Corner post office, at which point what is now known as Heller's Corner lies two miles to the left. The map provided herein will clarify this point.

18. ASPMA, I, 26–27; GUTHMAN, 191. See also IRVIN, 393–96, from whose letter the quotation is taken.

19. Captain Armstrong was near enough, where he was hidden, to hear and see at night the celebration of victory held in the Miami camp. This detail is given in Dillon's version of Armstrong's journal, not in Meek's. Armstrong's estimate of the Indians was "about 100." Harmar's journal in MEEK, 89–96, increases this to "not more than 150" and reports that Captain Armstrong returned on October 20, "much fatigued."

20. TURNER (Ayer 689) credits Hardin's defeat to "800 Miamis, Puttowatamies, Chippaways, Ottaways, Delawares, and Shawanoes" but fails to make clear whether this was the Heller's Corner fight or the three rivers fight. Indian losses are given as "twenty five killed and fifty wounded." This appears to be grossly inaccurate along with other information compiled by Turner from Indian sources on other

battles from Braddock's Defeat to Wayne's Victory (i.e., 1754–94.) The same can be said of several other sources, including Matthew Elliott's contemporary report, given in HORSMAN, 61. See also PECKHAM (3), 227–41.

It is of interest that TURNER can be identified as the husband of Ann Wells, eldest daughter of William Wells. Welsington was the high-sounding name he used for the property of Wells at Fort Wayne which he controlled and occupied in 1817.

21. ASPMA, I, 34–36.

22. BARCE, 168. The plan was well conceived but not so well executed. The militia did not support the regulars, being employed instead at chasing small groups of Indians whose object was to lead them away from the main battle.

23. HOPKINS, 63–64. Hopkins wrote, "The Indians being stationed behind trees on the west side shot them in their attempt to get across. We were shown the tree behind which the Little Turtle took his station. . . ." Captain Armstrong estimated the width of the St. Joseph River at twenty yards and that of the Maumee at seventy yards. See MEEK, 83.

24. See Ebenezer Denny's journal in MEEK, 102–8.

25. Harmar's official reports to the secretary of war are in ASPIA, I, 104–6.

26. HOPKINS, 64. William Wells pointed out the tree where Turtle's nephew was killed. This does not constitute proof that Wells himself took part in these battles, but it does establish a strong presumption that he was a participant. Wells did not state the Indian losses but gave Harmar's loss as 300 men, a considerable exaggeration. Hopkins saw many skulls and other human bones, some bearing tomahawk marks, still scattered along the banks of the St. Joseph some fourteen years after the battle.

27. BRICE, 315. Richardville also said that the Indians, concealed among the trees and bushes along the river, held back their first fire until the regulars had all approached the bank of the stream. Brice, however, is inaccurate in placing the main conflict at the crossing of the Maumee instead of at the ford of the St. Joseph.

28. ASPIA, I, 104. Harmar had carried out instructions to burn the villages, but he had certainly not impressed them with the military strength of the United States.

29. ASPMA, I, 20–36. Testimony taken concerning reports of Harmar's excessive drinking did not support such charges.

30. MEEK, 89–96. Harmar's description of the militia action during the second battle does not agree with facts brought out by the court of inquiry.

31. HORSMAN, 65–67.

32. THORNBROUGH (3), 259–64, 266–67. Major Hamtramck to General Harmar, November 2, 1790, and November 28, 1790.

33. HORSMAN, passim, makes clear that the British Indian Department distributed food to Indian gatherings on a much larger scale than had been customary in earlier times.

10

St. Clair's Defeat, 1791

By JANUARY 1791 Secretary of War Henry Knox reported to President Washington that Harmar's Defeat had rendered it necessary for the federal government to plan another expedition against Kekionga. This time he recommended that a permanent military post be established there from which the Indians could be controlled.[1] In March, Congress confirmed the appointment of Major-General Arthur St. Clair to head the expedition. General St. Clair was governor of the Northwest Territory and a veteran of the American Revolution; his military experience included service with British General Jeffrey Amherst at Louisburg and British General James Wolfe at Quebec in the French and Indian War.[2]

An expedition to Kekionga obviously required a strengthening of the regular army and new levies of militia, as well as arrangements for provisioning on an extensive scale, which meant several months of preparation. In the meantime, a force was being recruited at Louisville (the Falls of the Ohio) to strike a swift blow at Ouiatenon in order to discourage any plans the Indians might have for an offensive to disrupt the main expedition. This army of about 800 mounted militia was recruited in the same Kentucky counties that had furnished the bulk of Harmar's force and was commanded by Brigadier-General Charles Scott, whose military experience had begun with Braddock's Defeat in 1755. Many of Harmar's men reenlisted for service with Scott, including Colonel John Hardin.

The Wea Miami were aware that a force from Louisville was planning to attack Ouiatenon, but apparently they were unable to agree upon what they should do about it until it was too late. Their head chief at this time was Baptiste Constant, who was more French than Indian and who owed his position to the influence of Alexander McKee. His British connections may have been a deterrent to decisive action, since the British, in the hope of retaining control of the Indians of the Heartland, were now bent on mediation. Colonel Hamtramck, at Vincennes, reported that on June 4, 1791, a Wea chief, whom he did not name, and twenty followers appeared at Fort Knox and begged him to put a stop to General Scott's expedition. Their request exceeded Hamtramck's power to grant, even if he had been disposed to do so.[3] Furthermore, Ouiatenon had been destroyed by Scott on June 1, three days before the request was made. Clearly, the Wea Miami were demoralized before the attack. Their inaction was in sharp contrast to the performance of Little Turtle at Kekionga under similar circumstances.

Scott and his men had crossed the Ohio at the mouth of the Kentucky River on May 23 and headed northward through the wooded hills of southern Indiana toward Ouiatenon, which they reached on June 1. General Scott detached Colonel Hardin with 200 men to cross the Wabash below Ouiatenon and attack the Kickapoo village near the old French fort and trading post. Neither Ouiatenon nor the Kickapoo village was deserted, although the Indians were totally unprepared for the attack. At Ouiatenon 32 warriors were killed and 58 women and children captured. None of the attackers died, and only 5 were wounded. At the Kickapoo town Hardin killed 6 warriors and took 52 prisoners. Both villages were burned and the cornfields destroyed the following day.

Colonel James Wilkinson was detached the night of June 2 with 360 men to march to Kithtippecanuck (Petit Piconne) on the Tippecanoe River, eighteen miles away. This Pepikokia Miami village was also destroyed, and Wilkinson and his men then rejoined Scott within twenty-four hours. Scott's report mentions that many books and papers were put to the flames.[4]

The destruction of the Piankashaw village on the Vermilion in 1790 and of Ouiatenon and Kithtippecanuck in 1791 completed the severing of these Miami bands from the tribal leadership at Kekionga. More than anything else the Wea Miami lacked capable military leadership. They had no one of Little Turtle's ability to direct their movements against Scott as Turtle had directed his warriors against Harmar. Ouiatenon never regained its former importance.

Scott left Ouiatenon on June 4 and arrived at Louisville ten days later, having freed sixteen prisoners whom he considered too infirm to travel.[5] St. Clair was unable to get his army underway for Kekionga by July 10, as he had planned. St. Clair's delay and the fact that Scott had been mixed up about his geography resulted in a second expedition to the Wabash on August 1 under James Wilkinson. Scott had originally intended to destroy Kenapakomoko as well as Ouiatenon. But when Kithtippecanuck was destroyed by Wilkinson, Scott had been confused and reported that this was "the Eel River village."[6] Later, when Scott's error was perceived, Wilkinson was commissioned as brigadier-general and sent against Kenapakomoko with 500 mounted volunteers.

Wilkinson rode out of Cincinnati and headed northward to the portage between Loramie's Creek and the St. Marys River, in a feint toward Kekionga. Then he went directly west to Kenapakomoko and succeeded in taking it by surprise, for the warriors had left to join the forces that Little Turtle was gathering to oppose St. Clair. Wilkinson killed half a dozen Miami men and captured thirty-four women and children, losing two men himself. Among the captives were the wife of Kaweahatta (The Porcupine) and the wife and baby of William Wells (Apekonit). Wilkinson, after demolishing the town and the crops, revisited Kithtippecanuck and Ouiatenon, where he destroyed such crops as had been replanted. He then returned to Louisville with his prisoners.[7] The raid was of small military value compared to the one against Ouiatenon, for the Kilatika Miami had already joined the forces gathering at Kekionga.

Both expeditions illustrate the type of warfare at which the frontier militia excelled, which was similar to the Indian raids that they were avenging. However, the frontiersmen required more men and horses than the Indians did to accomplish the same end of burning villages and taking captives. Furthermore, while it was a way of life with the Indians, for the frontier militia it was an interruption of their normal activities, one that was compensated for by the opportunity to have a good look at very desirable Indian lands.

Little Turtle was in Detroit near the end of June 1791 but was present at the Maumee Rapids in early July as the grand council of the Indians gathered to receive their annual presents from the British. In accordance with the British diplomacy of the moment, Alexander McKee succeeded in persuading them to modify their demand for the Ohio River as a boundary line. They indicated a willingness to accept a line running up the Ohio from the mouth of the Tennessee to the mouth of the Muskingum and then up the Muskingum-Cuyahoga line. The Miami consented to this modification because it involved no loss of land to them. Joseph Brant, the Mohawk chief, was chosen to convey this news to Lord Dorchester at Quebec, and the "Western Confederacy" selected a delegation to accompany him. When they met with Lord Dorchester on August 17, he agreed to attempt mediation with the United States.[8] However, neither Brant nor Dorchester was able to interest the United States in such a proposal. The United States had already sold a great deal of land beyond the Muskingum in southern Ohio. The sale of a million acres between the Little Miami and the Great Miami to Judge John Cleve Symmes in 1788 had been made

102

without purchasing the land from the Miami and was the reason for that tribe's inveterate hostility toward the Americans.

With General St. Clair's expedition against Kekionga expected to set out at any time, it is unlikely that Turtle went to Quebec. Furthermore, family concerns may have kept him near to home for this is undoubtedly the time that he became closely associated with William Wells, who was soon to marry his daughter, Sweet Breeze (the capture of Wells's first wife and child by Wilkinson was noted earlier). There was certainly no barrier among the Miami to taking a second wife under the circumstances in which Wells found himself. Among the Miami, men usually married at the age of twenty-five and women at eighteen. If we assume that Little Turtle married at the customary age in 1772 and that his eldest child, a daughter, Sweet Breeze, was born in 1773, she would have been eighteen in 1791, at which time Wells found himself suddenly without a wife.[9] Whether the couple felt a romantic attraction or whether Little Turtle facilitated the marriage is unknown. Turtle could have cultivated the friendship of Wells in order to learn things from him that he needed to know and understand about white people. He may have suggested to his daughter that she take an interest in a young man whom he himself liked and admired. Or the young people may have taken the initiative themselves. Whatever the case the attachment was an enduring one, not only between Wells and Sweet Breeze, but also between Wells and Turtle.

The marriage of Sweet Breeze and Wells produced four children: Ann (Ahpezzahquah) was probably born in 1793 and Rebekah (Pemesahquah) in 1795; a son, William Wayne (Wapemonggah), born about 1797, was named for Anthony Wayne, who had died on December 15, 1796; and Mary (Ahmahquauzahquah) was born on May 10, 1800. Sweet Breeze, whose name is rendered as Wanangepeth, with the usual variations of spelling, died in 1805. There seems no reason to question that she was a daughter of Little Turtle, for her descendants through her youngest daughter, as well as other members of the Wells family, were quite positive in this belief.[10] Some writers have stated that Sweet Breeze was a sister of Little Turtle. The disparity of ages is too great to support such a claim, which may have arisen from the fact that the Miami kinship system took no account of generations, so that a man's sister was equated with his daughter.

The Maumee valley was teeming with Indian warriors in the late summer of 1791. All through August and September there was a gathering of the tribes from near and far such as had not occurred since 1755, when their fathers had assembled at the Forks of the Ohio to defeat General Braddock. St. Clair's expedition was so long in getting started and so slow in its advance that by October some of the Lake Indians and Prairie Indians began to show signs of restlessness. But morale continued to be high as Indian scouting reports revealed that St. Clair's army was not as large as they had expected it to be.

It is impossible to know the numbers of fighters furnished by the tribes represented. The Wyandot lived nearby in the Sandusky valley, some of the Ottawa lived on the lower Maumee, and the Shawnee villages that had been near Kekionga in 1790 were now on the middle Maumee and the Auglaize. The Delaware came from their White River villages and other Shawnee from the hills of southern Indiana. Chippewa, Potawatomi, and Ottawa from the Michigan peninsula were there in considerable numbers. A few Wea and Piankashaw Miami joined the Miami proper, and some Kaskaskia and Kickapoo were on hand as well. There were certainly a few Mississauga from the north shore of Lake Erie and probably a few Seneca from the south shore, but Brant and his Iroquois were not present. The total number of effective warriors gathered to oppose the long-awaited invasion was about 1,400 although larger estimates have been made by white historians.[11]

St. Clair's offensive was three months late as his new recruits were slow to arrive at Cincinnati from Pittsburgh. Recruiting had been carried out in the larger towns of the East Coast to bring existing regiments of the regular army somewhere near their full strength. Six-month enlistments were also accepted to form new regiments. So many of these soldiers lacked adequate training that when General Harmar, now retired, looked them over, he decided they were poorer material than he had led the previous year. He was very pessimistic about the expedition and did not conceal his gloomy views, telling his former aide, Captain Ebenezer Denny, that he might be lucky enough to survive the campaign.[12]

Not only was the quality of the soldiers judged to be poor, but the original hope for an expedition of over 4,000 men had been scaled down to 2,300 by September, of whom 300 were Kentucky militia. The call for 1,000 militia had produced only 300, largely because, after the Scott and Wilkinson expeditions during the summer, not many Kentuckians were willing to volunteer for still further service that year.[13] The contracts for supplying St. Clair's army were given to William Duer, a New York politician and businessman whose principal interest was profiteering. From any other point of view his operations were extremely inefficient.[14]

St. Clair had moved from Fort Washington at Cincinnati to Ludlow's Station six miles north, where the forage for horses was better and where it was easier to keep the soldiers sober. He left Ludlow's Station on September 6 and marched twenty-three miles in nine days to the Great Miami River, where two weeks were spent building Fort Hamilton. On October 4 he resumed his northward advance, halting between October 12 and 24 to construct Fort Jefferson, six miles south of present-day Greenville, Ohio. On October 24 the army moved north once more and encamped, on the evening of November 3, on a small stream thirty miles from Fort Jefferson, where the town of Fort Recovery, Ohio, now stands. Although St. Clair believed he was on the St. Marys River, within fifteen miles of Kekionga, he was actually on the Wabash, not far from its source, and more than fifty miles from his objective.[15]

St. Clair had proceeded according to plan in building the two forts, and the slow pace of his advance was in itself no detriment to eventual success. The weather had worsened as he marched, however, and the morale of his army had declined as well. Desertion was high, and disciplinary measures failed to check the loss. On October 31, 60 men deserted, and St. Clair sent Major Hamtramck with his First Regiment of regulars to overtake them and bring them back. This was a serious error in judgment, for Hamtramck's First Regiment was the best in the army, which was reduced to about 1,400 men as it camped on the Wabash. On October 27 Piomingo, a Chickasaw chief, arrived belatedly with a few Chickasaw to act as scouts. St. Clair sent them into Indian country on October 29 with orders to penetrate to the Maumee and bring back captives from whom something might be learned of the enemy force and its plans. This too was an error in judgment, for it deprived the army of a badly needed scouting service. Neither Hamtramck nor Piomingo was able to return before the Indians had annihilated St. Clair's army.[16]

While the American army approached it was kept under constant surveillance by the Indians by means of small scouting parties. In late October the Indians moved up the Maumee to its head, and there the important decision was made that Little Turtle would be their supreme commander. A considerable number of Indians had wanted the command to go to Buckongahelas, a renowned Delaware war chief who was older and more experienced. Fortunately Buckongahelas was not a petty or a jealous man. He had been tremendously impressed by Little Turtle's victories over Harmar and asserted that he himself preferred Little Turtle and would willingly serve under him.

Following this decision, Little Turtle reviewed his warriors on an extensive plain along the St. Marys River in what is now the southern portion of the city of Fort Wayne. He gave instructions to the various tribal war chiefs to divide their men into messes of twenty, of which four were designated as hunters to supply each mess with food. The hunters were to come in each day at high noon with their game. On October 28 the Indian army of 1,400 men (seventy messes) moved up the St. Marys to meet St. Clair's army, which their runners reported had left Fort Jefferson on October 24.[17]

Thus, Little Turtle took his large command southward, not in close order, but spread out over a considerable area in small groups that could keep in touch with one another. In this way he was able to have his men on all sides of St. Clair's army within three days; and he was also aware that Hamtramck's regiment had been detached on October 31 to pursue the deserters southward. This piece of information motivated his bold strategy. Indians had often attacked white armies as they struggled through the forests in single file or lured them into an ambush on the march. The Turtle, who had not forgotten how he had surprised La Balme, who had believed himself secure behind earthworks, now decided he could employ the same strategy on a much greater scale against St. Clair. He decided to attack the enemy in camp.

The only problem was that St. Clair had artillery, of which the Indian warriors were fearful. The artillery was not located in a protective fort, however, and was vulnerable to attack. Little Turtle had one man whom he trusted and regarded as capable of carrying out a well-laid plan: William Wells, his son-in-law. He gave Wells a handpicked force of his own Miami warriors with instructions that they should concentrate their fire upon the gunners who manned the cannon and should not desist until the last of the big guns was silent.[18] The time for attack was fixed at dawn, November 4. All that remained was to position his seventy messes of men under cover of darkness without the American army becoming aware that it was being almost totally enveloped. Even though the Indians were accustomed to moving with the utmost stealth and silence, to move so many into various positions was not easy.

General St. Clair was fifty-seven years old and troubled with gout; at times on the march he had to be carried in a litter. He had sent orders to Colonel William Oldham, who commanded the militia, that he was to dispatch scouts an hour before daylight on November 4, but the orders were not carried out. (Recall that Oldham was the friend of Hayden Wells, the father of William Wells, with whom the Wells family had moved to Kentucky.) The militia was encamped on a somewhat elevated plain that rose beyond the Wabash River, which was small and easily fordable. The rest of the army was camped nearer the river, where the town of Fort Recovery is now located. Both of the camping sites were clear of trees. General St. Clair's tent was on the right wing with that of his second-in-command, General Richard Butler. The left wing was commanded by Colonel William Darke, a veteran of Braddock's campaign. The artillery was posted in the center.

Richard Butler, the eldest of five brothers, had served in the Revolutionary War and was a capable and popular soldier; however, he believed that he, not the governor, should have been given charge of the expedition.

106

On the night of November 3, Captain Slough of the regular army scouted around the encampment with a small detail of men and reported to General Butler that a number of Indians had been seen skulking among the trees. He offered to carry this intelligence to General St. Clair, but Butler dismissed him and told him to get some rest. Slough supposed that Butler would inform St. Clair, which he did not do. Butler's negligence was to prove fatal, for he, like William Oldham, was killed in the ensuing battle.[19]

Although the American army was astir on the morning of November 4 when Little Turtle gave the signal to advance, the Indian attack came as a total surprise. A Mississauga chief from Canada, Wapacomegat, distinguished himself by leading the charge against Colonel Oldham's militia, who were quickly routed and turned back with heavy loss upon the main camp, thereby throwing it into great confusion.[20] Immediately the Indians, hidden in the tall grass which covered the treeless area, began firing from both sides into the main camp, falling to the ground to reload. William Wells and his Miami warriors picked off the artillery gunners as they fired several shots, but the Indians were emboldened by the confusion that convulsed the camp and closed in on the gunners with their tomahawks. Officers here and there succeeded in rallying their men for a counter-attack at close quarters, and whenever they did so the Indians gave ground promptly.

The Indians, firing from three sides, concentrated their shots on the active officers whom they could easily distinguish. General St. Clair had six bullet holes in his clothing but was not wounded. General Butler, severely wounded, was killed while still trying to direct the right wing. Colonel William Darke, who commanded the left wing, led two bayonet charges and survived, but he lost a son. Samuel Wells, the eldest brother of William Wells, fought in the battle and was unharmed. All but one artillery officer was killed.

The battle raged for three hours with the carnage among the Americans about twenty times that among the Indians.[21] At 9 A.M. General St. Clair ordered a retreat. With great difficulty a way was cleared to the road and the retreat soon became a flight, with many men throwing away their arms in order to run faster and the Indians pursuing hotly for about three miles. It was William Wells's later recollection that he had wielded his tomahawk until his arm became so tired he could hardly lift it.[22] Little Turtle gave the signal that the killing should stop and sent runners bearing the message for his men to return. White participants attributed the cessation of the pursuit to the desire of the Indians to plunder the camp rather than to the humanity of their leader.[23] As the remnants of St. Clair's army approached Fort Jefferson they were met by Major Hamtramck and his regiment, who restored some semblance of order to the panic-stricken survivors, who finally reached the fort "a little after sunset."

St. Clair, reporting to the secretary of war five days later, frankly called the retreat "a flight" and said that the artillery as well as the camp supplies had been abandoned.[24] A congressional inquiry later exonerated St. Clair, made no reference to Butler's negligence, and placed the blame on the failure of the contractors to deliver goods in time for an earlier campaign. Total casualties were 913 out of 1,400 present, including 68 officers; the dead alone numbered 634.[25] Supplies valued at $33,000 were lost. The Indians, not knowing what else to do with them, buried the cannon they had taken. Among the bodies on the battlefield were those of many women. It is estimated that there were 200 camp followers with the American army, of which nearly half were killed.[26] The losers took what consolation they could from the instances of heroic action on the part of many individuals in the midst of the panic that seized the majority. It was the most overwhelming defeat in American military history.

St. Clair resigned his military commission but continued to act as governor of the Northwest Territory. Despite the fact that Congress glossed over his failure, public opinion held him responsible for the defeat. Although this is a fair judgment, there are other considerations. Congress correctly placed blame on the contractors for the late start, but Congress, the administration, and public opinion were all to blame for insisting on a campaign in 1791. The fatal error was an underestimation of the Indians as fighters and, as a consequence, the use of ill-trained troops. The mistakes made by St. Clair and his subordinates would not have brought disaster if Little Turtle had not perceived and taken advantage of them, a fact that white historians have failed to appreciate. Many writers also have been confused by the claims for credit for the victory made by Blue Jacket, the Shawnee war chief.[27] To add to the obfuscation, Joseph Brant's biographer claimed that Brant was in command, although he was not even in the West at the time.[28]

Many writers have discussed Harmar's and St. Clair's defeats without reference to Little Turtle, as if the Indians had no commander. Some have added insult to injury by placing him in command only in time to be defeated by Wayne in 1794, which is a strange perversion of fact. Others have even seized upon the tradition that Tecumseh, then twenty-one years of age, was a scout among the Shawnee during the campaign, elevating him to the nonexistent position of "chief of scouts" for the Indians and crediting him with a share of the victory. While Americans like to remember Braddock's Defeat as an instance of British military stupidity, they do not care to face up to the fact that St. Clair's Defeat was an even greater disaster. Little Turtle's unique achievement of attacking an American army while encamped on an offensive campaign and overwhelming it to the point of disintegration has been minimized all too often.

Alexander McKee and Matthew Elliott, the two Tory traders who were in charge of Indian affairs for the British at Detroit and on the Maumee, accompanied the Indian expedition against St. Clair and witnessed the Indian victory. Two British officers, Captain Bunbury and Lieutenant Selby, also went along as military observers and advisors, but the British were extremely careful to avoid any overt participation, a fact that did not escape the notice of Little Turtle.[29]

The various tribal bands returned to their villages loaded with booty and scalps in time for a short period of celebration before the onset of the winter hunting season. Small bands of warriors raided the frontier settlements in their customary way without fear of meeting organized opposition. The American government now showed a disposition to make peace on a basis of compromise, but the Indians in their elation reverted to their former demand for recognition of the Ohio River as the boundary of white settlement. Little Turtle alone turned his mind to the possibility of negotiation.

NOTES

1. ASPMA, I, 36. On January 10, 1791, Simon Girty, with 200 Wyandot and Shawnee, attacked Dunlap's Station, or Coleraine, but was driven off after a siege of twenty-seven hours. This has often been wrongly ascribed to Little Turtle. See THORNBROUGH (3), 272.

2. See ST. CLAIR, I and II, which contain much biographical material. He was born in Scotland, the grandson of the Earl of Roslyn. A man born to wealth and station, he died poor in 1818, remembered only for his great defeat in 1791.

3. THORNBROUGH (3), 267, 283–84. Hamtramck to Harmar, November 28, 1790, and June 15, 1791.

4. ASPIA, I, 131–32. Scott to Knox, Lexington, June 28, 1791.

5. Ibid., 133. List of prisoners taken by General Scott at Ouiatenon.

6. Ibid., 132. EDMUNDS (4), 241–53, perpetuates General Scott's geographical error confusing Kithtippecanuck and Kenapakomoko. The villages were some forty miles apart; neither was located on the Wabash River itself, though both were near it.

7. ASPIA, I, 133–34. Wilkinson to Knox, Frankfort, August 24, 1791. Unfortunately Wilkinson did not append the list of his prisoners to his report. Knowledge of the families of Wells and The Porcupine comes from the negotiations conducted in their behalf by General Rufus Putnam in 1792.

8. HORSMAN, 66–67.

9. The fact that Little Turtle's granddaughter Kilsoquah in her old age denied knowledge of more than three children of Little Turtle does not negate the existence

of Sweet Breeze, for her death occurred about five years before Kilsoquah's birth. She would, therefore, have known of but two sons and one daughter.

10. Knowledge of Sweet Breeze was preserved by the Wolcott family, who were her descendants, and by the Heald family, who were descendants of Samuel G. Wells, oldest brother of William Wells. See WENTWORTH, 45–46, Appendix A. The order of birth of Wells's children is known but not the precise dates of birth, except in the case of Mary Wells Wolcott, who is said also to have been known as Sweet Breeze, like her mother. The Miami term for "a sweet breeze" does not occur in any of the Miami vocabularies. The term meaning "sweet" is given as *uahka-panggah* in the Thornton vocabulary. A silhouette in possession of the Chicago Historical Society, said to have been made in 1810, is reputed to be a likeness of Sweet Breeze, but if the date is accurate it must be Mary (Polly) Geiger, whom Wells married in that year, five years after the death of Sweet Breeze.

11. HOPKINS, 65. This is the total given by Wells in 1804, which includes those assigned to supply meat by hunting. If the hunters and scouts are excluded, the number would be about 1,000. Some hunters and scouts may have joined in the battle.

12. DENNY, 237–57. Denny's journal covers the period July-October 1791. Denny stated that many recruits came from the streets and jails of eastern cities.

13. The Kentucky militia did not include many of those who had served with Harmar but did include William Wells's oldest brother, Samuel, who was a good officer.

14. The uncertainty of the supply of rations contributed to the low morale of St. Clair's army. See WOEHRMANN, 67–68.

15. WILSON, 9–29. Bradley and his men arrived at Fort Washington on September 9 and marched to join St. Clair at Fort Hamilton, arriving on September 16. They helped to build Fort Jefferson and formed part of the garrison of that fort, thus missing the battle.

16. Ibid., 28. Bradley mentioned Hamtramck's regiment passing Fort Jefferson but was ignorant of its mission. VAN EVERY mentions the arrival and departure of the Chickasaw scouts.

17. HOPKINS, 65–66. William Wells told these interesting and important details of the Indian campaign to Gerard T. Hopkins in 1804.

18. BARCE, 203. According to WILSON, 22, St. Clair had "ten peices of artillery."

19. ASPIA, I, 137. St. Clair to Knox, November 9. 1791. St. Clair mentions both Oldham and Butler, in his postscript, as having been remiss.

20. SCHOOLCRAFT, 299.

21. SARGENT, 237–73, provides the fullest firsthand account of the battle; ROOSEVELT, 151–74, is the most vivid secondary account. DRAPER, 8J128, gives the recollections of William McCasland.

22. HILL, 36.

23. HOPKINS, 133–34.

24. ASPIA, I, 137. St. Clair to Knox, November 9, 1791.

25. VAN EVERY, 241, compares the casualties with those of other defeats at the hands of Indians. Captain Bradley says, "Braddock's Defeat . . . is not to be compared to this." See WILSON, 34.

26. ASPMA, I, 36–44, gives the report of the congressional committee of inquiry.

27. KNOPF, 532. Wayne to McHenry, Detroit, October 3, 1796. Concerning the chiefs who are going to Philadelphia to meet their Great Father, the president of the United States, Wayne wrote: "Among whom is the famous Shawanoe Chief *Blue Jacket,* who, it is said had the Chief Command of the Indian Army on the 4th of November 1791 against Gen. St. Clair. The *Little Turtle* a Miamia Chief who also claims that honor, and who is his rival for fame and power—and said to be daily gaining ground with the Wabash Indians—refuses or declines to proceed in Company with *Blue Jacket.*" Wayne took no position on the merits of the Blue Jacket–Little Turtle controversy. The Shawnee war chief's claim to have commanded against St. Clair lacks any such solid documentation as there is for Little Turtle. On the other hand, it is clear that he commanded against Wayne at Fallen Timbers following Little Turtle's resignation.

28. Joseph Brant never claimed to have commanded against St. Clair, but his biographer, William L. Stone, made the claim on the basis of speculations to this effect in American newspapers. Brant remained in Canada after his visit to Quebec in August 1791 and went to Philadelphia in June 1792, still trying to mediate between the Indians and the United States.

29. VAN EVERY, 239; HORSMAN, 69.

11

The Family Compact: First Phase, 1791–94

ON MAY 25 AND 26, 1868, Lyman Draper interviewed Darius Heald at his home near O'Fallon, in St. Charles County, Missouri. Draper was engaged in his favorite occupation of talking to people who had some recollection of early days on the midwestern frontier and recording these conversations for the Wisconsin Historical Society. Heald was the son of Captain Nathan Heald, who had commanded at Fort Wayne from 1807 to 1810 and at Fort Dearborn at the time of the famous massacre in 1812. His mother, Rebecca Wells, a daughter of Samuel Wells, of Louisville, and a niece of William Wells, had married Nathan Heald in 1811. Captain Heald died in 1832, Rebecca Wells Heald in 1857. Their son was the repository of considerable information of interest to Lyman Draper, not the least important of which was a brief but revealing statement concerning William Wells and his Indian friend and father-in-law, the Miami war chief Little Turtle.

In Heald's words, as set down by Draper, "Wells made an agreement with Little Turtle and a few others not to kill each other in war. Also to do what they could for peace. Wells and Little Turtle actually met several times during the Wars before 1795. Friendly meetings on neutral ground neither trying to learn anything from the other."[1] Concerning this Family Compact, Paul A. Hutton has written, "The Wells family contended that William Wells and Little Turtle hoped to bring peace between the two races and that it was agreed between them that Wells would join the Americans and work for peace while Little Turtle tried to sway the tribes in that direction. This story is supported by the continuing friendship of the two and by the fact they both advocated peace after 1792."[2] Hutton's conclusion is a fair and reasonable appraisal of the situation that developed

112

between the defeat of St. Clair by the Indians in 1791 and Wayne's victory over them in 1794.

The legendary and far less believable form in which the Family Compact tradition survived was current for a long time in Fort Wayne and was reported by Wallace Brice, writing in 1868, the same year in which Draper interviewed Darius Heald. According to this version, Wells parted from Turtle under a "Big Elm" along the Maumee and rode eastward to join General Wayne after saying these words, "I now leave your nation for my own people. We have been friends. We are friends yet, until the sun reaches a certain height [which was mentioned]. From that time we are enemies. Then if you wish to kill me, you may. If I want to kill you, I may."[3] This dramatic recital, not at all supported by later events, is important only as an indication of the widely held view that Turtle and Wells made an agreement, which took place after Wells announced his intention to rejoin his own people. The nature of the agreement was misjudged in this popular version, but it was correctly stated by Darius Heald, although in very general terms.

There is nothing improbable about individuals working to bring about peace while a war is being fought, although it is difficult for individuals actually engaged in fighting to do so without the imputation of giving aid to the enemy. Still, many wars among civilized nations have been fought with sword in one hand and olive branch in the other. Individual actions were less subject to control by their chiefs among Indians than among whites, and numerous examples of individuals who spared enemies for personal reasons in war might be cited. It is probable that whatever agreement was reached between Wells and Turtle was an honorable one from the Indian viewpoint and possibly from the white viewpoint as well. Certainly both men continued to fight while at the same time exerting their other capabilities toward peace in a manner that aroused no strong objection from their fellow fighters on either side.[4]

There are two distinct periods during which such a Family Compact might have been made. The first, and less probable time, was that between November 4, 1791, and sometime in March 1792. St. Clair's Defeat had produced a profound effect upon both Little Turtle and William Wells. Turtle had actually been so moved by the slaughter on that fatal day that he ordered an end to the killing. Wells cannot be said with certainty to have known that his brother Samuel was among the opposition or that his father's old friend Colonel Oldham was among the dead, but it is quite possible that he may have learned of these things after the battle. Such knowledge was probably not sufficient, however, to cause him, at this time, to cast his lot with the whites. He was well aware that his first wife and their child were being held captive by white men, and he definitely felt a

113

responsibility to do all that he could to secure their freedom. It would be easier, of course, to accomplish this end if he were to resume his place in white society. He decided to rejoin his Indian father, The Porcupine, whose wife and two sisters were also captives, and take some action that they might agree upon. It is reasonable to assume that he did so after fully discussing the matter with Little Turtle and, perhaps, with Turtle and The Porcupine together.

In March 1792 Wells and The Porcupine went down the Wabash to Vincennes and opened discussions with Colonel Hamtramck, who, following St. Clair's campaign, had resumed the command at Fort Knox. Before setting out on their journey, The Porcupine gave Wells his complete freedom (recall that Wells was originally a captive) in order that he might go wherever necessary to negotiate the release of the women and children of Kenapakomoko.[5] At Fort Knox, The Porcupine signed a declaration of friendship with the United States, as did chiefs from Ouiatenon and Kithtippecanuck, who sought the release of prisoners taken by General Scott.[6] Hamtramck did not have the power to act in this matter, however, and referred the Indians to General Rufus Putnam of Marietta, recently appointed head of a peace commission.

The Porcupine and other chiefs returned to their villages, and Wells went to visit his brother in Louisville. Apparently, Hamtramck had notified Samuel Wells of his brother's presence while negotiations had been in progress, and Samuel came to Fort Knox to conduct his brother to Louisville. William spent a month at Samuel's home before contact with Putnam was established. Samuel Wells had prospered and was living in comfortable circumstances, his children enjoying greater advantages than their parents had had. The contrast with Indian life must have weighed heavily on William's mind, and he was forced to admit that, despite the attractions of Indian life, there was not much promise of betterment for the future as compared to a future among the whites. He concluded that a fatal flaw in the Indian culture was that so little attention was given to either past or future. With rare exceptions his Indian friends lived entirely in the present— a rather carefree life, but a very risky one. Increasingly he began to feel that if he could find some employment he would do well to return to white society.[7]

When General Putnam finally arrived at Cincinnati, where the prisoners were held, he found William Wells awaiting him. He needed an interpreter, and since no one else was available "he sent for Wells and took him into the service of the United States." Thus, a first step was taken in the direction toward which Wells had been inclined for some time. However, on July 13, 1792, at Fort Washington, Wells had a strong tug in the opposite direction when he was reunited with his Miami family, who received him "with many tears," undoubtedly tears of joy.[8] His dual loyalties remained with him for the rest of his life, a matter never to be more than partially resolved.

On July 26, 1792, Putnam informed the secretary of war that Wells had revealed to him the site where the ten pieces of artillery had been buried by the Indians following St. Clair's Defeat. This gave evidence that Wells was to be trusted by the United States. Because he knew Little Turtle to be favorably disposed toward peace, Wells also urged that peace negotiations be opened with the Miami at the earliest opportunity. Further, Wells told Putnam that Kaweahatta (The Porcupine) "is a very sensible man; that the British account him the best speaker among all the Indian nations; that he is the greatest chief, and had more influence than any other man in the Wabash country."[9] This information was also reliable, for The Porcupine was indeed a much respected chief, the only Miami head chief who had been in power under the French regime and had survived through the British era and into the American period of control. The statement that Little Turtle favored peace was an indication that Wells and Little Turtle had certainly discussed the subject of war and peace, although they may not yet have arrived at their Family Compact.

On August 16–18 five barges left Cincinnati for Vincennes. They carried the Indian captives, under an escort of sixty soldiers, General Putnam (the peace commissioner), William Wells (his interpreter), and the Moravian missionary John Heckewelder, who kept an account of their journey. Wells did much of the hunting to supply meat for the large party. Somewhere along the Ohio, between Louisville and the mouth of the Wabash, Heckewelder observed and recorded fully a remarkable incident involving Wells and a wounded bear. It is known from early French sources that the Miami had mastered the art of subduing the black bear and driving the animal to their villages before killing him, thus saving themselves the labor of carrying the meat. On this occasion Wells had wounded a large bear and then approached the animal and struck it on the nose with the ramrod of his gun. He then spoke very earnestly to the bear in the Miami language and upbraided him for whimpering and carrying on in his wounded condition. He explained to Heckewelder, "I told him that he knew the fortune of war, that one or the other of us must have fallen; that it was his fate to be conquered, and he ought to die like a man, like a hero, and not like an old woman; that if the case had been reversed, and I had fallen into the power of my enemy, I would not have disgraced my nation as he did, but would have died with firmness and courage, as becomes a true warrior."[10] Whether or not the bear regained his composure before Wells finished him off, Heckewelder does not say. However, the incident provides some insight into the character of William Wells, as it had been shaped by his dual exposure to the ideas of both white men and Indians.

At Vincennes, Putnam released the prisoners and negotiated a peace treaty with some of the Wabash tribes, including the Eel River Miami. The Indians refused to include in the treaty a recognition of the legitimacy of any white settlements north of the Ohio River. The treaty was signed by thirty-one chiefs on September 27, 1792, but the Senate failed to ratify it, by a vote of 21–4, on January 9, 1794.

The treaty had stated, "The United States solemnly guarantee to the Wabash and Illinois nations or tribes of Indians, all the lands to which they have a just claim; and no part shall ever be taken from them but by a fair purchase and to their satisfaction." The Senate objected to the fourth article which declared, "That the land originally belonged to the Indians: it is theirs and theirs only. That they have a right to sell and a right to refuse to sell. And that the United States will protect them in their said just rights."[11] Apparently, it was the opinion of the Senate that Indians did not have the right to refuse to sell their land. It is difficult to say how well this treaty was adhered to by the Indians who signed it, but as the Piankashaw, the Wea, and the Eel River Miami, and the Kaskaskia and the Kickapoo provided no effective support for the campaign against General Wayne, it is probably fair to say that it was instrumental in neutralizing the Wabash and Illinois tribes.

Meanwhile, at Au Glaize in May 1792, the Miami told Matthew Elliott that they wished to leave Kekionga and settle near Au Glaize. They indicated that they needed food, and Elliott agreed that the British would provide food as well as guns and ammunition. As a result, a Miami village was established on the north bank of the Maumee, a few miles west of the junction of the Auglaize with the larger stream. It was early enough in the season for the women to plant corn in considerable quantity. This village was known as Little Turtle's Village and was not far from a Shawnee village at the junction. It is unlikely that Kekionga and Le Gris's Village were completely abandoned. Pacan undoubtedly remained at Kekionga. The warriors were joined by many women and children, for they needed the labor of the women to increase provisions. Little Turtle wanted to be in closer touch with the chiefs of other tribes and with the general negotiations being carried on to determine whether peace should be made or whether the war should be continued. The prevailing sentiment was for war, and the time had not yet come when Turtle could openly advocate peace.[12]

In April 1792 General Wilkinson, at Fort Washington, had sent a flag of truce to Kekionga with two men named Freeman and Gerrard. Also in May, two officers left Fort Washington for Au Glaize bearing flags of truce. One of these was Captain Alexander Trueman, who had been selected and instructed by the secretary of war, Henry Knox; the other was Colonel John Hardin, chosen by General Wilkinson. The officers traveled north together, into Indian country, and separated in the vicinity of Loramie's Creek. Trueman continued north through the Black Swamp toward Au Glaize, while Hardin bore northeast, headed for Upper Sandusky. All four soldiers were captured by Indians and put to death. Of Freeman and Gerrard it was reported that they were being conducted to Au Glaize but that they asked so many questions about the trails and location of the rivers and villages that their captors decided they were spies, not peace commissioners. Their deaths occurred near Kekionga, and it was reported that the chiefs at Au Glaize were displeased that their followers had violated the flag of truce.[13]

Of the two, word of Trueman's death was reported fairly early at Vincennes. It was eventually learned that Hardin had permitted the Indians to tie him to a tree in order to demonstrate his peaceful intention and had then been subjected to torture and death.[14] It is not likely that the Miami were involved in the deaths of Trueman or Hardin; Trueman was probably captured by the Shawnee, Hardin by the Wyandot. The deaths of these good officers and brave men were inexcusable and contributed to the failure of peaceful efforts at a time when the American government was making a genuine effort to negotiate. It is fair to say, however, that in the event that peaceful overtures were unsuccessful, the government had probably hoped to utilize its emissaries as gatherers of information useful in war.

Before General Putnam left Vincennes he persuaded Wells to accept a similar peace mission, despite the fact that the fate of these four men was already well established. For the sum of $300 Wells agreed to go to Kekionga to try to persuade the Miami and the Delaware of White River to participate in peace talks similar to those just concluded with the Wabash and the Illinois tribes at Vincennes. If successful he was to receive a bonus of $200; if unsuccessful he was expected to furnish such information as he could about the numbers and morale of the Indians. Wells could rely upon his relationship with Little Turtle to afford a degree of safety, but even so it was a mission fraught with some danger.[15]

Wells left Vincennes on October 7, 1792, and did not return for several months. Meanwhile, Putnam, in Marietta, was worried that Wells might also have been killed by the Indians. Traveling to Pittsburgh in January 1793, on his way to Philadelphia but unable to visit General Wayne at Legionville, he expressed his fears for Wells's safety in a letter to Wayne.[16] On reaching Kekionga, Wells found that he would need to continue to Au Glaize to find Little Turtle and Sweet Breeze. This he did and remained with them until January 1793, at which time he presented his invitation to peace talks to the chiefs of the various tribes in council. As British influence was strong at the council, his overtures received a negative reply.

In November 1792 Wells had talked with Oliver M. Spencer, an eleven-year-old boy who was a prisoner at the Shawnee village at Au Glaize. Spencer had been captured on July 7, 1792, on the Ohio River between Cincinnati and Columbia, where his parents had settled in 1790. His father was a Revolutionary War officer of some substance and with influential connections. The Spencers had reported their son's capture to General Wayne but in the ensuing six months had learned nothing of his whereabouts. His captors were two Mohawk brothers whose mother lived among the Shawnee at Au Glaize, where Spencer had been taken. Their sister was the wife of George Ironside, a well-known English trader at Kekionga and along the Maumee.

Wells, whom Spencer called "a prisoner at large among the Indians," promptly sent word of the boy's whereabouts to Colonel Hamtramck, at Vincennes, who notified the parents through General Wilkinson, at Fort Washington. They were able to work through the government to secure their son's release, and he reached home in October 1794, having spent more time in Canada, on the roundabout route prescribed by British officials, than he had spent as a captive among the Indians.[17]

There is a gap in information about Wells between January and August 1793, at which time he was employed on a fresh mission by Colonel Hamtramck. Probably Wells extended his stay at Little Turtle's Village, or perhaps at Kekionga, beyond January, not only because of difficult travel conditions, but also to discuss many things with Little Turtle. For several reasons this is a somewhat more likely time than the earlier period for the Family Compact to have been completed. Wells had committed himself to working for the American government. He may also have decided against resuming life with his first wife at Kenapakomoko and dissolved their marriage, though he maintained some responsibility for their son. He seems also to have assured Little Turtle and Sweet Breeze that he would return to them after the conclusion of peace. In 1792 or 1793 Sweet Breeze gave birth to her first child, a daughter.

Little Turtle certainly would have been able to counsel him from the Indian viewpoint about some of these domestic arrangements. Wells answered questions about the Americans that were helpful to Little Turtle in making up his mind about future policy. They must have agreed, as honorable men who trusted each other, that each should go his own way and do what he had to do and that whatever either had to do would make no difference to their friendship or their future relations. This is the only reasonable explanation for the way they faced the world together from this time, so that their contemporaries puzzled over the question of whether their words and actions were those of Wells or those of Little Turtle. It also seems clear that they agreed not to kill each other if they met in battle, an understanding that Wells also had with The Porcupine.

From this point on, historians, too, have had difficulty in separating the actions of Wells and Little Turtle. Most would agree that Wells was a romantic, whereas Turtle was a realist. Turtle may have understood this himself and viewed Wells at first simply as a convenient tool he could employ. Turtle, however, was limited by advancing age, by the difficulty of language in dealing with whites, and by the problems of maintaining followers among his own people. As the years passed he became more dependent on Wells, and Wells became more a man of thought, without losing his character as a man of action. History provides few instances of more complete identification of purpose than these two men achieved from this time until their deaths, which occurred only a month apart. Once peace was achieved they saw eye to eye and acted shoulder to shoulder.

There is a moral question as to whether either was false to the side he had chosen for the duration of the war, in which both were actively engaged. It can only be said that each man seems to have been satisfied with the behavior of the other, and no reproaches on this score were ever exchanged. Later there were to be accusations by Indians regarding Little Turtle and regarding Wells by the whites. Yet Turtle worked in harmony with Pacan and Le Gris, and Wells gave complete satisfaction to both Putnam and Wayne.[18]

Had Wells returned to Vincennes in the winter of 1793 he would have been sent to Philadelphia, in accordance with General Putnam's request. The failure of his peace conference proposal pleased the British, who now began to plan for a conference of their own later that year.[19] His job completed, Wells's time was his own. Everything pointed to his return to Vincennes in the late spring or early summer of 1793.

In the meantime, a Grand Council of Indians was planned for August 1793 at Au Glaize, at which not only the British Indian agents McKee and Elliott were expected but also three members of a new American commission composed of General Benjamin Lincoln, Beverly Randolph, and Timothy Pickering. General Anthony Wayne and his well-trained Legion had finally reached Fort Washington. Wayne was eager to know the results of the three-way consultation, for his orders were not to jeopardize the prospect of peace by any military movement into Indian country. Wayne and Hamtramck arranged that the latter would send Wells to attend this great meeting, with orders for him to report directly to Wayne as soon as definite results were known. Once again Wells went to Au Glaize, but this time as an observer for the American army—in other words, as a spy.

"Peace conference" was actually a euphemism for the negotiations that had begun as early as May 22 with the arrival of the Mohawk chief Joseph Brant, who expected to dominate the meetings. Brant was in favor of a boundary line along the Muskingum. His hopes were shattered by the influence of Alexander McKee, aided by Matthew Elliott. These two British agents had great influence among the Shawnee and through them were able to retain the support of the Delaware, the Wyandot, and the Miami for the Ohio River boundary. Brant was selected as the emissary to the American commissioners who were at Fort Niagara. He succeeded in persuading them to come to Elliott's farm at the mouth of the Detroit River, but they were not permitted to come to McKee's store at the foot of the Maumee Rapids or to Sandusky, to which locations the meetings were shifted from Au Glaize. John Graves Simcoe, governor-general of the newly created province of Upper Canada (1791), officially backed Brant and unofficially backed McKee. In fact, Simcoe was even willing to consider the possibility of gaining Kentucky from the United States. The American commissioners were not prepared to make any appreciable concessions for peace, and when, on August 17, they rejected the Indian stand for the Ohio River boundary, negotiations finally ended.[20]

The Indians were impressed by the British ability to retain Detroit, Michilimackinac, and Niagara, in defiance of the Americans, and by McKee's ability to deliver food, powder, and ball. They were divided by Brant, an interloper in the West, whom they resented. Not recognizing that Little Turtle's mind grasped the realities of peace better than any of the other chiefs, the Indians made the mistake of turning to him only to lead them in war. Without this recognition Little Turtle was forced to leave the conduct of negotiations to men of far less penetration than himself. He was willing to accept either the Muskingum or the Ohio boundary but was forced, by his mistrust of Brant and the necessity of supporting his wartime allies, into holding fast for the Ohio River line. Brant had taken no part in St. Clair's Defeat, and although he had been invited he had no real business at the conference. Without the presence of Brant, Little Turtle would have had an opportunity to advocate a peace based on a compromise boundary. As his prestige was high at this time, he might well have counteracted the Shawnee influence.

Wells appeared at Fort Jefferson on September 11, accompanied by one Indian. On the same date, at Fort Washington, Wayne received a letter from the commissioners dated August 23, from Fort Erie, with the news that peace negotiations had failed. Wells arrived at Fort Washington, where Wayne interviewed him on September 14, 15, and 16. It must be remembered that Wells had to conceal the fact that he had been acting as a spy for Wayne; thus he could not afford to travel too directly or with too great an appearance of haste. Wayne examined him on three successive days in order to ascertain whether he told a consistent story. Wells passed this grilling with flying colors and was thereafter trusted implicitly by the general.[21]

Wayne was much interested to learn Wells's opinion that the Indians would be able to field an army of at least 1,600 men, that they would be well equipped for warfare by the British, and that the British advice and influence had been and continued to be the principal barrier to peace.[22] So impressed was Wayne with William Wells's ability and trustworthiness that in October 1793 he commissioned him captain of a special force of spies, recruited by Wells himself and directly under Wayne's orders and responsible to him alone. Although concerned in one more peace effort, Wells was from this time on an important cog in Wayne's military machine. Since Wayne regarded October as too late for an offensive campaign to begin, his army garrisoned and repaired the forts built by St. Clair, built some new ones, and went into winter quarters from Fort Washington (Cincinnati) to Fort Recovery, built on the site of St. Clair's Defeat.

NOTES

1. DRAPER, 23S62–65.
2. HUTTON, 190.
3. BRICE, 147–48.
4. DUNN, 116–17, indicates acceptance of the existence of a compact between Wells and Little Turtle.
5. HECKEWELDER, 45. The fact that these negotiations were handled by Wells and The Porcupine, not by Wells and Little Turtle, is strong evidence that Wells had a wife and child among the Eel River Miami who were not Turtle's daughter and grandson. Some romantics wish to believe that Sweet Breeze was Wells's first wife, but these negotiations, in which Turtle had no part, weigh heavily against such fancies.
6. CARTER (1), II, 374–75, 380–83. Wells left Vincennes with Samuel Wells on June 17, 1792. See BUELL, 296.
7. VOLNEY, 372–74, 378–79, gives some idea of Wells's thoughts, as expressed to Volney in 1797.
8. HECKEWELDER, 45, 49. Heckewelder stated that the prisoners taken by Scott and Wilkinson had cost the government $60,000 to maintain during their year of captivity, which seems excessive. Having done his duty toward his wife and their child, Wells may now have felt it necessary to speak of his having taken a second wife; or he may simply have taken his departure without explanation, after conducting them back to Kenapakomoko. It is also conceivable that Wells maintained two families about sixty miles apart.
9. ASPIA, I, 238–39.
10. HECKEWELDER, 256.

11. DILLON, 293–95.

12. TANNER, 15–39, identifies seven separate villages near Au Glaize with a total population of 2,000 people. Her note, p. 20, attributing a white wife (Polly Ford) to Little Turtle appears to be based on oral tradition not committed to paper until 1937. I have been unable to find any supporting evidence. Her note, p. 36, on the other hand, giving evidence that Blue Jacket could not have been a white man, seems to me to rest on solid ground.

13. KNOPF, 22–23. If the Miami were responsible for this violation of the flag of truce, as seems probable, it may have provided an added reason for their removal to Au Glaize, for fear of retaliation. Little Turtle would certainly have been one of the chiefs to disapprove such action, and he may have influenced others to do so as well.

14. ASPIA, I, 229–30, 238, 494, gives about all that is known of the deaths of Captain Trueman and Colonel Hardin. Trueman was scalped and stripped; Wayne, at Pittsburgh, received word of his death on August 3, 1792, from Francis Vigo, at Vincennes. Wayne was shocked because the Indians usually respected a flag of truce. See KNOPF, 56–58. Both Hardin and Trueman were said to have allowed themselves to be bound to demonstrate their good faith.

15. BUELL, 370, gives Putnam's official letter of instruction to Wells for this mission. The Grand Council at Au Glaize was already in session, for on the day that Wells departed from Vincennes the Wea chief Messquakenoe (Painted Pole) delivered a speech that indicates why American peace efforts were unsuccessful. He said, "We know very well what the Americans are about and what are their designs. Last fall when the Great Spirit was good enough to assist us, to throw them on their back, we got their great chiefs papers and instructions. . . . All the Chiefs here present heard them interpreted to us. If the Americans had been successful, they were to build a strong fort at the Miami Towns, if they succeeded, they were to proceed to the mouth of the River and build a strong fort there. They were afterwards to set about building boats and to drive all of the Indians out of the Country, to clear the Lake of them and drive them far back into the Country. But if any of the Nations came and offered their hands, the American Chief was to put them at his back and give them hoes in their hands to plant corn for him and his people and make them labor like their beasts, their oxen, and their pack-horses." CRUIKSHANK, I, 227.

16. BUELL, 375–77. Putnam requested that if Wells returned his expenses be paid to join him in Philadelphia.

17. QUAIFE (2), passim. Wells is referred to on pp. 51 and 114.

18. The conclusions presented here are based upon the knowledge that exists concerning Wells and Little Turtle as set forth in the correspondence of Wells with the War Department, for the most part in his capacity as Indian agent, which will be surveyed in later chapters of this work.

19. CRUIKSHANK, I, 282–83. Alexander McKee to John Graves Simcoe, January 30, 1793.

20. A full analysis of the conference is in HORSMAN, 76–91. The report of the American commissioners is in ASPIA, I, 340–61.

21. KNOPF, 272–73. Wayne wrote to Knox, "It's true, that I have made it his *interest*—to be and continue faithful to the United States, for this Campaign at least." Wayne was a strong believer in gaining loyalty by means of generous pay for services rendered. No better method has been found.

22. SMITH (3), 217–26. During this period, Wells and William Henry Harrison, junior aide-de-camp to General Wayne, became good friends. Harrison actually helped Wells to improve his reading and writing, and Wells in return imparted a good bit of information on the customs of the Indians to Harrison.

12

Wayne's Victory, 1792–94

FOUR MONTHS AFTER St. Clair's Defeat the Congress of the United States passed legislation providing for the creation by recruitment of the Legion of the United States. On April 12, 1792, President Washington appointed Major-General Anthony Wayne to command this new army. Wayne promptly accepted and in early June arrived at Pittsburgh, where the Legion was being assembled and trained. Like Harmar and St. Clair, Wayne was a Pennsylvanian and a veteran officer of the Revolutionary War. He was forty-seven when he became commander-in-chief of the Legion; as did St. Clair, he suffered severely from gout. His record in the Revolution had been distinguished for daring, but Washington was careful to impress upon him the need for caution to avoid such a disaster as St. Clair had suffered.

The Legion was to be composed of 291 officers and 4,272 men, if fully recruited. There were four sublegions of infantry, plus dragoons and artillery. More than $350,000 was appropriated for Legion use during the year of its creation alone. Although the Legion was not recruited to full strength, by November 28 Wayne was able to move down the Ohio from Pittsburgh and set up a camp known as Legionville. Here he intensified the training to such an extent that he was regarded by the enlisted men as something of a martinet. Deserters were harshly dealt with, and officers who offered to resign found their resignations promptly accepted. With pay and supplies coming through fairly regularly, however, morale increased. When Wayne was ordered to take his troops to Cincinnati on April 20, 1793, he was able to comply promptly, arriving on May 5 "after a passage of six days" down the river. Here Wayne established a camp at Hobson's Choice, near Fort Washington and Cincinnati, where drill was continued until mid-September, when the failure of the peace conference became

124

known. An advance toward Indian country was ordered along the line of the forts established earlier by St. Clair.[1]

After St. Clair's Defeat, Little Turtle adopted and began putting into practice an entirely different method of warfare than had previously been used by the Indians. Whether this was a plan of his own or whether he had heard it spoken of by British army officers is difficult to say. In view of the fact that he did not speak English, it is more probable that he devised it himself from observations of St. Clair's campaign. His plan was to attack the convoys that brought food and other supplies to the American army and to continue doing so until the Americans were forced to abandon their offensive campaign.[2]

His plan was well adapted to the realities of the situation he faced. Turtle had badly defeated two armies, but the result had been that the Americans put a stronger army in the field each time. He was convinced that eventually the Americans would prevail by virtue of their greater numbers, but he could not convince his more short-sighted allies of this. He was fully aware that the American supply line was vulnerable because of its length and that the uncertainty of delivery increased in proportion to the size of the army being maintained in the field. Like Napoleon he realized that an army marches on its stomach, and reasoned that if the supply line could be disrupted often enough to prevent the arrival of food supplies, the American army would be plagued with deserters and forced to abandon the campaign. Such a strategy had the advantage that it would supply the Indians with horses. The chief flaw of this hit-and-run technique, however, was the lack of enough time to destroy those supplies which could not be carried off.

An additional risk was that some of the Indians might not confine themselves to the attack of convoys but would be tempted to use the plan whenever they found a small force that could easily be overwhelmed, regardless of whether there was any military advantage. For example, a mowing party of twelve was attacked near Fort Jefferson on June 24, 1792. Four men were killed and eight captured by about fifty Indians. Except for what intelligence could be learned from the captives, there had been no advantage gained from such a raid.[3]

It was often difficult to find out when a convoy was expected, although such information could be learned at times from captives. In November 1792 Little Turtle commanded a party of 200 men against the town of Columbia, on the Ohio River near Cincinnati, where supplies often were unloaded. Near Fort Hamilton, however, two captives were taken and from them it was learned that Colonel John Adair was returning from Fort Jefferson with a pack train that had convoyed supplies there. An ambush set for Adair about midway between Fort St. Clair and Fort Hamilton failed when Adair did not arrive because he had camped near Fort St. Clair. Plans were changed again, and Adair, who had 100 mounted soldiers with him, was attacked early on the morning of November 6. An attack so near the fort was unexpected and Adair's militia fled to the fort, which Adair referred to as "a place of safety for the bashful." The Indians were making off with 160 captured horses when Adair rallied his men and pursued them. The Indians turned and drove him off, however, inflicting a loss of 6 men, among whom was Colonel Richard Taylor, father of a future president.[4]

In 1805, when Adair was registrar of the land office at Frankfort, Little Turtle and Wells passed through Frankfort and the two former enemies had a friendly conversation, in the course of which General Adair attributed his defeat to having been taken by surprise. Little Turtle, who had a considerable reputation for witty remarks, is said to have replied affably, in keeping with the tone of the conversation, "A good general is never taken by surprise."[5]

Indians were interested in a type of warfare that provided an opportunity for taking scalps or captives, in the capture of horses and cattle, or in seizing booty that attracted them. They were not interested in the destruction of food supplies in a systematic way. Adair's convoy had been returning from a trip to supply Fort Jefferson, at that time the most advanced post. Apart from the capture of many fine riding horses, Turtle's victory was not of great military importance. Later attempts to disrupt Wayne's supply line were too infrequent to be very effective.

When it became clear that efforts toward peace had failed, General Wayne took up his line of march on October 7, 1793, from Hobson's Choice, with a view to establishing winter quarters for the Legion nearer Kekionga and Au Glaize. His advance was unimpeded by the Indians until October 17, when Wayne reached Fort Jefferson and found it very short of supplies and transport. He was forced to halt until food could be brought in. Lieutenant Lowry, with ninety men, attempted to convoy twenty wagons to the Legion but was attacked by forty Indians on October 17, seven miles beyond Fort St. Clair. Lowry, another officer, and twelve men were killed. The Indians captured seventy wagon horses and rode off with such plunder as they could carry, without setting fire to the wagon train. Wayne was thus able to bring the food supplies in undamaged within a few days. Closely repeated attacks such as this would have given Wayne a serious problem, but with increasing vigilance and constant attention on the part of his quartermaster, General John O'Hara, he was able to surmount the difficulties. Wayne was further aided by the suspension of attacks on convoys during the winter months; they were not resumed by the Indians until May 1794. The Miami were forced by sheer necessity to give attention to their own food supply and engaged in their usual winter hunt in the buffalo country to the west of Kekionga.[6]

126

Wayne established his headquarters in a strongly fortified camp six miles beyond Fort Jefferson, at Greeneville, during late October and November of 1793, taking care to have the men construct their own huts first and leaving his own quarters to the last. A chain of redoubts completed the protection of the camp, which presented a compact and well-ordered appearance. By December 23 Wayne was able to detach eight companies of infantry and some artillery under Major Henry Burbeck to the scene of St. Clair's Defeat, about twenty-three miles northwest of Greeneville, where Fort Recovery was erected. It was garrisoned under the command of Colonel Gibson, and in the spring of 1794 the cannon lost by St. Clair were dug up and utilized for its defense.[7]

Information as to the location of those ten pieces of artillery had been divulged first to General Putnam and then to General Wayne by William Wells, a point of great importance in assessing the genuine character of Wells's shift from the Indian side to that of his own people. The Indians were unaware that the cannon had been recovered and were to spend some time in a fruitless search for them at a critical period some six months later. This affords proof that Wells was not transmitting military intelligence to the Indians as "a double agent."

On the other hand, true to his Family Compact with Little Turtle, Wells was engaged in one more effort toward peace. Wayne had pretty well given up hope of further negotiations, although he was still under orders from the United States government to persevere in such efforts. When a captive Indian woman was released by Wells to go to the Delaware villages on White River, the son of Buckongahelas, the Delaware war chief, and two other Delaware warriors came to Greeneville on January 13, 1794. In order that peace negotiations might begin in earnest, they arranged a truce of thirty days, during which they undertook to try to round up and surrender all white prisoners among the Indians. In the absence of Alexander McKee, the British agent, the Delaware secured the consent of the chiefs at Au Glaize, and runners were sent to all the hostile tribes to begin the roundup of prisoners. Two problems prevented the success of this effort: the prisoners were widely scattered, so the task could not be accomplished in the allotted time; and Wayne refused to extend the truce. Then McKee returned and convinced many of the chiefs to withdraw their cooperation. Although Wayne suspected from the outset that it was simply a maneuver to gain time, it is more likely that the effort was begun in good faith by the Indians but was brought to an end by British influence.[8]

Lord Dorchester, governor-general of Lower Canada, had returned in September 1793 from an extended visit to England. In a speech made on February 10, at Quebec, he flatly stated that there was no boundary between Great Britain and the United States in the Indian country and predicted that Great Britain would go to war with the United States before the end of 1794 in order to force the Americans to agree to a boundary that would be satisfactory to the Indians.[9]

A week later, Lord Dorchester ordered Colonel John Graves Simcoe to build and garrison a fort at the foot of the rapids of the Maumee River, about five miles from its mouth and near Alexander McKee's trading post. As governor-general of Upper Canada, Simcoe was opposed to such action, but as a subordinate to Lord Dorchester he had to obey orders. This sequence of events was traced in the diary kept by Mrs. Simcoe. On Saturday, February 1, she wrote, "I am in great spirits today, as the Governor talks of going to Detroit in March and spending a month there very gaily." On Sunday, February 9, she continued, "I am quite impatient to set out for Detroit." But on Saturday, February 15, she noted that her husband had just received an express from Lord Dorchester, ordering him to establish Fort Miami, and recorded, "This order puts an end to my scheme of going to Detroit, which is an exceeding great disappointment to me."[10] It was probably around this time that Mrs. Simcoe, who was an accomplished artist, made a sketch of Pacan, the Miami head chief, at her residence at Fort Niagara.[11]

During April 1794 Governor Simcoe supervised the construction of Fort Miami, usually called Fort Miami of the Lakes. On April 14, at Au Glaize, he read Lord Dorchester's speech to the Indians, thus reinforcing to his audience the completely false assurance that they could count on the active entrance of Great Britain on their side in their war against the United States. All thoughts of peace were discarded, and as McKee supplied black wampum belts, indicating war, for general circulation, Indian warriors began to assemble at Au Glaize in ever increasing numbers from far and near. Plans were made for an offensive that would isolate Wayne by cutting off his supplies. As usual, it was to Little Turtle that the Indians looked for effective leadership. The promising peace movement set afoot by Wells and Little Turtle had been reversed by the belligerence of British officialdom in Canada. Unknown to the Indians, the Canadian attitude was not supported by the government of Great Britain.[12]

Wayne was ignorant of the activities of the Indians and their British abettors in the first half of the year 1794. From his headquarters at Greeneville he was occupied chiefly with the three essentials to which his eventual success must be attributed. His supply line of nearly 100 miles had to be maintained intact. To this end, although pack horses were still employed, he had widened the road used by St. Clair so that wagons could be used and provided strong convoys and constant warning to be on the alert. He had accumulated rations at Greeneville and stored them at the forts along the way. Although this was the weak point of his campaign, and although

Little Turtle and the British officers realized this, he had been able to prevent any important disruption of his line of communication and supply.

The Legion continued to be drilled regularly at Greeneville with a view to invasion of the Indian country. No longer were they being taught to maintain close order. Wayne believed that an open order of march, so long as it was disciplined and practiced and the men felt confident about it, lessened the likelihood of a successful surprise attack.[13] He also obtained new uniforms of which the Legion was very proud; esprit de corps was raised and desertion reduced. Furthermore, Wayne was not sparing with praise for tasks well performed. He had an insoluble problem in the person of General James Wilkinson, his second-in-command, however, who constantly sought to undermine the confidence of officers in their commander-in-chief and attach them to himself. Wayne was able to ignore this until after the crucial battle had been fought because he retained the full support of at least half of his officers. He functioned well despite Wilkinson's conspiracy as he retained the solid backing of Secretary of War Knox and President Washington throughout the campaign.[14]

Wayne was fortunate to have an unusually efficient and daring group of spies under the direction of Captain William Wells. Many of these men, like Wells himself, had spent some years as captives among the Indians. They were able to dress as Indians, speak as Indians, apply Indian war paint and pass as Indians, roaming almost at will in Indian country, taking captives who were forced to give needed information. They did not hesitate to kill small parties of Indians after mingling with them and making sure of at least one captive. A company of rangers under Captain Ephraim Kibby performed more general scouting services, but Wells, with his elite group of about twenty men, was responsible to Wayne directly.[15] Wayne also employed seventeen Chickasaw and a few Choctaw, who, while performing similar services to those of Wells and his men, operated independently. As a consequence of the work of his scouts and spies, Wayne was better informed of the preparations and intentions of the Indian confederacy than they were of his activities.

The exploits of Wells and his men were long remembered and often told on the early frontier. The most celebrated of his band were William May, Robert McClellan, and brothers Nicholas and Christopher Miller. Of these, all but McClellan, a young man famous for his athletic prowess and later a member of the Overland Astorians, had been captives among the Indians. Christopher Miller was captured from among the Indians by one of Wells's scouting expeditions and persuaded by his brother to change sides. On one occasion Wells encountered his foster father, The Porcupine, and his family on the St. Marys River, but he recognized them in time to prevent their deaths at the hands of his men.[16] Although most of their operations were in the Black Swamp between Greeneville and Au Glaize, it is probable that Wells, at least, penetrated to the villages on the Maumee, for he received on several occasions information from John Kinzie, a trader with whom he was well acquainted.

The Indians were so annoyed, particularly with Wells and May, that they asked help from Alexander McKee in dealing with them.[17] They were accustomed to holding an advantage in scouting and spying operations, so it was most significant that through the employment of Wells, Wayne shifted this advantage to his side. Wells employed the tactics that he had learned from the Miami themselves during the years of his captivity.

Little Turtle had expected that Wayne and his army would begin the advance toward Au Glaize prior to the middle of June. His plan was to watch for a good opportunity to do one or both of two things before the Americans reached Au Glaize. The first was to by-pass Wayne's advance with a portion of the Indian forces and cut his supply line by overwhelming any convoy that might bring food supplies by pack-horse train. The second was to ambush the army at some favorable spot along the Auglaize River. Ideally, both these plans might be attempted in the order mentioned. If neither plan succeeded and Wayne reached Au Glaize, it would still be possible to retire to the protection of the recently constructed British fort at Roche de Bout, where a battle might be risked with British aid that would draw England into the war, no matter what the outcome.

Wayne, on the other hand, could not advance until the arrival of General Scott with some 1,500–2,000 mounted militia from Kentucky, which would double his strength. His orders from the secretary of war were to take the field offensively by July 15, or July 20 at the latest, by which time Scott was expected to be on hand with his reinforcements.[18] When Wayne did not move out from Greeneville by June 15, Little Turtle was forced to consider taking the offensive himself, for the large number of Indians assembled at Au Glaize and Roche de Bout had created a supply problem which overtaxed the ability of the British traders. The large number of Lake Indians, as the Ottawa, the Chippewa, and the Potawatomi from the far north were called, not only had to be fed but were a disruptive influence on the families of the tribes living along the Maumee.

The Wyandot lived nearby on the Sandusky; they came in prepared for action on June 15.[19] A council of war was held and it was determined to organize an advance party and also to involve the British whites and half bloods by forcing them to join the war party. Between June 18 and June 20 the Indian forces had been set in motion, but with between 1,500 and 2,000 warriors from many tribes available, no unified command was possible.[20] The Delaware decided to advance separately by a more westerly route in order to intercept any offensive against their villages on the White

River. They lost touch completely with the main force and did not establish contact again until after the main force had been repulsed at Fort Recovery.[21]

The advance was slow because the hunters needed time to bring in food. Large numbers of deer and turkey were supplied, but from the outset there was a shortage of corn.[22] Three British officers in scarlet uniforms who accompanied the expedition advised the Indians to adhere to Little Turtle's plan to destroy first any convoys operating between the forts. However, the Lake Indians wished to attack Fort Recovery, the most advanced post, and they had their way. Bear Chief, an Ottawa, seems to have been the principal advocate of this course of action.[23]

Both the Chickasaw scouts and Wells's spies were aware of the advance of the Indian army in open files about ten rods distant from one another. Wells, May, and one of the Miller brothers brought this news to Wayne at Greeneville on June 28, together with the information that Mountain Leader, one of the Chickasaw scouts, had been killed and scalped by the enemy.[24] Wayne was thus prepared for an attack at Greeneville, but on June 29 the Indians veered westward and on the morning of June 30 attacked Fort Recovery instead.

The Indians had arrived in the vicinity the evening before and learned that a convoy with 300 pack horses loaded with flour had just arrived and would be leaving the next morning. Major McMahan, along with 140 soldiers and 300 pack horses attacked about one-half mile from the fort. The major and 15 of his men were killed and the pack horses were captured. A sortie from the fort was forced to flee, along with the remainder of McMahan's men, back to the fort for safety. This would have been a good time to have swung south to Fort Jefferson, but in the flush of victory the Lake Indians were out of control and attacked Fort Recovery, a stockade of logs with blockhouses at intervals. There were cannon in all the blockhouses, some of which were those recovered by Wells's information, unknown to the Indians, some of whom spent considerable time searching in vain for these artillery pieces. The Indian attack was repulsed, according to a British source, with a loss of 17 warriors; Wayne reported a much larger, although indefinite, loss. Fighting continued on a lesser scale throughout the day. Wayne recorded that the Indians killed and ate a large number of the pack horses that evening and spent the night recovering their dead, so that after the assault was abandoned only 8 bodies were found.[25]

During the night a large number of Chippewa, who had just caught up with the main army, insisted on renewing the attack the next day. They were repelled by the cannon, as on the previous day, and it was then decided to give up the attack and retire to Au Glaize. The Delaware rejoined the

131

army on July 2 and undertook to cover the retreat by assuming all scouting duties. The importance of the St. Clair artillery cannot be overstated. One of the British officers wrote that with two barrels of powder and one of the cannon the fort could have been breached and taken.[26]

The authority of an Indian war chief in Little Turtle's position was by no means as great as that of a general among the whites. The only possibility of retaining control in a situation such as developed was by sheer force of personality, which was impossible with a war party of this size composed of many tribes. Furthermore, Little Turtle himself had reached the conclusion that the Indians could not win the war without the active military participation of the British. He may have thought that the only way to convince those who advocated attacking a fort defended by artillery was to let them learn the hard way, through inevitable failure. The Lake Indians, fiercest advocates of direct attack, changed their minds and headed for their distant homes. The best that could be done was to persuade some of their chiefs to remain at Au Glaize, with the hope that they might be able to summon their warriors later on for another action.[27]

Little Turtle himself went to Detroit almost at once, following the repulse at Fort Recovery, and there confronted Colonel Richard G. England with the question of how much aid the Indians could expect from the British. Colonel England was highly impressed with the intelligence and demeanor of the great Miami war chief, calling him "the most decent, modest, sensible Indian I ever conversed with," but he was unable to answer the question. Little Turtle then became specific and asked for twenty redcoats and two cannons. With these he promised to go again to Fort Recovery with the Miami, the Wyandot, the Delaware, and the Shawnee and destroy the fort. Colonel England refused this minimal request, since it would plunge Britain into war with the United States. Little Turtle then said flatly that unless the British backed up their war talk with at least that much aid, the Indians could not stop Wayne's expedition. In reporting to Lieutenant Governor Simcoe, Colonel England concluded, "I of course talked him over for two or three days and dismissed him seemingly contented."[28]

Little Turtle had confirmed what he had long suspected, namely, that the British wished only to use the Indians for their own purposes against the Americans and that, from Lord Dorchester down to McKee and Elliott, no British official's words could be relied upon. From this time on he became an open advocate of peace in the Indian council meetings. Unfortunately, the Shawnee were completely under the control of McKee and Elliott; Girty and the Wyandot were strongly impressed by Fort Miami of the Lakes, constructed so near their own territory; the Delaware, having led an earlier abortive peace move, were now inclined to side with the majority. Thus, Turtle was unable to sway his allies toward peace.

General Charles Scott and the vanguard of his long-awaited mounted militiamen from Kentucky arrived at Greeneville on July 26. Wayne had been impatient to take the offensive ever since the repulse of the Indians at Fort Recovery. The Legion and half of Scott's 1,600 men began their march into Indian country on July 27, leaving the other half of the militia, which had not yet reached Greeneville, to catch up as soon as possible.[29] Wayne moved first to the St. Marys River, where he spent three days building Fort Adams (near present-day Mercer, Ohio), during which time the remainder of the Kentucky volunteers arrived with heavy ordnance and rations for thirty days.[30] Both wagons and pack horses were used, and woodsmen were employed to prepare a road over which wagons might be taken. Wayne now had about 3,600 men, including the scouts. Wells was sent to scout the route ahead, which was down the Little Auglaize River to the main stream of that name and thence to its junction with the Maumee at Au Glaize (modern-day Defiance, Ohio). Wells's report indicated that the route was favorable at this time of year and that the Indian villages along the Auglaize had been deserted.[31]

On August 3 a tree fell on Wayne's tent and laid him out cold, but he soon recovered and ordered the march to be resumed on August 4.[32] On August 8 the junction of the Auglaize and the Maumee was reached. Here, too, the Indian villages were deserted, as their former inhabitants were well aware of Wayne's advance.[33] The women and children of the Shawnee and the Ottawa had been sent to Sandusky; those of the Delaware had returned to the White River; and the Miami women had gone to Kekionga and thence taken refuge among the Potawatomi. The warriors were assembled at Roche de Bout, at the foot of the Maumee rapids near the British fort. Wayne congratulated the army upon having arrived at what he aptly called "the Grand Emporium of the hostile Indians of the West" because of the extensive cornfields, which stretched for several miles up and down the Maumee.[34]

On August 9 the army encamped at the site of Blue Jacket's Village, where it remained for several days during the construction of Fort Defiance. Meanwhile, William Wells was ordered to scout the Indian army and the British fort fifty miles down the Maumee and to capture an Indian to see what could be learned. Taking Christopher Miller, Robert McClellan, William May, and Dodson Thorp, dressed and painted as Indians, Wells carried out this mission on August 11, taking a Shawnee and his wife as prisoners. On their return trip the scouts noticed a small Delaware village about twenty miles from Fort Defiance and decided to see what could be learned there. When Wells overheard one Indian remark to another that he recognized May, the scouts were forced to shoot their way out of the village. They killed two Delaware and effected their escape, but not before McClellan was wounded in the shoulder and a bullet had shattered Wells's left wrist. Miller rode to Fort Defiance, whence a party of dragoons was sent to bring in the wounded scouts. The Shawnee prisoner revealed that about 600 warriors were at McKee's store and that Elliott had gone to Detroit for reinforcements and supplies and would return on August 11; that 400 Ottawa and Wyandot were expected also; and that the British fort was well defended by cannon. It was also learned that the Indians had accurate knowledge of Wayne's army and were undecided whether to fight him or to step aside and let him confront the British fort, or possibly even to join the Americans.[35]

Wayne now decided to make one more peace effort. He sent Christopher Miller with a white flag to urge the Indians not to be deceived any longer by the British and to make peace at once. The Indian reply was to request a ten-day truce to consider the matter, during which time Wayne was asked to remain at Fort Defiance. Wayne rejected this and set the army in motion once more on August 15.[36] His belief, in which he was probably correct, was that the Indians were simply trying to gain time to strengthen their numbers. It must have been at this council meeting that Little Turtle made his strong plea for peace, rather than on the eve of the battle. He is reported to have said, "We have beaten the enemy twice under different commanders. We cannot expect the same good fortune to attend us always. The Americans are now led by a chief who never sleeps. Like the blacksnake, the day and the night are alike to him for during all the time he has been marching on our villages, notwithstanding the watchfulness of our young men, we have not been able to surprise him. Think well of it. There is something whispers me, it would be prudent to listen to his offers of peace."[37]

In all likelihood the return of Matthew Elliott from Detroit with Captain Caldwell and a company of Canadian rangers, as well as additional cannon for Fort Miami of the Lakes, resulted in the disregard of this advice.[38] When some chiefs in the council accused Little Turtle of cowardice, his response was to resign as leader of the allied Indian army in favor of the Shawnee war chief Blue Jacket, while also asserting that he would abide by the decision to fight and would himself lead the Miami warriors as usual.[39] Convinced as he was of the unreliability of British support, of the strength of Wayne's army, and of the certainty of defeat, Turtle thus put himself in a position to become the leader of the Indians after the battle; at the same time he could point out that he had done his part to the very end.

Wayne and his army arrived at Roche de Bout on August 18. The temporary earthwork that was built up where the supplies could be left under a strong guard was called Camp Deposit, some forty-one miles from Fort Defiance. When William Wells was sent with his spies to reconnoiter the

Indian camp, they found the enemy in such numbers that they fled for their lives. William May's horse gave out and he was captured. The next day he was tied to a tree and used for target practice, until about fifty bullets had struck him and it was obvious he was no longer alive.[40]

On August 18 the Indians judged a battle to be imminent and, as was their custom, began to fast. They had taken up a strong position near the Maumee about three miles above the British fort, in a tangled swath of fallen trees occasioned by a tornado some years before. They numbered about 1,300 or 1,400; the expected reinforcements from the Chippewa and the Iroquois had not put in their appearance.[41] Wayne's halt to form Camp Deposit was an unanticipated delay, and on August 20 his orders to resume the march at 5 A.M. were also delayed by at least two hours by a sudden rainstorm. William Wells, who knew the habits of the Indians, advised Wayne to move forward as planned, because he was sure that many of the Indians would take advantage of the rain to go to the fort or to their camps for food. This was precisely what happened, and when Wayne's advance encountered the Indian army at Fallen Timbers about 10 A.M., only 900 Indians were on hand for the battle, which began at once and lasted approximately one hour.[42]

Major Price, at the head of 180 selected men from the Kentucky mounted militia, formed the vanguard of Wayne's army. The four sublegions comprised the main body, with General Wilkinson commanding the right wing and Colonel Hamtramck the left. Wayne had direct charge of the center and overall command, which he exercised by means of his aides-de-camp. The main body of the mounted militia under General Scott was in the rear. The probable order of the Indian army, beginning from the extreme left, near the Maumee, was the Miami, the Delaware, the Shawnee, the Ottawa, and the Wyandot, with Captain Caldwell's fifty rangers on the extreme right.[43]

Contact was made on the American right wing when Major Price's men were fired upon by the Miami and the Delaware, who rose from the tall grass, fired, and dropped to the ground to reload while a second and then a third line of Indians rose and fired. Price's men recoiled and fled back into the ranks of the advancing Legion, creating some confusion. At this point, had the Indians been at full strength, they might have been able to turn the situation to their advantage, but they were too few in number and had no reserve to concentrate on the weak point that their attack had developed.[44] General Wilkinson was able to rally those who had recoiled and continue the steady advance of the Legion. In this he was aided by the three years of intensive disciplining that the Legion had received under Wayne's rigorous training.[45]

Wayne's and Hamtramck's men also continued to advance. Since the Kentucky mounted militia under Scott, Todd, and Barber could not be employed in the fallen timber, where the Indians stood their ground, Wayne ordered them to ride to the rear of the Indians by a circuitous route.[46] He also ordered the Legion to attack with bayonets after discharging their weapons. Hamtramck, on the American left, encountered stubborn opposition from the Wyandot, supported by Caldwell's rangers on the Indian right, but was able to overcome it. Nine Wyandot chiefs and two Ottawa chiefs were killed, and Tarhe (The Crane), the leading Wyandot chief, was wounded before they gave way. Four of Caldwell's men were killed and a fifth was captured.[47] The Indian left, after its initial success, was forced to fall back by Lieutenant Percy Pope, who dropped several shells from his howitzer into the fallen timber just before the bayonet charge by the Legion took place.[48] Scott's encircling movement could not be completed in time to cut off the Indian retreat, which was made with great haste in the direction of the British Fort Miami of the Lakes.

Among the Americans, 89 men were wounded and their losses totaled 44 dead, including Captain Mis Campbell and Lieutenant Harry Towles. Although Wayne reported the Indian loss as more than double his own, British sources indicated that it was not greater than 50 dead. According to McKee, the Americans scalped and mutilated the Indian dead. He also believed that not more than 400 Indians had actually participated in the battle. The British complained that the Shawnee, who had been the most belligerent before the battle, did not actually take part in it.[49]

When the defeated Indians fled to the British fort they expected to find a refuge; instead they found the gates closed against them. This so enraged Buckongahelas, the Delaware war chief, that he openly expressed his contempt for the British, a contempt he retained for the rest of his life.[50] Wayne, although authorized to use his judgment about attacking the British fort, decided not to attack. He spent three days encamped near it, exchanging acrimonious messages with Colonel Campbell, its commander. But as he was well aware that an attack would jeopardize the negotiations of John Jay in London at this time, he judged it better to gain the fort by negotiation. After destroying McKee's store and all crops in the vicinity, he returned to Fort Defiance, where "with infinite pleasure" he penned his official report of "the brilliant success of the Federal Army," eight days after the battle.[51]

Wayne remained at Fort Defiance until September 14, strengthening the fort, sending some of the Kentucky militia to convoy cattle and flour from Greeneville, and laying waste to thousands of acres of Indian cornfields in the neighborhood of Au Glaize. The corn was useful to both the men and the horses of his army, but he was determined to leave none for use

136

by the Indians. He remarked that he had never seen such "immense fields of corn, in any part of America, Canada to Florida."[52]

On September 14 the army began its march up the Maumee, arriving at the former Miami villages, now deserted, on September 20. Here Wayne began construction of a fort on the right (south) bank of the St. Marys River, just above the junction of the three rivers. The army was put on half rations before the fort was completed, but various journals report that general good health prevailed, for there was a large amount of cleared land and good forage if the horses did not overeat of the tall grass. The fishing was also good.[53] On October 22 a ceremony was held, and after fifteen rounds had been fired from the cannon, Colonel Hamtramck, who was to command the fort with four infantry companies and an artillery company, named the new structure Fort Wayne.[54]

Wayne and his army marched back to Fort Defiance and thence to Greeneville, over the route by which the campaign had begun. They arrived at their starting point on November 4, the anniversary of St. Clair's Defeat. As they returned, small parties of Indians often approached bearing white flags, an indication that Indian resistance had crumbled and peace negotiations would now be possible.[55] Thus, the Battle of Fallen Timbers began to assume an importance far beyond the numbers engaged, the casualties, or the magnitude of the battle. Historically, it was one of the decisive battles of American military experience.

The importance of the battle became clear, however, only with the passage of time. General James Wilkinson continued to disparage Wayne. He referred to the battle as a mere skirmish that Wayne had thoroughly mismanaged from start to finish. Although Wayne had been aware of Wilkinson's plotting all along, he had ignored it as much as possible. But the time was approaching when he would be forced to take some notice of Wilkinson's scheming and disloyalty.[56] In this he was fortunate that the administration appreciated his efforts and permitted him to continue in charge of peace negotiations with all the confidence they had bestowed upon him in his conduct of the military campaign. Wayne justified their confidence by concluding the Treaty of Greeneville in 1795.

NOTES

1. KNOPF, 15–277, passim. The precise date of Wayne's arrival at Pittsburgh is not given, but Knox had learned of it by June 22, 1792. Wayne's last letter from Hobson's Choice is dated October 5, 1793, which gives the approximate time of his movement northward.

2. VOLNEY, 357. Volney says that Little Turtle explained this strategy to him in the course of one of his interviews in 1797.

3. WILSON, 42. Whites may at times have attributed such raids to Little Turtle, but it is inconsistent with what is known of his character to do so without positive evidence.

4. Ibid., 45–49. BUTTERFIELD, 272–74, says that Alexander McKee had planned to send Simon Girty with 247 Wyandot and Mingo on this expedition but that the Great Council of the allied tribes at Au Glaize recalled Girty and sent Little Turtle with 200 Miami and Shawnee instead. QUAIFE (2), 115, notes that 50 Shawnee joined the Miami for this expedition under Little Turtle. On December 29, 1792, Colonel R. G. England wrote from Au Glaize to Governor Simcoe, at Detroit, that Little Turtle had arrived on the Maumee with twenty-six horses and four cattle captured at Fort St. Clair and that both Fort Hamilton and Fort Jefferson had been reinforced since Adair's defeat. CRUIKSHANK, I, 271.

5. YOUNG (1), 65–67.

6. KNOPF, 278–80; WILSON, 54–55. Wayne understood the essentials of the Indian food supply problem and was confident that his situation was superior to theirs in this respect.

7. KNOPF, 297–98. Wayne recognized, as St. Clair did not, that Fort Recovery was on the headwaters of the Wabash.

8. CRUIKSHANK, II, 132–33, 139, 141, 174; KNOPF, 304, 308–9. There can be no doubt but that more than a month was required to bring in the prisoners. Little Turtle's influence was gaining among the Indians, aided in this case by Buckongahelas, but no peace movement could withstand the false promises of military aid made by McKee, which were bolstered by the official speech of Lord Dorchester in Quebec.

9. VAN EVERY, 300–301, states that Little Turtle "headed the deputation of chiefs from the Maumee" to whom Dorchester made his speech but gives no source for the statement. No such statement is made by writers who do give their sources in discussing the event.

10. ROBERTSON, 216–17.

11. Mrs. Simcoe's diary does not mention this circumstance, so there is no way to tell whether the sketch was made in 1794 as Pacan traveled to Quebec. It is, indeed, the most probable time. If Pacan made the trip to Quebec it is unlikely that Little Turtle accompanied him; as the Miami war chief he would have remained at Au Glaize. If he had made the trip Mrs. Simcoe would probably have sketched him as well as Pacan, for Little Turtle was well known by this time as the conqueror of Harmar and St. Clair.

12. HORSMAN, 94–96.

13. GUTHMAN, 124–27. Wayne did not use patrols or picket guards. The men were trained to alert one another in the Indian fashion, an innovation that may have come about by the advice of Wells.

14. KNOPF, 377. Many journals kept during the campaign display a pro-Wilkinson bias; for example, that of Lieutenant William Clark.

15. HUTTON, 194, lists the names of nineteen scouts serving under Wells.

16. For an account of these other exploits of Wells's command, see McDONALD, 183–96. The Porcupine probably died within a year or so after this incident, for he did not sign the Treaty of Greeneville.

17. MICHIGAN, XX, 346–47, 356–57. A deserter from Wayne's army told Alexander McKee that "Wells and May, two spies, with 16 others . . . are paid $40 for every Indian scalp besides a dollar each per day and $1000 for the scalp of Simon Girty." Girty lived to a ripe old age, with his scalp intact, but there is no doubt that he was one of the most hated white men among the Indians. Although Alexander McKee at first gave credit to a rumor that Wells and May had been killed at Fort Recovery, he soon learned that they had been at Greeneville during that action.

18. KNOPF, 344.

19. HORSMAN, 96. The Wyandot were accompanied by Simon Girty.

20. None of the journals kept by American officers provides an account of the Fort Recovery attack by a participant. Reliance has been placed on the "Diary of an Officer in the Indian country," known only by the initials J.C., which is reproduced in CRUIKSHANK, V, 90–94. Wayne's official report of the action is found in KNOPF, 345–49.

21. HORSMAN, 97–99.

22. VAN EVERY, 321.

23. TURNER (Ayer 689), 56. See also SMITH (1), 277, where it is reported that it was learned from an Indian prisoner that, when the Lake Indians said they could take such a place as Fort Recovery, the Shawnee laughed and told them to go ahead and try it, which they did, with disastrous results.

24. MICHIGAN, XX, 366.

25. KNOPF, 346–47.

26. HORSMAN, 99.

27. Ibid.

28. CRUIKSHANK, II, 333–34. R. C. England to J. G. Simcoe, July 22, 1794.

29. KNOPF, 349–50.

30. SMITH (1), 249–61. The unknown author of this journal was extremely anti-Wayne and pro-Wilkinson. It is, nevertheless, as the editor remarks, "a veritable mine of information of the Wayne campaign." It is more informative than either Draper Mss. 5U or 16U in the Wisconsin State Historical Society Library, both of which have been consulted for the present work. The published versions of the Draper Mss. 5U and 16U are listed in the bibliography as CLARK and UNDERWOOD. The Clark journal also exhibits a rather strong pro-Wilkinson bias; the Underwood journal reflects a lesser Wilkinson influence. BOWYER displays less bias but is also less informative.

31. SMITH (1), 261.

32. Ibid., 262. A similar accident had occurred at Legionville, where a tree fell on Wayne's tent during a storm.

33. Ibid., 272–73.

34. Ibid., 273–74.

35. Ibid., 275–76; DRAPER, 5U; McDONALD, 192–95; CRUIKSHANK, II, 371, all take note of this adventure of Wells and his men. The information gleaned from the prisoner was accurate. The possibility of joining the Americans could only have been suggested by Little Turtle. There is some question as to whether Wells was shot in the left or right forearm. Hutton, citing several Draper Mss., says left; Wayne, KNOPF, 533, says right; McDONALD says "the arm on which he carried his

rifle." The wound did not prevent his continued scouting, though it earned him a pension.

36. SMITH (1), 277–78, 283. Wayne simply ignored the request for a truce by continuing his march and making no reply.

37. BRICE, 148–49; VAN EVERY, 323. The comparison of Wayne to a blacksnake was a clever appeal for support from the Delaware, who called Wayne by this name. The Miami called him *alomseng,* or Big Wind (i.e., tornado).

38. HORSMAN, 102. A hundred workmen were also sent to strengthen the fort. Caldwell's rangers numbered only fifty-three.

39. Many writers mistakenly persist in saying that Little Turtle commanded at Fallen Timbers. Little Turtle had no liking for the blustering Blue Jacket, and it was a clever move on his part to withdraw in favor of Alexander McKee's favorite, who had tried to claim credit for St. Clair's Defeat. Wayne referred to him as "the infamous Blue Jacket." See KNOPF, 296, 384.

40. HUTTON, 198.

41. HORSMAN, 103. Wayne's report to Knox that he had defeated over 2,000 Indians with about 900 of his 3,600 available troops, KNOPF, 352–53, simply exhibits the usual desire of victorious generals to magnify their achievements. The Chippewa refused to come and about 100 Iroquois showed up after the battle.

42. The fact that numerous historians have stated that the battle lasted two hours, and some have stated that it continued for three hours, necessitates a review of the primary sources on this matter. To the accounts by participants mentioned already may be added a "Memorandum of Occurrences in the expedition under Gen. Anthony Wayne, 1794" by Nath(anie)l Hart, of Woodford (Va.), in DRAPER, 5U. A comparison of six primary sources is set forth in tabular form as follows:

Source	March begun	Contact with enemy made	Duration of battle
Bowyer	"7 A.M."	"11 A.M."	(not stated)
Clark	"7 A.M."	"after about 2 hours"	"more than an hour"
Hart	"7 A.M."	(not stated)	"about one hour"
Underwood	"7 A.M."	"after 3 or 4 miles"	(not stated)
Unknown	"7 A.M."	"after 4 miles"	"10 o'clk to 11:05 o'clk"
Wayne	"8 A.M."	"after 4 or 5 miles"	"one hour"

The only reasonable conclusion from this comparison is that the order was given to be prepared to march at 7 A.M. but that the march did not get under way until 8 A.M.; that the march "much embarrassed by the thickness of the woods on the left and by the number of steep ravines on the right" (Clark) covered four miles in two hours, at which time the vanguard was fired on by the Indians; that this first contact was made at 10 A.M.. (unknown officer); and that pursuit of the Indians for two miles through "a thick woods" (Wayne) was halted at 11:05 A.M. (unknown officer), after which camp was made about one mile from the British fort (Clark). From this analysis it may further be concluded that all secondary accounts giving a longer time for the duration of the battle are in error. Captain Daniel Bradley, stationed at Fort Jefferson, stated that it lasted only forty minutes. See WILSON, 69. Such a shortened time is probably to be ascribed to boasting after the battle.

43. The Indian order of battle can only be deduced from the known position of Caldwell and the Wyandot on the right. Their line extended over a two-mile front, in three lines, so that they were spread pretty thin, which accounts for their hasty withdrawal. The total number of 900 is that of Antoine Lasselle, a trader among the Miami, who was captured and recognized by Colonel Hamtramck. Since he was captured while hiding near the Maumee, it seems reasonable to place Little Turtle and his 175 Miami on the extreme left, near the river. This means that they began the battle and also that the howitzer was directed at them, and that Captain Mis Campbell was killed at the head of his cavalry charge near the river, when the Miami were finally routed. For Lasselle's statement, which insisted that the Indians were averse to a battle but persuaded by McKee and Elliott, see SMITH (1), 296. See also ASPIA, I, 494.

44. This was the opinion of Captain William Clark, DRAPER, 5U, entry for August 20, 1794.

45. SMITH (1), 291–93. This journal gives such an extended account of General Wilkinson's exertions that it has been suspected, despite some contrary indications, that General Wilkinson wrote it himself. No amount of heroic behavior by St. Clair and many of his officers had sufficed. It was the discipline of the Legion that was the deciding factor, along with the lack of an Indian reserve. Instead of supporting the Indian left, Blue Jacket and his Shawnee tried a flank movement to the right, which failed utterly, as only the Wyandot stood their ground.

46. Captain Thomas Underwood, DRAPER, 16U, entry for August 20, 1794, says, "General Scott was ordered, to try and seround the indians, but they got aprized of it and retreated as fast as possible." Clark expressed the opinion that Wayne should have ordered Scott's movement much earlier or planned it in advance.

47. For the losses among the Wyandot and the Ottawa, and of the Canadian militia, see HORSMAN, 104.

48. The action of the howitzer may have discouraged the Shawnee from supporting the Indian left. The only narrative to mention this important action is that of Captain Underwood, DRAPER, 16U, entry for August 20, 1794.

49. HORSMAN, 104–5. While it is scarcely to be believed that the Shawnee failed to participate, it is certain that they played no conspicuous part in the battle.

50. DAWSON, 82. When Buckongahelas was threatened by Major Campbell with denial to pass Fort Miami of the Lakes with his followers in canoes in order to send a white flag to Fort Wayne later in 1794, he told Major Campbell that he no longer feared the British cannon since they had been afraid to fire upon General Wayne.

51. KNOPF, 351–55.

52. SMITH (1), 310–26. Wayne's remark about the Indian cornfields is reported in ASPIA, I, 490.

53. Captain Underwood's journal, DRAPER, 16U, entry for October 1, 1794. Bowyer reported but 500 acres of cleared land, but Underwood says there were 1,200 acres.

54. Ibid., entry for October 22, 1794.

55. KNOPF, 358–63.

56. Ibid., 377-79. Wayne eventually sent an officer to Philadelphia to express orally his report on the conduct of General Wilkinson. Wayne lacked the proof that his second-in-command was in the pay of Spain, so Wilkinson was able to pursue his career of self-promotion for many years, until the discovery of such proof finally ruined him.

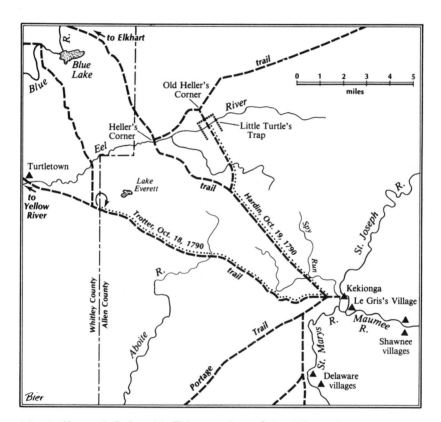

Map 3. *Harmar's Defeat (1)*. This map shows Colonel Trotter's reconnaissance toward Turtletown and Colonel Hardin's ambush and defeat by Little Turtle at Heller's Corner in 1790.

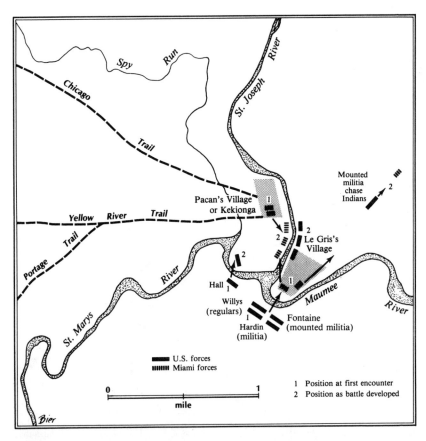

Map 4. *Harmar's Defeat (2)*. Shown here in some detail is the battle at the head-waters of the Maumee, which ended Harmar's campaign. Little Turtle directed the Indians from the right bank of the St. Joseph River below Kekionga.

Figure 8. *Josiah Harmar.* The original portrait was painted by Raphael Peale. Although Harmar destroyed the Indian villages at the head of the Maumee River, his two defeats by Little Turtle forced him to retire to Cincinnati. Reproduced by permission of the Indiana Historical Society. M211, negative no. A103.

Figure 9. *Arthur St. Clair.* The original portrait is by Charles Wilson Peale. Governor St. Clair's defeat by Little Turtle in 1791 was one of the greatest disasters in American military history. Reproduced by permission of the Indiana Historical Society. M211.

Figure 10. *The Treaty of Greene Ville.* The original of this notable work by Howard Chandler Christy hangs in the State Capitol Building in Columbus, Ohio. Overall, including the frame, it measures seventeen by twenty-two and three-fourths feet. It was installed in the capitol in 1945. Reproduced by permission of the Ohio Historical Society. SC 404(a).

LINE DRAWING OF THE PRINCIPAL FIGURES IN THE PAINTING

1. Anthony Wayne	6. Meriwether Lewis	11. Buckongehelas	16. David Jones
2. Little Turtle	7. Isaac Zane	12. Leatherlips	17. Henry De Butts
3. William Wells	8. Tarhe, The Crane	13. Bad Bird	18. John Mills
4. William Henry Harrison	9. Blue Jacket	14. White Pigeon	19. The Treaty of Greene Ville
5. William Clark	10. Black Hoof	15. The Sun	20. Greene Ville Treaty Calumet

Figure 11. *Key to the Christy Painting (Figure 10).* The principal characters can be identified readily by means of this key. The work is one of historical authenticity. Reproduced by permission of the Ohio Historical Society. SC 404(b).

Figure 12. *Anthony Wayne*. This portrait is attributed to Henry Elois. Wayne displayed equal skill as a general and as a negotiator, but, unfortunately for Little Turtle and William Wells, he did not long survive his success in waging war and making peace. Reproduced by permission of the Historical Society of Pennsylvania.

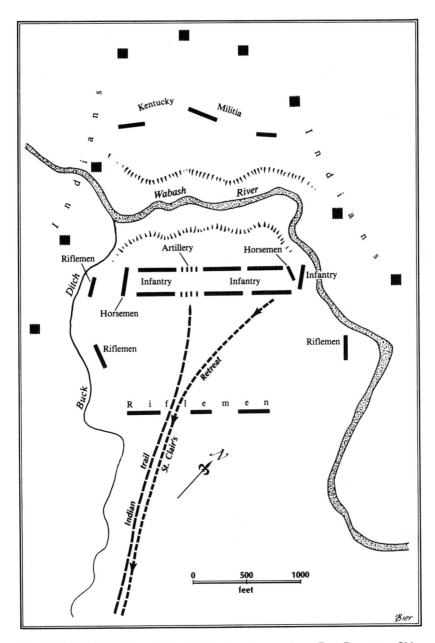

Map 5. *St. Clair's Defeat, 1791.* The battle site was where Fort Recovery, Ohio, stands. An impressive monument, commemorating both St. Clair's Defeat and Wayne's later victory, was erected there pursuant to an act of Congress in 1912.

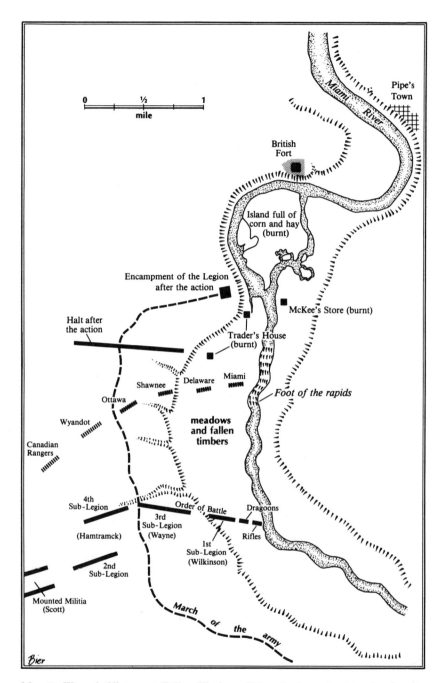

Map 6. *Wayne's Victory at Fallen Timbers.* Although the action lasted only one hour, Fallen Timbers was one of the decisive battles of American history. Little Turtle had counseled peace and resigned his command of the Indians before the battle, in which he nevertheless participated.

PART THREE

THE STATESMAN

13

The Treaty of Greeneville, 1795

Wᴏʜᴇɴ Wᴀʏɴᴇ ʀᴇᴛᴜʀɴᴇᴅ ᴛᴏ Gʀᴇᴇɴᴇᴠɪʟʟᴇ and the Legion went into winter quarters there in early November 1794, it was by no means certain that all the Indians were prepared to negotiate a peace, although there were strong indications that some of them were eager to do so, even before Wayne had arrived. The first overture in this direction was made by Shamakunesa (The Soldier) and Charley (Katunga), who had succeeded, upon the death of old Kaweahatta (The Porcupine), to the leadership of the Eel River Miami. They had established contact with Wayne, under protection of a flag of truce, within a month after the Battle of Fallen Timbers.[1] Following this, on September 26, the Wyandot chief Tarhe (The Crane) caused a letter, asking for peace, to be written for delivery to Wayne. This letter Wayne answered and subsequently received further pacific overtures from the Wyandot in December.[2] Then, the Ottawa, the Chippewa, and the Potawatomi were heard from, and messengers were sent to them in return.

In the winter of 1795, Pacan, Little Turtle, Blue Jacket, and Buckongahelas are reported to have journeyed to Detroit to complain to Simcoe about the scarcity of food supplied by the British.[3] Little Turtle may have arranged this in order that the other chiefs might be convinced that the British were no longer making strong war talk to the Indians. This was indeed the case, since Jay's Treaty had been signed in London on November 19, 1794, as Simcoe was, by this time, well aware. With Fort Wayne and Fort Defiance to contend with, McKee could no longer send food supplies by the usual route.

The result of this final conference with the British officials was that Buckongahelas and the Delaware decided in favor of peace and so informed

Wayne. Blue Jacket was more obstinate and began to talk of moving the Shawnee to Chicago, with the ultimate design of moving beyond the Mississippi. Pacan, the Miami head chief, now had Colonel Hamtramck, whom he had once sought to cultivate at Vincennes, at Fort Wayne. His former bad treatment at the hands of the Americans still offended him. As head chief he had to do what was best for his people, but to preserve his dignity he suggested that the peace conference be held at Kekionga. This invitation Wayne declined, for it would have been difficult to convey food supplies for a large conference to Fort Wayne. Furthermore, he had his own dignity to preserve. Pacan was forced to yield. He decided not to go to Greeneville himself but to be represented by Richardville (Peejeewah, The Wild Cat, or The Lynx), his nephew, heir-apparent, and deputy head chief.

The Miami favored meeting at Kekionga, believing that it was appropriate to bury the tomahawk where it had first been raised. The symbolism did not appeal to Wayne, who feared that it might be buried where it could too easily be dug up again. One reason for thinking that the Miami were not to be trusted was that Le Gris was extremely slow in showing any disposition to attend a peace conference. Wayne planned to use as interpreters William Wells for the Miami and Christopher Miller, one of Wells's famous scouts, for the Shawnee. Still another interpreter was Jacques Lasselle, a brother of Antoine Lasselle, the trader captured at Fallen Timbers. All three of these men were employed, together with Antoine Lasselle, in visiting tribes to invite them to make peace at Greeneville in the summer of 1795. Colonel Hamtramck credited Jacques Lasselle with persuading Le Gris to promise to attend the peace conference.[4]

At one point during the proceedings at Greeneville, The Sun, a Potawatomi chief, said, "You have been told the Potawatomi are always foremost in mischief. I now tell you that was not a true representation. The Potawatomi sit at the center; nothing takes its beginning from thence. It is the three people who lived at the Miami villages, who assumed to themselves the privilege of going before; but this can not be unknown to you."[5] His speech was one of the few instances of dissension to surface among the tribes at the meeting. While it might be interpreted as a reference to Pacan, Le Gris, and Little Turtle, it is more probable that it refers to the Miami, the Shawnee, and the Delaware tribes and their leadership in forming the Indian alliance. Recall that in 1790 the Shawnee and the Delaware each established two villages near the two Miami villages that were already at the three rivers.

The fact that The Soldier was the first to "take Wayne by the hand" is another interesting point. The Eel River Miami were identical with the Kilatika Miami of earlier times, but the name had vanished from use when the British took over from the French in 1763. They were actually one of the six original Miami bands, of whom the Wea and the Piankashaw had by this time achieved a separate tribal status. They were also the band that had captured and adopted William Wells.

One result of the Family Compact between Little Turtle and Wells was that they secured recognition for the Eel River Miami as a separate tribe entitled to a separate governmental annuity of $500, the amount allowed also to the Wea and the Piankashaw. The Miami proper received $1,000, which was the same as that allowed to the Shawnee, the Delaware, the Wyandot, the Ottawa, the Chippewa, and the Potawatomi tribes, each of which was more populous than the Miami, even including the Kilatika, the Wea, and the Piankashaw. Thus the Miami-speaking Indians drew $2,500 in annuities, while each of the other tribes in the Indian Confederacy drew $1,000.

Wells cooperated with his father-in-law because he wished to do something for the old friends among whom he had been so kindly treated at Kenapakomoko. Little Turtle's object was to see that the Miami retained the leadership in peace that he had earned for them in war. Although this did not work out as he had planned, it was nevertheless a master stroke of diplomacy that was not even suspected until long after the event. The fact that The Soldier was the first to indicate a desire for peace leads to the conclusion that his action was probably prompted by Little Turtle in order to gain favor for the acceptance of the Eel River Miami as a separate tribe.[6]

The conference was slow in getting started. The Indians began to arrive during the first week in June, which was the end of corn-planting time. A number of Ottawa, Chippewa, and Potawatomi came before June 15, as did some of the Delaware. The main body of Potawatomi arrived on June 17, and Buckongahelas, with the main body of Delaware, came on June 21.[7] The interpreters certified that 1,130 Indians were in attendance at the treaty deliberations. By tribes they were distributed as follows: Wyandot, 180; Delaware, 381; Shawnee, 143; Ottawa, 45; Chippewa, 46; Potawatomi, 240; Miami and Eel River, 73; Wea and Piankashaw, 12; and Kickapoo, 10.[8] The Delaware and the Potawatomi delegations obviously contained large numbers of freeloaders, who came primarily for the refreshments. The Chippewa were by far the most populous tribe, but they lived a great distance away. The small number of Wea, Piankashaw, and Kickapoo attests to the demoralized condition of these tribes that had occurred by reason of their proximity to the Kentucky settlements and Fort Vincennes, as well as their willingness to let the Miami speak for them.

Le Gris and Little Turtle, with seventeen Miami, arrived on June 23, and several days were spent getting acquainted and celebrating the American Independence Day while others arrived or were awaited. The Wyandot and the Shawnee had not arrived; finally, on July 9, Wayne, who was eager to get down to business, asked whether he should begin discussions without them. Little Turtle suggested waiting, and July 13 was set as the date for officially convening the meeting. The Wyandot arrived before that date, but the Shawnee did not appear until after the conference had begun.

Wayne's question indicated the importance he assigned to Little Turtle's presence. By long-established protocol among the Indians, the Wyandot were accorded the right to speak first at any deliberation. This custom was carefully preserved by Little Turtle in his suggestion that business be deferred until mid-July. In spite of the added cost of food and drink the delay entailed, Wayne made no objection. However, neither Little Turtle nor Wayne was disposed to wait for Blue Jacket and his Shawnee, who did not make their appearance until July 18.[9] Thus, while showing consideration for the primacy of the Wyandot, which was approved by the other tribes, in the eyes of Wayne and of the Indians themselves Little Turtle established himself, rather than his chief rival, Blue Jacket, as the dominant leader of the conference.

Anthony Wayne had no such problem to solve, for he had the sole and undisputed right to conduct negotiations on behalf of the American government. His military rival and constant critic, General Wilkinson, was not even present, having been deliberately kept away by Wayne by virtue of the fact that all military duties devolved on Wilkinson while the commander-in-chief was busy with diplomatic affairs.

William Wells, with the aid of seven others, was chief interpreter. He interpreted for the Miami, including the Eel River, the Wea, and the Piankashaw, and also for the Kickapoo and the Kaskaskia. Isaac Zane and Abraham Williams, though both were illiterate in English, translated for the Wyandot. Jacques Lasselle and Christopher Miller interpreted for the Shawnee, Robert Wilson for the Delaware, and Baptiste Sans Crainte and M. Morin for the Ottawa, the Chippewa, and the Potawatomi. Also in attendance at the conference were Francis Vigo, Francis La Fontaine, Antoine Lasselle, Henry Lasselle, and Charles Beaubien, traders who knew the Indian languages. Wayne's military aides, Henry De Butts, William Henry Harrison, and Thomas Lewis, were, for a change, engaged primarily with taking notes rather than carrying messages. Wayne was also assisted by four military officers from the Legion, chief among whom was Quartermaster General James O'Hara. The others were Paymaster Caleb Swan, Major John Mills, and Captain George Demlar. An army chaplain, David Jones, also participated.[10]

General Wayne, up to the time of the Treaty of Greeneville, was well known as a good army officer but not for success in civilian life. His campaign against the Indians enhanced his military reputation, setting to rest any doubts that may have been felt about the soundness and prudence of his actions. The Treaty of Greeneville, however, proved him to be far more able in argument and in diplomacy than had been anticipated. Although he had some guidance from Timothy Pickering, who had succeeded Henry Knox as secretary of war, Wayne had thoroughly prepared himself for the conference. He applied without error his knowledge of Indian psychology and firmly kept the entire proceedings under his own control. His attention to punctilious behavior, which earned the doubts of some of his colleagues, was exactly the proper course for earning the highest regard from the Indians. He had the enormous advantage of having been their conqueror, but he did not abuse this position in any way. He was the perfect host and master of ceremonies, while at the same time he insisted upon obtaining every concession from the Indians that his government demanded. In the end, he left them feeling that they had been treated with both courtesy and fairness. They could pledge with sincerity to observe the peace, without feeling that it had been imposed upon them in any way. Wayne put on a great performance, even while he was suffering severely from the gout, which took his life less than a year and a half later.[11]

Wayne's performance was nonetheless rivaled by that of Little Turtle, who by reason of his superior intelligence towered above all the chiefs assembled at Greeneville. He emerged in his recorded speeches as the only Indian chief capable of standing up to Wayne and debating with him on equal terms. Other chiefs spoke, but none spoke to the points at issue as they were raised by Wayne. Indeed, Wayne found himself at times speaking in reply to Little Turtle and defending himself from the brilliant and direct onslaughts of his opponent. Nor was Turtle less mindful of courtesy than Wayne; he was as John Johnston, the government factor at Fort Wayne, aptly called him, "the gentleman of his race."[12]

There could have been no greater contrast between Lincoln and Douglas on the hustings in Illinois or Gladstone and Disraeli in the House of Commons than was presented by Anthony Wayne and Mishikinakwa, the Miami chief. Wayne wore the dress uniform of an American general; with gold epaulets on the shoulders of his blue coat, cut away to reveal his white trousers, he was a model of sartorial elegance from the cockade of his tricorne to the toes of his highly polished black boots. Little Turtle, who wore white men's apparel in later years, now, in the hot weather of the Lightning Moon, wore no clothing but his breech cloth and moccasins; he also had on a bear-claw necklace, metal armlets on his upper arms, large metal ear hoops, a large medallion suspended by a second neck chain, and a headpiece of thirteen eagle feathers fastened in his hair by means of three snake rattles. In his own way he was as impressive as General Wayne, and certainly his knowledge and his manner of speech were no less authoritative.[13]

Wayne had the forethought to provide himself with a copy of Jay's recently signed treaty with Great Britain, a portion of which he read in order to prove to the Indians that England had agreed to evacuate Fort Miami of the Lakes, Fort Niagara, Fort Michilimackinac, and Fort Detroit.[14] This only served to enhance Little Turtle's position among the Indians, for he had advocated peace with the United States for some time on the ground that no faith could be placed in British promises.

The progress of the debate between Wayne and Turtle is of sufficient importance to warrant an examination of it as it unfolded day by day. When the Wyandot arrived on July 12, their request that the opening of the conference be deferred from July 13 to July 15 was granted.[15] Wayne, thoroughly familiar with previous treaties, had decided to demand that those treaties, and especially the Treaty of Fort Harmar (Muskingum), be the basis for a settlement. Beyond this the United States would ask only for military reservations at strategic spots. Upon opening the conference he stressed that his government was willing to accept the line already established by the Treaty of Muskingum. On July 18 Little Turtle pointed out that he and the Miami had no knowledge of this treaty, not having been party to it. He asked Wayne to explain it and to comment as to whether or not the parties to it had been satisfied.[16]

The arrival of Blue Jacket that evening necessitated a private meeting between him and Wayne on July 19. The next day Wayne made a full disclosure of the Muskingum Treaty. The Chippewa and the Potawatomi claimed they had never received any payments under that treaty and accused the Wyandot of having sold land that belonged to them.[17] Wayne spoke in a conciliatory manner, and the offended tribes, after a night of eating and drinking well, became more cooperative. On July 21, however, Little Turtle said that although he was satisfied with Wayne's explanation of the Muskingum Treaty, he had been told by the Delaware that the British had given all the Indian land to the Americans in 1783. He felt this contradicted Wayne, who had just explained how the Americans had purchased it from the Indian tribes.[18] On July 22 Turtle lost no time in following up this bombshell with another. He outlined the broad boundaries of the Miami lands and asked for comment from both Wayne and the other tribes. He concluded by saying, "I came with an expectation of hearing you say good things, but I have not yet heard what I have expected."[19]

At this point, Tarhe (The Crane) made a speech about taking the tomahawk out of the head of the United States, where the British had told them to place it, but he also injected the idea that the land belonged in common to all Indians rather than to particular tribes. This was an old

150

concept that Brant and the British had fostered. It was acceptable neither to Wayne, who was instructed by his government to oppose it, nor to Little Turtle and the Miami. Wayne adjourned the meeting, promising to speak the next day after pondering the questions that had been raised. [20]

Blue Jacket made a move on July 23 to supplant Little Turtle as the dominant Indian speaker by seating himself and the Shawnee between his "uncles," the Wyandot, and his "grandfathers," the Delaware. Furthermore, he asked Wayne to address himself to the Wyandot, as keepers of the Sacred Fire, and to allow them to pass his information to the other tribes. To this last request Wayne paid no attention, except to pass the belts first to the Wyandot.[21] On the following day Wayne made a long speech in which he quoted the Jay Treaty provisions that bound the British to retire from American soil. He did not reveal, of course, that the treaty had not been ratified by the Senate and might yet fail. He removed the tomahawk from the head of the Indians as tenderly as Tarhe had removed it from the head of the Americans. But he also demanded sixteen military reservations within Indian country, on the ground that the Indians had previously sold land to the French and the British for similar use. Wayne had now put all his cards on the table. Tarhe at once urged that peace be made on this basis without delay. Little Turtle opposed it immediately, saying that these were matters which required careful consideration.[22]

On July 28 the roles were reversed. Tarhe spoke first and reported that the Wyandot, the Shawnee, and the Delaware were not yet prepared to answer. He requested more time for deliberation. Little Turtle arose and professed great surprise that the three tribes were not ready to make peace. The Miami, he asserted, had deliberated and were ready. Wayne had said that he had thrown the tomahawk into the ocean and at this the Miami were pleased, for in the past it had been buried in shallow water where it washed upon land and had been taken up again by foolish young men. Little Turtle lit the calumet and presented it to the Shawnee, who he said had not yet smoked it. The Chippewa and the Potawatomi also supported his desire for peace. Little Turtle had outmaneuvered Tarhe and Blue Jacket completely.[23]

On the following day the Wyandot, the Delaware, and the Shawnee gave Wayne a letter asking that he decide the boundaries of land in the Indian country and that he apportion the land among the tribes. Little Turtle, speaking for the Wea, the Kickapoo, and the Potawatomi, requested that the western line be altered so as to run from Fort Recovery to Cincinnati rather than from Fort Recovery to the mouth of the Kentucky River. The change would allow the Indians to retain the fine hunting lands of the Whitewater River valley in what became known as the Indiana "gore" following the formation of the state of Ohio. He also corrected Wayne on the matter of selling land for forts to the French and the British. This had never been done; the French and the British had only been permitted to use the land. On the specific point of Fort Pickawillany, Little Turtle said that it had been built by Mishikinakwa, meaning his father (not himself, as the official interpreter misunderstood him to mean). Little Turtle wished to reduce the military reservation at Fort Wayne, and on this point he succeeded, so that Kekionga was not included; but on other points no concession was made.[24] Wayne ably replied, pointing out the necessity of controlling the portage at Fort Wayne and the awkwardness of a line ending at Cincinnati. He assured the Indians that traders acceptable to them would be available at the various military reservations. His reply, made on July 30, noted that the Indians knew their own boundaries and that he could not undertake to settle such matters for them. He then put the question of a peace treaty to a vote, and all the tribes voted in the affirmative.[25]

The days from July 31 to August 3 were spent in harmonious peace talk and ceremony. Complimentary remarks were made by many chiefs, and medals and silver ornaments were distributed to them. The signing took place on August 3, but since the Indians were in no hurry to depart, the final adjournment was made on August 10. Wayne spoke to the Indians concerning complaints he had received from French traders about horse stealing. As a result, in order to show that he meant to observe the treaty, Buckongahelas brought in two of three stolen horses and promised to recover the third.[26]

On August 12 Wayne held a private meeting with the Miami and the Eel River warriors, who were about to depart. Little Turtle made a graceful speech in which he apologized for the direct manner in which he had debated with Wayne but said that it had been his duty to represent his people as well as he could. He expressed a hope that Fort Ouiatenon might be rebuilt. He also said that he would live near Fort Wayne and would be available at any time to the commandant of the fort. Finally, he asked that William Wells be made resident interpreter at Fort Wayne, as he possessed the confidence of the Miami as well as the confidence of the general, "their Father."[27]

Although Little Turtle dominated the other Indian chiefs at Greeneville by his superior grasp of the realities of the situation, by his statecraft, and by his ability as a speaker, his arguments were advanced in behalf of a lost cause and had little effect upon the outcome, the actuality of which was dictated by Wayne. The cause was lost not at Greeneville, nor even at Fallen Timbers, but when the Indians failed to take advantage of Turtle's defeat of St. Clair and frittered away their time listening to Brant and the British instead of putting their confidence in Little Turtle and treating with the American commissioners as Wells had treated with General Putnam.

The Treaty of Greeneville consisted of ten articles, which may be summarized briefly. Article one provided for a cessation of hostilities. Article two called for mutual restoration of prisoners. Article three set the boundary of the Indian country so that the Indians retained the northwestern portion of what is now the state of Ohio. It enumerated the sixteen cessions of land within the Indian country where forts and trading posts might be established and also gave Americans the right of travel between these forts and trading posts.

Article four of the treaty relinquished the American claim to other land between the Ohio and the Mississippi with three exceptions of lands already granted. It provided for annuities of $1,000 to the stronger tribes and $500 to the lesser tribes. Article five stated that the Indians were under the protection of the United States and might sell their lands only to the American government. Article six bound the government to protect Indian lands from white squatters. Article seven allowed the Indians peaceful hunting privileges within lands they had ceded. Article eight bound the government to provide licensed traders among the Indians. Article nine stated that violators of the treaty would be punished by both the government and the Indians upon complaint of the injured parties. And by article ten the Treaty of Greeneville supplanted those treaties made between 1783 and 1795.[28]

The Treaty of Greeneville was a fair one under the circumstances. Little Turtle is said to have remarked at the signing that he was the last to sign it and would be the last to break it. The Miami was the last of the important tribes to sign, and Little Turtle was the last of the major chiefs, but he was actually the seventy-seventh of ninety signatories. The treaty, despite the ineffectiveness of certain provisions, prevented war until 1811. It was weakened in its original intent by the aggressive efforts of the United States government to purchase Indian lands and remove the tribes beyond the Mississippi River, efforts begun and relentlessly pursued by the Jefferson administration.[29]

NOTES

1. Aspia, I, 567.

2. Ibid., 526–28.

3. Anson, 133.

4. Slocum, 222–24. Several of Colonel Hamtramck's letters from Fort Wayne in 1794–95 are reproduced in this work. They shed some light on affairs among the Miami at this time. Richardville was definitely for peace. Hamtramck called Le Gris "a sensible old fellow" despite his seeming lack of interest in making peace.

5. Aspia, I, 574.

6. TROWBRIDGE, 4. Trowbridge wrote to Governor Lewis Cass, March 6, 1825, "The idea which you have been pleased to suggest with respects to the division of the Miamies and Eel Rivers, by the late Capt. Wells, corresponds with an account I have heard, but the Wuyautonakee or Weas, were not made a separate tribe for the same purposes: their separation was long, long before and was the effect of chance."

7. ASPIA, I, 564.

8. Ibid., 582.

9. Ibid., 566.

10. KAPPLER, II, 32–34, gives the signatories in full. All of those enumerated here signed the treaty.

11. KNOPF, passim, presents much the best concept of Wayne during his western campaign by means of his official correspondence. His biographers do not do justice to his western campaign.

12. KNAPP, 361.

13. This description is made from a woodcut of Little Turtle appearing as the frontispiece in YOUNG (1), and reproduced here as Figure 3. The author identifies it only as "a cut from a very old book which had been reproduced from a painting made for him while in Philadelphia. This painting was destroyed when the Capitol building was burned by the British in the War of 1812." It differs greatly from the lithograph in the Smithsonian Institution, which is also reputed to have been based on the painting by Gilbert Stuart made in Philadelphia in 1797. See also the Howard Chandler Christy painting which hangs in the State Capitol Building, Columbus, Ohio, reproduced herein as Figure 10.

14. KNOPF, 418.

15. ASPIA, I, 567.

16. Ibid.

17. Ibid., 568–69.

18. Ibid., 570.

19. Ibid., 570–71.

20. Ibid. Tarhe (The Crane) was perhaps urged by the Shawnee and the Delaware to broach the subject of common ownership, but it was a tactical error since both the Miami and the federal government were opposed to this concept.

21. Ibid., 571–73. Blue Jacket's maneuvers were clearly intended to reduce the influence of the Miami, but because both the Americans and the Miami were against the idea of common ownership of Indian land, these maneuvers did not succeed.

22. Ibid., 573–74.

23. Ibid., 575–76.

24. Ibid., 576–78. The reservation at Fort Wayne was made to include more land on the St. Marys River to compensate for allowing the Miami to retain the site of Kekionga. Wells chose to locate the land granted to him to include Kekionga and along Spy Run, which was named for him.

25. Ibid., 577–78. A less astute man than Wayne might have made the error of accepting the invitation of Tarhe to apportion the Indian lands among the tribes, which would have satisfied no one and would have given the tribes added cause for complaint in the future.

154

26. Ibid., 579–82.

27. Ibid., 583. A report of this meeting was made by Henry De Butts, Wayne's aide-de-camp, as a supplement to the Treaty of Greeneville. Little Turtle's remarks confirm his determination to devote himself to cultivating good relations with the Americans.

28. Ibid., 562–63. The signatures are not printed in this reference. The text of the treaty, complete with signatures, is found in KAPPLER, II, 30–34.

29. SHEEHAN (1) makes a full exploration of this subject, which will be discussed in the later chapters of this work insofar as the Miami tribe is concerned.

14

The Family Compact: Second Phase, 1795–1802

FOLLOWING THE COMPLETION of the Treaty of Greeneville, Little Turtle and William Wells returned to Fort Wayne. Turtle reestablished his village at Turtletown, about fourteen miles west by northwest of the recently erected fort. Wells, in his capacity of interpreter, took up residence west of the St. Joseph River, half a mile above the junction, on Indian land through which flowed a small stream, henceforth to be known as Spy Run, a name derived from Wells's service as a captain of spies for General Anthony Wayne.[1] Spy Run entered the St. Marys about as far south of the headwaters of the Maumee as Kekionga had been located north of it on the St. Joseph. The land occupied by Wells included the site of Kekionga and was adjacent to the military reservation. The reservation did not include the former Le Gris's Village, nor did it extend beyond the St. Joseph. It did extend beyond the St. Marys, upriver from the mouth of Spy Run.

In 1808 Wells was given, by act of Congress, the right to preempt a half section of land near Fort Wayne, but at the time of his death in 1812 he had not yet exercised the right. After his death his children acted to preempt the land on which he had lived since 1795. During his lifetime apparently no one had challenged his right to the land, and it may be argued that Wells preferred to occupy it as an adopted Miami and hold it by his right as an Indian rather than to exercise his legal right to buy it from the United States.[2] Upon his return to the area he was reunited with Sweet Breeze, Little Turtle's daughter, and their two daughters. Two more children were born to them, a boy in 1797 or 1798 and a girl in 1800. There can be no doubt that he and Turtle frequently conferred with each other and discussed their plans for the future.

General Wayne left Greeneville on December 15, 1795, and returned there on July 16, 1796, after having spent several months at his home west of Philadelphia. He went once more to Fort Miami of the Lakes, and on August 7, 1796, he received the surrender of that British fort. Wells and Little Turtle may have traveled there with Colonel Hamtramck for the ceremony, which would certainly have given them pleasure. Wayne then proceeded to Detroit, which was also transferred to American possession.[3]

Certainly Wells and Turtle were in Detroit by October 3, 1796, when Wayne wrote to James McHenry, Pickering's successor as secretary of war, that they were there and were preparing to travel to Philadelphia to meet President Washington. Blue Jacket was present for the same purpose, but he and Turtle would have nothing to do with each other. The Wyandot chiefs were traveling separately by land and the Delaware were not mentioned, although the "Lake tribes" and the "Wabash Indians" were represented. Wells and Christopher Miller were to act as interpreters.[4] No details of their journey have been found, but it is known that they reached Philadelphia in late November.

Wayne recommended Wells for a pension, on account of the wound he incurred just before the battle of Fallen Timbers, and it was granted in the amount of twenty dollars per month. At this time Wayne was keeping an eye on a French traveler, Constantin Volney, who had come to Detroit by way of Vincennes and the Wabash route. His suspicion that Volney might have a scheme to unite Canada with Louisiana was unfounded. Volney returned to Philadelphia, where he met Wells and Little Turtle. Wayne never reached Pittsburgh, where he had decided to establish his headquarters. Instead, he arrived at Fort Presq'ile (Erie, Pennsylvania) in mid-November, had a renewed attack of the gout that had troubled him for years, and died there on December 15, 1796.[5]

Of Little Turtle, Wayne wrote, "He possesses the spirit of litigation to a high degree, possibly he may have been tampered with by some of the speculating land jobbers. . . ."[6] Little Turtle may have made remarks to Wayne which indicated that he had a better understanding of the value of land and of the white man's concept of landownership than most of the chiefs of his time. It is probable that Wells and Turtle had already formulated, at this early date, the plan to gradually sell off Miami land in order to finance a "civilization program" for their tribe, while at the same time retaining enough of this great asset until such time as their fellow tribesmen were thoroughly prepared to make a living by agriculture. The term litigation, as used by Wayne, cannot be taken literally, for Turtle had no suit at law against any one. It must be interpreted as meaning that Wayne found Turtle to be argumentative about the Miami land claim and disposed to assert what he believed to be his rights and those of his tribe.

As subsequent developments would soon demonstrate, Wayne was correct in this judgment.

Wayne's death was unfortunate for William Wells and Little Turtle. They missed him in the years to come, when they tried to maintain the Treaty of Greeneville and found no one among the whites who was much concerned about it. Wayne also had been fully aware of the abilities of Wells and had seen to it that he was well paid for his services. During his two years as a spy and interpreter for Wayne, Wells had earned, taking his subsistence allowance into account, about $1,000 a year.[7] Little Turtle and Wells had planned that the latter would have charge of the relations of the federal government with the Miami, and Wayne might have been instrumental in bringing this about. As it turned out, their plan for civilizing the Miami was thwarted by the fact that Wells was never able to gain the complete control necessary for such a program.

Neither Wells nor Little Turtle was entirely altruistic in their design. Wells certainly hoped to gain a good living in this way, and Turtle no doubt wished to do so as well. There is reason to believe, however, that both men had the good of the tribe at heart and felt that they were the only tribal members with enough foresight and ability to accomplish a change.[8] In this they were undoubtedly right, and they were also correct in their belief that only a member of the tribe could possibly succeed in changing the traditional way of life of the Miami. No outside force could accomplish it, nor could Wells or Turtle alone attempt it with much hope of success. But together they had a chance.

On November 29, 1796, the visiting chiefs were given an audience by President Washington. It is possible that Little Turtle was given a separate interview, for he was presented by Washington with a ceremonial sword, which he valued and which was buried with him.[9] A rather curious memorandum, dated Philadelphia, December 9, 1796, and signed by W. Wells, reads, "I promise for what I have received and for what I may receive to promote to the extent of my power the interest of the United States with the northwestern Indians."[10] Some years later Wells stated that he had received an appointment as a temporary resident agent of the United States at Fort Wayne but that, although he had functioned as such, he had never been paid. He sought to collect arrears of $300 per year for his services, but his claim was disallowed by the War Department. It is probable proof of Wells's truthfulness that the memorandum quoted bears on its reverse side the notation, "300 doll's." It is reasonable to conclude from this evidence that the president or the secretary of war had been asked by Little Turtle to make this appointment and that it had been granted on the condition signed by Wells.

Dr. James McHenry, secretary of war until 1800, was also impressed by Little Turtle, as the following letter bears witness.[11]

To Mr. Little Turtle

War Department

30 May 1800

Friend and Brother:

Being about to retire from the Department of War and return to my house and fields near Baltimore in Maryland, I could not think of leaving the office without conveying to you my earnest request, that you will continue to the U.S. your friendly and honorable attachment. I shall sincerely and earnestly recommend to my successor to cultivate the good will of all our brethren and in particular your friendship.

It would have given me pleasure had it been proper to have taken home with me your picture, which I have preserved in my office. This however cannot be permitted, it must remain with my successor but I shall carry with me the remembrance of your fidelity, your good sense, your honest regard for your own people, your sensibility and eloquent discourse in their favour, and what is precious to me as an individual a belief that I shall always retain your friendship.

I give you my hand and pray the great spirit to protect and make you happy.

Farewell brother.

If anyone is disposed to regard McHenry's letter as simply official blandishment for the sake of public policy, it would be well to supplement it with another letter that Dr. McHenry wrote to William Wells when he learned that Little Turtle had come east once more.[12]

Baltimore, 26 Dec. 1801

Dear Sir:

Be pleased to inform my friend the Little Turtle of the pleasure it gives me to learn that he is in Baltimore and that I may again take him affectionately by the hand. I propose, if convenient to him and his brother chiefs, to wait upon them at their lodgings tomorrow morning at 10 o'clock and shall expect them and you to dine with me at my house at 4 o'clock.

I am Dear Sir very truly

your ob sv

James McHenry

Mr. Wm Wells

It is clear that McHenry, retired and with his party out of power, had nothing in mind but a renewal of friendship and a pleasant evening spent in the company of one whom he admired. Although it seems to be indicated by the memorandum already quoted, it is difficult to reconcile McHenry's friendly attitude with Wells's subsequent claim that his appointment as temporary resident agent had been made and his duties fulfilled but that his salary remained unpaid. Nor do we know how the memorandum itself escaped from the office of the War Department. McHenry served through most of the Adams administration, so there should have existed a continuity of policy. The matter seems to defy reasonable explanation.

This concern of Wells may have prompted the second visit by Wells and Turtle to Philadelphia a year later, at approximately the same time of the year as their first visit, but if so Wells received no satisfaction. The change in the presidency was sufficient to make a second visit desirable, for they had not made the acquaintance of John Adams on their first visit. In 1796 they had shared the limelight with many other chiefs; on the second visit, Little Turtle alone was lionized for three months in the capital city, not only by the inhabitants, but by other visiting celebrities. As this episode of Turtle's life forms the subject of the first chapter of the present work, our attention may now be given to the most vexing and ruinous of all Indian problems, that of alcoholism, or drunkenness as it was then called.

Between 1798 and 1800 Little Turtle became convinced that the Miami would never succeed in making the transition to a settled agricultural way of life such as he envisioned for them unless they could be prevented from obtaining whiskey. They had long been acquainted with alcoholic beverages. Under the French they drank wine and brandy; from the English they received port wine and rum. Under American authority they obtained increasing quantities of rye whiskey, which was made in large amounts in the Monongahela country of western Pennsylvania, and liquor distilled from Indian corn, which was being produced in Bourbon County and the adjacent bluegrass counties of Kentucky. The price of this frontier whiskey was about twenty-five cents a gallon, but Indians were charged double that price or more. Both Volney and Harrison, among others, have left vivid accounts of the effect of liquor on the behavior of Indians, which was not different from that on whites, except perhaps in degree.[13]

The effect of liquor on anyone drinking it is to remove the inhibitions imposed by the customs and taboos of his society and cause him to act in an unrestrained manner. Thus, he is almost certain to do things while in a drunken condition that he will regret as soon as he becomes sober. Religious, moral, and legal literature had for some centuries been creating disapproval of drunkenness among whites; however, this was nonexistent among Indians. A white man was prone to commit a crime when he got drunk; an Indian was almost certain to do so. There were many moderate drinkers among whites, but few among Indians. As a general rule, white women did not drink strong liquor; but Indian women did, although their opportunity for getting it was somewhat less than it was for men. When a considerable number of Indians had access to a considerable amount of

160

whiskey, the result was invariably a considerable number of maimings and murders, nearly always of one another.[14]

Little Turtle was not a teetotaler. He enjoyed good eating and drinking, along with good company and conversation. There are no reports of his ever having been drunk, but there are such reports concerning Pontiac, Brant, Le Gris, Blue Jacket, and, in fact, virtually every well-known chief of every tribe.[15] Little Turtle associated with white men more than most of the other chiefs, so had he ever been seen in a drunken condition it surely would have been mentioned. There are stories of his wit, of his eloquence, of his courtesy, of his dignity, of his bravery, but none accusing him of drunkenness. Turtle realized, however, that he and Pacan, the head chief, were among the few Miami who did not drink to excess. He had secured for the Miami the largest annuities on a per capita basis, only to find that this was rapidly transforming them into a nation of drunkards. The rest of the tribes were going to hell in a whiskey keg, but the Miami were going there in a barrel. Turtle saw only one way out of the situation, and that was to cut the dog's tail off right behind its ears. He became one of the first prohibitionists of record in the United States and urged the federal government to prohibit the sale of liquor to Indians. He also urged state legislatures in Kentucky and Ohio to do the same.[16]

Wells was also a moderate drinker, and even his worst enemy, John Johnston, never accused him of drunkenness. He agreed with Turtle that the Indians were doomed unless they were prevented from buying liquor. Thus, although both men realized the difficulties besetting their plan to transform the Miami into farmers, they nonetheless believed that, with the power of government supporting them, it could be done. There was one difference between them and later prohibitionists: they did not believe that drinking was sinful or morally wrong. Their concern was not morality but survival.[17]

The year 1800 saw the election of Thomas Jefferson as president and the decline of the Federalist party, especially on the American frontier. It also saw the creation by Congress of the Indiana Territory. Ohio remained the Northwest Territory and became a state in 1803. Because Wells was unsure whether this affected his status as interpreter at Fort Wayne and as Indian agent, he decided, after Jefferson's inauguration, to go to Washington, D.C., which had replaced Philadelphia as the seat of government, to try to obtain a permanent and paid appointment.[18] Little Turtle went with Wells to meet President Jefferson and to urge him to take action favorable to the Miami before it was too late. As usual, they traveled in late fall and returned in early spring, spending the winter of 1801–2 in the capital. They were accompanied by Five Medals, chief of the Potawatomi village on the Elkhart River (at what is now Waterford, just south of Goshen), and by several other chiefs.

Turtle and Wells were able to meet with President Jefferson on more than one occasion. Jefferson had a scientific interest in the Indian languages, and at his request William Thornton met with Little Turtle and Wells on January 11, 1802, to compile a vocabulary of Miami words somewhat more extensive than that compiled by Volney. Wells supplied most of the words but Turtle also cooperated since the president wished it.[19]

On January 4 the chiefs met with Jefferson, and Turtle delivered the principal speech for the occasion. He very ably rested all his points upon the Treaty of Greeneville and the desire of the Indians to abide by its provisions. He called attention to the fact that white people were breaking the treaty by settling beyond the line in Indian country. Jefferson indicated that a government trading house might be established in Indian country, and Turtle asked that it be placed at Fort Wayne because "the farther a trading post is established from the white people the better it will be for both." He mentioned that British traders were still operating in the area and charging high prices. He also requested a blacksmith for Fort Wayne and plows and other implements to be placed in the hands of "the Interpreter," William Wells, for distribution. Then he asked for a council house to be built at Fort Wayne where the Miami and their visitors might assemble when annuities were to be distributed.

Turtle emphasized that none of the requests would avail unless liquor was forbidden to be sold to the Indians. "Father," he said, "your children are not wanting in industry, but it is the introduction of this fatal poison, which keeps them poor. Your children have not the command over themselves that you have, therefore before anything can be done to advantage this evil must be remedied." Finally, he mentioned the Quakers as people who were interested in helping the Indians but had as yet done nothing. In conclusion he asked for an interview with the secretary of war, Henry Dearborn, since Jefferson had indicated that the answers to their requests would be left to him.[20]

The immediate result of Turtle's speech was that Dearborn appointed Wells the Indian agent at Fort Wayne, as of January 1, 1802, at a salary of $600 per year and four rations per day. He was responsible for distributing the annuities to the Miami, the Eel River Miami, the Wea Miami, the Delaware, and part of the Potawatomi. Wells had gone well prepared to argue his case. Letters of recommendation from Colonel J. F. Hamtramck, now commandant at Detroit, and from William Henry Harrison, newly appointed governor of the Indiana Territory with headquarters at Vincennes, had already been received by Dearborn. Hamtramck related his own part in persuading Wells to change sides in the late war and stressed

Wells's brilliant work as a spy, as well as the satisfaction he had given as an interpreter. Harrison described Wells as "a sober, active, and faithful public servant" and noted that his knowledge of Indian customs and languages was greater than that of anyone else. He also mentioned Wells's family connections in Kentucky.[21]

By late December 1801 Wells and Little Turtle had met with the Quakers in Baltimore; there is reason to think that this meeting had been suggested by Jefferson at his initial conversations with them in Washington. In speaking to the Quakers, Turtle stressed their common belief in a Great Spirit and plainly stated that the whites who had come among the Indians had "very much cheated and imposed upon us. They found us simple and ignorant, and have taken great care to keep everything from us, in order to profit by our ignorance." He pointed out that liquor had destroyed so many Indians "that it causes our young people to say, 'We had better be at war with the white people.' This liquor that they introduce into our country is more to be feared than the gun or the tomahawk; there are more of us dead since the Treaty of Greeneville, than we lost by the years of war before, and it is all owing to the introduction of this liquor among us."[22] As a result of his speech, the Baltimore Quakers sent a memorial to Congress urging prohibition of the sale of whiskey to the Indians. Although Congress passed a resolution empowering the president to act in the matter, which Jefferson did, the prohibition lacked any enforcement and had little effect.[23]

The journey back was made by way of Louisville, where Wells visited his relatives and purchased some black slaves to take to Fort Wayne.[24] Wells and Turtle undoubtedly felt they had made much headway in getting support from the Jefferson administration. Jefferson had defended the Indians against charges of degeneration and inferiority, advanced by a French scientist named Buffon, that were widely accepted in Europe. He was also on record as favoring intermarriage of whites and Indians, which accorded with his general belief in the equal rights of all men. What Wells and Little Turtle did not know was that there was a wide gap between Jefferson's theory and his practice. Nor did they yet realize that Jefferson's political supporters on the frontier were to be found among those who were most strongly anti-Indian in their views.[25]

Jefferson did not comprehend that Little Turtle was no more supported in his desire to change the Indians to the white way of life among his own people than Jefferson was supported in his liberal philosophy by his political backers, particularly when it came to applying that philosophy to the Indians. Both Little Turtle and Jefferson were intellectually far ahead of their followers. That Jefferson's actions were at times inconsistent with his beliefs became evident to Little Turtle and Wells almost as soon as they arrived home.[26]

Turtle's request for a government trading post at Fort Wayne was granted, but the post was not placed under the charge of William Wells. The secretary of war instead appointed John Johnston to the position of government factor, effective July 1, 1802, and ordered Wells to build a government factory and residence for Johnston. The new factor was to become the most devious and inveterate enemy of Wells almost from the outset. Nor was Wells placed in charge of Turtle's "civilization program," which was turned over by the president to the Baltimore Quakers. Turtle and Wells had no alternative but to try to accommodate themselves to these divisions of authority. Cooperation with Johnston was rendered impossible from the beginning by his hatred of Wells. The Quaker who was sent to the area proved to be a difficult person, one who fell under the influence of Johnston instead of being guided by Wells and Turtle, so that after a promising start cooperation with that organization faltered.[27]

It is not contended that Wells and Turtle would have succeeded had they been trusted by the Jefferson administration. However, they, and they alone, had a chance of success and deserved to be given that opportunity. The governmental division of authority would prove fatal to any real achievement.

NOTES

1. BRICE, 95, 148. Wells's residence was within the former village of Kekionga, as was the council house he constructed, but the village was not rebuilt.

2. This view is strengthened by the fact that the council house of the Miami, built by Wells after authorization by the government, was constructed on the land occupied by Wells. It was erected in 1804 and destroyed by fire in July 1809. THORNBROUGH (1), 44–45.

3. KNOPF, 477–88.

4. Ibid., 532–33.

5. Ibid., 478.

6. Ibid., 532.

7. HUTTON, 199. A ration was computed at seventy-two dollars per annum, and Wells was entitled to draw double rations during this period.

8. Dr. James McHenry, in a letter reproduced here in full, refers to Little Turtle's "honest regard for your own people." Wells, throughout his life, was partial to the Miami, with whom he had cast his lot. For this reason it seems proper to regard the plans of the two men as an extension of their Family Compact, not only chronologically, but also numerically, so that the tribe was included.

9. See the article on Little Turtle's grave relics in WHITLEY, (December 1976), 16–18.

10. This memorandum, found in NORTHWEST, is photographically reproduced in WOEHRMANN, following p. 156.

11. Rough draft in NORTHWEST.

12. Ibid., except that this letter is a final draft.

13. SHEEHAN (1), 236, quotes Harrison's statistic that 600 Wabash Indians consumed 6,000 gallons of whiskey annually.

14. SHEEHAN (1), states that white men could not explain the greater effect of liquor on Indians. This paragraph is an attempt to do so.

15. VOLNEY, 380, states that during his stay at "Fort Miami," Blue Jacket (whom he calls Blue Jockey), while drunk, killed a man against whom he had held a grudge for twenty-two years.

16. There were certainly very few advocates of prohibition in the United States at this early date. The first Temperance Society was formed in New York in 1808. Prohibition by law was first enacted in Maine in 1851, then repealed in 1858. Turtle discerned the advantage gained by traders over the Indians through the use of liquor. See YOUNG, 148–49; also GUTHMAN, 122.

17. Wells, a Kentuckian, also owned slaves. The Indians traded in Indian, white, or black slaves captured in war. Neither liquor nor slavery was widely regarded as a moral issue at this time, although the sentiment was present and growing.

18. Wells first wrote to Governor St. Clair and learned that Fort Wayne was within the newly designated Indiana Territory. St. Clair to Wells, August 13, 1800, in NORTHWEST. This apparently impelled the trip to Washington, but doubtless he and Turtle were aware of President Jefferson's reputed interest in Indians. They clearly knew of the Quaker interest. Whether Wells had favored Jefferson's election is not known. Turtle was also accompanied by his nephew, The Toad, who died soon after their return. Two brothers of Little Turtle also died about this time. HOPKINS, 53.

19. THORNTON states this information on the title page of his vocabulary.

20. HILL, 14–18, reproduces Little Turtle's speech to President Jefferson as translated by William Wells. Turtle's explanation was simple: "Father, your children do not have the command over themselves that you do. . . ." I have given one explanation; there are others.

21. For Harrison's recommendation, see WOEHRMANN, 145. For Hamtramck's recommendation, see Ibid., 146.

22. HOPKINS, 164–65, 169–73.

23. WOEHRMANN, 110–12.

24. HUTTON, 203. It was probably at this time that Little Turtle addressed the Kentucky legislature on prohibiting liquor sales to the Indians.

25. President Jefferson went so far in his desire to acquire land from the Indians as to suggest to Governor William Henry Harrison, in a letter dated February 27, 1803, that "to promote this disposition to exchange lands" he should cultivate the Indian relation with the government factories and "be glad to see the good and influential individuals among them run into debt, because we observe that when these individuals get beyond what the individual can pay, they become willing to lop them off by a cession of lands." Quoted in SHEEHAN (1), 171. Jefferson had a

life-long battle with debt himself, so he spoke from personal experience, but the advice completely negates Jefferson's vaunted philanthropy.

26. By appointing John Johnston as government factor at Fort Wayne, Jefferson and Dearborn went counter to the request made by Turtle on behalf of Wells.

27. The Quakers were well intentioned but their choice of William Kirk was unfortunate. Kirk's failure will be discussed later in this work.

15

The Militant Whites, 1803–10

On May 7, 1797, William Henry Harrison, at the age of twenty-four, was given his captain's commission and the command of Fort Washington, near Cincinnati. On June 1, 1798, having married Anna, daughter of John Cleves Symmes, owner of a million acres of land in southwest Ohio, he resigned from the army to accept an appointment as secretary of the Northwest Territory from President John Adams. He resigned from that post in October 1799 to take a seat in the House of Representatives as territorial delegate, a position to which he had just been elected. Harrison's rapid rise was not surprising in view of his descent from a well-established family of able planter-politicians. His family had maintained its place among the interlocking families of the Virginia tidewater which had controlled the destiny of that colony for several generations. Able, energetic, and ambitious, Harrison played a key role during the year he served as delegate for the Northwest Territory in Congress by persuading that body to enact two important pieces of legislation.[1]

The first, known as the Public Land Act of 1800, provided for the sale of federal lands at two dollars per acre in minimum amounts of 320 acres, with four years in which to pay; in 1804 the minimum was reduced to 160 acres. In 1800, of course, almost all of the federal land available was within that part of the Northwest Territory which was to become the state of Ohio. The second piece of legislation created two territories where there had been but one. They were divided by a line from the mouth of the Kentucky River to Fort Recovery and thence due north to the Canadian border. The portion east of this line was known as the Northwest Territory and was still under Governor Arthur St. Clair; the portion west of the line was called the Indiana Territory. In 1800 the population of the new territory was only 5,641 and was concentrated around the old French settlements of Vincennes and Kaskaskia, and in Clark's Grant, opposite Louisville, where American settlement had begun; the Northwest Territory had a population of over 42,000. By 1803 the state of Ohio was created from a portion of the Northwest Territory and the remainder was added to the Indiana Territory. Harrison was promptly appointed governor of the Indiana Territory and commissioner of Indian affairs, a post for which he was obviously available, although he had earlier insisted that, should it be offered to him, he would refuse it.[2]

Harrison received his appointment from President Adams, but by the time he set out for Vincennes, the seat of government for the Indiana Territory, he was well aware that Thomas Jefferson, not Adams, would soon be president. He also knew that Jefferson had received the overwhelming support of the new western states of Kentucky and Tennessee as well as the frontier portions of older states. With an unerring eye for the main chance, Harrison switched his political allegiance from the Federalist to the Jeffersonian party. He was twice reappointed by Jefferson to three-year terms and once by Madison, so that he served as territorial executive from his appointment in May 1800 to his resignation in December 1812. As governor he reported to the president, but as commissioner for Indian affairs he was responsible to the secretary of war, and it is chiefly in this capacity that Harrison dealt with Little Turtle and with William Wells.[3]

Thomas Jefferson, one of the best examplars of the eighteenth-century philosophical movement known as the Enlightenment, had long been recognized for his intellectual interest in the aboriginal tribes, for his philanthropic and humanitarian views toward them, and for his tolerant attitude toward the individuals who comprised these tribes. He had a scientific interest in their languages and customs and was an advocate of gradual assimilation through intermarriage and through a civilizing program that would convert them from hunters to farmers.[4]

That Harrison was aware of the president's attitude toward the Indians was reflected in his early reports to Jefferson and to Henry Dearborn, the secretary of war. In his first report to Dearborn, Harrison called attention to the fact that the citizens of Kentucky had so constantly and habitually hunted on Indian lands north of the Ohio River, in violation of the Treaty of Greeneville, that the game upon which the Indians depended for their existence had become scarce. He pointed out that one white hunter would kill more game than five Indians. The Indians also complained that "their people had been killed, their lands settled on . . . & their young men made drunk and cheated of their peltries. . . ." He warned that such actions forced the Indians into the willing clutches of the British traders in Canada and asked for the reactivation of Fort Knox, at Vincennes, with a force large enough to impress the Indians and enforce their treaty rights.[5] The federal government did not accede to this request at the time it was made, but Fort Knox was garrisoned with less than twenty men a few years later.

Harrison gave a vivid description of the effects of liquor upon the Piankashaw, the Wea, and the Eel River Miami, who frequently visited Vincennes, and pointed out that when in a drunken condition they often murdered members of their own tribe, especially their chiefs. On July 20, 1801, he issued a proclamation that forbade the sale of liquor to Indians in and around Vincennes, but there is no evidence that any attention was paid to it, for the traders knew there were no means of enforcement. The president suggested to the governor that a reward be offered for the apprehension of any white who had murdered an Indian, but there is no record of any white having been convicted of this crime in the Indiana Territory.[6]

At the outset, Harrison seemed genuinely concerned about the condition of the Indians and was disposed to protect their treaty rights. But he became indifferent to these matters by the close of his first term when he realized that Jefferson and his administration had more interest in acquiring land from the Indians than in rendering them acceptable to white society. Harrison agreed with the desirability of pressing a program of land acquisition as rapidly as possible and became such a willing instrument of this policy that no other person in American history has rivaled his record. The program ran counter to that of Little Turtle and William Wells, who wished to hold the Miami lands as long as possible and to sell land only after the Miami had been taught to support themselves entirely by agriculture, for then they would need less land than they needed for hunting. Jefferson wished to acquire the lands first and thus force the Indians into agricultural pursuits.[7]

Jefferson also underwent a change of attitude toward the Indians after the purchase of nearly one million square miles, known as the Louisiana Territory, from Napoleon in 1803. He mistakenly believed that many generations would pass before the advance of white settlement would require these lands for farming. He ceased to believe that the Indians might be assimilated by the whites within the near future and advocated that they should instead be removed from their native habitat and given land on the prairies beyond the Mississippi or the great plains beyond the Missouri. Here he felt they could live without contact with whites, other than missionaries, who would convert and civilize them.[8] How a man with such a strong attachment for his native Virginia could have failed to realize that the Indians of the Heartland had similar strong feelings for their native woodlands, lakes, and streams, is difficult to comprehend. His blindness to

169

this fact would bring the tribes of the Heartland close to extinction in the next half century.

A survey of the treaties secured by Harrison in the years from 1802 to 1810 will clarify the way in which the Jeffersonian system was put into practical operation. In the summer of 1802, Governor Harrison invited the chiefs of the Eel River, the Wea, and the Piankashaw Miami, and also of the Kaskaskia, the Kickapoo, and the Potawatomi tribes to attend a conference at Vincennes to discuss a land grant recognized in general terms by the Treaty of Greeneville, which stated that "the post of St. Vincennes on the river Wabash, and the lands adjacent, of which the Indian title has been extinguished should henceforth belong to the United States." The basis for this grant was an agreement made in 1742 between the French commandant and the Piankashaw Miami and was for the use of the French *habitants* rather than a cession to the French crown. In 1775, when the Piankashaw sold a rectangular piece of land lying on both sides of the Wabash River to the Wabash Land Company, the prior grant was remembered and expressly reserved from the rectangle within which it lay. The American government had refused to recognize the validity of this sale to the Wabash Land Company.

The chiefs who assembled in 1802 were reluctant to authorize any land sale. However, under pressure from Harrison, who distributed $1,500 in gifts to them and their followers, the chiefs agreed to convey to the United States the land formerly sold to the Wabash Company, comprising about 1.6 million acres in present Indiana and Illinois. The cession was made provisionally only and required ratification at a second conference to be held in the summer of 1803.[9]

Harrison certainly realized the cession was supported on tenuous legal grounds since there was no proof that either the French or the British crowns had held possession of the land and since the United States could only assert a legal claim upon this basis. He may not have understood that, by extending his negotiations beyond the Piankashaw Miami, he was broadening the concept of Indian landownership beyond the point recognized and claimed by the tribes themselves. The Potawatomi, the Kickapoo, and the Kaskaskia tribes all recognized that the land in question belonged to the Piankashaw Miami and was within the general bounds of the Miami land claim asserted at the Treaty of Greeneville by Little Turtle. Although at that time Wayne had remarked upon the broad extent of the claim, it had not been questioned by either the other Indian tribes or by the United States government.[10]

In the late spring of 1803, Harrison journeyed to Fort Wayne where the cession was confirmed, not only by those who had met during the previous year at Vincennes, but also by the Delaware, the Shawnee, and the Miami proper. For the latter, Little Turtle and Richardville, aided by Wells, who acted as interpreter, played a key role in persuading the other tribes to agree to the cession. Wells and Turtle recognized the importance of getting along with the governor and the desirability of abiding by the Treaty of Greeneville. They felt that it was reasonable that the United States control the land in the immediate vicinity of the territorial capital and hoped that, by being cooperative with the governor, they would be in a better position to retain the rest of the Miami lands. The acquiescence of Richardville indicated that he was well disposed toward the United States and that he could give assurance that Pacan would make no objections.[11] In their assessment of Harrison, however, Turtle and Wells were completely mistaken. Far from appreciating their cooperation, Harrison embarked upon a program of land grabbing that forced them into unwilling opposition to the Jeffersonian policies. The Indians were soon to discover that not only did the governor speak with a forked tongue but he wrote with a forked pen.

The ratification of the Vincennes cession was signed on June 7, 1803, at Fort Wayne. Had Harrison been more patient, had he been willing to remain until the Miami proper and the Delaware had settled their differences about the status of the White River lands, long occupied by the Delaware with Miami consent, it is possible that the spirit of cooperation inspired by Wells and Turtle among the Miami might have induced them to confirm these lands to the Delaware.[12] This would have simplified future negotiations from the white point of view and produced a Miami-Delaware coalition that might have been of advantage to both tribes.

But Harrison was eager to return to Vincennes, where on August 13, 1803, he induced the Kaskaskia, who feared extermination by the Potawatomi, to cede, without consultation with the Peoria and other divisions of the once powerful but now greatly reduced Illinois tribe, all the land that lay south of the Illinois River not drained by the Wabash. This amounted to nearly eight million acres in what is now Illinois. In return, Harrison took the Kaskaskia under his protection. Flushed by this stroke of good fortune, and having the administration of the Louisiana Territory temporarily under his control, Harrison was able to deal with the Sauk and the Fox tribes for the land north of the Illinois River and to induce them to promise to remain west of the Mississippi and even to cede, on November 2, 1804, their claims in present-day northeastern Missouri. Signed at St. Louis, this treaty, which was made with only a few chiefs, gained fifteen million acres in Illinois, Missouri, and Wisconsin in return for an annuity of $1,000 per year and a few other concessions. It also became the source of future trouble leading to the Black Hawk War in 1832.[13]

Although these two treaties constituted Harrison's most spectacular land acquisitions, he was not without success in enlarging the government's domain at the expense of the Miami. On August 18 and 27, 1804, he acquired all the Ohio River hunting grounds of the Piankashaw Miami from the mouth of the Wabash to Clark's Grant, opposite the Falls of the Ohio. Harrison purchased the same land first from the Delaware, who did not own it, and ten days later from the Piankashaw, who did own it. In fact, Harrison's treaty with the Delaware not only stated that they had proven their ownership to the land in question but that Harrison, acting for the federal government, recognized that the Delaware were also the rightful owners of all the White River lands on which they resided only by the courtesy of the Miami, as the Delaware themselves well knew. Faced with this statement, the Piankashaw, who were reduced in numbers and whose survivors were now mostly habitual drunkards from long association with the American traders, had little recourse but to accept what seemed an accomplished fact.[14]

The situation was quite otherwise among the Miami proper, where consternation prevailed not only among the Miami generally but also in the mind of Little Turtle and of Wells. Harrison knew that they were disturbed by his Treaty of Vincennes, but he did not comprehend that it was his dealing with the Delaware, who owned no land, that disturbed them. He wrote to the secretary of war, "Whether the opposition to those Treaties originated with himself [Little Turtle] or with Mr. Wells I cannot determine but that the opinions of the one are always the opinions of the other." In this observation, which gives strong support to the concept of a continuation of the Family Compact, Harrison was entirely correct.

When he charged that Turtle and Wells were without influence among the Miami proper, however, and that their influence was confined to the Eel River Miami and the Potawatomi village of Five Medals (Onoxa), Harrison was mistaken. He recognized that Pacan and Richardville were the principal Miami chiefs, but he did not know that at this time they agreed with Turtle and Wells in desiring amicable relations with the government, relations which they felt were threatened by Harrison's dealings with the Delaware. Richardville cooperated with Turtle and Wells, in 1803 at Fort Wayne, in persuading the Miami to ratify the Vincennes cession despite their view that the Delaware had no rights in the matter. Harrison did nothing at Fort Wayne to indicate that he was aware that the cause of the Miami dissatisfaction lay in his failure to recognize that the Delaware tribe occupied Miami lands which they had no right to sell. However, he admitted to Secretary Dearborn that he recognized the historic justice of the Miami position.[15]

Recognition in 1804 of the Delaware tribe as owners of not only the Piankashaw hunting grounds on the Ohio but also the whole of the White River drainage forced Turtle and Wells into reluctant opposition to Governor Harrison. Their recourse was to appeal to President Jefferson by means of a letter written by Wells, signed by Little Turtle, and sent to General James Wilkinson. In this letter they stated accurately that Harrison was confirming land titles to landless Indians and then buying the land from them for a pittance, and that he was undermining the control of the established chiefs by recognizing lesser chiefs and even creating new chiefs. They further suggested that, rather than sell their lands, the Indians might fight for them once more, if foreign aid were available. The letter was forwarded by Wilkinson to the secretary of war, who from this time forward became the inveterate enemy of Wells. Although Wells had believed that the president would set matters right, it is not certain that Jefferson ever saw the letter. Wells had gone too far, of course, in his empty threat of war, and after reflection he and Turtle decided that they would have to make their peace with the governor.[16]

Meanwhile, Harrison had let his imagination run riot. With no basis whatever he accused Wells of jealous rivalry and Turtle of wishing to become the head of a great Indian confederacy.[17] He soon realized how far from the truth these accusations were, but he had already transmitted them to Dearborn. Because he was not disposed to admit his error of judgment, the damage in Washington was permanent.

Harrison had discovered that John Johnston, the government factor at Fort Wayne, was eager to vilify William Wells. The cause of Johnston's animosity remains a mystery. Seven months after Wells became Indian agent at Fort Wayne, Johnston had taken up his residence there as government factor at a salary of $750 per year plus three rations per day. Wells had superintended the building of the government factory and Johnston's house. Since Wells never criticized Johnston to Harrison or Dearborn, as Johnston constantly criticized him, it is possible that Wells was unaware of Johnston's hatred for him. It is peculiar that Johnston, who reported both to the governor and to the secretary of war, criticized Wells for doing the same, although as Indian agent Wells was required by law to do so. It is also odd that after Wells acquired the land on which Pickawillany had once stood, Johnston obtained land adjacent to Wells and lived there during later years. Perhaps Johnston considered Wells a white renegade, in spite of his valuable services to Wayne. Although Johnston received a greater salary as factor than Wells did as Indian agent ($750 to $600 at first, and later $1,000 to $750), Wells received more rations and also drew a salary as interpreter and a pension as a wounded soldier.

Perhaps Johnston, who considered himself superior in attainments, was envious of Wells.[18]

Johnston was the only source of derogatory information concerning Wells that Harrison had, and it is possible that the governor, when he visited Fort Wayne in 1803, may have indicated dissatisfaction with Wells and Turtle and may have encouraged the factor to keep an eye on them for him. At various times Johnston charged that Wells was debauching the Indians with whiskey; that he made more than $6,000 by illegal trade in a single year; that he regularly kept for himself most of the annuities due the Kickapoo, the Delaware, and the Potawatomi; that he was illiterate and incapable of serving the government; that he had defrauded the Eel River Miami; and that, altogether, he had enriched himself at the expense of the Indians and the government by more than $50,000. Harrison relayed these charges to Dearborn, who accepted them as fact without investigation.[19]

Governor Harrison involved himself in contradictions. For example, he reported that Turtle and Wells controlled the Eel River Miami, which could not have been true if they were defrauding them. He also claimed that they had more influence with the Potawatomi than with the Miami proper, which could not have been true if Wells was pocketing the Potawatomi annuities, which were smaller per capita by far than those of the Miami. Since Wells purchased the goods for distribution to the Indians from the government factory, most of Johnston's charges were obviously false. Johnston himself sometimes purchased liquor from the army for the factory when he ran short of stock. When Wells produced a letter from Alexander McKee, the British superintendent of Indian affairs, complaining to the Indians of Wells's efforts to persuade them to use less liquor, Johnston suggested at once that Wells had fabricated the letter. Certainly, when Wells died in 1812 the size of his estate did not substantiate Johnston's charges of peculation on a grand scale.[20]

Only two irregularities were ever proved against Wells. First, he did not keep a detailed record of his expenditures in a way that satisfied the secretary of war. When Dearborn took him to task for this, Wells began to keep itemized records, and on this score there were no further complaints. However, on the specific charge that he had employed soldiers as railsplitters and had used some of the rails for his own private fencing, Wells readily admitted that he had done so but that he did not consider it a crime.[21] As to his literacy, another complaint of Johnson's, his letters are readable, his handwriting clear, and his spelling average for the time.

In 1804 Harrison sent John Gibson and Francis Vigo from Vincennes to Fort Wayne to invite the Miami to meet with him the following year in the hope of settling their differences. Chief Richardville told the emissaries that Wells had advised the Miami to stand up for their rights.[22] In Harrison's view this amounted to treachery, but Wells believed that as Indian agent he was properly counseling them in their best interests, as was his duty. Harrison's view of an Indian agent's duty did not include the government's responsibility for the welfare of the Indians, whom he regarded as possessing no rights. When Gibson and Vigo visited the Delaware villages on the White River at Muncie and Anderson Town, they found that the Delaware had second thoughts about their ownership of the lands they occupied. It became clear to Harrison that he had acted hastily and unwisely in recognizing their right of ownership when they were afraid to assert it themselves to the Miami.

Little Turtle was the only chief who had fully understood and accepted the white theory and law of landownership and had staked out the Miami's land claim clearly in 1795 so that it was a matter of public record. He was prepared to deal with the whites on their own terms and sell or not sell as he judged best for his tribe. Harrison had undermined Turtle's position by accepting quitclaim deeds from other tribes for Miami land and giving them annuities and what other considerations they asked for in return. In doing so he had embarrassed Little Turtle among his own people and injured the credibility of Wells as their agent. Little Turtle and Wells extricated themselves from this predicament at considerable cost to the Miami and to their standing among the other tribes.[23]

Pursuant to the arrangements made by Gibson and Vigo, Governor Harrison invited the Wea Miami, the Eel River Miami, and the Miami proper to come to Vincennes in August 1805 for a general conference to settle the question of landownership. The Delaware and the Potawatomi were also invited to this meeting. Wells was the official interpreter for the Miami. Richardville and Little Turtle attended, although Pacan did not. After the fashion of the Virginia tidewater families, Harrison had built for himself, near Vincennes, a stately residence, which he called Grouseland; as the meeting was held upon his private grounds, the resulting treaty was called the Treaty of Grouseland. The Indians were lavishly entertained by their host, and goods in the amount of $1,000 each were distributed to the Miami proper, the Delaware, and the Potawatomi, with $500 each going to the Wea Miami and the Eel River Miami.

The Delaware acknowledged that they did not own the White River lands whereon they lived but were there by courtesy of the Miami. In return the Miami withdrew their objection to the Treaty of Vincennes of the previous year, whereby the Delaware had sold that portion of Indiana lying south of the Buffalo Trace. The right of the Piankashaw Miami to sell this same land had never been denied. In addition, the Miami proper, the Wea Miami, and the Eel River Miami agreed to sell the remaining portion of their hunting grounds along the Ohio River from the Falls of the Ohio to the mouth of the Kentucky River, in return for increased annuities and for Harrison's pledge that the United States recognized all land lying in the Wabash River drainage as the exclusive property of the Miami. Of the land ceded at Grouseland, a portion opposite the Falls of the Ohio had already been granted by the federal government to General George Rogers Clark in recognition of his Revolutionary War services and had already been taken up by white settlers.[24]

Following private conversations with Wells and Turtle, the governor reported to Dearborn that past differences with them had been resolved and that he was convinced that they would work amicably with him in the future. Harrison did not exert himself, however, to convince Dearborn that his own charges against Wells and Turtle had been exaggerated, and Dearborn continued to mistrust Wells on the basis of the charges Harrison and Johnston had already lodged against him. Harrison may have felt that he had bought the loyalty of these two men, for Wells's pay as agent at Fort Wayne was raised from $600 to $750 per year, while Little Turtle's annual pension was increased from $100 to $150. In addition, the government constructed a house for Little Turtle on the Eel River, a mile or so upstream from Turtletown. It was a grave error on Harrison's part, however, to be so obtuse about the motives of both Turtle and Wells.[25]

The governor made another mistake when he failed to ask Richardville, the highest-ranking chief present among the Miami proper, to head the list of signers of the treaty. This disregard of Richardville continued, and in 1810 John Badollet, who was in charge of the public land office at Vincennes, wrote Albert Gallatin, "I myself have observed one Pishooah or Richarville a half blooded indian who speaks french as well as I do, is with [his] uncle Pacawn, a grand chief of the Miamis & besides very much of a gentleman, I have seen that man, for some hidden reason affectedly thrown in the back ground and treated with very little ceremony which usage he has deeply felt."[26] Since Richardville was to guide the destiny of the Miami until 1841, Harrison's treatment of Pacan's nephew and successor as Miami head chief had far-reaching effects.

Badollet also criticized Harrison's handling of Indian negotiations in general. It was his opinion that "Gen'l Gibson and Col. Vigo could purchase more land in two hours than the Gov'r in ten years," and he credited Gibson and Vigo with helping to settle the Miami-Delaware landownership question which Harrison had obviously mishandled.[27] These criticisms, though deserved, did not alter the fact that Harrison was a successful land grabber who created much ill will among the Indians. On December 30, 1805, the Piankashaw Miami, who had not been invited to Grouseland, were assembled at Vincennes and persuaded to cede that portion of their land which lay in the Wabash River drainage in present-day southern Illinois. This cession brought the last few miles of the Ohio River under white control.[28]

Governor William Hull, of the Michigan Territory, which was created early in 1805, sought to emulate Harrison, concluding the Treaty of Detroit on November 17, 1807, in which the Ottawa, the Chippewa, the Potawatomi, and the Wyandot ceded all of southeastern Michigan to the United States. The fact that the southern boundary of this tract was the Maumee River, as far west as the mouth of the Auglaize, was of some concern to the Miami, but they do not appear to have been invited to Detroit.[29]

Harrison made no more Indian treaties until 1809. During the intervening years he was involved in much political controversy, principally over black slavery in the Indiana Territory, which he favored although a majority of the settlers did not. His aggressive land acquisitions from the Indians provoked criticism by some of his opponents, but he was conscious that he had the majority of the settlers on his side in this matter. By 1809 he had decided that it would be good politics to acquire additional Indian lands, even though white settlement was not as rapid as to make this necessary.

The Indians, however, did not respond favorably to his invitation to come once more to Vincennes. There was dissatisfaction among them about the treaties that had already been made, and none were eager to sell more land. The followers of the Shawnee Prophet and his brother, Tecumseh, opposed further sales of land. Harrison was unwilling to recognize that his own policies and those of Jefferson had been responsible for Indian unrest. He determined that if the Indians would not come to Vincennes, then he would go to Fort Wayne. He traveled there on horseback over the new road connecting Vincennes to Cincinnati, so that he might do some political campaigning along the way. At his father-in-law's house at North Bend he went northward to Fort Wayne, taking two weeks for the entire journey and arriving at Fort Wayne on September 15, 1809.[30]

Nearly 1,400 Indians were encamped nearby to learn what the governor had in mind; fully half of these were Potawatomi, but the Delaware were there in force, as well as the Miami proper and the Eel River Miami. Richardville sent word that illness prevented his attendance, but Pacan and Little Turtle were present. Wells was the chief interpreter, but he had been replaced as Indian agent by his old enemy, John Johnston, who was also serving as factor. Harrison visited the separate encampments and ascertained that the Delaware and the Potawatomi were willing to sell the land he wanted. However, the Miami were solidly united in opposition to his proposition. They were unmoved by the threat made by Harrison's favorite employee, Winamac, a young Potawatomi whom the governor had recognized as a chief, although he was not one, that if the Miami did not comply with the governor's wishes he would drive them into the lake. Because the influence of Little Turtle and Wells had melted away with the loss of the agency by Wells, Harrison could not attribute to them the recalcitrance of the Miami; neither could not explain the Miami opposition.[31]

Finally, Harrison visited the Miami chiefs in their own camp and told them that he was aware that something unknown to him was troubling them, and he asked to know what it was. He called first on Charley, the Eel River chief, whom he had known since 1794. Charley arose with a copy of the Grouseland Treaty and explained, "Here are your own words, in this paper you promised that you would consider the Miamis as the owners of the lands on the Wabash why then are you about to purchase it from others?" Harrison finally understood what he should have known all along, and once more he reaffirmed that the Miami were the sole owners of the land in question. He went so far as to say that if they insisted upon it the whole compensation would be given to them, but that this would certainly be offensive to the Potawatomi and the Delaware.[32]

On his assurance that the treaty would recognize the Miami as sole owners and the other tribes as receiving compensation only as their allies, the Miami chiefs agreed to sell two large areas. The greater of these lay north of the Vincennes tract and extended the boundary of federal land up the Wabash as far as the mouth of the Raccoon Creek, although its eastern limit was much farther south. Since it actually belonged to the Wea Miami the sale was conditioned upon their ratification and that of their neighbors, the Kickapoo. The lesser tract, which was the sole possession of the Miami proper, extended the federal boundary twelve miles west of the Greeneville Treaty line, which had formed the western boundary of the Indiana "gore." Together the two tracts amounted to 2.9 million acres.[33]

Harrison traveled back to Vincennes by way of the Wabash River and met with the Wea Miami to secure their consent to the sale. Later, on December 9, 1809, he acquired not only the consent of the Kickapoo but also an extension of the westerly tract into what is now Illinois.[34] Thus, the Wabash was controlled on both sides by the United States as far as Raccoon Creek, and some of the Wea villages were forced to move upriver. Federal control was also brought closer to the militant Shawnee village at Prophetstown, near the mouth of the Tippecanoe River.

The cession of the easterly tract was entirely at the expense of the Miami proper and was a cruel blow in return for the steadfast support Little Turtle had given since 1795 to the American government. Yet Turtle had no choice but to agree to the Treaty of Fort Wayne, even though he knew, and was afterward to say, that the government had no particular need to acquire the land at this time. Turtle was caught between the militant Indian extremist Tecumseh and his followers, and the rapacious white land grabbers encouraged and endorsed by Jefferson and Harrison. Wells had lost his agency and had volunteered his services as interpreter in an effort to regain his post. He succeeded only in receiving an appointment as interpreter at a salary of $365 per year.[35]

The Treaty of Fort Wayne greatly strengthened the movement led by Tecumseh and The Prophet. It brought Little Turtle and Wells to the lowest point of their influence among the Miami, yet Harrison and John Johnston continued to blame Wells and Turtle for stirring up dissatisfaction with the treaty.[36] The lack of appreciation for their efforts must have sorely tried the patience of these two loyal, able, and moderate men, who nonetheless remained true to their chosen policy of cooperation with the American government.

By 1800 there were 220,000 people in Kentucky and half that number in Tennessee. Thousands more were migrating from Pennsylvania, Maryland, Virginia, and North Carolina into the new states of Kentucky, Tennessee, and Ohio. Some were pressing into the Indiana Territory.[37] The majority disliked and feared Indians and supported rapid acquisition of their lands by the government, which found the sale of public lands immensely profitable. Harrison boasted that he had acquired over 2.5 million acres for less than two cents an acre, which the government would sell for two dollars an acre. Although many of the Indians understood that they were being swindled, they were powerless to do anything about it. All they could do was to make the best bargain possible under the circumstances. They arranged for perpetual annuities rather than outright cash sales and sold in as small amounts as possible, but this availed little in stemming the tide of the advancing white frontier.

Had Wells and Turtle been able to secure the cooperation of the government, the Miami, at least, might have fared better, and other tribes might have profited by their example. Jefferson did not recognize in Wells his own philosophical ideal of assimilation by intermarriage. Harrison failed to recognize the right of Turtle and Wells to express their intelligent views and he choose not to listen to and be guided by the advice of these loyal men. Clearly, Jefferson and Harrison pursued the path of expediency rather than that of morality. They chose to follow public opinion rather than shape, lead, or guide it.[38]

NOTES

1. GREEN provides reliable facts on Harrison but is uncritical of his Indian policy.

2. BARNHART and RIKER, 316. Harrison did not get along well with Governor Arthur St. Clair. As governor of the new territory he was St. Clair's equal, not his subordinate.

3. For Harrison's various appointments and reappointments see ibid., 314, 316, 332, 349, 355.

4. For a thorough consideration and critical analysis of Jefferson's Indian policy, see SHEEHAN (1), passim. The contrast between Jeffersonian theory and practice is brilliantly shown.

5. ESAREY, I, 26–29. Harrison to Dearborn, July 15, 1801.

6. BARNHART and RIKER, 326. Harrison had stated to Dearborn that many frontier settlers "considered murdering the Indians in the highest degree meritorious." See ESAREY, I, 25.

7. Jefferson spoke to Little Turtle on one of his visits to Washington, D.C., as he spoke on other occasions to other chiefs, expressing the same rather self-righteous sentiment: "I have . . . always believed it an act of friendship to our red brethren whenever they wished to sell a portion of their lands, to be ready to buy whether we wanted them or not, because the price enables them to improve the lands they retain, and turning their industry from hunting to agriculture the same exertions will support them more plentifully." See SHEEHAN (1), 169. The practice was to force the Indians to sell whether they wished to or not, and especially to force them to sell before they had managed to be able to turn from hunting to agriculture.

8. Jefferson originally objected to the practice of converting the Indians to Christianity first and then trying to civilize them. See SHEEHAN (1), 125. In this he was right, since it is much easier for people to change their technological practices than to change their abstract ideas, because the former are subject to proof while the latter are not. In practice, Jefferson turned the civilizing process over to the missionaries because it was cheaper.

9. The agreement reached in 1802 concerning the Vincennes tract was not recorded as an official treaty and was not operative until the Treaty of Fort Wayne ratified it in 1803. This illustrates the extreme reluctance of the Indians to sell land. They were disposed to regard the Greeneville Treaty of 1795 as literally marking the end of white expansion.

10. Wayne's passing remark was not the subject of any further discussion at Greeneville. It is a measure of Little Turtle's foresight that he alone among the Indians understood the white man's concept of property in land and established a claim for the Miami in exactly the same way that a white diplomat would have done.

11. Chief Jean Baptiste Richerville was half French and well educated. Richardville, as the name is usually written, worked closely with Wells and Turtle at the outset but was much less cooperative as time went on.

12. BARNHART and RIKER, 338–39. The text of the treaty and signatures thereto are found in KAPPLER, 64–66.

13. KAPPLER, 67–68, 74–77. JACKSON, 203–22, examines Harrison's methods in procuring the treaty with the Sauk and the Fox Indians.

14. KAPPLER, 70–72, 72–73. The treaty with the Delaware required Piankashaw consent, and the Piankashaw treaty referred to their obstinate refusal to recognize Delaware ownership. It is clear that the Piankashaw gave consent only after the Delaware had been paid for selling Piankashaw land, when they concluded that they

had better be paid as well. Buckongahelas, the old Delaware war chief, signed for that tribe but died in 1805 before the Treaty of Grouseland.

15. ESAREY, I, 76–77. Harrison to Dearborn, March 3, 1803, discussed the question of the Delaware claim, which Harrison interpreted to suit himself so as to lay the blame for Miami dissatisfaction on Little Turtle and Wells.

16. LRSW, Reg. Ser., Record Group 107. Wilkinson to Dearborn, December 13, 1804, with Wells to Wilkinson, October 6, 1804, enclosed.

17. ESAREY, I, 76–84. Harrison to Dearborn, March 3, 1803. Either Esarey misdated this letter or the date was misprinted. The correct date is 1805 and is so given in CARTER (1), VII, 288, and in LRSW, Reg. Ser., Record Group 107. Harrison to Dearborn, March 3, 1805. See also Jefferson to Harrison, April 28, 1805, in ESAREY, I, 126–28.

18. Johnston, at this period, was not sympathetic to the Indians, although in later life he became more so. He denied saying anything to Gibson and Vigo that "impeached Wells's character." See CARTER (1), VII, 343–44. Johnston to Harrison, February 28, 1806. In the same letter, however, he attributes to Wells "the application of Little Turtle to the President for the purpose of superceding your Excellency."

19. ESAREY, I, 147–51. Harrison to Dearborn, July 10, 1805, contains a number of these charges against Wells, which Harrison is careful to say originated with John Johnston. See also ibid., 393–94, Harrison to Dearborn, December 3, 1809, and 430–32, Johnston to Harrison, June 24, 1810. WOEHRMANN ably reviews the Johnston-Wells controversy. See especially Johnston's accusations, pp. 149, 151–52, 157–58, 162, 163–64, 167–68.

20. McKee's letter to the Potawatomi, written in November 1804, is found in ESAREY, I, 111–12. A copy of Wells's will and an inventory of his estate was kindly furnished to me by Professor Paul A. Hutton. The worth of Wells's slaves and personal property was less than $5,000; the amount and worth of his land is difficult to estimate. He was not poor, but from what is known of his sources of income he could have and probably did acquire his possessions honestly. It must be considered, too, that he undoubtedly followed Indian rules of hospitality at Fort Wayne, at considerable personal expense beyond what he could collect from the government.

21. Wells's admission of the fence rail charge may possibly indicate that he had done this with the knowledge and consent of the commanding officer at Fort Wayne but did not wish to implicate him. Wells got along well with a succession of commandants at the fort, and some of them wrote letters attesting to his good character.

22. ESAREY, I, 141–47, Gibson and Vigo to Harrison, July 6, 1805. PRUCHA, 54–57, makes clear that the legal basis for Indian agents and their duties was more the result of early practice than explicit law but that agents were expected to impress Indians with the desire of the government for peace and justice. The justice of Miami rights under the Greeneville Treaty, when pointed out by Wells and Turtle, however, was ignored by both Harrison and Dearborn. An appeal to the Supreme Court did not occur to them, but such an appeal might have been made with better success at this time than under Jackson's presidency, when the Cherokee won a decision only to have it ignored by the president.

23. ESAREY, I, 141–47. Little Turtle made a definite statement to Gibson and Vigo that he was acting only as the interpreter for the Miami, not as their spokesman, but it is questionable whether they or Harrison realized that he was telling them that Pacan and Richardville were the head chiefs and, therefore, the authorized tribal spokesmen.

24. KAPPLER, 80–82. It is often stated that the Miami recognized the right of the Delaware to make the sale of the previous year, but this is not true. What the Miami did was to recognize the treaty of 1804 with the Delaware as an accomplished fact which they were now forced to accept. The Delaware relinquished any right to sell more land in the future, and the Miami extracted additional annuities for themselves in return for accepting what they realized they could not change. Harrison reported that he had agreed to "a general amnesty and act of oblivion for the past" with Wells and Turtle.

25. The suggestion of increased pay for Wells and an increase in allowance for Little Turtle came from Jefferson. ESAREY, I, 126–28. Jefferson to Harrison, April 28, 1805. The War Department had already authorized an increase for Wells and other agents, but it did not take effect until 1805.

26. THORNBROUGH (2), 168. Badollet to Gallatin, September 25, 1810.

27. Ibid., 133. Badollet to Gallatin, November 13, 1809.

28. KAPPLER, 89–90.

29. Ibid., 92–95. The Miami lodged a protest concerning their lack of compensation for other portions of the Maumee valley later purchased from other tribes, but they do not seem to have protested Hull's Treaty.

30. THORNBROUGH (2), 131–32.

31. Ibid., 172–73. Badollet to Gallatin, June 24, 1810. Badollet wrote, "I think that I informed you once, that rumours were afloat concerning the late treaties with the indians, as having been concluded under circumstances not very short of compulsion. These rumours have kept increasing and the Governor himself added weight to them by boasting in the presence of witnesses that one Winemack (or some such name), a young Potawatamie lately made chief by him, had declared to the Miamis that if they did not sign the treaty he would drive them into the lake." Badollet's identification makes it clear that it was Harrison's paid informant, Winamac, who was present with Harrison at the Treaty of Fort Wayne, not the chief of that name who signed the Greeneville Treaty. The two are frequently confused.

32. ESAREY, I, 362–78, especially 374. Journal of the Proceedings of the Indian Treaty at Fort Wayne and Vincennes, September 1–October 27, 1809. CLIFTON, 197–98, and EDMUNDS (5), 169–70, discuss the Treaty of Fort Wayne from the various Potawotami perspectives. It is to be noted that Pacan signed this treaty for the Miami.

33. The Wea Miami, who were the owners of the larger tract, were not present at Fort Wayne. The Piankashaw had formerly sold this tract to the Wabash Land Company, but the Wea had established some villages farther south since 1775. Finally, by the Treaty of Fort Wayne the Miami recognized joint ownership with the Delaware of the White River lands, and it was agreed that neither could sell without the consent of the other. By this provision Turtle and Wells hoped to strengthen the Miami position.

34. KAPPLER, 103–4, 104–5.

35. ASPIA, II, 82–83. John Johnston, testifying on September 6, 1815, said that Indian good will could not be secured while the government insisted that the Indians make land cessions. He cited the Treaty of Fort Wayne under which the government took a large tract on the Wabash in 1809 before it was needed, quoting Little Turtle as having said at the time that he could see no use in taking this land except to enable the government to get rid of the Indians living there.

36. Wells had already lost his agency for being too independent in his views. Turtle was now to lose face with the Miami for his persistent loyalty to the United States. Wells and Turtle exerted themselves to prevent the Miami from supporting Tecumseh, but Harrison and Johnston reported that the Miami would remain pro-American without crediting Wells and Turtle for their efforts.

37. Michigan and Illinois were lopped off from the Indiana Territory during the decade 1800–1810. The population of the Indiana Territory increased from 5,641 in 1800 to 24,520 in 1810; by 1820 there were 147,178 people in the state of Indiana. Thus, the rapidity of frontier settlement was directly proportional to the reduction of Indian lands. The frontier settler did not want to take his family to live in close contact with the Indians, peaceful or otherwise.

38. Harrison, indeed, had some appreciation of their services, but he had so influenced Washington officialdom against them that he could not very well stop what he had begun without hurting himself. Jefferson actually gave very little of his attention to Indian affairs. For an evaluation of Jefferson and Harrison that agrees with the one presented herein, see BILLINGTON, 273–77. Billington wrote, "Thomas Jefferson, whose frontier background transcended his well known humanitarianism, was to blame for these [land-grabbing treaties]. . . . Jefferson's agent [in the Northwest] was Governor William Henry Harrison, whose avaricious desire for Indian lands was tempered by neither sympathy nor humanitarianism."

16

The Militant Indians, 1805–10

GOVERNOR HARRISON'S INDIAN TREATIES with various tribes had added a total of nearly thirty million acres to the public lands of the United States. The Indian reaction to this policy could not have been expected to be peaceable. It was only the great influence and tremendous exertions of Little Turtle and William Wells, aided by a few other chiefs, that succeeded in rendering such a policy acceptable at all, but their support was not adequately recognized by the government. It is not surprising that President Jefferson and Governor Harrison, as representatives of great Virginia landowning families, should have spearheaded this aggressive policy, so popular among the land-hungry frontiersmen; nor that Tecumseh, a Shawnee warrior, and his one-eyed brother, Tenskwatawa, a medicine man who came to be known as The Prophet, headed the opposition among the Indians, as the Shawnee were an essentially landless and migratory tribe. The Shawnee had moved northward from Georgia and Florida in the early eighteenth century, settling in central Pennsylvania. Pushed westward by the advancing frontier, along with the Delaware, they later settled in the upper Ohio valley.

Tecumseh was born about 1768, near present-day Springfield, Ohio, on lands formerly occupied and still claimed by the Miami. His brother The Prophet was the survivor of twins who were born in 1771. Their father was killed in 1774 at the battle of Point Pleasant; their mother may have been a Creek woman.[1] The area of their birth was ceded to the United States by the Treaty of Greeneville in 1795, after which the principal Shawnee town was at Wapakoneta on the Auglaize River. Shawnee bands ranged across central and southern Indiana and into Illinois. Tecumseh himself lived on the Whitewater River and then on the White River near

184

the Delaware towns in 1803 and 1804. During these early years The Prophet was notable only as a drunkard, but in 1805, at Greeneville, he had a visionary experience which led him to reform and to announce that he spoke with the voice of the Great Spirit. His message was anti-American: he claimed that the Great Spirit had created Indians, French, Spanish, and English, but not the evil Americans. He urged the Indians to cease drinking whiskey and to return to the old way of life they had followed before the coming of white men. His doctrine did not extend so far as to include giving up the use of firearms, however, and as soon as British traders became aware of the anti-American movement, they supplied The Prophet's followers with weapons.[2]

Tecumseh joined his brother, and in the fall of 1805 they arranged a mass meeting of all the tribes, excluding the Miami and the Delaware, at Wapakoneta, where The Prophet spoke. Wells became aware of the meeting from reports of the Indians who passed through Fort Wayne on their way to Wapakoneta, and he promptly reported the news to Governor Harrison.[3] Matthew Elliott, the old Tory leader, learned of it as well, and in 1806 he established a British trader, Frederick Fisher, at Greeneville, who reported to him and who also was used by the Shawnee brothers to transmit messages to Elliott at Amherstburgh (Malden).[4]

The brothers were not successful in winning the support of Black Hoof, the principal Shawnee chief, nor of Tarhe (The Crane), principal chief of the Wyandot. The distant tribes were more responsive, and large numbers of them visited Greeneville throughout the years 1806 and 1807. Early in 1806, accusations of witchcraft made against two Delaware men, a chief named Tetaboxti and a Christianized Indian, so excited the towns on White River that the two men were burned at the stake.[5] Governor Harrison sent a message to the Delaware tribe in which he condemned The Prophet's teaching and actions. Harrison also challenged him in these words: "If he really is a Prophet, ask of him to cause the sun to stand still—the moon to alter its course—the streams to cease to flow—or the dead to rise from their graves." Unfortunately for Harrison, The Prophet knew the date of an approaching eclipse of the sun in late 1806 and announced that on that day he would cause the sun to hide its face in darkness. When this did occur, The Prophet scored a great triumph over Harrison in the minds of his followers. Henceforth they were true believers, and his fame spread over the entire Northwest.[6]

The number of Indians passing through and usually stopping at Fort Wayne during 1806 and 1807 caused a great deal of trouble for William Wells as Indian agent. The fact that they had to be fed was expensive to the government and put a strain on food supplies. The fort had a small garrison, and there was always danger of a surprise attack by some of the

Indians. Although Wells's attempts to turn back as many as possible from going to see and hear The Prophet met with some success, most were not to be deterred.[7]

Wells was also justice of the peace, and as such he performed a marriage ceremony in June 1805 for the surgeon at the fort, Dr. Abraham Edwards, who was wedded to Ruth, daughter of Colonel Thomas Hunt of the Fifth Infantry. In 1881 their son, born at Fort Wayne in 1807, related the following story, told to him by his mother, of an occurrence which probably took place in 1806.

> [Indians camped at Fort Wayne] invited the officers of the Fort to come out to witness a grand dance and other performances, previous to their departure for the Indian conference. Wells advised the commander of the Fort not to go, as he did not like the actions of the Indians; but his advice was overruled. . . . After many preliminary dances and talks, a large and powerful chief arose and commenced his dance around the ring, and made many flourishes of his tomahawk. Then he came up to Wells, who stood next to my mother, and spoke in Indian, and made demonstrations with his axe that looked dangerous, and then took his seat. But no sooner than he did so, Wells gave one of the most unearthly war-whoops she ever heard, and sprang up into the air as high as her head, and picked up a jaw-bone of a horse or ox that lay nearby, and went around the ring in a more vigorous and artistic Indian style than had been seen that evening; and wound up by going up to the big Indian and flourished his jaw-bone, and told him he had killed more Indians than he had white men, and he had killed one that looked just like him and he believed it was his brother, only a much better looking and better brave than he was. The Indians were perfectly taken by surprise. Wells turned to the officers and told them to be going. He hurried them off to the Fort and had all hands on alert all night. When questioned as to his actions and what he said, he replied that he told the Indians what I have related. Then he inquired of those who were present if they did not see that the Indians standing on the opposite side of the tent had their guns wrapped in their blankets. If I had not done just as I did, and talked to that Indian just as I did, we would all have been shot in five minutes. . . . He saw the game when he first went in, as his Indian training taught him, and he waited just for the demonstration that was made as the signal for action. Wells saw no time was to be lost and made good his resolves and the big Indian cowed under the demonstrations of Wells. . . .[8]

This incident illustrates not only the thorough knowledge that Wells had of Indian psychology but also his ability to put into practice what he knew in order to outwit them. Whenever their plans were discovered the Indians held a council to formulate a new course of action. Wells was much more disturbed by The Prophet's rise to power than were other white officials. He was perfectly aware of the nature of the danger posed by such a

186

movement and was never deceived by the pretensions of peace and freedom from British influence that the Shawnee brothers put forward for several years.

The situation of Greeneville within the state of Ohio was an added complication. The town was on the "white" side of the Greeneville Treaty line and the congregation of a large number of Indians there was cause for alarm among the settlers of the region. They sent a petition to Wells asking him to remove the Indians to some other location.[9] Wells was inclined to comply, but he needed authorization and assistance from the War Department to do so. In 1807 he offered several times to undertake personally such a mission, but he was ignored by Dearborn. Governor Harrison was also uninterested in such a project, probably because Greeneville was in Ohio and any place to which the Indians might be moved would be in Indiana Territory. His failure to back Wells in his offer to Dearborn was to prove embarrassing to him later on when the Indians themselves decided to locate on the Wabash, in closer proximity to Vincennes.

In April 1807 Wells sent Anthony Shane, a half-blood Shawnee, to invite the Shawnee brothers to come to Fort Wayne to hear a message from the War Department. Tecumseh replied very haughtily and demanded that Wells come to Greeneville instead. Wells was not disposed to do this and sent Shane back with the War Department message; it suggested that with financial aid from the War Department the Indians remove out of the area open to white settlement. After making disparaging remarks about Shane, whom he did not consider to be a suitable emissary, Tecumseh took this occasion to propose his doctrine that the Indians did not recognize any of the treaty boundaries because not all of them had consented; therefore, they would remain where they were. Thus he repudiated even the Treaty of Greeneville.[10] This was the first announcement of Tecumseh's land doctrine, which he developed more fully after the Treaty of Fort Wayne in 1809.

Wells estimated that 1,500 Indians had passed through Fort Wayne by midyear of 1807.[11] The Chesapeake-Leopard affair with the British occurred on June 22, 1807, and became known in Ohio by August 1807. Since this involved the impressment of seamen from an American naval vessel by a British naval vessel, it was widely assumed that war with Britain would ensue. Indian visits to Malden thus increased. The Jefferson administration chose to negotiate, however, and the latter portion of 1807 saw a great decline in Indian activity. The governor of Ohio sent commissioners to Greeneville to parley with the Indians, and Tecumseh accompanied them back to Chillicothe, where he declared that his intentions were entirely peaceable.[12]

Wells continued to be more concerned than most officials. On July 14, 1807, he informed Dearborn that 2,000 Indians were expected to assemble at Greeneville and that this could not be prevented except by "driving the Shawnese prophet as he is called and his band from that place which cannot be done with words." Again he volunteered to deal with the problem if authorized to do so. In the same letter he said, "The Indians are religiously *mad* and beleaves all the Shawnese (Prophet) says to them and it is much feared that his ententions are not friendly to peace. . . . He defies the United States to interrupt him and makes the indians beleave that if the government moves him from Greenville there will be an end of the world."[13] As usual, Dearborn did not reply.

Governor Harrison, however, sent a letter to the Shawnee tribe in August 1807 in which he asked them to drive The Prophet out as "he speaks not the words of the Great Spirit but those of the devil and of the British agents." The Prophet, in reply, denied that he was in collusion with the British and asserted that the Indians came to Greeneville of their own volition.[14] Although his suspicions were not entirely allayed, this time Wells was less perturbed. Little Turtle, on whom he relied for information, reported that secret meetings were being held among the Miami—meetings to which he, White Loon, The Owl, and Charley, of the Eel River Miami, were not invited because of their known friendship for the United States.[15] Wells felt less alarm chiefly because he had succeeded in preventing Marpock, a Potawatomi war chief whose village was on the Illinois River, from going to Greeneville, and he believed that Marpock would influence others.[16]

On December 5, 1807, Wells informed Dearborn "that speeches from the British agents at Malden are at this time passing through this country informing the Indians that their father King George had sent seven large vessels to America loaded with Soldiers to releave his red children from oppression and restore their country to them again." He also stated definitely that The Prophet was a British agent and had been invited to Malden.[17] This information elicited a reply from Dearborn, who instructed Wells to continue to keep an eye on The Prophet and to arrest any British agents who might be found in American territory. When at the end of the year he sent his account of money expended to the War Department, Wells added a reference to "the restless state of the Indians *but not of this agency.*"[18]

Despite Dearborn's lack of appreciation for his efforts, Wells carried out his superior's instructions and kept his eye on The Prophet. He gave Dearborn the first information of The Prophet's decision to leave Greeneville, in a communication dated March 6, 1808: "Sir: The Shawnese Prophet is about to move to the Wabash 120 miles Southwest of this place [Fort Wayne] and has sent for the sax-foxes-Iahowes-Winnebagoes & Malomenees to meet him at that place. Should he effect this, there is no doubt but He will put the tomahack in their Hands and derect them to strike the white people—and those Indians that will not listen to him—I will leave nothing undone to defeat his plans—and preserve peace."[19]

The Miami were naturally alarmed at The Prophet's intention to move to the Wabash, for this area was recognized as belonging exclusively to them. The Prophet claimed to have been invited by the Potawatomi to establish his village at the confluence of the Tippecanoe and the Wabash, near the site of the old Pepikokia village of Kithtippecanuck, or Petit Piconne. This may have been true, for the Potawatomi now occupied the full extent of the Tippecanoe River. In April 1808 Little Turtle visited The Prophet, who with sixty followers was already en route to the new location. Wells reported the visit to Dearborn, saying, "The Little Turtle has just had a meeting with the Prophet on the Massacemwey [Mississinewa] 60 miles southwest of Fort Wayne. The Turtle and other [Miami] chiefs forbid him to move from Greeneville to the lower Wabash but he defies them with a bold speech though Turtle says outcome is doubtful as Prophet is desperate."[20]

Wells had called attention many times to the fact that for two years the Indians had hunted and planted little because of their constant preoccupation with The Prophet and his movement.[21] The plain truth was now evident: to remain longer at Greeneville was to starve. Even the Miami, who were least affected by the religious madness, were very short of food in the early months of 1808. Wells found it necessary to issue to the Indians during the first three months of that year some 2,315 pounds of bread, 153 pounds of beef, 492 pounds of pork, 43 quarts of salt, 116 quarts of whiskey, and 91 rations of meat and bread.[22] In view of this problem, Little Turtle's opinion that The Prophet was desperate becomes comprehensible. It also accounts for the small number of Indians he was able to take with him, particularly when compared to the hundreds who had flocked to him earlier.

The new village was established in May, too late for planting. However, The Prophet, with forty followers, visited Vincennes in August 1808, probably as much for the purpose of receiving food from the governor as for any other reason but also emphatically to announce his peaceful intentions.[23] The governor was not altogether persuaded, for he knew that Tecumseh and five warriors had visited Matthew Elliott and William Claus at Malden in early June and had remained to attend a gathering of over 1,000 Canadian Indians in July. Tecumseh explained to the British that although he and his brother were anti-American, they were reluctant to be pro-British because they still remembered how the British had failed to keep their promises to the Indians in 1794.[24]

189

Wells proposed a visit to Washington, D.C., which Jefferson approved, for the fall of 1808. He and his party set out from Fort Wayne on November 5 and began their return in mid-January 1809. The travelers included Little Turtle and Richardville, for the Miami; Captain Hendrick, a Stockbridge Indian (Mohican), who was the civilization agent among the Delaware; Beaver, a Delaware chief; Black Hoof, head chief of the Shawnee; Raven, a Potawatomi chief; and the Potawatomi chief Marpock, with his two wives, from Illinois. President Jefferson addressed them with his usual speech, which Wells and Turtle had heard before. Wells was unable to win approval from Henry Dearborn for any of his proposals. In fact, Dearborn had already decided to replace Wells as agent but chose to do so by letter rather than in person. Marpock was drunk most of the time and was therefore difficult to manage.[25] Altogether, the trip was a costly failure.

Wells returned by way of Louisville, where he remained for a time for personal and family reasons, arriving back at Fort Wayne in April. On April 12 John Johnston, the government factor, delivered a letter from Dearborn. That letter, written soon after Wells had quitted Washington, terminated his appointment as Indian agent. Johnston was appointed in his stead.[26]

The loss of the post was a bitter blow to Wells, who complained that it left him in debt. He was retained as interpreter at a salary of $365 per annum because William Henry Harrison realized that Wells was by far the best source of information on The Prophet, Tecumseh, and all other matters pertaining to the Indians. Harrison and Johnston had undermined Wells at the War Department, but Harrison wished to continue to use Wells for his own purposes.

It is notable that The Prophet paid Johnston a visit at Fort Wayne in late May 1809, although Tecumseh had refused earlier to visit Wells there. A month later, in late June, The Prophet visited Governor Harrison again at Vincennes.[27] As a result of this visit and of the information he continued to receive from Wells, Harrison recruited two militia companies for the defense of his capital city. The tenor of Wells's reports in 1809 was that because The Prophet was proposing attacks on white settlements he was losing support among the Chippewa, the Ottawa, and the Potawatomi, who were not at this time prepared to go to war. Wells continued to stress the precarious state of the food supply of the Indians, noting that these conditions were worse at Prophetstown than elsewhere.[28] He concluded that the more warlike The Prophet became, the less support he was likely to have.

There is some ground for accepting Wells's analysis. Tecumseh, at this time, began to assume the leadership that had hitherto clearly belonged to his brother. While the brothers differed greatly in appearance and personality, the characteristic they shared was their highly effective skill as orators. Neither was a chief, yet each built up a personal following by the ability to speak with dignity and persuasion. The Prophet was rather heavyset, blind in one eye, and had coarse facial features; Tecumseh was fairly tall and muscular, of a dignified and commanding presence, and had rather handsome features. The religious fanaticism created by The Prophet was an effective background for Tecumseh's doctrine, which declared that all Indian tribes owned their lands in common and none could sell without the consent of all. From common ownership of land it followed that there should be common action by the various tribes, action which could be brought about through political confederation.

Tecumseh's self-imposed task of unification was doomed to failure from the outset, for neither common landownership nor political confederation had any basis in fact among the Indians. Perhaps he borrowed the idea of the "united states," or "seventeen fires" as the Indians called them, for white leaders pointed out the strength of such a combination. Although Tecumseh worked at confederation, there is no reason to believe that he was as near to accomplishing it as he confidently asserted. The white fear that Tecumseh might succeed was unrealistic, for common sense and a knowledge of Indian tribal government should have told them it could not be done. Indeed, Tecumseh's confederacy was never brought to completion.[29]

By comparison with Tecumseh and The Prophet, Little Turtle and William Wells, with their plan to civilize the Miami, were realists indeed. But they failed because the government would not give them a chance, whereas the Shawnee brothers did not succeed because their plans were too grandiose. Furthermore, Little Turtle and Wells were forward-looking in their plans, whereas the Shawnee brothers were backward-looking in their desire to return to Indian ways of an earlier time.

Governor Harrison's purchase of additional lands by the Treaty of Fort Wayne in the fall of 1809 brought Tecumseh to the foreground. It is clear that Harrison neither anticipated the great impetus that the final act of his rapacious land acquisition policy would give to the militant Indians nor understood why they were so outraged when it was completed. Presidents Jefferson and Madison showed no greater comprehension of the matter than did Harrison. The Treaty of Fort Wayne was not made in response to any immediate need or demand for land by settlers. It brought the boundary between white and Indian lands within sixty miles of Prophetstown and compensated not only the Miami, who were the owners of the land acquired, but also the Delaware and the Potawatomi, who were not.

The Shawnee were not participants in this treaty or in any earlier treaty made by Harrison. The Miami, who had no desire to sell the land at this time, were pressured to do so by such members of the Potawatomi as Winamac, who was employed by Harrison for that purpose. Indians of unquestioned loyalty to the United States, such as Little Turtle, were placed in an embarrassing position. Furthermore, William Wells had been ignominiously dismissed as Indian agent at Fort Wayne. The British were able to exert more influence on the Indians than ever before and control of the antiwhite movement was effectively transferred from the mystic preacher, The Prophet, to his brother Tecumseh, the warrior.[30]

Through the early months of 1810 a war belt sent by the British was circulated among the tribes in Michigan, Wisconsin, and even beyond the Mississippi.[31] Delegations from these tribes began to visit Prophetstown just as they had formerly come to Greeneville. The Prophet still spoke to them, but Tecumseh was also speaking now with authority and persuasion. In August 1810 he came to Vincennes with 300–400 followers to reply to a message in defense of the Treaty of Fort Wayne that Harrison had sent to Prophetstown.[32] There followed a remarkable confrontation of the two militant leaders, Indian and white, in which Tecumseh was impressive but allowed himself to be outmaneuvered by Harrison.

Tecumseh was emboldened by the fact that the Wyandot had at last moved closer to his position. Earlier in 1810 they had killed one of the Wyandot lesser chiefs, Leatherlips, who had been accused by The Prophet of witchcraft.[33] On August 12, 1810, Tecumseh told Harrison that he and his brother had from the first planned to wrest authority from the village chiefs and transfer it to the warriors. He admitted that he had threatened to kill those chiefs who had signed the Treaty of Fort Wayne. He repudiated all treaties on the ground that no single tribe could sell land that the Indians owned in common and disclaimed any intention of making war on the United States. But, in a way calculated to inflame his followers, he did review the history of Indian relations with the Americans since the beginning of the American Revolution, pointing out the wrongs committed by whites against Indians. In his reply, Harrison defended the Treaty of Fort Wayne on the ground that the Miami were the sole owners of the land purchased, a position he had only recently adopted. He added that if the Great Spirit had intended the Indians to hold their lands in common, he would have given them a common language.[34]

When the interpreter translated what Harrison had said Tecumseh became very excited and interrupted with a violent speech of his own. In order to avoid an armed clash, the governor told Tecumseh he would have no more to do with him, and he broke off the meeting. Later, Tecumseh sent messengers requesting that he be allowed to explain his conduct, to which Harrison consented. Tecumseh claimed to have been influenced by two white men to say that the governor had lied, which was what the interpreter said had been his words. The white men had told him that many citizens of Vincennes opposed Harrison and his policies and had assured him that Harrison would soon be out of office. This was probably true, for Harrison had many political enemies. Tecumseh reiterated that he would never accept the Treaty of Fort Wayne. Those chiefs of the Wyandot, the Kickapoo, the Potawatomi, the Ottawa, and the Winnebago who were present spoke in support of this position. Harrison promised to lay the matter before President Madison but reminded the Indians that there was no possibility the treaty would be reversed.[35]

Following the council, Harrison visited Tecumseh at his camp, where Tecumseh warned him that if the president did not reverse the treaty he would be forced to ally himself with the British, an action he would prefer not to take. In November 1810 Tecumseh, accompanied by 169 warriors of many tribes, told Matthew Elliott, in Malden that in one more year his confederacy would be completed and that he would be ready for war. He stated that Harrison had forced him into the open and that there was no longer any need for secrecy.[36]

Harrison knew that he had pressed Tecumseh to the point of open avowal of his intentions. The Prophet had always denied any connection with the British, but Tecumseh was more forthright and less deceitful than his brother. He was also more arrogant and unable to conceal his contemptuous feelings for the governor and his hatred of Americans generally. Harrison, from this time, began definite preparations for a war that he was certain would come and in which he decided to take the offensive rather than await attack. Tecumseh had failed to discern the possibility of such action.[37]

During his conference with Harrison, Tecumseh had said that "a man of sense," whom he did not identify, had told him that Harrison had de-liberately excluded Tecumseh and The Prophet from the negotiations at the Treaty of Fort Wayne, that Harrison had said The Prophet was a bad man and no traders could operate in his village, and that it was Harrison's intention to confine all the Indians to a very small piece of land. Harrison reported to Eustis, secretary of war under President Madison, that "the man of sense" referred to by Tecumseh was William Wells. He considered his identification to be "beyond all doubt" but gave no reasons for his conclusion.[38] It must be remembered that Wells had never had anything to do with Tecumseh, nor Tecumseh with Wells, and that Wells had been the earliest and most persistent critic of The Prophet. There is no record of Tecumseh visiting Fort Wayne or of Wells visiting Prophetstown in the period between the Treaty of Fort Wayne and Tecumseh's trip to Vin-cennes nearly a year later. It is almost certain, therefore, that Harrison was unjust to Wells in this matter.[39]

It must be stressed that Little Turtle and Wells were caught between the militant Indians exemplified by Tecumseh and the militant white men represented by Harrison. Clearly, their loyalty was to the United States, but the government never trusted them. Their sympathies were with the Indians, but the militant Indian movement was repugnant and ridiculous to their moderate way of thinking. Although Wells had been deprived of his agency, there is not the slightest evidence that either he or Little Turtle ever wavered in their support of the government. They adhered steadily to the course they had chosen from the outset, and nothing deterred them from following the path of reason in an unreasonable world.[40]

NOTES

1. See TECUMSEH, 25. R. David Edmunds, *The Shawnee Prophet* (1983), confirms these facts as the most reliable regarding the Shawnee brothers' birth and parentage. All books on the subject are based largely upon DRAKE (1), which was based on information from Anthony Shane and from Stephen Ruddell.

2. TECUMSEH, 105–17. It was at this time that The Prophet changed his name from Laulewasikaw (The Noise Maker) to Tenskwatawa (The Open Door).

3. BRICE, 170. In 1805, when The Prophet first became active, Harrison urged Dearborn to dismiss Wells because of his letter, written for Little Turtle to Wilkinson, protesting Harrison's land purchase from the Delaware. Harrison and Wells resolved their differences in August 1805, however, and Harrison, writing to Dearborn on July 11, 1807, reminded him of how fully Wells had kept them informed concerning the activities of The Prophet.

4. HORSMAN, 168–69.

5. WESLAGER, 342–44.

6. ESAREY, I, 191–95.

7. WOEHRMANN, 185. Captain Hendrick, a Stockbridge Indian (Mohican) living among the Delaware, told Wells that The Prophet was angry with Wells for preventing Indians from visiting him and said that Wells should have a rope put around his neck.

8. WENTWORTH, Appendix D, 56–57. A. H. Edwards to John Wentworth, Sheboygan, Wisconsin, June 10, 1881. This incident could not have occurred after June 1, 1810, on which date Dr. Edwards resigned his commission.

9. WOEHRMANN, 178.

10. DRAKE (1), 91–93. Also DRAPER, 11YY49.

11. BRICE, 172–73. Most of the Indians had new British rifles.

12. Ibid., 173–75. Blue Jacket was associated with Tecumseh at this time.

13. CARTER (1), VII, 465. William Wells to Henry Dearborn, July 14, 1807. In contrast to the offers of Wells to lead an expedition to drive the Shawnee brothers from Greeneville, John Johnston suggested removing them by poison! Wells made no offer to assassinate Tecumseh and The Prophet, though certain writers have accused him of it.

14. ESAREY, I, 249–51.

15. Ibid., 239–43. Five Medals, chief of the Potawatomi on the Elkhart River, was also among those excluded.

16. CARTER (1), VII, 555–60. Wells to Dearborn, April 20, 22, 23, 1808. Wells spent about $800 of government money on Marpock, who said, "My friend, you have caught me like a wild horse is caught, with a lick of salt you hobbled me. I can no longer range the woods as I please. You must now git a Bell and put on my neck when I shall always be in your Hearing. . . ." I have used Wells's spelling of Marpock, which is more properly spelled Main Poche (Puckered Hand). His actions are more fully narrated and his character more fully discussed in CLIFTON, 194–99, and in EDMUNDS (5), 166–68, 174–75, 181–85.

17. CARTER (1), VII, 499–500. Wells to Dearborn, December 5, 1807.

18. Ibid., 510. Wells to Dearborn, December 31, 1807.

19. Ibid., 531–32. Wells to Dearborn, March 6, 1808.

20. Ibid., 558.

21. WOERHMANN, 184, 188.

22. CARTER (1), VII, 542.

23. BRICE, 178–79.

24. HORSMAN, 170–72.

25. WOEHRMANN, 189–90; HUTTON, 212–13.

26. CARTER (1), VII, 647–48. John Johnston to Dearborn, April 15, 1809. Johnston wrote, "Sir: I had the honor to receive your letter of the 27th January covering an appointment for me as Indian Agent at this Post, together with a letter of discharge for William Wells, the late agent, which was handed to him on the 12th Inst. . . ."

27. WOEHRMANN, 191–92.

28. There is reason to think Wells was right about this, for Harrison referred to the large and starving following that The Prophet was forced to feed. After the battle of Tippecanoe, Harrison destroyed between 100 and 200 acres of corn at Prophetstown. This was a small amount under cultivation, in view of the constant stream of visiting Indians who came there. John Johnston agreed with Wells in regard to the shortage of food among the Indians.

29. This is not to disparage Tecumseh's efforts but rather to stress the difficulties of communication over distances which rendered a confederacy impossible in any practical sense.

30. HORSMAN, passim. Tecumseh was also dependent on whether or not the British were anticipating an American war. Often when the Indians were worked to a high pitch of warlike fervor, the British had to restrain them; at times the opposite was true.

31. Ibid., 171.

32. WOEHRMANN, 199. The Prophet was abusive toward Harrison's messengers, but Tecumseh responded by saying he would go to Vincennes.

33. TECUMSEH, 170–73. It is uncertain whether Tarhe (The Crane) authorized the killing of Leatherlips or not. Harrison thought not.

34. ESAREY, I, 459–69.

35. BRICE, 189.

36. HORSMAN, 180.

37. ESAREY, I, 491. In his annual message to the territorial legislature, Harrison admitted his error in formerly believing The Prophet to be friendly to the United States.

38. WOEHRMANN, 163, 200.

39. These conclusions are my own. Tecumseh's "man of sense" remains unidentified.

40. EDMUNDS (4), passim, refers to Little Turtle, Black Hoof, Tarhe, and Five Medals as "government chiefs," which seems to imply that they owed their position and authority to the federal government. They were legitimate chiefs by Indian tribal custom and were not dependent on the United States for their power or influence. They had made peace at Greeneville in 1795 and meant to keep the terms of that treaty. Little Turtle's situation was different from that of the other chiefs mentioned in that he was a war chief seeking to influence affairs in peacetime by working with and through the Miami civil chiefs without arousing their resentment. The deference accorded him by the United States government was a help that easily became a hindrance.

17

The Family Compact: Third Phase, 1803–10

PERHAPS THE MOST CONVINCING EVIDENCE for the continuation of the Family Compact that existed between Little Turtle and William Wells is to be found in their persistent efforts to get government support for a "civilization program" that would be placed in their own hands. So far as it is possible to determine, the original impetus in this direction came from Turtle's conviction that the Indians could not survive without changing their way of living. Turtle and Wells advocated peace with the United States, gradual sale of the land by consent of tribal chiefs, and use of money gained thereby to change the Indian way of life. They planned to work with the village and tribal chiefs.[1]

Little Turtle and Wells must have returned to Fort Wayne from Washington, D.C., in 1802 with some feelings of satisfaction, for Wells, who was already the resident interpreter, had been appointed Indian agent as well. An act of Congress, passed on March 1, 1793, provided for such appointments of persons to reside temporarily among the Indians and furnish them with such goods, money, domestic animals, and implements for farming as might be authorized by the president. Agents were also expected to disburse the annuities guaranteed to tribes by various treaties, convene Indian councils to receive and discuss messages from the government, report to the government matters of importance concerning the movements and activities of Indian tribes, and in general to act as intermediaries between the Indian tribes and the federal government.[2] Wells and Turtle could assume, therefore, that the civilization program which they advocated would be administered by Wells, an assumption that turned out to be too optimistic.

On July 1, 1802, an Indian factory was established at Fort Wayne, with John Johnston as factor. A factor was essentially a businessman whose duties were to take in peltry from the Indians, paying them in goods furnished by the government; he was not required to show a large profit, but he was not expected to operate at a loss either. Nor did the factory have a monopoly of the Indian fur trade, for private traders might still procure government licenses to go among the Indians with goods to exchange for furs. Either the factor or the Indian agent could issue such licenses, or they could be and usually were issued by the superintendent of Indian affairs, who was also the territorial governor. This system was inimical to the civilization program because private traders were always well stocked with liquor. Wells was ordered to build the government factory for storing goods and also a private residence adjacent to it for the factor.[3]

From the outset Wells and Johnston had trouble getting along. No specific cause for this has ever come to light, but it was not long before Johnston was writing to Governor Harrison and to Secretary of War Dearborn in criticism of virtually everything that Wells did. Johnston's efforts to dislodge Wells were unremitting, but so underhanded were his methods that the two men worked together at Fort Wayne for some time before their difficulties became public knowledge.[4]

The trouble between Governor Harrison and Wells was of a different sort, and there is no doubt as to the cause: Wells and Harrison had different concepts of the duties of an Indian agent. Harrison's view was that agents were responsible only to the government; Wells thought that agents had responsibilities to the Indians as well as to the government. Harrison believed that Wells and Turtle had no business to question his land acquisition policy, but in their view they had every right to do so. The law was intended to operate so that the agent could present the opinions of the Indians to the government as well as the views of the government to the Indians. In practice, it was difficult for an agent to do so without incurring the government's displeasure.[5]

To Little Turtle the civilization program was of vital importance, for he was convinced that unless the Indians could be persuaded to live by agriculture and stock raising they were doomed to extinction. Turtle and Wells believed that they could persuade and teach the Miami to adopt the white man's ways well enough to give them a fair chance of survival. In order to do this they had to have the control of the government program and the backing of the government. They did not succeed in getting either.[6]

At the outset they were disposed to go along with the Quaker administration of the civilization program because they had heard good reports of it and because President Jefferson obviously wished the Quakers to be in charge. However, Little Turtle was never deterred from his central objective. In his meeting with Jefferson in 1802 he mentioned the friendly Quakers but in addition asked the government to provide tools and a resident blacksmith, and he requested that Wells be placed in charge of the civilization program at Fort Wayne. He also extended a verbal invitation to the Baltimore Quakers to visit Fort Wayne in order to see for themselves what needed to be done. Later, on September 18, 1803, he repeated his invitation in writing.[7] The response was fairly prompt, and on February 23, 1804, Gerard T. Hopkins, George Ellicott, and young Philip Dennis set out for Fort Wayne, where they arrived on March 30, 1804. Hopkins and Ellicott remained only two weeks, but Philip Dennis stayed until autumn in order to demonstrate to the Miami the methods of farming used by the whites.[8]

Gerard Hopkins kept a journal of his trip and brief visit to Fort Wayne, during which he met with Little Turtle and the Potawatomi chief Five Medals, as well as some of their people. As Turtle explained, the attendance was somewhat small because many were engaged at this season in making maple sugar.

Hopkins affords an unusual sidelight on the personality of Little Turtle. The Quakers had been shown the spot near the junction of the three rivers from which the chief had directed his warriors in 1790 in defeating General Harmar. It was the season when the lake sturgeon swam up the Maumee and entered the St. Joseph and St. Marys rivers in great numbers to deposit their eggs. Little Turtle was in good humor, and in company with Wells, Johnston, and Hopkins jokingly proposed that they ought to build a wall across the Maumee at the junction in order to keep the sturgeon penned in the upper streams. He laughed and said, "We will eat sturgeon all summer and get very fat."[9]

Wells took Philip Dennis to the Forks of the Wabash where Chief Richardville afterward established his home. Dennis began plowing, planting, and cultivating crops on the fertile land located there, a site chosen specifically to avoid any trouble that might arise from favoring one village over another. Indian men are said to have come from nearby villages to watch Dennis work, but none of them would help him. After harvesting his crops Dennis returned to the East.[10] Although the Quakers were willing and well intentioned, their good example was not enough for the Indian men to learn from them. The Indians were not willing to follow the lead of strangers, and in addition they needed someone in authority who was ever present, not only to persuade them to try, but to see that they kept on trying. The efforts of Wells to explain this to Dearborn met with no success.

After Wells and Little Turtle settled their difficulties with Harrison in August 1805, at Grouseland, the government built a house for Turtle a mile or so up the Eel River from Turtletown. It was a log structure, about eighteen by twenty feet.[11] For the next three years, some of the Miami annuities were used to defray the cost of maintaining a blacksmith and a carpenter at Fort Wayne. Annuity money also was used at Turtletown and at Dennis's Station, and perhaps elsewhere, to employ whites to help with various activities related to the civilization project.[12] However, it became clear that little progress could be made without the appropriation of government money for such activities. Accordingly, Wells once more proposed a plan to Dearborn whereby the various tribes interested in becoming civilized might be gathered in twelve settlements and each tribe be given someone whom the Indians knew and had confidence in to supervise the work and the expenditure involved.[13]

It was probably in the winter of 1805–6 that Sweet Breeze, daughter of Little Turtle, wife of Wells, and mother of a son and three daughters by him, died after a marriage of about fifteen years. The reason for this conclusion is that the children spent the next three years at the home of their uncle Samuel Wells in Kentucky. Here they received some schooling and a rather thorough training in good manners. Some letters bearing witness to this, written to their father by Ann and Rebekah, the two oldest children, have been preserved.[14] Their mother remains a person of whom only her lovely name is known. In fact, her very existence might be questioned but for the solid evidence of her four children. Although she was the original link in the Family Compact, her passing did not in any way weaken that bold design to bridge the gap between the races.[15]

It is thought that about this time Little Turtle took a second wife, said to have been a niece of his first wife, who was still living. Possibly the house built for him by the government may have been a cause for this expansion of his household.[16]

In the spring of 1806 a Quaker, William Kirk, and his brother, Mahlon, came to Fort Wayne and remained in the vicinity until fall. They were presumably laboring among the Indians on behalf of the Baltimore Quakers to further their civilization project. While there is no question but that Little Turtle and Wells cooperated with Philip Dennis as well as they could, they not only refused cooperation with Kirk but actively opposed him. What remains in doubt is whether this was their attitude from the outset or whether their attitude was changed in response to something Kirk did to offend them.

The Kirks visited the Delaware towns on White River before returning to Baltimore, but their reception was discouraging. Nonetheless, William Kirk made such a favorable report to the Baltimore Quakers that in 1807 they succeeded in receiving an appropriation of $6,000 from Congress and an appointment for Kirk as civilization agent at Fort Wayne. He and his brother, with five helpers and supplies purchased in Cincinnati, arrived at Fort Wayne on April 20, 1807, at a time when John Johnston was absent. Wells consented to act as interpreter for them and appears to have secured promises of cooperation from Richardville and Five Medals.

Kirk then proposed to establish his farming operations among the Mississinewa Miami and at the Potawatomi village of Five Medals, not at Turtletown nor at Dennis's Station, both nearer to Fort Wayne. Kirk's agricultural judgment was good because the places he chose possessed better land and drainage. His political judgment, however, was very poor, for Little Turtle was offended and made such strenuous objections that Richardville and Five Medals dared not oppose him. Since Wells knew that Turtle was the main advocate of the civilization project, he sided with his partner in the Family Compact and opposed Kirk's plans, going so far as to forbid him to go to Five Medals's Village. John Johnston, having returned to Fort Wayne, now sided with Kirk and made further complaints against Wells to Dearborn. While this imbroglio was going on, the season for planting passed and nothing was accomplished.[17]

Dearborn, at the War Department, condemned Wells for his opposition to Kirk, accepting Johnston's accusations against Wells, as he had always done. Wells, however, fought back with considerable skill and some success. He accused Kirk of having appropriated Little Turtle's plan as his own in order to get the appointment and the money from the government. In a letter to Dearborn, Wells pointed out that Kirk was living at his house as his guest in 1806 when he met Turtle and learned of his plan, and also at the time when he accused Wells of noncooperation in 1807. Said Wells, "This man may be a Quaker but I cannot beleave he is one of the Best Sort. . . ." He further pointed out, "I was the only advocate in this country of civillizing the Indians and the only person that had made any attempt at it. . . ." Finally, he stated that the Miami would not work with Kirk even if the president himself came and told them to do so.[18]

Wells buttressed his position with the backing not only of Little Turtle but also of The Owl, Richardville, Five Medals, and many other chiefs, all of whom sent President Jefferson a letter, the accuracy of which was attested to by John Johnston's signature. The Indians expressed their lack of confidence in Kirk because he had arrived too late for planting and had spent half of his funds before arrival. Wells, who no doubt composed the letter, also wrote to Dearborn, offering to come to the nation's capital to prove his charges against Kirk to the government and the Baltimore Friends. Wells claimed that Little Turtle and other Miami "took fire" at Kirk's charges against Wells because they feared they had thus far spent their annuity money for nothing.[19]

In his first report to Dearborn, Kirk's request for more money led the secretary of war to transfer him to the Shawnee at Wapakoneta, where, with the patronage of Johnston, who had influence among the Shawnee, he did very well. At the end of 1808, however, despite his success with the Shawnee, Dearborn dismissed Kirk because of his inability to account satisfactorily for funds expended.[20]

It was no part of John Johnston's duty as factor to report on the character of the Indian agent William Wells, but he had done so both to Governor Harrison and to Secretary of War Dearborn from the beginning of his residency at Fort Wayne, and he continued to do so over the years. The most serious charge that he made was that Wells was dishonest. Governor Harrison was careful to make no such charges himself, but he repeated to Dearborn those charges made by Johnston. As a result, Dearborn became convinced that Wells was untrustworthy. Wells was accused of holding Indian annuities, selling liquor to the Indians, and cheating the government in various other ways. Little Turtle was also accused of keeping Indian annuities that should have been distributed to the tribe.[21] None of these charges were ever substantiated. In the known cases of delayed annuities either Wells reported that he was delaying them for some specific reason, or it has been shown that the money had not been sent because of some error in Washington.[22]

Historians are entitled to dismiss all such accusations as unproven, for they were never investigated. Constant repetition of unproven charges, however, has often led historians to suspect that there must be some truth in the accusations. Such a conclusion is unjustified. Furthermore, even if the charges made against Wells and Turtle were true, it would need to be shown that they used the money for their own purposes. Both men followed the Indian rules of hospitality and provided food to any hungry Indian, so that some of their private income probably went for this purpose in times of scarcity of food. A case could be made, therefore, that Wells and Turtle should be extenuated, if they used government money illegally for this purpose; but most emphatically it has never been shown that they did so, even in a single case. Quite unjustly, when Wells reported more money spent for food for hungry Indians than Dearborn thought was necessary, he was admonished and told that if he had not opposed Kirk, plenty of food would have been available. Rather than planting, many Indians had spent their summer idly with the Shawnee Prophet, and Dearborn thus shifted the blame to Wells.[23]

At the close of the year 1807, Wells became tired of being lectured by Dearborn about the Kirk affair. He had received a rebuke from Dearborn in which the latter had written, "Either you possess no kind of useful influence with the chiefs in your agency or that you make an improper use of what you possess. In either case, you cannot be considered well qualified for the place that you hold."[24] Wells, suspecting that his place as Indian agent was endangered, characteristically mounted an offensive of his own. He noted that all the other Indian agents had housing furnished by the government but that he had had to provide his own dwelling, including his firewood; he therefore requested that a new dwelling be provided for him. He also reminded Dearborn that in 1801 the president had promised him the rank, pay, and emoluments of a colonel but that he had received far less than he was assured; he therefore requested that the arrears due him now be paid. Further, he asked that payment for his services as interpreter at several of Harrison's treaties be made.[25] Since Jefferson and Harrison were still in office, Wells would hardly have made such claims if they had not been true, although of course the president and governor might plead that they had no recollection of these matters.

Dearborn made no reply to Wells, but he did write Harrison that he feared "Wells is too attentive to pecuniary considerations" and that he had "lost much of my Confidence in his integrity." Wells was planning a trip to Washington in the fall of 1808, at which time he hoped to have redress in these matters. Meanwhile, he sent in his quarterly accounts and called Dearborn's attention to the fact that the proper vouchers were enclosed and that all annuities had been delivered to the Indians on time.[26]

Sometime after the death of Sweet Breeze, Wells made another Indian marriage, but there is no reliable information regarding the wife that he chose. It is conceivable that he was reunited with his first Indian wife, but there is no evidence for this except the fact that a letter to Dearborn dated March 6, 1808, enclosed a letter of Captain Hendrick's, which contained "an allusion to the Death of my son who was kild by accedent a few days ago."[27] This could only refer to the child by his first wife, since his son by Sweet Breeze was still alive. Obviously, he had been in touch with this son over the years, but it would be unwarranted to conclude that he was also in touch with the boy's mother. Sometime in the first half of 1808, however, he became the father of a girl, named Jane Wells, who lived most of her life on the Wabash at Peru, Indiana. It is a reasonable assumption that her mother also lived in that area.[28]

The trip to Washington made by Little Turtle and other chiefs under Wells's guidance in 1808–9 was a disappointment. Wells's young son by Sweet Breeze, William Wayne Wells, who was about twelve years old, accompanied them. None of Wells's requests were met by Dearborn. Even his offer to administer the civilization program without additional salary was disregarded. Dearborn had made up his mind to dismiss Wells but lacked the courage to do it personally; instead, he accomplished it by letter, not to Wells, but to Johnston for delivery to Wells. This appears to have been an act of personal dislike on the part of Dearborn, for he was leaving office on March 4, 1809, and might well have left the matter to his successor.

This trip was the last of Little Turtle's many visits to the capital and was a difficult one for him because of his increasingly painful gout. However, the otherwise unprofitable visit did produce one of the best descriptions ever made of him.

> The Little Turtle and Rusherville, the Beaver and Crow (Delawares) and the two Shawnee (Blackhoof was one) were dressed in a costume usually worn by our own citizens of the time—coats of blue cloth, gilt buttons, pantaloons of the same color, and buff waistcoats, but they all wore leggings, moccasins, and large gold rings in their ears. The Little Turtle exceeded all his brother chiefs in dignity of appearance—a dignity which resulted from the character of his mind. He was of medium stature, with a complexion of the palest copper shade, and did not wear paint. His hair was a full suit, and without any admixture of gray. . . . His dress was completed by a long red military sash around the waist and his hat (a chapeau bras) was ornamented with a red feather. Immediately on entering the house he took off his hat and carried it under his arm during the rest of the visit. His appearance and manners, which were graceful and agreeable in an uncommon degree, were admired by all who made his acquaintance.[29]

John Johnston, no friend of Little Turtle while he lived, although he did not hate him as he did Wells, had laudatory things to say of him many years after his death. He wrote a description that substantiates and strengthens the one just quoted.

> Little Turtle—I consider him the superior of Tecumtha in all the essential qualities of a great man . . . a distinguished orator, Councilor and Warrior, my acquaintance with him was long, intimate and gratifying; as a public speaker I thought him the most animated, graceful and close reasoner of any of his color. I had heard his knowledge of the migrations, history, government, customs and territorial rights of the various tribes was accurate and extensive. In a Council with the Commissioners of the United States, he had not an equal among his people. Governor Harrison often admitted his great tact and talent and the trouble he gave him in the acquisition of the Indian lands. His person was of the medium size, graceful and well formed, had a peculiar squint of the eyes, when speaking, they flashed with fire, energy and zeal, his gesture was natural, noble and dignified; words flowed like torrents, never embarrassed or at a loss or fault in his subject, dressed with taste, a fur cap, blue frock coat and scarlet sash.[30]

Little Turtle and the other Indians returned from Washington to their respective homes. Wells traveled by way of Louisville where he remained for several weeks. On March 7, 1809, he married Mary (Polly) Geiger, whom he had apparently met at some time prior to this, while visiting his children at the home of his older brother, Samuel Wells.[31] She was the daughter of Colonel Frederick Geiger (1753–1832), who had moved from Maryland to Louisville about 1790.[32] Wells had probably terminated his marriage to the mother of Jane Wells a few months after Jane's birth. Among the Miami a marriage could be ended by either man or wife by a simple leave-taking with one's personal possessions. William and Polly Wells returned to Fort Wayne in early April, bringing with them Wells's four children by his marriage with Sweet Breeze. On April 12, 1809, Wells was handed his discharge by Dearborn, courtesy of John Johnston. It must have been a most unexpected and unwelcome wedding present.

Wells was a fighter and immediately began his campaign to regain his agency. His thorough preparation for waging this political battle arouses admiration. He learned that Johnston had been his secret enemy for years, for Johnston was now not only factor but Indian agent at Fort Wayne and had been given an assistant agent who was paid $350 a year. The assistant, John Shaw, turned out to be nearly as bitter an enemy of Wells as Johnston himself.

Wells began by simply continuing to make reports to Harrison and Eustis, the new secretary of war, as if he were still agent.[33] Next, he secured through Little Turtle the support of all the important Miami chiefs. Then he asked for letters in his behalf from General Wilkinson, from Captain Nathan Heald, who commanded at Fort Wayne, from a number of other local army officers, and, finally, from Governor Harrison himself. Each wrote to Eustis.[34]

Governor Harrison, who had himself more than once suggested that Dearborn dismiss Wells, was nonetheless surprised when that occurred.[35] Aware of the danger posed by the militant movement led by Tecumseh, he realized that Little Turtle was the mainstay of the Miami against Tecumseh's influence and that Wells was his own most reliable source of information on this movement. He was also interested in more land grabbing and accepted the offer of Wells to act as interpreter at the Treaty of Fort Wayne in the latter part of 1809. He gave Wells a foothold at Fort Wayne by making him official interpreter there at $365 per year, an appointment which Eustis confirmed.

John Johnston, meanwhile, was not idle. He repeatedly blackened Wells in his letters to Eustis, saying there could not be a worse man, that Wells was so crooked that he would not believe him if he knew he was telling the truth, that he could not understand why Governor Harrison wanted to employ him, that Wells had amassed $50,000 by cheating the Indians, and that Eustis should not believe any of the testimonials of character that Wells was sending him. Johnston claimed that the Miami were pleased to have him as agent in place of Wells. He suggested that Wells had lied about the danger from Tecumseh and The Prophet in order to enhance his own reputation.[36] In this Johnston went too far, because it was obvious to Eustis and Harrison that Wells had been right all along about the Shawnee brothers and their intentions. Johnston reversed himself on this matter and suggested that if Eustis would give his approval, he could arrange to have both of the brothers assassinated by Indians.

The anti-Wells attitudes of Dearborn, Eustis, and Harrison are readily explainable. Dearborn had employed Johnston as a clerk at the War Department before Johnston was appointed factor at Fort Wayne. Whenever Johnston and Wells differed, Dearborn accepted the views of his former clerk.[37] Eustis was new to the controversy, did not want to become involved in it, and was inclined to accept the policy decisions already adopted at the War Department. Harrison had never forgiven Wells for defending the right of the Miami to refuse to sell their land. He was a politician and suspected Wells of political ambitions that might run counter to his own.

It is more difficult to account for Johnston's extreme feelings against Wells. He was influenced by anti-Miami sentiment among the Shawnee at Wapakoneta, but this cannot have been of primary importance. Johnston had failed in business and, although he blamed the failure on his brother, it might have hurt him to see others succeed more than himself.[38] Because he regarded Wells as a renegade he thought him undeserving of his military pension and his land grant.[39] Possibly Johnston was lacking in courage and detested Wells because he seemed not to know the meaning of fear. Whatever the cause of the factor's unscrupulous bitterness toward the Indian agent, the result was most unfortunate for the plans of Little Turtle and the future of the Miami, for Johnston would stop at nothing in seeking to damage Wells so long as he could do it underhandedly.

An example is found in Johnston's report to Dearborn that the army surgeon at Fort Wayne, Abraham Edwards, had advised him to report Wells to the government. Yet the fact is that Edwards had signed a testimonial for Wells. One is forced to conclude that Dr. Edwards had merely said, "Take it up with the government," when Johnston had sought to enlist him against Wells. Johnston told Eustis that those who wrote on behalf of Wells were acting against their country.[40]

Meanwhile, after the Treaty of Fort Wayne, Wells and Turtle once more fell under the suspicion of Governor Harrison, who seems not to have understood the difficult position he had put them in by the unnecessary sale of lands that he had forced the Miami to make. Johnston reinforced this with the report that Wells and Turtle were intriguing to replace him. At a council that Johnston held in October 1810, Pacan, the Atchatchakangouen Miami head chief, told Johnston that if the United States wished to hold the land purchased by the Treaty of Fort Wayne, it would have to build a bridge across it. Johnston replied that they would build a bridge with armed men, if need be.[41] Johnston and Harrison seem to have missed the significance of Pacan's statement. The Miami were in real danger of joining Tecumseh; the government was in real need of Little Turtle and Wells, whom it had cast aside. Yet just prior to this Johnston had written to Harrison, saying, "The Turtle is contemptible beyond description in the eyes of the Indians," and that he would not allow him to go to Washington to see the president for he had been there too often already.[42]

Johnston could not prevent Wells from going to Washington, however, and, characteristically, Wells told Johnston before he left Fort Wayne that Senator John Pope of Kentucky had promised to retrieve the agency for him.[43] Undoubtedly Wells's father-in-law and his brother Samuel had urged Senator Pope in his behalf. In the winter of 1810–11, Wells made his journey to the capital and with the support of Pope won at least a partial victory. Eustis said he was unable to replace Johnston with Wells because of objections that Harrison had made to Dearborn concerning Wells's conduct of the agency. Wells showed that Harrison's objections no longer held, and Eustis left the matter to Harrison. With Pope applying political pressure Wells was made subagent for the Miami. John Shaw received a similar appointment for the Potawatomi, and John Conner for the Delaware. Later, in August 1811, John Johnston resigned the agency at Fort Wayne and became agent for the Shawnee at Piqua.[44]

Before his resignation Johnston also went to Washington and prevailed upon the War Department to appoint Benjamin Stickney, a New Englander, to the Fort Wayne agency. Eustis now told Harrison that he could transfer Wells elsewhere, but Harrison was fearful of Tecumseh and The Prophet and decided to keep Wells at Fort Wayne.[45] Although Wells had indicated that he preferred the position of civilization agent to recovering his agency, no attention was paid to his preference.[46] This is significant because it indicates the genuine concern that both Little Turtle and Wells felt for the Miami. The government, however, was more concerned with the growing prospect of war with Great Britain and had lost most of its interest in the civilization project. Harrison certainly had no concern for it and was actively preparing to take the offensive against the Indian militants at Prophetstown. Where Little Turtle had hoped for a peaceful transition of the Miami to the white man's economy, the government officials had succeeded only in producing chaos.

Whether Turtle and Wells could have made any progress with the Miami, if their own ideas on civilizing them had been financed by the government under their own supervision, it is impossible to say. They did have a plan as to how to proceed and sufficient knowledge of the tribe and influence among them to have had a better chance of success than anyone else. There is no doubt that they expected to make their own living from the administration of the plan. The cost of their administration, whether viewed as legitimate by the government or not, would have been far less than the percentage usually paid for such work. It is regrettable that Jefferson and his administration did not give them the chance.[47]

NOTES

1. By contrast, the Shawnee brothers planned to overthrow all village and tribal chiefs and seize control for themselves.

2. THORNBROUGH (1), 11.

3. Ibid., 12

4. Ibid., 14–21. If Wells kept a letter book during the period of his agency it has not been found.

5. It is unfortunate that William Wells was unsuccessful in maintaining a more independent status as agent. Had he succeeded, the whole history of governmental relations with the Indians would have been changed for the better. As it turned out, Indian agents became virtually powerless to act for the welfare of the Indians. Agencies were increasingly sought by unscrupulous men who cheated both the government and the Indians and often got away with it for years.

6. SHEEHAN (1), 44–45. Sheehan observes that Jefferson's program imposed on the white man the obligation to make it happen and on the Indian the desire to abandon his past and become a white man. It should be noted that only a minority of whites or Indians fulfilled this condition. The great mistake of Jefferson, Harrison, and Dearborn was their failure to recognize that Little Turtle and Wells fulfilled this requirement.

7. HOPKINS, 164–65, 169–73.

8. Ibid., passim, especially 46–49, 52–53, 69, 70–80. Hopkins enjoyed a dinner of boiled turkey and roast turkey with cranberry sauce in Wells's home, prepared and served by Wells's wife. His mention of the fact provides what is probably the only contemporary reference to Sweet Breeze.

9. Ibid., 90. Another story about Little Turtle was told by John Johnston. In the 1780s when the chief was raiding white settlements in Kentucky and Ohio, the Miami had taken captive a white man, who pleaded to be allowed to accompany them in a raid on the white settlers, a request that was granted. The Miami warriors, led by Turtle, were creeping up on an isolated settlement of a few cabins in a clearing. The settlers were unaware of their approach through the bushes. Just as Turtle was about to give the signal to spring from concealment, the white captive ran toward the settlers, waving his hands and yelling, "Indians! Indians!" at the top of his voice. HILL, 161–67. Little Turtle was very fond of telling this story and always laughed heartily about it because the joke was on him. Such stories illustrate his affable nature and his sense of humor.

10. THORNBROUGH (1), 37. The site of Dennis's Station, sometimes referred to as Little Turtle's Farm School, was seven miles below the Forks of the Wabash,

four miles east of present-day Lagro. Richardville's house can still be seen near the Forks. It is owned by Mr. Luke Sheer, of Huntington, Indiana.

11. YOUNG (2), 113.

12. WOEHRMANN, 117. A small trading post was also located on the Eel River, one-half mile east of Little Turtle's house, established by the government for his convenience.

13. CARTER (1), VII, 510-11. Wells to Dearborn, December 31, 1807. Wells estimated that $3,600 would suffice for a beginning.

14. These letters were presented to the Allen County-Fort Wayne Historical Society by Oliver Farrand, grandson of Rebekah Wells Hackley, in 1921.

15. A silhouette of Mrs. William Wells owned by the Chicago Historical Society is said to be a likeness of Sweet Breeze but is more probably one of Polly Geiger Wells, since it is said to have been made in 1810 and the features and hair styling appear to be those of a white woman rather than an Indian woman (see Figure 14).

16. HILL, 161.

17. LRSW, Reg. Ser., Record Group 107. Kirk to Dearborn, May 28, 1807; Wells to Kirk, copy to Dearborn, June 18, 1807; Johnston to Dearborn (private), May 31, 1807. The location of the projects was important. Richardville and Five Medals would not support the project unless their villages were chosen for the farm sites. Had the government been earnest and efficient all of these sites would have been developed.

18. CARTER (1), VII, 469-70. Wells to Dearborn, August 20, 1807.

19. Ibid. See also WOEHRMANN, 124-27.

20. THORNBROUGH (1), 19; WOEHRMANN, 130-31.

21. ESAREY, I, 141-47. Harrison to Dearborn, July 10, 1805.

22. THORNBROUGH (1), 68-69; Harrison to Eustis, October 3, 1809.

23. CARTER (1), VII, 555-60. Wells to Dearborn, April 20, 1808.

24. Ibid., 467. Dearborn to Wells, August 5, 1807. On microfilm "considered" appears to be "conceded," but the meaning is the same in either case.

25. LRSW, Reg. Ser., Record Group 107. Wells to Dearborn, September 30, 1807; Wells to Dearborn, December 31, 1807.

26. Ibid. Henry Dearborn was appointed by President Madison to the lucrative post of collector of the Port of Boston upon his resignation as secretary of war. When he gave up that post in 1813 to resume his military career as senior major-general, he took care to have his son appointed in his place. His son held the post until the death of Henry Dearborn in 1829. Wells may have been "too attentive to pecuniary considerations," but he was surely exceeded in that respect by Dearborn himself. See DAB, III, 174-76.

27. CARTER (1), VII, 531-32.

28. CENSUS, 1850, 1860, 1870. Jane (Wells) Griggs's age is given as forty-two in 1850, which places her birth early in the year 1808.

29. The quotation is in DUNN, 44-45. Dunn gives the year as 1807 but it should be 1808, when Turtle visited the Baltimore Quakers for the last time.

30. HILL, 59-60.

31. HUTTON, 213.

32. ESAREY, I, 623.

33. This was an astute tactic, for Wells furnished better information on Tecumseh's activities than anyone else, as Harrison realized.

34. WOEHRMANN, 157–66, is a full account of Wells's battle for reinstatement.

35. Harrison had suggested the removal of Wells as early as 1805. He wrote a very damaging letter to Eustis, December 3, 1809; see ESAREY, I, 393–94. Thereafter, he shifted his ground to some extent.

36. LRSW, Reg. Ser., Record Group 107. Wells to Eustis, June 25, 1809, contains the testimonials on Wells's behalf. Johnston's most damaging attacks were in ibid., Johnston to Eustis, July 1, 1809, and Johnston to Eustis, November 6, 1810. The latter gives a biographical sketch of Wells, wholly unfavorable to him. Harrison to Eustis, October 3, 1809, contains his straddling position in this matter.

37. APPLETON, III, 457.

38. HILL, 22.

39. Ibid., 36.

40. THORNBROUGH (1), 103–4.

41. HILL, 35. Of 1,779 Indians at this meeting, 387 were Miami. The Mississinewa Miami refused to accept their annuity in order to show their displeasure with the Treaty of Fort Wayne. Johnston arbitrarily distributed their annuity among other Miami chiefs. It should not be forgotten that Pacan, as well as Little Turtle, had signed the Treaty of Fort Wayne.

42. ESAREY, I, 432. Johnston to Harrison, June 24, 1810.

43. HUTTON, 215.

44. WOEHRMANN, 166.

45. ESAREY, I, 508–10. Harrison to Eustis, April 23, 1811. Harrison tried to explain his inconsistency with regard to Wells. It was Harrison who appointed him subagent.

46. ESAREY, I, 218. Wells to Harrison, June 1807. Wells offered in this letter to administer the civilization program without salary. See also LRSW, Reg. Ser., Record Group 107, Wells to Eustis, June 25, 1809, in which Wells thinks he would be more useful as "Head of Civilization."

47. The fact that the Cherokee, the Creek, the Choctaw, and the Chickasaw made enough progress at this time to become known as civilized tribes, and that the Mohican, the Oneida, and other northern tribes made similar progress, demonstrates that the civilization project was not an impossible one. Nevertheless, success elsewhere does not prove that Little Turtle and Wells would have succeeded among the Miami. It would be foolish, however, to believe that they were bound to fail. It is reasonable to conclude that they would have had the best chance of success and the least chance of failure among anyone who might have been put in charge of such a program.

18

Tippecanoe, 1811

LITTLE TURTLE HAD REACHED the zenith of his career at the Treaty of Greeneville, a culmination of fifteen years as a successful war chief of the Miami. By the beginning of 1811 he was at the nadir of his career, following fifteen years as a diplomat, during which he had adhered faithfully to the United States and to his self-imposed task of trying to encourage the Miami to start on the road to becoming a civilized agricultural people. His failure to make progress in this direction was due almost entirely to circumstances beyond his control. His steadfast support of the United States had been increasingly undermined by the desire of the government to gain possession of all Indian lands as rapidly and as cheaply as possible. His chosen partner and alter ego, William Wells, had aided him to the extent of his very considerable ability but had been unable to gain control of the civilization project. Their best efforts had only succeeded in securing greater annuities for the Miami than those paid any other tribe. This led to that tribe's more rapid decline because of the increased ability of its members to purchase liquor. The most crippling blow, however, was Wells's loss of the Indian agency, for this gave strong support to the argument of Tecumseh and The Prophet that it was impossible to rely on the friendship of the United States and that Great Britain offered a more dependable alliance.

Wells had been able to demonstrate enough strength to recover his position among the Miami. This was sufficient, along with the traditional Miami policy of neutrality, to prevent any Miami band, even the Wea Miami, from joining the alliance that Tecumseh was trying to form. Harrison had purchased Wea Miami land along the Wabash by the Treaty of Fort Wayne, and it was their land upon which Prophetstown was located.

Lest it be thought that the charges brought against Wells by Harrison and Johnston were in any way indicative of Wells's guilt or incapacity as Indian agent, it should be noted that such charges were made almost as a matter of course in frontier politics. No better illustration of this can be found than in the case of William Henry Harrison. He was able to clear himself by bringing suit for slander against a Vincennes trader, William McIntosh, whom he described as a "Tory merchant." McIntosh was not the only one to make charges against Governor Harrison. As far back as December 1809, Dr. Elias McNamee had written a letter to the president of the Senate in which he accused Harrison of speculation in public lands, using money to buy off his political opponents, trying to introduce slavery into the Indiana Territory, and engaging in the Indian trade illegally while superintendent of Indian affairs.[1] John Badollet, in charge of the public land office at Vincennes, believed that these charges were true, and in addition he accused Harrison of deliberately provoking the Indians to war.[2]

Harrison brought suit against McIntosh for slander in late 1810; the case came to trial on April 11, 1811. He had accused Harrison of defrauding the Indians in his various treaties with them, especially the Treaty of Fort Wayne in 1809, of creating chiefs for his own purposes and in order to exclude the real chiefs, and of having produced the disturbances in Indian country that were so alarming to the white settlements. Harrison was astute enough to allow his political record to be examined thoroughly by the questions of defense lawyers for McIntosh, without objection from his own. When he emerged with a judgment of $4,000 in damages against his opponent, he also emerged triumphant over his political enemies in the territory.[3]

William Wells played an important part in Harrison's victory. He came from Fort Wayne to Vincennes and testified on the governor's behalf. Since he had been interpreter at most of the treaties and had been Indian agent under Harrison as superintendent, his testimony was extremely helpful if not actually the determining factor in the outcome. Yet, in writing to the secretary of war in late April, just after the trial, Harrison said, "Could I be allowed to dispose of Wells as I thought proper my first wish would be to place him in the Interior of our settlements where he would never see and scarcely hear of an Indian." Harrison went on to say that because such a proposal was impossible, and because Wells's activity and talents were not to be doubted, he recommended Wells be allowed to function as sub-agent for the Miami at Fort Wayne. Thus, Harrison paid his debt to Wells for his testimony but continued to maintain in Washington that Wells was an unprincipled and dangerous man.[4] He sent Wells at once to the Illinois country to investigate some murders by the Potawatomi in which it was thought The Prophet might be involved. While there, Wells met Tecumseh, who made no effort to conceal that he was engaged in a hostile movement to stop the white advances. When Wells predicted that he would not be able to accomplish his design, Tecumseh claimed Wells would live to see it happen.[5]

Harrison was now free to take more decisive action against the Shawnee brothers. He sent messages to the more friendly tribes urging them not to join Tecumseh and to Tecumseh warning him against any hostile actions. At the same time he began to build up his military strength at Vincennes and to discuss with the secretary of war the possibility of erecting a fort above Vincennes in the new purchase and making a demonstration of strength in the direction of Prophetstown.

On July 27, 1811, Tecumseh came again to Vincennes with over 100 followers. Almost all the Wea Miami followed him there, bringing the total to over 300. Harrison paraded his militia to impress the Indians and then met with Tecumseh, who assured him of his peaceful intentions but warned him not to cross the border into the Indian lands. Tecumseh restated his position of the previous year and also asserted confidently that he was going to spend some months with the Creek and the Choctaw in the south; he expected them to join with him in alliance against further land acquisition by the United States.[6] Tecumseh's open confidence consorted ill with his professions of peace. Once the Shawnee leader had set off for the south, Harrison redoubled his own activity.

Because President Madison had expressed a strong desire for a peaceful resolution of the Indian troubles, Harrison directed Wells to convene a meeting, on September 4, 1811, of the Miami proper, the Eel River Miami, and the Wea Miami. The head chief of the Wea Miami, Lapoussier, who owed his position to British influence, admitted that while he held the hand of the president he also held the hand of The Prophet, but that the hand of the latter was held slack and was not held against the United States. He minimized the danger to the United States from any foreign power but indicated that the Wea would defend their lands against invasion "and die with the land." Charley, the head chief of the Eel River Miami, felt that Lapoussier should not have spoken without first consulting the others. Little Turtle, Great White Loon, and other respected chiefs spoke in favor of peace. At one point when Little Turtle was speaking Lapoussier made a threatening gesture toward him with his tomahawk. Little Turtle lost none of his composure and replied that Lapoussier might kill him if he wished, but he should know that the Little Turtle would not die alone.

Turtle, though friendly as always to the United States, made a direct reply to the message by which Governor Harrison had convened the meeting. Harrison had said, "I shall draw a line. Those that keep me by the hand must keep on one side of it and those that adhere to the Prophet on the other." Turtle replied, "The land on the Wabash is ours we have not put the Prophet there, but on the contrary we have endeavored to stop his going there . . . you say you will draw a line between your children and the Prophet we are not pleased at this because we think you have no reason to doubt our friendship."[7]

With the exception of Lapoussier and the Wea, who had gone to Malden to visit the British immediately after the meeting, the conference assured Harrison of the neutrality of the Miami. Despite the president's wishes for peace, and without the express authorization of Eustis at the War Department, Harrison then determined upon an expedition against Prophetstown. Eustis had ordered the Fourth United States Army Regiment of 500 men from Pittsburgh to Vincennes in mid-July. Following the arrival in Vincennes of Lieutenant-Colonel John Parker Boyd and his regiment of regulars, Harrison marched northward, on September 27, 1811, with nearly 1,000 men, about one-third of them regulars and two-thirds volunteers.[8]

Although Harrison was acting on his own authority, he kept Eustis informed of his intended movements after he was underway. However, it normally took a month for communications between Vincennes and Washington to reach their destination.[9] At Terre Haute, Harrison lingered for most of the month of October, building a fort which had been authorized and was named Fort Harrison. Here he received cautious approval from Eustis, authorizing him to order The Prophet to disperse and to compel him to do so if he should refuse.[10] Apparently this was what Harrison was waiting for, and he prepared to march northward once more, leaving a garrison at the fort. His army was dwindling through sickness and desertion, however, and he had already sent urgent messages to Louisville asking for Kentucky volunteers. Some of these units, notably mounted riflemen raised and led by Samuel Wells, brother of William Wells, and Colonel Frederick Geiger, Wells's father-in-law, joined him at Fort Harrison or between there and Prophetstown.[11]

Leaving Fort Harrison on October 29, Harrison crossed to the western side of the Wabash at the mouth of Raccoon Creek on October 31. This was the extreme northern limit of the land purchased by the Treaty of Fort Wayne. Here he built a blockhouse where the boats and some provisions were left. A delegation of Miami chiefs who had met Harrison to assure him of their continued friendship proceeded up the trail on the east side of the Wabash.

Harrison had already sent the Wea Miami chief Little Eyes, with a small band of his scouts, from Terre Haute to Prophetstown to spy for him and to try to persuade The Prophet to agree to a council. In this last task they failed, and they also failed to make contact with Harrison because they traveled on the opposite side of the Wabash. They apparently met the

214

Miami chiefs and were across the Wabash within hearing distance of the battle which ensued.[12]

By crossing the Wabash where he did, Harrison was able to approach across prairie country instead of through the wooded land east of the river. He thus avoided any possibility of ambush by the Indians, who had followed his movements. He was now beyond the Indian boundary line with an armed force of over 700 men and was in violation of Indian treaty rights. The Indians at Prophetstown were apprehensive as to his intentions, which were obviously not peaceable.[13]

Harrison's route lay to the northeast, paralleling the Wabash at a distance of five miles. He neared Prophetstown on the afternoon of November 6, where he was met by a delegation of Indians from the village, who after some discussion agreed to meet in council with him the next day. The Prophet himself was not with this delegation, nor was he a party to the agreement. The parley took place about a mile and a half west of Prophetstown. Harrison's officers now scouted the immediate vicinity and selected a flat elevation overlooking Burnett's Creek about a mile from Prophetstown. The town was strung out along the Wabash, a mile below the mouth of the Tippecanoe River, from which the ensuing battle took its name. The old Pepikokia Miami village had been located only a mile or so up the Tippecanoe but was no longer extant. Immediately north of Harrison's campsite and west of the Tippecanoe was a small prairie still known locally as Pretty Prairie.

Because the Indians had indicated the campsite eventually chosen as a suitable one, it has been widely believed that Harrison was lured into a trap. Anyone viewing the spot, however, will see at once that the best site available had been selected.[14] Harrison himself said it was a good one, although he later professed not to have been entirely satisfied. This was hindsight and was also an effort to place part of the blame for the high casualties suffered in the battle on the location. In truth, his army would have been far more vulnerable but for the fact that the side facing Burnett's Creek on the west was very steep and only three sides of the camp could be attacked.

Some accounts claim that Harrison had surrounded Prophetstown before the parley took place.[15] This would have been possible, for the town was situated 200 yards from the Wabash on the second ledge rather than on the actual bank of the river. But it is probable that the Indians only feared that this might occur and that this fear gave rise to their being willing to set a council meeting for the next day. They could then either attack Harrison or abandon the village during the night, if they did not wish to extend the parley into a general council meeting.

There is evidence that Indians and whites attempted, without much success, to spy on each other during the early hours of darkness. A rumor existed that a black cart driver of Harrison's went to Prophetstown and gave information to the Indians. According to one version, he reported that the governor intended to attack the next day, which caused the Indians to decide to attack Harrison.[16] Another version suggested that he told the Indians that Harrison had no cannon, which emboldened them to attack.[17] The first version is unlikely inasmuch as the informant could hardly have known Harrison's intentions; the second seems more plausible but raises the question as to whether or not he gave the information on his own account or was acting for Harrison to provoke an attack. Either is possible under the circumstances. The man is said to have returned to Harrison's camp and was not punished.

Harrison was definitely not taken by surprise. He had ordered the soldiers to sleep fully dressed and with weapons readily available. The camp was in a rectangular form, and in case of alarm the men were told simply to advance five paces and thus form a line on every side. Harrison's quarters were at the center of the camp. The soldiers may have been less apprehensive than Harrison, however, for most were inexperienced. They may also have thought that the presence of women and children in Prophetstown indicated that an attack was not imminent.[18]

Information gathered from the Indians after the battle indicated that The Prophet had incited the attack by assuring his followers that his medicine was strong enough to counteract the bullets of the whites and that they would emerge not only victorious but unharmed. He is said to have kept to himself during the battle, engaged in prayers to the Great Spirit and various incantations to bolster the morale of his warriors. This may have been true, since he was blamed by the Indians for his failure to make good his promises of victory and subsequently lost credit throughout Indian country. He was reported to have blamed the failure of his medicine upon the onset of his wife's menstrual period.

The attack came nearly two hours before dawn on November 7. Harrison was already awake and pulling on his boots. Some of the men were stirring and replenishing the campfires. All were soon aroused and the lines were formed. The initial attack, accompanied by blood-curdling yells and war whoops, struck the northwest corner of the camp where the men of Major Samuel Wells and of Colonel Frederick Geiger were stationed. Geiger was wounded while still in his tent, but Wells was unscathed. Casualties were numerous because the campfires afforded light for the Indians who attacked from the darkness. The first attack was repelled, but the Indians kept firing all along this side of the camp with considerable effect. Soon a second attack began on the opposite side, and before long firing was general on three sides of the camp. Colonel Abraham Owen, Major Jo Daviess, Captain Spier Spencer, and Harrison's friend, Captain Thomas Randolph, were killed. Their names were given by the legislature to Indiana counties while the memory of their death was still fresh.

Harrison mounted and directed the fight with coolness and confidence. He took a bullet through his hat and his horse was shot. For a while the outcome was in doubt as casualties mounted to 20 percent of the force. There was some confusion but no panic. After the repulse of the initial attack the Indians did not get inside the camp again. Shortly after daybreak the Indians abandoned their effort, for they were also suffering losses in the light of day, and they may have run short of ammunition as well. Harrison eventually reported 61 dead and 118 wounded. About half of the dead had been mortally wounded during the battle and had died in camp or on the way back to Vincennes. He counted 36 Indians dead on the battlefield.[19]

Harrison remained in camp anticipating a renewal of the attack, but the Indians had no thought of this. Binding The Prophet with cords, they abandoned Prophetstown and made camp on Wild Cat Creek some twenty miles eastward. When he realized that the Indians had left, Harrison burned Prophetstown and departed for Vincennes, where he arrived on November 18 and penned his report to the War Department.

Rumors were rife all over the frontier region that Harrison had been defeated. John Johnston ascertained from the Miami and other Indians at his agency at Fort Wayne that not more than 350 Indians had participated at Tippecanoe. He prematurely publicized, in the Cincinnati newspaper *Liberty Hall*, his criticism of Harrison for what he assumed was a defeat, and other papers copied the report. Harrison was incensed at Johnston.[20] Wells agreed with Johnston as to the number of Indians engaged but did not put his views in print. Harrison was embroiled in a controversy at Vincennes with political opponents who wished to credit Colonel Boyd and his regular army men with having saved Harrison and the militia at Tippecanoe. Thus, he took time to gather all the evidence he could that the Indians were more numerous. He first reported 600, which, through his utmost efforts, was later increased to 700, thus making the number of whites and Indians virtually equal.

Although the number of Indians probably conformed closely to the estimates of Johnston and Wells, there was little basis for transferring Harrison's laurels, such as they were, to Colonel Boyd.[21] The militia stood up well enough under fire and so did the regulars. The Indian account given to Matthew Elliott, in Malden, by a Kickapoo chief seems to have been reliable, except for minimizing the number of Indian dead, which was placed at only 25. The chief claimed that the Winnebago and the Kickapoo furnished nearly all the warriors and delivered the two vigorous attacks, the Kickapoo from the north and the Winnebago from the south. He further stated that only about 100 Indians from these two tribes actually fought but that about 200 more, chiefly Potawatomi and regular residents at Prophetstown, engaged in stealing horses and plundering.[22] Obviously the chief was interested, as Harrison was, in exaggerating the part his own people played and in minimizing the part of the "regulars" at Prophetstown, but the total number is more believable than Harrison's various estimates. It is also clear that Harrison's camp was caught between an effective cross fire and that only the poor timing of the Indian attacks from north and south gave Harrison's men a fighting chance. Had the attacks been simultaneous the outcome might well have been different.

The battle of Tippecanoe bears a similarity to Little Turtle's famous defeat of St. Clair twenty years earlier. In both cases the whites were attacked while encamped. There are notable differences, however, which served to produce a different outcome: Harrison was more alert and more effective than St. Clair; the Indians had no one to direct them at Tippecanoe, as Little Turtle had directed them against St. Clair; the Indians had triumphed, even over cannon, in 1791, whereas they failed, even in the absence of cannon, in 1811; in the earlier battle the Indian attack was concerted by Little Turtle, while at Tippecanoe, without leadership, the Kickapoo either opened fire too soon or the Winnebago took too long in getting into position.

Captain Josiah Snelling took one Indian prisoner who, when questioned with appropriate threats, named three chiefs, Winamac of the Potawatomi and White Loon and Stone Eater of the Miami, as having participated in the battle. The involvement of Winamac and his small band of Potawatomi was a severe blow to Harrison, for Winamac was an Indian he had made a chief for his own purposes and had paid as an informer for several years. It was well known that Winamac had stolen horses and cattle and committed murders which were then blamed on The Prophet and Tecumseh. Harrison had never admitted his poor judgment in employing Winamac, but now he was forced to do so.[23]

It is difficult to believe that Great White Loon, a close friend of Little Turtle, and Stone Eater, a Wea Miami chief, took part in the battle. They had always resisted The Prophet and been friendly to the United States. John Johnston reported to Harrison that none of the Miami or the Delaware, and only a few Potawatomi, were engaged. In January 1812 Little Turtle assured Harrison by letter that none of the Miami or the Eel River Miami had taken part.[24]

In order to believe that these two chiefs participated one must assume that they were among the Miami chiefs who had traveled down the Wabash to affirm their loyalty to Harrison and then separated from the rest of the Miami party on their homeward journey to join The Prophet. Although Indians were sometimes overcome by war fervor and took part in battles in which they had nothing personal at stake, in this particular case White Loon, especially, would have contradicted his own convictions and his own long friendship with Little Turtle by joining the fight. Harrison did not name these chiefs as participants, as he did Winamac, but he apparently believed that they were present. One other possibility exists: they may have been present merely as observers but were recognized by Captain Snelling's captive and reported as participants. The matter cannot be settled, but the weight of evidence inclines against their participation.

The battle of Tippecanoe could easily have been avoided. The entire responsibility rested on Harrison, who chose the time and place and forced the issue. There was no more reason for aggressive action against the militant Indians in 1811 than there had been for the preceding seven years; in fact, there was less reason than there had been in 1808 or 1810. There was some public opposition to the campaign, but it was supported by a majority on the frontier. Harrison had determined to act and had forced an unwilling president and secretary of war into some semblance of support.

Did Harrison's action at Tippecanoe benefit the United States? This is arguable. It certainly prevented any concerted action between the British and the militant Indians of the United States when the War of 1812 began. It formed a sort of watershed, however, in governmental Indian policy and public opinion toward the Indian. From this time on there was much less said and done about civilizing the Indians than had been true earlier.

It is important for us to note that this defeat greatly enhanced the prestige of Little Turtle and William Wells among the Miami. From a low point in tribal esteem they were suddenly elevated to the position of having been right all along in opposing Tecumseh and The Prophet and in advocating friendship with the United States. Given a few years of peace in which to operate, they might at last have reached the point from which they could have brought their cherished dreams of converting the Miami to the white man's way of life to fruition. This was not to be. Within eight months of Tippecanoe came war with Great Britain. And with that war came death.

NOTES

1. CARTER (1), VII, 662–86. The charge of engaging illegally (and profitably) in the Indian trade was the same that John Johnston had made against William Wells. Harrison had insinuated to the secretaries of war that the charge was true.

2. THORNBROUGH (2), 120–23, 130–31, 237–38.

3. ESAREY, I, 509–10. Harrison to Eustis, April 23, 1811.

4. Ibid., 508–9.

5. WOEHRMANN, 209.

6. ESAREY, I, 542–46. Harrison to Eustis, August 6, 1811.

7. Ibid., 577–81. Le Gris was present at this meeting. He had not been mentioned in any correspondence for several years, and this is the last knowledge we have of him. ANSON, 156.

8. A field report of October 12, 1811, at Terre Haute listed 345 regulars, 415 Indiana militia, 120 dragoons, 84 mounted riflemen, and 13 scouts, for a total of 977. ESAREY, I, 592–94. Another listing of the same date was Boyd's Regulars, 265, Bartholomew's Militia, 314, Davies's Horse, 85, Spencer's Mounted Riflemen, 67, Dubois's Spies, 11. Ibid., 597. The classifications are apparently the same, with the lower total in the second listing indicating that it included only those reported as fit for duty.

9. Time required for communication between Washington, D.C., and Fort Wayne was usually about forty days.

10. CARTER (1), VIII, 133–34. Eustis to Harrison, September 12, 1811.

11. A full listing of the rosters of the various units composing Harrison's army is found in BEARD, 102–21, and in PIRTLE, 111–31.

12. ANSON, 157–58.

13. Treaty violation by Harrison is usually conveniently overlooked. There was a congressional inquiry into the matter, but nothing came of it.

14. I first visited Battle Ground in the fall of 1923; I visited the site most recently in May 1981. John Tipton, who participated in the battle, later bought the site and still later gave it to the state of Indiana.

15. ESAREY, I, 616–18. Matthew Elliott to Isaac Brock, June 12, 1812.

16. THORNBROUGH (2), 205–6.

17. ESAREY, I, 720.

18. GREEN, 128.

19. ESAREY, I, 614–15, 618–30. The latter constitutes Harrison's full official report.

20. ESAREY, II, 12–13. Harrison to Eustis, January 12, 1812. Johnston's original letter to Eustis was dated November 28, 1811. The *Liberty Hall* account was published on January 3, 1812.

21. THORNBROUGH (2), 207–22.

22. ESAREY, I, 616–18. Elliott to Brock, January 12, 1812.

23. THORNBROUGH (2), 198–200, 232–33. The two Potawatomi chiefs called Winamac (Catfish) are often a source of confusion. CLIFTON, 199–201, and EDMUNDS (5), 176–77, assume that the one who fought at Tippecanoe was the war chief whose village was on the Huron River in southeastern Michigan, who signed the Treaty of Greeneville, and who conducted the seige of Fort Wayne. On the contrary, it was Harrison's trusted spy, whose village was on the Tippecanoe River, some forty miles above the site of the battle. The facts are as follows. Harrison had sent Winamac ahead to Prophetstown. He did not return and Harrison was told that he had joined the Miami chiefs going south on the other side of the Wabash. ESAREY,

I, 620. This is unlikely since the Miami detested him and had offered to kill him, if Harrison would authorize it. ESAREY, II, 44.

On December 3, 1811, nearly a month after the battle of Tippecanoe, "Winemac, a Potawatomi from near the Prophet's Valley," showed up at Malden, where he assured Matthew Elliott that no battle had been fought when he left Harrison's camp eight days earlier. ESAREY, I, 660. Elliott knew from other reports that he was lying. Apparently he was trying to establish an alibi for his participation.

By December 27, 1811, Harrison had come to believe that "all the Potawatomi living on the Wabash (excepting the chief, Winemac) were in the action." ESAREY, I, 684. By January 14, 1812, Harrison wrote to the secretary of war, "It is agreed by everyone that the whole of Winnemac's party of the Potawotami fought against us." ESAREY, II, 12. No exception was made for Winamac.

Finally, on May 6, 1812, Harrison upheld an action of Captain Snelling, who had detained Winamac and nine followers at Fort Harrison on the ground that they would be killed by the citizens of Vincennes for their participation at Tippecanoe. Harrison agreed and wrote, "It is thus that we are served by these scoundrels." ESAREY, II, 44. He could hardly have written more on the subject without advertising the extent to which he had been duped by Winamac.

24. ESAREY, II, 18–19. Little Turtle, for the Miami and the Eel River Indians, to Harrison, January 25, 1812. Great White Loon was Little Turtle's son-in-law. Stone Eater was a member of a Miami delegation that went to Fort Harrison and Vincennes to express regret that the battle had taken place.

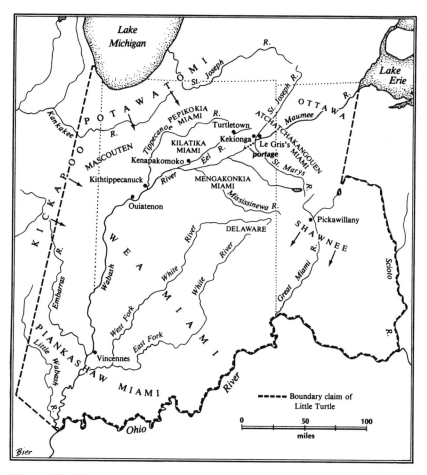

Map 7. *The Miami Domain.* This map shows the extent of the Miami Domain as outlined by Little Turtle in 1795. Also shown is the portage connecting the Maumee-Wabash Line of travel and the encroachment of other Indian tribes upon the Miami Domain.

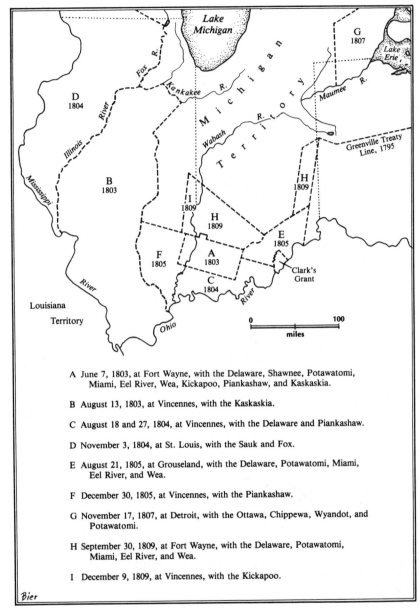

Map 8. *American Treaties of Land Acquisition, 1803–9.* All but one of these treaties was concluded by William Henry Harrison, governor of the Indiana Territory. The exception was a treaty concluded by William Hull, governor of the Michigan Territory.

Figure 13. *William Wells.* This miniature is the only likeness of William Wells, Indian agent and Little Turtle's son-in-law. The uniform indicates that it was probably made between 1805 and 1810. Reproduced by permission of the Chicago Historical Society. ICHi 14160.

Figure 14. *Mrs. William Wells.* This silhouette is traditionally reputed to be of Sweet Breeze, wife of Wells and daughter of Little Turtle. The date of 1810 and the hair style render it virtually certain that it is a profile of Polly Geiger, Wells's white wife, whom he married in 1810, five years after the death of Sweet Breeze. Reproduced by permission of the Chicago Historical Society. ICHi 12872.

Figure 15. *Tecumtha (Tecumseh)*. Governor Harrison's great antagonist was killed in battle during the War of 1812. This sketch is believed to have been made shortly before Tecumseh's death because he is shown in the coat of a British brigadier-general. Reproduced by permission of the Indiana Historical Society.

Figure 16. *Tems-Kwah-ta-wah (The Shawnee Prophet)*. Tecumseh's younger brother, The Prophet, provided the religious background for Tecumseh's plan of uniting all the tribes against the Americans. His incitement of the Indians at Tippecanoe nearly succeeded, but the failure doomed any further chance of success. Reproduced by permission of the Indiana Historical Society. Negative no. C546.

Figure 17. *William Henry Harrison.* The original of this portrait is in the Harrison House at Vincennes. It is attributed to Rembrandt Peale and depicts Harrison as he appeared in his earlier years. Reproduced by permission of the Indiana Historical Society, from the W. H. Harrison Collection.

Figure 18. *John Johnston.* This portrait was made in Philadelphia in 1820; the original is in the Ohio Historical Society. Johnston, Indian factor at Fort Wayne, joined with Harrison in undermining William Wells and Little Turtle in their efforts to gain control of a civilization program for the Miami tribe. Reproduced by permission of the Ohio Historical Society. SC 2433.

Figure 19. *Jean Baptiste Richerville (Richardville)*. J. O. Lewis painted this portrait of Richardville in 1827, along with the portraits of many other Miami chiefs. Half French, Richardville was Pacan's nephew and his successor as head chief of the Miami proper. Reproduced by permission of the Indiana Historical Society. Negative no. A129.

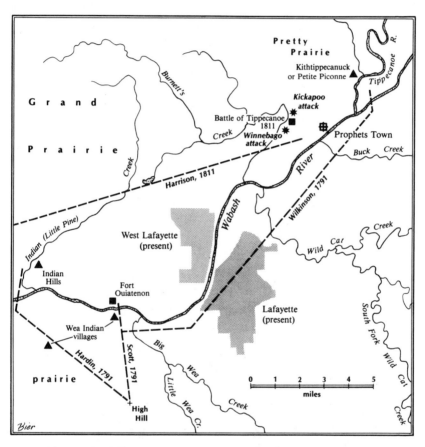

Map 9. *The Battle of Tippecanoe.* The map shows Harrison's line of march in 1811, as well as Prophetstown and the scene of battle. Also shown are the former Miami towns, Ouiatenon and Kithtippecanuck, destroyed by Scott in 1791.

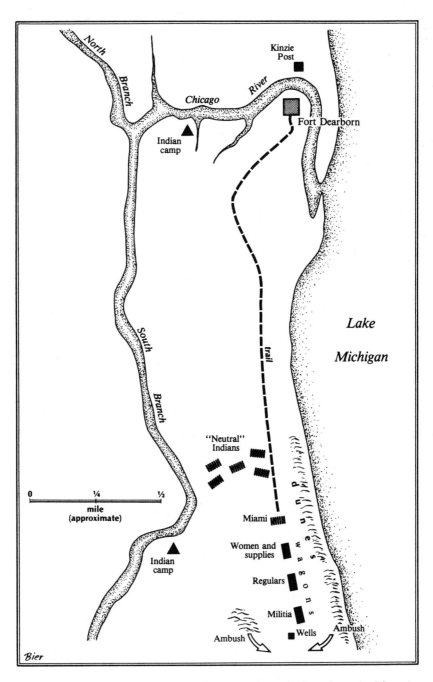

Map 10. *The Fort Dearborn Massacre.* This map shows the line of march of Captain Heald when he evacuated Fort Dearborn in 1811 and was overwhelmed by hostile Indians. Although Captain Heald and his wife, Rebecca Wells Heald, survived, Captain William Wells died a heroic death.

PART FOUR

THE TRAGEDY

19

A Frontier Tragedy, 1812

WHEN TECUMSEH RETURNED in January 1812 from his extended visit to the Creek and the Choctaw, he was disappointed to learn that, contrary to his express instructions, his brother had risked a battle during his absence. He did not appreciate at once, however, the impact of the battle of Tippecanoe. The Indians were fully aware of the damage they had inflicted on Harrison's army and the consternation this had caused in Kentucky and Ohio. Prophetstown was rebuilt and reoccupied; the British were as friendly and active as before. Tecumseh asserted that if he had been present when Harrison had invaded the Indian country, he would have met the governor with assurances of peace.[1] In short, he attempted to carry on as before and thought that he might now be able to persuade the Delaware and the Miami to join his movement. But he was mistaken, for once more he was thwarted by Little Turtle and William Wells.

Early in February, Wells informed Harrison that Tecumseh was very active and had sent runners to the tribes in Illinois and to the southern tribes. Wells believed that the plan was to persuade the Illinois tribes to send their women and children beyond the Mississippi while their warriors assembled at Prophetstown for an attack on Vincennes.[2]

Meanwhile, President Madison sought to capitalize on Tippecanoe by asking Harrison to invite Tecumseh and The Prophet to Washington to make peace. Harrison had misgivings about the president's plan but sought to make it more workable by extending the invitation not only to the militants but also to the chiefs of the loyal tribes, such as the Miami, the Delaware, and the Wyandot. He specifically stated that Little Turtle and Five Medals might go if they wished. [3]

Nothing came of the president's plan, for the Shawnee brothers refused to go to the capital city. Benjamin Stickney, the new Indian agent at Fort Wayne, tried to organize a meeting of the friendly chiefs to consider the invitation, but Little Turtle was afflicted so badly with gout that he could not attend. The few chiefs who came to Fort Wayne on April 18 had as their spokesman the Eel River Miami chief Charley, who pointed out that they did not need to go to Washington because they had caused no trouble but had loyally kept the agreement made at the Treaty of Greeneville. Furthermore, these were troubled times, many of the old chiefs were dead, and those who were still alive found it hard to maintain their authority.[4] The implication was clear that Charley felt they were needed more at home than in the nation's capital.

Charley's message was reinforced by a speech made voluntarily and unexpectedly by Five Medals to Stickney on May 12, 1812. Stickney, a newcomer, found it rather puzzling. Five Medals's message was that the trouble had arisen from the government's demand that the Indians sell their lands, which in turn had caused the Shawnee brothers to be so militant. Five Medals asked Stickney to convey the message to Harrison and concluded by saying, "Tell it on paper and make it strong."[5] If Harrison understood the message he could not afford to admit it; indeed, he did not. Five Medals was en route to a meeting on the Mississinewa where Tecumseh was expected. Obviously, Little Turtle's longtime friend from the Elkhart River was troubled enough to speak very plainly.

Stickney became aware of a stranger's presence in the Fort Wayne neighborhood during April and May 1812. He decided, correctly, although he lacked proof, that the man was a spy for Matthew Elliott, at Malden. The stranger, who claimed to be a Wyandot chief named Shetoon, was actually Isadore Chaine (or Chene), half French and half Huron. He had spent some time at Little Turtle's house in March, where he probably tried to win Turtle over to the British side—an impossible task, as he was to find out.[6] Shetoon was in touch with Tecumseh and played a part in assembling a meeting in mid-May on the Mississinewa. Twelve tribes were represented at this gathering: the Wyandot, the Chippewa, the Ottawa, the Potawatomi, the Delaware, the Miami proper, the Eel River Miami, the Wea Miami, the Piankashaw Miami, the Shawnee, the Kickapoo, and the Winnebago; 600 warriors were present. This was clearly a major effort on the part of Tecumseh and his British backers to win support from the old chiefs of the tribes who had, for the most part, opposed a militant policy toward the United States.

William Wells conducted Little Turtle and Five Medals to the meeting. It required a strong effort on the part of Turtle to make the journey of sixty miles, for his gout had become disabling. Tecumseh was the principal orator and spoke in his usual manner. He placed the responsibility for Tippecanoe upon his brother and blamed the Potawatomi, in particular, for irresponsible behavior. While still professing peaceful intentions, he promised that the Shawnee, the Kickapoo, and the Winnebago would fight for their homes and that when the time came all tribes "would rise as one man." The Delaware took the lead in opposing Tecumseh, supported as always by the Miami and, in this case, no doubt to Tecumseh's surprise, also by the Kickapoo. Tecumseh did not rally support, for the old chiefs held to the policy laid down by Little Turtle at Greeneville and adhered to steadfastly since that time. However the council did take action to protest the sale of liquor by white traders. When Shetoon returned to Fort Wayne, Stickney learned what he could from him. He then sent him to Elliott with a letter stating that he was allowing Shetoon to return but not revealing that he knew what Shetoon's business had been.[7]

Tecumseh appeared in Fort Wayne on June 17 and conferred with Stickney for several hours. He stated that he was going to Malden for powder and lead but still professed peaceable intentions; his plan was to visit other tribes on his peaceful mission. Wells reported more specifically that Tecumseh would bring twelve pack horses laden with ammunition back to Prophetstown and that he was trying to persuade a band of Chippewa to settle there, although the Miami had refused to give permission for such a settlement.[8]

Governor Harrison, meanwhile, had taken Winamac back into his employment and sent him to Peoria and Chicago to spy on Indian activities in Illinois. Winamac reported that there were several hundred warriors in both places and that some recent murders of whites had occurred. His conclusion that the Indians there had not paid any attention to Tecumseh was strange in view of the rest of his report.[9]

For several months the United States and Great Britain had been drifting closer to war over the issues of the impressment of seamen by the British and of the British prohibition of trade by American vessels with France (recall that the British were engaged in a struggle with Napoleon, the emperor of the French). On June 1 President Madison sent his war message to Congress; on June 4 the House declared for war by a vote of seventy-nine to forty-nine, as did the Senate on June 17 by a vote of nineteen to thirteen. The president approved the Declaration of War on June 18, and it was publicly proclaimed the next day. Unaware that the United States had taken this action, on June 23 Great Britain revoked the Orders in Council that had provoked the Americans. Their action came too late.[10]

Although official word did not arrive until July 19, the news that war had been declared reached Fort Wayne from unofficial newspaper reports on July 6.[11] It found Little Turtle at Wells's house, where he had ridden from his home, between twelve and thirteen miles distant, at the end of June in order to receive medical treatment from the army surgeon at the fort. For fifteen years he had suffered from the gout, but this time he seems to have had a dropsical condition as well.[12] It is probable that he realized that his health was failing fast. Indeed, he may have had a premonition of death and wished to die at Wells's house, for it was located on the former site of Kekionga and there was a burial ground near that former Miami village. Many friends and relatives are likely to have joined him and encamped in "the old orchard" near Wells's home. Although he certainly knew of the Declaration of War against Great Britain, Turtle's thoughts about it are not known. He may have realized that it would terminate his great design for civilizing his tribe in the hope that they might live in harmony with the whites. As he felt the end of his life approaching, he was carried at his own request outside the house and reposed on the ground under the shade of a tree, where he died on July 14, 1812.

Little Turtle's death was reported by Stickney to Eustis, to John Johnston, and to Harrison. To Eustis he wrote, "On the 14th inst. Little Turtle breathed his last at his camp near Fort Wayne. Conceiving it was for the public interest, I have had him buried with the honors of War, and gave such presents as the nature of the case appeared to require, for which his nation and family made a public expression of their gratitude." To John Johnston he wrote, "I had him buried on the 15th with the honors of War and every other mark of distinction in my power. The gout was his disorder; and he died with more firm composure of mind than any other person I have seen." His letter to Harrison added nothing further. In Stickney's accounting to the War Department are found two entries:[13]

Cunningham & Howell for making a coffin for Little Turtle	$2.00
Burney & Milligan for digging grave for do	$1.00

No doubt Little Turtle would have been pleased with the military funeral that Stickney arranged with the cooperation of Captain James Rhea, commander of the fort. Such a tribute from his former enemies would have appealed to his well-known sense of humor. In a more serious vein, he might have considered it as acceptance by the white men, whose manners and customs he had adopted as nearly as possible, even at the cost of some popularity with his own people. Although there are no actual details extant of Little Turtle's funeral, a military funeral at that time doubtless included marching by uniformed soldiers to the music of muted fifes and muffled drums, the firing of muskets in salute to the dead as the flag-draped coffin was lowered to the grave, and the solemn playing of taps by the bugler as the grave was filled with earth.

The venerated Mishikinakwa was given an Indian burial, and for this William Wells and his Indian family must have been responsible. In the traditional manner his body was wrapped in a fine blanket, his hair was tied with a buckskin thong, and he was given his most valued possessions and such useful articles as he might require for his journey to the spirit world. These possessions, at least the nonperishable ones, included the dress sword given him by President Washington, eight silver armlets, two silver anklets, three silver medals, six pendants, two necklaces of silver beads, twenty-three silver crosses, four silver brooches, and a pair of large silver ear hoops. The articles of utility included a small pocketknife, a large clasp knife, a drinking cup, a spoon, a pair of scissors, a hammer, a gun, a bullet mold, a pistol, a flint lock, an axe, a tomahawk, a pair of steel spurs, three large skinning knives, a copper kettle, a flask, and a bottle of vermilion war paint.

All of these articles were found when the bones of Little Turtle were disinterred a century later, in July 1912. The discovery was accidental and occurred when laborers began excavating for the cellar of a house to be built for a veterinary doctor, George W. Gillie, at 634 Lawton Place, Fort Wayne, Indiana, on a site between the St. Joseph River and Spy Run Creek. They found several skulls and other human bones, which they kept as curiosities. Dr. Gillie then discharged the workers and with the aid of his contractors, the two Lochner brothers, continued the work himself. They found the enumerated items and concluded that the grave was that of Little Turtle. Later, Jacob Stouder purchased all of the articles that he could and used them for an illustrated lecture on Little Turtle, which he gave for several years. The skeleton was reburied under a marble slab. Before his death, Stouder placed the items he had collected in the permanent custody of the Allen County–Fort Wayne Historical Society, where they are still exhibited.[14]

The death of Little Turtle occurred at a most unfortunate time, one of crisis for his tribe. The war with Great Britain drew a majority of the Miami warriors to the British side. The chiefs attempted to maintain a neutral policy, but the strategic location of the Miami lands rendered this impossible. Had Little Turtle lived, with his prestige restored by the reverse suffered by The Prophet and Tecumseh, he might have been able to hold the Miami on the side of the United States. Wells could not do this alone, but it is probable that together the two men could have done so.

Turtle's death forced Wells to do some serious thinking about his own future. After having been agent for several years, his current position as subagent and interpreter at Fort Wayne represented a loss of prestige; furthermore, it was not very lucrative. His last link with the Miami was now gone. His four children by Sweet Breeze had been educated for a life among the whites. His marriage to Polly Geiger had produced a son, Samuel Geiger Wells, and Polly was pregnant again. The war with England made Fort Wayne a place of some peril, should there be an invasion from Canada. Wells could see no future prospects at Fort Wayne and thus began to make plans to move to Louisville.

Just after the death of Little Turtle, The Prophet came to Fort Wayne with nearly 100 Shawnee, Kickapoo, and Winnebago. They were returning from Malden but sought to convince Stickney that they had abandoned the British and were going to support the Americans, "who talked straight everywhere except at Vincennes." Wells reported to Harrison that he believed that Stickney had been duped by The Prophet. Wells may have misjudged Stickney somewhat because two Kickapoo stole two horses from Wells, and The Prophet sought to palliate the offense by confessing it to the agent. Wells was in a bad temper at the loss and warned Harrison that the Shawnee brothers were contemplating an attack on Vincennes, while at the same time The Prophet promised not only to attend a pro-American council at Piqua, planned by Stickney, but also said that he would persuade Tecumseh to leave Malden and attend the council.[15]

Harrison learned through Colonel Frederick Geiger that Wells was thinking of resigning his post at Fort Wayne and moving to Louisville. He urgently pressed Wells to remain where he was on the basis that Wells would be more valuable than anyone else in the critical times brought about by the war.[16] Wells was responsive to Harrison's request but wished to assure the safety of his wife and children. His wife refused to leave Fort Wayne, however, and he compromised by sending his children by Sweet Breeze to Piqua. They were conducted there by Spemicalawba, or James Logan, a Shawnee friend who had been captured as a youth and educated among the whites, as Wells had been captured and adopted by the Indians. Militant Indians were gathering around Fort Wayne in rapidly growing numbers at the time the Wells children departed.[17]

Meanwhile, General William Hull, at Detroit, had invaded Canada and invited the Canadians to rebel against British control. His attempt predictably received no support among the Tories, who had settled in Canada after the American Revolution, so he marched back to Detroit, where he was soon besieged by the British forces and their Indian allies. Learning that Fort Michilimackinac had fallen to the British, Hull sent a messenger to Captain Nathan Heald, at Fort Dearborn, with orders for him to abandon that isolated post on the Chicago River and march either to Detroit or Fort Wayne. A copy of these orders was sent to Captain James Rhea, at Fort Wayne, instructing him to do anything he could to facilitate Heald's evacuation of Fort Dearborn. Rhea could do nothing, for he was a habitual drunkard and, as it turned out, was incapable of defending his own post.

An offer by William Wells to lead a band of Miami warriors to Fort Dearborn was accepted. Wells fully realized the danger he was facing, but Captain Heald was a good friend who had not only formerly commanded at Fort Wayne but was married to Rebecca Wells, William's niece and the daughter of his brother Samuel. There was a marked family resemblance between William Wells and Rebecca, who was only six years younger than her uncle.

Wells was able to persuade only about 30 Miami warriors to accompany him. They were doubtless enticed by the hope of bringing back goods from Fort Dearborn, for each Miami rode an Indian pony and led a pack horse. Corporal Walter K. Jordan, with five government pack horses, accompanied them with Captain Rhea's permission. Jordan reported that there were 100 Miami, which may indicate either that Wells had hoped more would come or that many started the journey but changed their minds before arriving at their destination.[18] The small party left Fort Wayne on August 8 and arrived at Fort Dearborn on August 13. Wells may originally have planned to cover Captain Heald's march to Fort Wayne with a larger force that would march independently of Heald's party but in close and watchful proximity to it.

At Fort Dearborn, meanwhile, the principal trader, John Kinzie, a man of long years in the Indian trade, tried to persuade Captain Heald to ignore the orders and defend the fort, if necessary, against the large number of Indians who were encamped round about. These were mostly Potawatomi, about half of whom seemed friendly, but there were bands of Kickapoo and Winnebago, who were definitely militant. While Kinzie's advice was motivated by self-interest, as he did not wish to endanger his family or lose his goods, it may have also represented a preferable alternative.[19] Fort Dearborn was located at the mouth of the Chicago River, and in addition to being well supplied and defensible it offered a possibility of escape by way of the lake to Fort St. Joseph. Captain Heald, however, felt that his orders were definite and that he had no discretion in the matter. Mrs. Heald said that the orders from General Hull were brought by an Indian who was also a British officer. This may have been Harrison's friend Winamac, who was present though not participating with the hostile Indians. If it was Winamac, he was still playing the role of a double agent.[20]

It is uncertain whether or not William Wells, after his arrival on August 13, urged Captain Heald to defend the fort. It is commonly stated and generally believed that he did, but Mrs. Heald said that although Wells was certain that the Indians were planning trouble, he did not advise against evacuation. He may have raised the point at the council of officers and then dropped it when he saw that Heald was not to be persuaded. On August 14 all the liquor at the fort and the guns and ammunition that could not be taken on the retreat to Fort Wayne were destroyed; the rest of the goods and supplies were distributed among the friendly Indians. Captain Heald believed that those Indians who received the goods did not join the hostile Indians but remained neutral bystanders during the attack on the following day. He and Wells endeavored to reach an understanding with the Indians such that, in return for the goods, the whole party would be allowed to proceed to Fort Wayne unmolested.[21]

Wells, who knew the Indians better than Heald, had less faith in the promises that were made. He was especially concerned by the action of Black Partridge, a Potawatomi chief, who returned a medal he had been given by the United States. Wells may actually have received verbal warnings from Black Partridge or other Potawatomi chiefs that the hostile Potawatomi could not be restrained, nor could the Kickapoo and the Winnebago. There is no doubt but that he entertained forebodings and was aware of the perilous situation. The Miami he had brought with him were also fully cognizant of the danger. It seems a reasonable conclusion that Wells negotiated with the friendly Indians and received some assurances in which he placed little reliance.[22]

The massacre which took place the following day was commented upon by John Kinzie's half-brother, also an Indian trader, Thomas Forsyth, who arrived the day after, on August 16. He claimed that the Indians were enraged by the destruction of the liquor and ammunition. It seems more likely that their hostility was fanned by the news from Tecumseh that Hull was besieged at Detroit and would probably surrender, which he did in fact do on August 16.[23]

Fort Dearborn was abandoned at 9 A.M. on August 15. The vanguard consisted of William Wells, who placed himself at the head of a dozen militiamen who had been stationed at the fort, followed by the regulars, whose officers were Captain Heald, Lieutenant Helm, and Lieutenant Ronan. After them came the wagons, laden with provisions for the journey and other supplies, including weapons and ammunition. The women and children, with the exception of Mrs. Heald, also rode in one or two of the wagons. Finally, the Miami warriors, with their pack horses laden, composed the rear guard under Corporal Jordan.[24] Those Indians who had received a share of the goods and with whom agreement had been reached, perhaps numbering 200, rode at the sides and at the rear of the wagons. The procession had progressed between a mile and a mile and a half, south along the lakeshore, when Wells and the militia halted. They were about a quarter of a mile in advance of the regulars. Wells had observed a large number of Indians emerging from behind low sand dunes on both the right and the left. The hostile Indians, some 400 in number, had formed a trap into which the less than 100 whites had been forced. The jaws of the trap were closing with murderous intent.

232

Characteristically, Wells now became a whirlwind of action. Quickly turning the Kentucky thoroughbred horse on which he was mounted, he dashed back toward Captain Heald, whirling his hat around in the air over his head. Rebecca Heald, on a good horse herself, beside her husband, understood that her uncle was giving the sign that they were surrounded. Wells gestured toward a low sand ridge on the east (lake) side and shouted orders for the wagons to be driven there. Captain Heald ordered the regulars massed in front of them. The twelve militiamen who formed the vanguard had been killed, and the Indians were swarming toward the wagons. Captain Heald formed his regulars and fired a volley into the oncoming Indians. Wells shouted to him to charge them and himself led a charge before which the Indians gave way to the right and the left. Wells wheeled to the left and the Indians gave way still more. Riding back, he led a few men in a second charge to the right, and this time received a bullet through his lungs.

Meanwhile, another large band of Indians had reached the wagons and was plundering them, killing twelve children and two women. Mrs. Heald sat on her horse between the regulars and the wagons. Wells rode near to her, but before he could reach her she was wounded in six places, one arm being disabled. When he managed to reach her his horse was shot and he was pinned under the animal as it fell. They were able to exchange a few words, and she realized that he knew he was mortally wounded. Then the Indians were upon them, and Wells was able to kill two with his pistols and another with his dirk before he was himself killed.[25]

Captain Heald had been shot in the hip and twenty-six of his regulars had been killed.[26] The captain and the remnant now surrendered and his wife was taken captive. She recalled that the Indians called her Epiconyare when she showed her spirit by refusing to let an Indian woman take her saddle blanket (the feminine form of Apekonit, which was the name the Miami had given her uncle as a boy captive). It meant that she had been recognized as a Wells. The Miami who came with Wells had ridden off at the first sign of trouble. Jordan was captured but later made his escape and returned to Fort Wayne.[27]

All accounts agree that the Indians cut out the heart of William Wells, divided it among themselves, and ate it—a tribute to his bravery. Whether this occurred on the spot or was reserved for a celebration that night depends on which of the contemporary accounts is believed.[28] One account says that his head was cut off and put on a pole.[29] In accordance with Miami custom, Wells had blackened his face that morning in anticipation of a fight to the death. The Indians counted fifteen dead, seven of whom were killed by William Wells.[30]

Captain Heald and his wife were saved by J. B. Chandonnais, a trader with Kinzie's operation, who was half French and half Indian. He claimed Heald as his own prisoner and bought Mrs. Heald from her captor for a mule and a quart of whiskey. He placed them on a boat that took them to Detroit, where Heald gave his parole. They were then sent by boat to Presque Ile and eventually reached Pittsburgh, where Heald made a report dated October 23, 1812.[31]

The news of Wells's death, brought by the returning Miami, reached Fort Wayne very early. By contrast, Fort Wayne was ignorant of Hull's surrender for two weeks, during which it was besieged by 500 Indians, including Five Medals and Winamac, two Potawatomi chiefs, and many of the Miami, although Pacan and Richardville were not involved. Captain Rhea was clearly incapacitated by liquor and was deprived of his command by his subordinates. They managed to thwart a stratagem of the Indians to kill Stickney and vigorously defended the fort when Stickney became ill of a fever and nearly died. Fearing the cannon, the Indians waited for Tecumseh to send aid that never came.[32]

Meanwhile, Governor Harrison moved with great vigor. He had resigned as governor on the advent of war, hoping to be given the supreme military command in the West, or at least a commission as major-general. Madison and Eustis failed to appoint him, but the state of Kentucky commissioned him as major-general of the Kentucky volunteers. He gathered troops in that state and marched from Cincinnati to relieve Fort Wayne. Spemica-lawba (Captain James Logan), Wells's Shawnee friend, managed to visit Fort Wayne and returned to Harrison with the news that the fort would hold out but was very short of supplies. On September 11 the Indians, learning of Harrison's approach, made a desperate, futile attack. The following day Harrison's relief force arrived to find the Indians had disappeared.[33]

Harrison forced Captain Rhea to resign and sent Colonel Samuel Wells to destroy Five Medals's Village on the Elkhart River and Colonel John Payne to destroy a Miami village at the Forks of the Wabash. The officers found both villages deserted. Turtletown, on the Eel River, was much nearer Fort Wayne, and it is doubtful that many Indians there had become hostile. Nevertheless, on orders from Harrison, Turtletown was destroyed by Colonel James Simrall, although Little Turtle's house, a mile east of the village, was spared out of respect for his many years of friendship to the United States.[34]

Little Turtle died at the age of sixty-five; his son-in-law and loyal friend, William Wells, was forty-two when he met his cruel and untimely, but heroic, fate. Their Family Compact had endured for life, and their passing was a frontier tragedy. Had they lived through the war and been able to hold the Miami to their "chain of friendship" with the United States, they would have had the opportunity to achieve their aspirations for their tribe. They would also have earned a very special status in the history of Indian-white relations. But this was not to be.

Despite their ultimate failure, Wells and Little Turtle were remarkable men—men of courage and achievement in war, of vision and practical sagacity in peace. They laid out a plan to be accomplished that was possible of attainment if the trust and backing of the federal government were present. That government, under Thomas Jefferson, should have given its support, for their program was wholly in accord with Jeffersonian theory. Their failure resulted essentially because Jefferson was too much the philosopher and too little the effective executive. Jefferson's subordinates, Dearborn and Harrison, were allowed to act on their own judgment and not pressed to conform to Jeffersonian ideals.

At Fort Wayne, Wells and Turtle were undermined by John Johnston. On the frontier, generally, it was never forgotten that Wells was a renegade and that Little Turtle was an Indian. Yet despite this adverse bias of the frontier mind, the two failed more from circumstances beyond their control than from anything else. Wells was an intelligent man but was primarily a man of action. His exploits as scout for Wayne and his heroic death were remembered by those of his own generation but forgotten with the passage of time. A county in Indiana, a street in Fort Wayne, and another in Chicago were named for him, but few today are aware of the origin of these names.

That Captain Wells had never taken up his preemption right nor sold any of the land on the site of ancient Kekionga gives ground for the speculation that Little Turtle had in mind not only an attempt to civilize his fellow tribesmen but also a project to retain this land, with his son-in-law's cooperation, in order to rebuild Kekionga and make it once more the capital and center of all Miami tribal activity. Such a plan would no doubt have encountered certain difficulties, but it was a grand conception and one that he may well have harbored. Turtle's death, and that of Wells, put an end to any hope of achieving the plan. It may be the explanation, however, of Little Turtle's wish to die at Wells's house. Only in this way could he be buried at Kekionga, where he had driven off General Harmar, who had burned "that glorious village," as Little Turtle referred to it at the Treaty of Greeneville. The dream of maintaining "that glorious village" in its historic setting thus was buried with him.

Little Turtle was not only an able leader in war and a capable diplomat but his thinking was statesmanlike. Yet among Indian leaders he has been overshadowed by men of less ability who were noted for spectacular failures in enterprises that were doomed from the outset. The name of his tribe is one of the most familiar in our geographic nomenclature, yet his own

235

name is less familiar in history than those of Pontiac, Tecumseh, Black Hawk, Sitting Bull, Chief Joseph, or Geronimo, and it has not been memorialized by the white man in the place-names of counties, towns, or streets. In a larger sense, however, the name of the territory and the state of Indiana bear eloquent testimony to the career of Little Turtle as a warrior and statesman, as well as to his valiant determination to hold for his tribe the Wabash-Maumee line. Perhaps it is fitting, therefore, to refer to him as the First Sagamore of the Wabash.[35]

NOTES

1. It is frequently stated that Tecumseh returned shortly after the battle of Tippecanoe, but no certain evidence of his return has been found before two months had elapsed. Tecumseh did not make this peaceful statement until May 15, 1812, and prior to that time his known actions had been warlike. ESAREY, II, 60–61.

2. Ibid., 27. Wells to Harrison, February 10, 1812.

3. Ibid., 15. Eustis to Harrison, January 17, 1812.

4. THORNBROUGH (1), 109–10, for Charley's speech. A letter from Stickney to Eustis, April 21, 1812, ibid., 113–15, mentions that Wells had been very friendly to the new agent and to the views of the government. Stickney also reported, "The Little Turtle has just sent his son to Wells and Wells has wrote a note to me," a very clear illustration of the close cooperation of Turtle and Wells with Stickney in this period of great uncertainty.

5. See ibid., 120–23, for Five Medals's speech and Stickney's reply.

6. An earlier effort on the part of the British to establish contact with Little Turtle had been made in May 1808. William Claus, a grandson of Sir William Johnson and a British Indian agent, expected to see Lafontaine, Richardville's son-in-law, and Little Turtle at Sandwich but was disappointed to find that Little Turtle was not with Lafontaine. MICHIGAN, XXIII, 52, 64. At this time the British sent a gold watch to Turtle in an effort to buy his support. The watch has been preserved. See WATCH, 17–32.

7. THORNBROUGH (1), 125–29, 133–34, 139–40. Also ESAREY, II, 50–53, 60–62.

8. THORNBROUGH (1), 140–43. Also ESAREY, II, 76–77. Stickney reported to Governor Hull; Wells to Governor Harrison.

9. THORNBROUGH (1), 149–52. Stickney to Harrison, June 30, 1812. At this time Stickney became embroiled in an argument with Harrison as to whether or not he was under Harrison's orders or solely under those of the secretary of war. Stickney was allowed a wider latitude in his correspondence than was ever accorded to Wells, but Harrison was able to assert his authority.

10. The War of 1812 was thus fought without real cause, and one battle was fought after peace had been made due to the slowness of communication.

11. THORNBROUGH (1), 152–54. Stickney to Captain Nathan Heald [at Fort Dearborn], July 6, 1812.

12. Possibly Bright's disease, although this ailment was not identified and named until 1827.

13. THORNBROUGH (1), 161, 165, 167, 178. The coffin makers and gravediggers were probably soldiers garrisoned at Fort Wayne.

14. Robert F. Lancaster, "Renowned Whitley County Man Got $3 Funeral," in WHITLEY, (December 1976), 16–18. This article appeared originally in *Outdoor Indiana*. A skull found at Lawton Place in 1911 was determined by the Smithsonian Institution to have been that of a twenty-three-year-old woman, not that of Little Turtle. Although no such scientific appraisal of the skeleton reburied in 1912 was made, the objects taken from the grave seem to afford satisfactory proof. L.T. and W., *Fort Wayne Journal-Gazette*, September 16, 1967.

15. ESAREY, II, 77–78, Wells to Harrison, July 22, 1812. THORNBROUGH (1), 162–64, Stickney to Eustis, July 19, 1812; 165-66, Stickney to Johnston, July 20, 1812; 168–69, Stickney to Harrison, July 24, 1812.

16. ESAREY, II, 33–34, 68–70.

17. HUTTON, 218.

18. BARNHART (1), 187–99, contains two versions of a letter by Jordan and reviews briefly other known accounts. QUAIFE (1), 211–16, concluded that General Hull's orders were received directly from Detroit and not by way of Fort Wayne. CARTER (1), XVI, 261–62, Thomas Forsyth to the Governor of Louisiana Territory, September 7, 1812, states that Captain Heald, conducting Indian chiefs to a conference at Piqua, encountered Winamac, escorted by Wells and his Miami, at Terre Coupee, and that they all returned to Fort Dearborn in consequence of Hull's orders, received at this time. Terre Coupee was about midway between Chicago and Fort Wayne, fifteen miles west of the Potawatomi village of Mishawaka. While such a scenario is not impossible, it is hard to believe that Captain Heald would have left Fort Dearborn in view of the prevailing indications of hostility on the part of the large number of Indians gathered there. Forsyth, whose information was from John Kinzie, also stated that Marpock (Main Poche) brought a wampum war belt from the British, at Malden, on August 14, which emboldened the Indians to attack on the following day. In my opinion General William Hull was responsible for the tragic outcome. Had his orders been discretionary, there is every reason to believe that Fort Dearborn, defended by artillery, could have withstood even a prolonged siege.

19. WILLIAMS, 343–52. KINZIE is the best-known account but contains many inaccuracies. Mrs. Kinzie was not present in 1812 at the "Chicago Massacre" and was biased against Heald.

20. Hull's orders did not arrive at Fort Dearborn until August 9, so they were known in Fort Wayne several days earlier. See QUAIFE (1), 138, for General Hull's orders to Captain Heald, July 29, 1812.

21. DRAPER, 23S58–62. Lyman Draper interviewed Darius Heald, son of Nathan and Rebecca Wells Heald, in 1868. KIRKLAND is based on an interview with Darius Heald in 1891. The Kirkland account contains some details not given to Draper, but the two accounts agree remarkably well considering the years that separated them.

22. CORBIN, 219–28. Corbin's story was dictated on July 8, 1826. He estimated the total number of Indians around the fort at 600 and says that Wells had made

an agreement with them to act as an escort, an agreement they did not carry out. He did not indicate that Wells had no firm faith in the agreement, however, as Mrs. Heald believed. Nor did he limit the agreement to the "friendly Indians," which was probably the case.

23. CARTER (1), XVI, 261–62. Thomas Forsyth to the Governor of Louisiana Territory, September 7, 1812. Forsyth also believed that Wells had favored the evacuation of Fort Dearborn. The various eyewitness accounts of the massacre are found in QUAIFE (1), 378–421.

24. Many historians have written that half of the Miami were with Wells in the vanguard and half of them were at the rear of the wagons. DRAPER, 23S58–62, which gives Darius Heald's 1868 version of his mother's recollections, states that Wells "and the militia" were in the advance. Darius Heald thought that by the term militia his mother meant the friendly Miami brought by Wells. However, Indians were never referred to as militia, as Mrs. Heald, an officer's wife, was well aware. The militiamen were all killed, as the vanguard was first to be attacked. The Miami, on the other hand, are said either to have slipped away or to have actually joined the other Indians (Jordan in BARNHART [1]).

These two actions are not irreconcilable. From their position at the rear they would naturally first mingle with those Indians who were neutral, mostly Potawatomi, and then be able to ride off, leading their pack horses, without attracting much notice. This would have been impossible if they had been in the vanguard. Had any of them been with Wells, some would have been killed. Since there were only thirty of them, they would probably have kept together, and Jordan must have been in their company to observe their mingling with the Potawatomi neutrals, some of whom may have joined the attack. It is possible that Wells had said farewell to his Miami friends on the previous day and had told them to save themselves in case his suspicions proved correct.

25. KIRKLAND, 23, 31–38. Also DRAPER, 23S58–62. There is some question as to whether Wells was able to extricate his leg from under his horse. As to the identity of the Indian by whom Wells was finally killed, Peesotum and White Hair, two Potawatomi, vied for the honor. Consensus favors Peesotum.

26. Captain Heald's report was published in NILES, 155, November 7, 1812. See ibid., 79–80, for an earlier and less correct report of the fall of Fort Dearborn.

27. BARNHART (1), 191–93. Jordan made his escape while camped on the Des Plaines River, northwest of Chicago.

28. CORBIN says, "Wells' heart and liver were eaten the night after."

29. Only Jordan, in BARNHART (1), says that Wells's head was displayed on a pole.

30. DRAPER, 23S58–62. Mrs. Heald thought her uncle blackened his face as a disguise, but this has not been generally accepted. It may have been done for both reasons. Wells himself told her, before he died, that he had killed seven Indians.

31. NILES, 155, November 7, 1812. Darius Heald told the details of Chandonnais's successful efforts to save the lives of the Healds. Chandonnais was acting on orders from John Kinzie, who had also arranged for the boat in which the escape was made.

32. WOEHRMANN, 225–30.

238

33. Ibid., 238–41.

34. DILLON, 494. These Indian towns were destroyed between September 13 and 19, 1812.

35. SAGAMORE, 78–79. An explanation of the designation "Sagamore of the Wabash has been made in the Preface.

The Miami During and After the War of 1812

Harrison's destruction of the villages near Fort Wayne provoked the Miami to send war belts to the Delaware asking their assistance in fighting the Americans. The Delaware were unresponsive, but Harrison, learning of the Miami request, extended his punitive measures against them by dispatching Colonel John B. Campbell with 600 men to destroy the Miami villages on the Mississinewa. Campbell first destroyed the Delaware village of Silver Heels, which was quite uncalled for, and then two Miami villages, including that of Metocina, the head chief of the Mississinewa (formerly the Mengakonkia) Miami. Then, on December 18, 1812, he was attacked by 200 Miami warriors under François Godfroy and was forced to abandon his campaign. While the Miami regarded this campaign against them as unjust, they could not deny that they had attempted to capture Fort Harrison, that some of their warriors had participated in the siege of Fort Wayne, and that a few had actually joined Tecumseh in Canada.[1]

Pacan, Richardville, and Metocina tried to keep the Miami neutral in the war, both before and after Colonel Campbell's raid, but without much success. The Americans insisted that the tribes within the United States must be their allies or be considered their enemies. The Wabash travel and trade route could not be allowed to remain in the possession of the Miami unless they were on the American side. After the fall of Michilimackinac, Fort Dearborn, and Detroit, the British were poised for an invasion, and the Indians recruited by Tecumseh flocked increasingly to their aid.

On November 22 Spemicalawba (Captain James Logan), the Shawnee

240

scout who had been brought up as a white man, was captured, with two Indian companions along the Maumee, by Alexander Elliott, the half Shawnee son of Matthew Elliott, and a party of seven Indians. Logan and his companions killed all but two of their captors, including Alexander Elliott, and made their escape, although Logan was mortally wounded. His name is perpetuated in the Indiana town on the Wabash at the mouth of the Eel River, called Logansport.[2]

The year 1813 opened inauspiciously for the American cause with the defeat and capture of General James Winchester on the Raisin River and subsequent Indian atrocities, which Matthew Elliott and General Henry Procter did not exert themselves to prevent.[3] General Harrison successfully defended Fort Meigs from May 1 to 9, 1813, against General Procter and a large number of Indians led by Tecumseh. In July he sent Colonel William Russell against the Miami villages on the Mississinewa. Russell met no resistance, burned several villages, and, reaching the Wabash, marched south to Vincennes with his 600 men.[4] Harrison thus ensured that there would be no uprising to the rear when he invaded Canada, which he was enabled to do by Commodore O. H. Perry's victory over the British naval force on Lake Erie on September 10.

Detroit was reoccupied on September 30. At the battle of the Thames River on October 5, Harrison defeated and put General Procter to flight. Here Tecumseh was killed, bravely fighting to the last, after Procter had abandoned the field.[5] Harrison was unable to follow up his success and retired to Detroit. The death of Tecumseh disheartened the militant Indians, who began to see that the British were less powerful than they had thought.

Harrison resigned his military command on May 11, 1814, in protest over the failure of the secretary of war, John Armstrong, to assign to him a more active command. Together with Lewis Cass, governor of the Michigan Territory, he convened about 4,000 Indians at Greeneville in July for a council. On July 22 the various tribes made peace with the United States and agreed to furnish aid in fighting the British, which became unnecessary when the war was ended by the Treaty of Ghent on December 24, 1814.

Pacan and Charley (Kitunga) spoke for the Miami at Greeneville. They tried to defend their neutral policy, but Harrison and Cass equated neutrality with deceit. Pacan, who was nearing seventy years of age, spoke of his personal sorrow at the loss of members of his family in the war. There was nothing the Miami could do but to submit and to express their regret that they had been unable to prevent some of their warriors from joining Tecumseh and the British.[6]

In the spring of 1816, Pacan sent word to all the Miami that he was going to establish a village on the Eel River. He invited them to bring their women and children there.[7] It is not clear whether the village was to be located at the former site of Kenapakomoko or not. But before his plan could be realized Pacan died. The principal chief of the Atchatchakangouen Miami for fifty-two years, he had been a steady and dignified leader, one who was able to maintain his influence as long as he lived. Although he made a minimum adjustment to changing times and was never clearly committed to the United States, as Little Turtle had been, he maintained the Miami policy of independent neutrality until it finally proved insufficient in the War of 1812.

Pacan was succeeded as head chief by his nephew, Richardville, who had long been associated with him. Richardville guided the destiny of the tribe until his death on August 13, 1841, at the age of eighty. He was well educated and spoke French and English fluently, but when he became head chief he began the practice of speaking only the Miami language. And the longer he lived the more he adhered to Indian customs. Possessed of a shrewd intelligence, it is possible that he had observed Little Turtle closely enough to realize that it was advantageous to deal with the Americans through an interpreter. This gave time for consideration before making a reply, especially if one pretended not to understand English and refused to speak it. However, his ability as a diplomat was of no avail in preserving Miami lands. At the Treaty of St. Marys, Ohio, signed on October 6, 1818, the Miami were punished for their failure to support the United States during the War of 1812. They were forced to give up most of central Indiana, an area of more than seven million acres, lying between the Wabash and the lands ceded by previous treaties.

The Delaware, on October 3, had released their White River lands and agreed to move beyond the Mississippi. Had the Delaware stood firm, as they might have done because of their loyalty in the War of 1812, the Miami might have emerged more fortunately, for these lands required the assent of both tribes before they could be alienated. When the Delaware decided to move, the Miami were placed in an impossible position.

South of the Wabash the Miami managed to retain only the Big Miami Reserve and several smaller reserves. The Big Miami Reserve consisted of a tract of about 1,600 square miles, whose northern boundary was the Wabash River from the mouth of the Eel River (Logansport) to the mouth of the Salamonie River (Lagro). With the exception of a narrow strip on the western side, which was ceded in 1834 along with other smaller reservations, this tract was retained as their winter hunting ground until 1840. The Eel River Miami accepted 100 square miles on Sugar Creek (Thorntown), which they retained only until 1828. The land north of the

Wabash, though held by the Miami, was populated mostly by the Potawatomi, except for the area between the Eel River and the Wabash.[8]

Richardville was able to have seven sections of land on the Wabash transferred to himself in fee simple. In later treaties he continued the practice, which also was adopted by other Miami chiefs who were partially white. This was an important development. It has generally been condemned as selfish and grasping. Certainly, at the time of his death, Richardville was the largest landholder and probably the wealthiest person in Indiana, and as such he was envied by the whites. But his policy can be defended on the grounds that the only way Indians could retain land was on an individual basis. Furthermore, as a Miami chief Richardville was expected to be hospitable toward his tribesmen, and he adhered to this old custom. There is no doubt that his lands were a refuge for many Miami and that they subsisted on his bounty to some extent. The settlers did not understand this.

Individual landownership was responsible for the fact that nearly half the Miami were exempt from moving to Kansas in 1846.[9] Those forced to move were given lands on the Marais de Cygnes River south of Kansas City, in what became Miami County. The remnants of the Wea Miami and the Piankashaw Miami had joined the Peoria and were living in Missouri. They were also transferred to Miami County, Kansas, but did not reunite with the Miami proper. Still later, the Miami and the Peoria also sold out and moved to the extreme northeastern corner of Oklahoma. Some chose to remain in Kansas, took title to lands in Miami County, and were not retained on the tribal roll.[10]

In Oklahoma an attempt to unite with the Peoria was only partially carried out, and there is still a Miami tribal organization there. For many years it was the only Miami tribal organization recognized by the government, but eventually the Miami who remained in Indiana received such recognition as well. The descendants of Richardville, of Metocina, of Godfroy, and of Lafontaine were fairly numerous and did not have to move. Some intercourse between the two tribal units, however, continued during most of the nineteenth century. One of Richardville's grandsons, Thomas F. Richardville, was a famous lawyer who, although he lived in Oklahoma, refused to sever his connections with the Miami in Indiana.[11]

Charles Beaubien was the second husband of Richardville's mother, Tacumwah (The Other Side). Their daughter, Josetta Beaubien Roubidoux, had many descendants of predominantly white blood. They were repudiated by the Indiana Miami in 1867 and their names struck from the tribal roll. Her eldest son was thereby denied the succession as head chief. Instead, Richardville was succeeded by his eldest daughter's husband, Francis Lafontaine. Another of his daughters married James Godfroy.[12]

Meshingomesia, eldest son of Metocina, went further and tried to prove that Richardville and Pacan were not lawful chiefs and that the principal chief of the Miami was himself.[13] Thus, the observation by Cadillac that the Miami would destroy themselves by the jealousy of their chiefs appears to have been well grounded. The present head chief of the Indiana Miami is a descendant of Metocina. Meshingomesia's repudiation of the leadership of Richardville and his successors was revolt against intermarriage of Indians with whites, of which there was less among the Mississinewa Miami. Nevertheless, the trend toward intermarriage continued even among this conservative band. Little Turtle, of course, had favored intermarriage.

The Indiana Miami exhibited the same strong attachment to their homeland that had been one of Little Turtle's most marked characteristics. His hope for a perpetuation of Kekionga as the Miami capital died with him, but he would have been pleased that many Miami chose not to migrate but rather retain land and remain in Indiana. Today there are more Miami in Indiana than in Oklahoma, reflecting a natural increase in population in their homeland that has perhaps been aided by the winning of several legal actions against the federal government for failure to perform treaty obligations. These suits resulted in payments which were divided among eligible tribal members. Here, again, it was Little Turtle who insisted from the outset that treaty obligations be kept by whites as well as Indians.

Little Turtle's repeated efforts to prohibit the sale of liquor to the Indians had been unsuccessful, as was true also of the efforts of the government in this direction. In 1839 Samuel Milroy, Indian agent to the Miami, reported that since 1822 the Miami in Indiana had been reduced to about 700 by the death of 450 men and 36 women by stabbing in drunken brawls. In that year the government factory system had been abolished and drinking among the Indians had increased. When the Miami were removed to Kansas in 1846 they were characterized by the Indian agent there as the most depraved by liquor of any of the tribes being moved. By contrast, the Wea Miami and the Piankashaw Miami had reached their low point a generation earlier and their survivors were more sober. Eventually, the Miami proper turned the corner, but not before they had further declined in population.[14]

NOTES

1. ANSON, 168–70, gives a good account of Campbell's campaign. The correspondence between Harrison and Campbell is found in ESAREY, II, 228–31, 248–49, 253–65.

2. HORSMAN, xii, 202–3. Spemicalawba is said to have been a nephew of Tecumseh. He is also said to have permitted himself to be captured in order to perform this exploit and stifle criticism by whites who did not trust his loyalty.

3. Ibid., 203–5.

4. ANSON, 173; ESAREY, II, 497–99.

5. ANSON, 173; HORSMAN, 213–14.

6. ANSON, 174–75. Anson remarks that this treaty "marked the end of Miami military power and influence." Among the signers for the Miami at the Second Treaty of Greeneville in 1814 was "Chekemetine or Turtle's Brother." It is uncertain whether or not this was a younger brother of Little Turtle. KAPPLER I, 105–7.

7. ESAREY, II, 725. Governor Thomas Posey to William H. Crawford, Secretary of War, April 20, 1816.

8. KAPPLER, I, 171–72.

9. Ibid. Howard County, Indiana, formed from the Big Miami Reserve, was first called Richardville, but the name was changed because of the opposition of white settlers. The town of Richardville in Howard County also changed its name to Russiaville (pronounced Roosh'-e-ville). For an estimate of Richardville's character, see ANSON, 188–90.

10. ANSON, 238–39, 246–47. See also WRIGHT, 182–83, 207–9, 209–10, 254–55.

11. ANSON, 248, 258–59.

12. Ibid., 272–73; CHAPUT, 114-16.

13. Meshingomesia succeeded his father and claimed that succession had followed this pattern for generations. This is contrary to all known evidence which places hereditary right in the female line among all the Miami bands. Modern chiefs are chosen by election in both Oklahoma and Indiana. One elected chief was deposed during the Kansas period of Miami history.

14. FOREMAN, 126, 129–31, 201, 204.

The Descendants of Little Turtle
and of William Wells

IT IS A MATTER OF SOME INTEREST to trace, insofar as the very meager sources of information permit, the fortunes of Little Turtle's descendants. His four children included two sons and two daughters. The daughters were probably the eldest and the youngest of the children. The names of the two sons are given by Samuel P. Kaler as Makeshenequah and Makattamonquah; by Calvin Young as Wakshingay and Katemongwah.[1] The first was the father of Kilsoquah; the second was the father of Coesse. Whether there were other grandchildren in these lines is unknown.

Among the twenty-three chiefs who signed the Treaty of 1838 was Katahmaungquaw, who was certainly Little Turtle's second son. His name is followed by Kohwazah, which is undoubtedly his son Coesse. Among the nineteen chiefs who signed the Treaty of 1840 was Koessay (a section of land was reserved to Kowassee by this treaty), but we do not find the name of his father, from which it may be concluded that he had died about 1839.[2]

In the list of signatories of 1838 the name of the eldest son does not appear. But in the Treaty of 1840 is found the name Waukashingquah, which bears a close resemblance to the version of the name of the eldest son as given by Calvin Young. Kilsoquah's father, then, was living in 1840 but may have died soon after.[3]

Kilsoquah was born in 1810, two years before the death of her famous grandfather; she died in 1915. Her birthplace was Markle, Indiana, and she lived most of her life near Roanoke, also in Huntington County. Her first marriage in 1826 was to John Owl, who died after a short time; they lived at Seek's Village, near the former site of Turtletown. She later married Anthony Rivarre (Shawpenomquah), by whom she had six children, the last born in 1849. In 1881 she traveled to Oklahoma, probably in order to share in a distribution of money owed the Miami by the government. She returned to Indiana with her youngest son, who lived with his mother following his wife's death. Her daughter Mary (Wahnogquanquah, or Snow) remained in Oklahoma, where she married. Guy Froman, chief of the Peoria tribe at the Quapaw agency in Oklahoma, is a grandson of this marriage and therefore a great-great-great grandson of Little Turtle.[4]

Kilsoquah's cousin Coesse died about 1853, having recovered the leadership of his village from Chief Seek. He had a son, who died at age sixteen, and two daughters. His wife and daughters lived on his land, just south of Columbia City, Indiana, for about ten years following his death. They sold part of the land through which the Blue River flowed just a mile or so above its junction with the Eel River. Later, they sold the remaining land and moved to the Indian community on the Wabash, east of Peru, Indiana. Coesse's name is perpetuated in a small village east of Columbia City, about two miles south of the former site of Turtletown.[5]

The youngest daughter of Little Turtle, Macutemonquah, married Great White Loon (Wahpemongquah), whose village was on the Aboite River. Great White Loon's name appears among the signers of the 1838 treaty as Wawpemaungquaw, but it is not on the treaty of 1840; again, it may be concluded that he had died about 1839. His family continued to reside on the Aboite River or in that general vicinity. Little Turtle's second wife married a Shawnee and moved to Kansas with that tribe, where she lived for many years.[6]

The will of William Wells was dated January 17, 1810. By its provision all his real and personal estate was bequeathed to "my beloved wife and my five beloved children Ann Wells–Rebecca Wells–William Wayne Wells and Polly Wells that I had by my former wife and my son Sam'l Geiger Wells that I have had by my Present wife and such other children as I may have by my said wife . . . and I constitute my said wife and my two brothers Sam'l Wells and Yelverton P. Wells or any two of them as executors . . . and guardians of my said children."[7]

The name of Jane Wells, the daughter born in 1808 to an unknown Indian woman, is not mentioned in the will. It may be that Wells considered her an illegitimate child; or it may indicate that it was the mother who divorced Wells, taking the child with her, rather than Wells who divorced her. For whatever reason (perhaps he had not told his wife, Mary [Polly] Geiger Wells, about the existence of Jane Wells), this child did not share in the will. Nor was this child, insofar as is known, related to Little Turtle. Nevertheless, Jane Wells, a Miami of half blood, was provided for in several treaties, and it may be well to discuss her life before passing on to those children enumerated in the will.

A section of land was reserved for Jane Turner Wells by the Treaty of St. Marys in 1818, at which time she would have been ten years old. The middle name of Turner may be related to the fact that she was present at the treaty signing with Dr. William Turner, the husband of Ann Wells, who was trying to get the appointment of Indian agent at Fort Wayne for himself. In the treaty of 1826, in which she is called Jane S. Wells, one half-section is reserved for her.[8] The treaty was signed on the Wabash at the mouth of the Mississinewa, not far from where Jane lived all her life. In 1830 she married John H. Griggs, who was born in New Jersey. Griggs was a hatter and apparently worked at his trade at least until 1850. In 1860 he was a justice of the peace in Peru, and in 1870 he was city assessor.[9]

Jane Wells Griggs maintained her status as a Miami. In 1854 the Treaty of Washington awarded her and her six children, who are enumerated, $7,689.22 which was due them because they had not collected the annuity payments to which they were entitled for several years.[10] The Griggs children and their probable years of birth are given as Warren A. (1831), Charles F. (1833), Anthony W. (1840), Eliza A. (1844), Martha J. (1846), and Maria (1848). Of these only Eliza was living with her parents in 1870. Charles F. Griggs had married and was a harness maker in Peru. He had one child at the time, named Warren A. for Charles's elder brother.[11] On May 7, 1880, John H. and Jane Wells Griggs celebrated their golden wedding anniversary, an event which received some publicity in Louisville. John died later in that year. Dessie Griggs, probably a descendant of Charles Griggs, was reported by Otho Winger to have been a county nurse in northern Indiana prior to 1942 and before her marriage.[12]

Jane Wells is of particular interest because she married and lived among the whites while maintaining her rights and those of her children as tribal members in Indiana, even after the tribal authority was relocated in Kansas and Oklahoma. In this respect she was representative of many, perhaps most, of the Indiana Miami who did not migrate. While the descendants of Sweet Breeze were aware of Jane and her family, they did not keep in close touch over the years, as was seen in the erroneous report in 1882 that Jane's husband's name was Matthew or Samuel, rather than John.

An inventory and appraisal of the personal property of William Wells, including slaves and indentures, was made in December 1812, with Captain Nathan Heald acting as one of the appraisers. Three black adults, one man and two women, and four girls and two boys were valued at a total of $1,500. The two indentures were valued at $280. Other personal property was appraised at $429.91 and brought $411.16 at a sale. The slaves and indentured servants were not sold at this time. An inventory of other assets totaled $4,171.30, of which $615 was cash on hand and the remainder in notes payable for loans to various individuals. Polly Wells signed this inventory in 1813 as executrix of the will.[13]

Wells also owned nearly 1,200 acres of land near Piqua, Ohio, and held preemption rights to 320 acres at Fort Wayne, where he had lived. The price of government land was $2 an acre at this time. Probably the government price would be a fair appraisal of Wells's land at the time of his death, which would have amounted to about $3,000. This would bring the total value of his estate to about $9,000, a considerable sum for the time but by no means large enough to support John Johnston's unproven charges that it was amassed by cheating the Indians and by engaging in illegal trading in liquor. Wells had earned on the average, for seventeen years of government employment, about $600 a year plus an allowance of four rations per day. This was just about enough to provide his living. The amount of cash on loan, a little over $4,000, was approximately the amount of his pension of $20 a month drawn since 1795 or 1796.

Polly Wells was pregnant at the time of her husband's death, and later in 1812 she gave birth to a son named Yelverton Peyton Wells, for his paternal uncle. In April 1817 Polly Wells married Robert Turner, of Louisville, a brother of the post surgeon at Fort Wayne, Dr. William Turner, who married Ann, Wells's eldest daughter, around the same time.[14] By the will of her father, dated December 12, 1831, and recorded September 12, 1832, "Polly Turner, wife of Robert Turner" received one-fifth of his estate, with remainder "if any left at her death, to her children, Samuel and Peyton Wells." Robert Turner was not named as an executor of Colonel Geiger's will, although his other two sons-in-law were so designated, along with his two sons. Samuel Geiger Wells did not long outlive his grandfather. His will, dated November 12, 1832, and recorded February 4, 1833, left his estate to his mother, with remainder to his brother Yelverton Peyton Wells, who was named coexecutor, along with his uncle, Jacob Geiger (1789–1857), whose first wife was Margaret Wells (1782–1820), daughter of his father's brother Samuel.[15]

Dr. William Turner was ambitious to become Indian agent at Fort Wayne and engaged in a defamatory campaign against Benjamin Stickney. He succeeded in becoming secretary to the commissioners who negotiated the Treaty of St. Marys in the fall of 1818, and he occupied Wells's former post of subagent for the Miami from March 1819 until May 1820, when he was discharged for "unsatisfactory conduct." Although Turner was a drunkard, his dismissal was actually precipitated by his ill-advised deposit of the annuities in a Cincinnati bank which failed.[16]

Ann Wells and her sister, Rebecca, two years her junior, were residents of Fort Wayne and seem to have been close companions all their lives. Ann and William Turner had no children. Rebecca married James Hackley, Jr., an army officer stationed at Fort Wayne. A Kentuckian, Hackley was commissioned a second lieutenant on March 12, 1812, and promoted to first lieutenant on March 13, 1813. He continued in the army after the close of the war and became a captain on May 17, 1816, but resigned his commission on December 31, 1818.[17]

It is certain that both Ann and Rebecca were married before the Treaty of St. Marys, on October 6, 1818, for a section of land was reserved to each of them by that treaty under the names of Ann Turner and Rebecca Hackley. Similarly, Rebecca's two children, Ann and Jack Hackley, were born prior to October 23, 1826, for at the Treaty of the Wabash, signed on that date, one section of land between the Maumee and the St. Joseph rivers was reserved to each of them by name. Also, one half-section each was reserved to Ann Turner and Rebecca Hackley. One of the puzzling aspects of the Treaty of St. Marys is that a section of land "on the south side of the Wabash where the portage path strikes the river" was reserved to Little Turtle. It is puzzling because he had been dead for six years. One wonders what the legal status of this tract is today.[18]

Captain Hackley, who committed suicide in 1831, may not have been the confirmed drunkard that Dr. Turner was, but neither was he a model of sobriety. It would seem that Ann Turner had ceased to live with her husband before his death and lived with her sister, Rebecca, for in the 1826 treaty she was referred to as "Ann Turner alias Hackley." The two sisters are remembered to have attended Presbyterian church services regularly in Fort Wayne during this period. Ann Turner died on July 26, 1834, and Rebecca Hackley died on June 14, 1835.[19] The Treaty of the Forks of the Wabash, signed on October 23, 1834, reserved a quarter-section of land for Rebecca.[20] Dr. Turner's death occurred on September 26, 1837.[21]

Rebecca Hackley's children moved in opposite directions. Ann made a marriage among the whites, of which nothing is known, but her son, Oliver Farrand, died in New York City in 1921. He preserved a few letters written during the years 1805–9 by his grandmother and her sister from Louisville to their father, William Wells, at Fort Wayne. Jack Hackley cast his lot with the Miami and moved with them to Kansas. He is known to have had a daughter, called Polly ("Sis") Hackley. In 1854 he was one of five delegates chosen to negotiate the Treaty of Washington for the Miami in Kansas, the Indiana Miami being represented by the same number. His signature appears as Lanapincha, or Jack Hackley, and he was the only delegate who was able to sign his name rather than make his mark.[22] At this time Hackley was employed as a miller at the Osage River agency.[23] Whether he remained in Kansas or later moved to Oklahoma is unknown.

William Wayne Wells was appointed to West Point, where he began his studies in 1817. Indiana became a state on December 11, 1816, but it is likely that Thomas Posey, the territorial governor, may have made or arranged his appointment, for he had served in Wayne's campaign and had known young Wells's father. William Wayne had been educated in private schools in Kentucky. He was intelligent and ambitious to pursue a military career. He graduated fourth in his class in 1821 and was commissioned second lieutenant in the artillery on July 1 of that year. He was promoted to first lieutenant on April 11, 1825, but over the years in the service he became an increasingly heavy drinker, a common habit among officers stationed at isolated posts. He resigned his commission on July 31, 1831, and died on September 8, 1832.[24] His Indian name was Wapemongah (White Loon). He was not married. His career had been one of great promise, and it is ironic that it was ruined by the effects of liquor, a problem his grandfather had so clearly perceived and sought to control.

The youngest of Sweet Breeze's children was Mary Wells, born at Fort Wayne on May 10, 1800, who was also called Polly, a familiar nickname for Mary in that period (probably derived from Molly, which was used so commonly that some alternative was required). Her Indian name was given by her descendants as Ahmahquauzahquah, which they said meant "a sweet breeze," although that has not been verified.

Her mother's name is variously reported to have been Wanangapeth, Wanmangopith, and Manwangapeth, all of which appear to be garbled forms of the Miami word meaning "sweet": *uahkapanggeh* (Thornton) or *ouak-apanke* (Volney), pronounced Wahkahpanggeh. All Miami words end in a vowel sound, so the word for sweet breeze, whatever it may have been, could not have ended with "th." The conclusion seems to be that Mary's Miami name meant something else and that her mother's name, Sweet Breeze, bore more resemblance to Wakapanke than to Wanangapeth.

Mary Wells was five years old when her mother died. The years 1805–9, which she spent in Kentucky with her father's relatives, were perhaps of more influence on her than on her siblings. Her marriage to James Wolcott, at St. Louis, on May 8, 1821, gives rise to the speculation that she may have spent several years with her relative Rebecca Heald and with Rebecca's husband, Major Nathan Heald, who, following Heald's honorable discharge on June 1, 1814, lived on a farm near St. Louis.[25] Wolcott, who was from Torrington, Connecticut, was a judge at Fort Wayne, where he and Mary presumably had met and been acquainted for some time before they married. They returned to Fort Wayne, where they lived until 1826, when they moved to Maumee, Ohio.

Mary Wells Wolcott died on February 19, 1843, at the age of forty-three, which was approximately the age attained by her older sisters. She had a more stable marriage and more descendants than they. Judge Wolcott survived her for thirty years, during which he remarried and had children by his second wife. Mary had a section of land reserved for her in 1818 but does not appear to have been provided for by subsequent treaties. One of her sons, Frederick Allen Wolcott, was killed at the battle of Atlanta, on July 22, 1864, but her other sons, William Wells Wolcott, Henry Clay Wolcott, and James Madison Wolcott, were still living in 1882. James was mayor of Maumee and wrote for the Chicago celebration of 1882, "We are proud of our Indian [Little Turtle] blood and of our Capt. Wells blood. We try to keep up the customs of our ancestors and dress occasionally in Indian costumes." He also sent to Chicago the tomahawk that Captain Wells had at the time of his death and presented the Chicago Historical Society with a number of books belonging to Captain Wells which contained his autograph.[26]

Mary's daughter, Mary Ann Wolcott, married Smith Gilbert in 1849. Her daughter, Frederika Gilbert Hall, lived until July 19, 1934, when she died at the age of eighty-four.[27] Henry C. Wolcott and James M. Wolcott died without issue. No information concerning William Wells Wolcott and other members of the Gilbert or Hall families has been found.

William Wells had acquired preemption rights to a half-section of land, including the former site of Kekionga, in what is now the city of Fort Wayne. On this site he had built his house and also a Miami council house, which burned down during the time John Johnston was agent. The preemption rights had been taken up by his heirs, who sold the land at $1.25 an acre in the 1820s, after the Land Law of 1820 reduced the price of government land.[28]

On November 28, 1840, when Richardville signed the treaty giving up the Miami tribal lands and agreeing that the tribe would move to Kansas, William Henry Harrison, who had done more to prevent the achievement of Little Turtle's plans than any other person, had just been elected president of the United States. Harrison's chief presidential distinctions were to make the longest inaugural address and serve the shortest term of any of the chief executives. He also has the distinction of having paid a superlative tribute to Little Turtle, of whom he wrote, "He took great interest in everything that appertained to civilized life and possessed a mind capable of understanding their advantages in a degree far superior to any other Indian."[29]

NOTES

1. KALER and MARING; YOUNG (1).
2. KAPPLER, I, 519–25, 531–34.

3. Ibid.

4. KALER and MARING, 79–83, contains Kaler's 1906 interview with Kilsoquah. John Owl was the son of the Miami Chief Owl, who was often quoted by Harrison as a source of information. ANSON, 279, confirms her Oklahoma visit; for Guy Froman, see ibid., 256, and the photograph between pp. 270 and 271. Kilsoquah was also known as Angelique Rivarre. She was probably christened Angelique when she became a Catholic, which may have been at the time of her second marriage.

5. KALER and MARING, 81. WUNDERLICH shows Coesse's land as being 310 acres. It is labeled "Coesse Dec'd."

6. KALER and MARING, 81.

7. WILL, I, 252. A copy of the will was kindly furnished to me by Professor Paul A. Hutton.

8. KAPPLER, I, 171–74, 280.

9. CENSUS, 1850, 1860, 1870, for Miami County, Indiana. Copies were furnished to me courtesy of the Peru Public Library.

10. KAPPLER, I, 644.

11. CENSUS, 1850, 1860, 1870.

12. WINGER (1), 26, stated that Jane Wells was the sole child of William Wells and Little Turtle's daughter Sweet Breeze. This has been shown to be a mistaken view.

13. WILL, Inventories and Settlements, III, 31–33. Slavery was not legal in Indiana Territory; nevertheless, in the territorial period numerous slaves were held by many residents, including Governor Harrison. The male indenture was valued at twenty-five dollars per year; the female indenture at ten dollars per year.

14. HEITMAN, I, 975; ROBERTS, 6.

15. WILL, II, 495, 507. Copies of these wills were furnished to me by courtesy of Dr. William Sholty, along with other materials, including information recorded in the Geiger family bible.

16. THORNBROUGH (1), 248–49, 255–56.

17. HEITMAN, I, 485.

18. KAPPLER, I, 171–74, 278–81.

19. WENTWORTH, 46. Earlier they had been Baptists, converted by the missionary Isaac McCoy in 1820. Their younger sister, Mary Wolcott, was an Episcopalian.

20. KAPPLER, I, 425–28.

21. HEITMAN, I, 975.

22. KAPPLER, I, 641–46. The Miami in Kansas in 1854 were reported by the Office of Indian Affairs as numbering 250, the Wea and the Piankashaw together as 251, and the Peoria and the Kaskaskia together as 255. By contrast, the Delaware numbered 1,132, the Shawnee, 931, and the Potawatomi, 4,300. BARRY, 1196. For "Sis" Hackley, see ROBERTS, 6.

23. BARRY, 1190.

24. HEITMAN, I, 1018. William Henry Harrison had one son who became addicted to liquor; he was sent on a trapping expedition to the Rocky Mountains in hope of a cure that did not take place.

25. Major Heald died in 1832, and Rebecca Wells Heald died in 1857. DRAPER, 23S58–62.

26. WENTWORTH, 46.
27. L.T. and W., *Toledo Blade,* July 19, 1934.
28. BRICE, 296.
29. Quoted in FORT WAYNE, 71.

Bibliography

ABERNETHY   Abernethy, Thomas Perkins. *Western Lands and the American Revolution.* 1937.

ALVORD   Alvord, C. W., ed. *Kaskaskia Records, Illinois Historical Collections.* vol. 5. 1909.

ANSON   Anson, Bert. *The Miami Indians.* 1970.

APPLETON   Wilson, James Grant, and Fiske, John, eds. *Appletons' Cyclopaedia of American Biography.* 6 vols. 1888–89.

ASPIA   *American State Papers, Indian Affairs.* 2 vols. 1832–34.

ASPMA   *American State Papers, Military Affairs.* 7 vols. 1832–61.

BALD   Bald, F. Clever. "John Francis Hamtramck." *Indiana Magazine of History,* 44 (1948), 335–54.

BARCE   Barce, Elmore. *Land of the Miamis.* 1922.

BARNHART (1)   Barnhart, John D. "A New Letter about the Massacre at Fort Dearborn." *Indiana Magazine of History,* 61 (1945), 187–99. Sergeant Jordan's letter.

BARNHART (2)   Barnhart, John D., ed. *Henry Hamilton and George Rogers Clark in the American Revolution with the Unpublished Journal of Lieut. Gov. Henry Hamilton.* 1951.

BARNHART   Barnhart, John D., and Riker, Dorothy L. *Indiana to 1816: The
and RIKER   Colonial Period.* 1971.

BARRY   Barry, Louise. *The Beginning of the West.* 1972.

BEARD   Beard, Reed. *The Battle of Tippecanoe.* 1911.

BILLINGTON   Billington, Ray Allen. *Westward Expansion: A History of the American Frontier.* 1967.

BLAIR   Blair, Emma Helen, ed. *The Indian Tribes of the Upper Mississippi Valley and Region of the Great Lakes.* 2 vols. 1911–12. Accounts by Nicholas Perrot, Bacquille de la Potherie, and Thomas Forsyth.

255

BOWYER   *A Journal of Wayne's Campaign . . . by Lieutenant Boyer.* 1866 (original edition, 1844).

BRICE   Brice, Wallace A. *A History of Fort Wayne, from the Earliest Known Accounts of This Point, to the Present Period.* . . . 1868.

BRUNO   Colerick, Edward F. "The La Balme Raid on Kekionga, 1780." *Old Fort News,* 27, no. 1. 1964. Reprinted from the *Indianapolis News,* March 17 and April 7, 1892. Recollections of J. B. Bruno.

BUELL   Buell, Rowena, comp. *The Memoirs of Rufus Putnam and Certain Official Papers and Correspondence.* 1903.

BUFFALO   Wilson, George R., and Thornbrough, Gayle. "The Buffalo Trace." *Indiana Historical Society Publications,* 15, no. 1. 1936.

BUSSARD   Bussard, Herbert J., comp. *Miami Indian Language* (236-word vocabulary). (1962). Indiana Historical Society Library. Ms.

BUTLER   Butler, Mann. "An Outline of the Origin and Settlement of Louisville." In: *The Louisville Directory,* for the year 1832.

BUTTERFIELD   Butterfield, Consul Willshire. *History of the Girtys.* 1890.

CALLENDER   Callender, Charles. "Great Lakes-Riverine Socio-political Organization." In: W. C. Sturtevant, ed., *Handbook of the North American Indians.* vol. 15. 1972.

CARTER (1)   Carter, Clarence E., ed. *The Territorial Papers of the United States.* 26 vols. 1934–62. vols. 2 and 3, *Northwest Territory;* vols. 7 and 8, *Indiana Territory;* vol. 16, *Louisiana Territory.*

CARTER (2)   Carter, Harvey Lewis. "A Frontier Tragedy: Little Turtle and William Wells." *The Old Northwest,* 6 (1980), 3–18.

CENSUS   Manuscript Census of Miami County, Indiana, 1850, 1860, 1870. Peru Public Library. Photocopies.

CHAPUT   Chaput, Donald. "The Family of Drouet de Richerville: Merchants, Soldiers, and Chiefs of Indiana." *Indiana Magazine of History,* 74 (1978), 103–16.

CHARLEVOIX   Charlevoix, Pierre François Xavier de. *Letters to the Duchess of Lesdiguieres.* 1721.

CLARK   McGrane, Reginald C., ed. "Journal of General Anthony Wayne's Campaign . . . 1794–95." *Mississippi Valley Historical Review,* 1 (1914–15), 419–44.

CLIFTON   Clifton, James A. *The Prairie People: Continuity and Change in Potawatomi Indian Culture, 1665–1965.* 1976.

CORBIN   Quaife, Milo M., ed. "The Story of James Corbin, A Soldier of Fort Dearborn." *Mississippi Valley Historical Review,* 3 (1916–17), 219–28.

CROGHAN   "George Croghan's Journals, 1765." In: Reuben Gold Thwaites, ed., *Early Western Travels.* 32 vols. 1904–7. vol. 1, 124–69.

CRUIKSHANK   Cruikshank, E. A., ed. *The Correspondence of Lieutenant Governor John Graves Simcoe, with Allied Documents Relating to His Administration of the Government of Upper Canada.* 5 vols. 1923–31.

DAB   Johnson, Allen. *Dictionary of American Biography.* 23 vols. 1928–36.

DARLINGTON   Darlington, William M., ed. *The Journals of Christopher Gist.* 1893.

DAWSON   Dawson, Moses. *A Historical Narrative of the Civil and Military Services of Major-General William Henry Harrison.* . . . 1824.

DENNY   Denny, William H. "Military Journal of Major Ebenezer Denny . . . with an Introductory Memoir." *Historical Society of Pennsylvania Memoirs,* 7 (1860), 205–409.

DILLON   Dillon, John B. *A History of Indiana from Its Earliest Exploration by Europeans to 1816.* 1859.

DRAKE (1)   Drake, Benjamin. *Life of Tecumseh and His Brother the Prophet; With a Historical Sketch of the Shawanoe Indians.* 1841.

DRAKE (2)   Drake, Samuel G. *The Book of the Indians of North America.* 3d ed. 1834.

DRAPER   The Lyman Copeland Draper Collection. Wisconsin State Historical Society Library.

DUNBAR   Dunbar, Seymour. *A History of Travel in America.* 4 vols. 1915.

DUNN   Dunn, Jacob Piatt. *True Indian Stories.* 1909.

EDMUNDS (1)   Edmunds, R. David, ed. *American Indian Leaders: Studies in Diversity.* 1980.

EDMUNDS (2)   Edmunds, R. David. "Pickawillany: French Military Power versus English Economics." *Pennsylvania Historical Magazine,* 58 (1975), 169–84.

EDMUNDS (3)   Edmunds, R. David. *The Shawnee Prophet.* 1983.

EDMUNDS (4)   Edmunds, R. David. "Wea Participation in the Northwestern Indian Wars." *Filson Club History Quarterly,* 44 (1972), 241–53.

EDMUNDS (5)   Edmunds, R. David. *The Potawatomi: Keepers of the Fire.* 1977.

ESAREY   Esarey, Logan, ed. *Messages and Letters of William Henry Harrison.* Indiana Historical Collections. 1922. vol. 7 cited as ESAREY, I; vol. 9 cited as ESAREY, II.

FOREMAN   Foreman, Grant. *The Last Trek of the Indians.* 1946.

FORT WAYNE   Beckwith, Hiram W., ed. *The Fort Wayne Manuscript: An Old Writing (Lately Found) Containing Indian Speeches and a Treatise on the Western Indians.* 1883.

GIPSON   Gipson, Lawrence Henry. *The British Empire Before the American Revolution.* 10 vols. 1936–58. vol. 4 (1942), *Zones of International Friction . . . 1748–54.*

GOODMAN   Goodman, Alfred T., ed. *The Journal of Captain William Trent.* 1871.

GREEN   Green, James A. *William Henry Harrison: His Life and Times.* 1941.

GUERNSEY   Guernsey, E. Y. [Map of] *Indiana. The Influence of the Indian upon Its History—with Indian and French Names for Natural and Cultural Locations.* 1933.

GUTHMAN   Guthman, William H. *March to Massacre: A History of the First Seven Years of the United States Army, 1784–91.* 1975.

HANNA   Hanna, Charles A. *The Wilderness Trail.* 2 vols. 1911.

HAVIGHURST   Havighurst, Walter. *The Heartland: Ohio, Indiana, and Illinois.* 1962.

HAY   Quaife, Milo M., ed. "A Narrative of Life on the Old Frontier: Henry Hay's Journal. . . ." *Proceedings of the State Historical Society of Wisconsin,* 63 (1915), 208–61. Reprinted in *Indiana Historical Society Publications,* 7, no. 7. 1921.

HECKEWELDER   "Narrative of John Heckewelder's Journey to the Wabash in 1792." *Pennsylvania Magazine of History and Biography,* 9 (1887), 466–75; 11 (1888), 34–54, 165–84.

HEITMAN   Heitman, Francis B. *Historical Register and Dictionary of the United States Army.* 2 vols. 1903.

HILL   Hill, Leonard U. *John Johnston and the Indians in the Land of the Three Miamis.* 1957.

HODGE   Hodge, Frederick Webb, ed. *Handbook of American Indians North of Mexico.* 2 vols. 1907.

HOPKINS   Hopkins, Gerard T. *A Mission to the Indians from the Indian Committee of the Baltimore Yearly Meeting to Fort Wayne, in 1804. Written at the Time by Gerard T. Hopkins, with an Appendix, Compiled in 1862 by Martha E. Tyson.* 1862.

HORNADAY   Hornaday, William T. *The American Natural History.* 1927.

HORSMAN   Horsman, Reginald. *Matthew Elliott, British Indian Agent.* 1964.

HUNT   Hunt, George T. *The Wars of the Iroquois: A Study in Intertribal Relations.* 1960.

HUTTON   Hutton, Paul A. "William Wells: Frontier Scout and Indian Agent." *Indiana Magazine of History,* 74 (1978), 185–220.

HYDE   Hyde, George E. *Indians of the Woodlands from Prehistoric Times to 1725.* 1962.

IRVIN   Irvin, Thomas. [A Letter of] "Harmar's Campaign." *Ohio Archaeological and Historical Publications,* 19 (1910), 393–96.

JACKSON   Jackson, Donald. *Thomas Jefferson and the Stony Mountains: Exploring the West from Monticello.* 1981.

JACOBS (1)   Jacobs, James Ripley. *Tarnished Warrior: Major-General James Wilkinson.* 1938.

JACOBS (2)   Jacobs, James Ripley. *The Beginning of the U.S. Army, 1783–1812.* 1947.

JACOBS (3)   Jacobs, Wilbur R. *Diplomacy and Indian Gifts: Anglo-French Rivalry Along the Ohio and Northwest Frontiers.* 1950.

KALER and MARKING   Kaler, Samuel P., and Maring, R. H. *History of Whitley County, Indiana.* 1907.

KAPPLER   Kappler, Charles J., ed. *Indian Affairs, Laws and Treaties.* 2 vols. 1904.

KELLOGG   Kellogg, Louise Phelps, ed. *Early Narratives of the Northwest, 1634–99.* 1917.

KENTON	Kenton, Edna, ed. *Travels and Explorations of the Jesuit Missionaries in North America, 1610–1791.* 1925.
KINZIE	Kinzie, Mrs. John H. *Wau-Bun, the "Early Day" in the Northwest.* 1932 (original edition, 1844).
KIRKLAND	Kirkland, Joseph. *The Chicago Massacre of 1812.* 1893.
KNAPP	Knapp, H. S. *History of the Maumee Valley; Commencing with Its Occupation by the French in 1680.* 1872.
KNOPF	Knopf, Richard C., ed. *Anthony Wayne: A Name in Arms, . . . The Wayne–Knox–Pickering–McHenry Correspondence.* 1960.
KRAUSKOPF	Krauskopf, Frances, ed. *Ouiatanon Documents, Indiana Historical Society Publications,* 18, no. 2. 1955.
LRSW	Record Group 107. Records of the Office of the Secretary of War. Letters Received, Registered Series. Letters Received, Unregistered Series. . . . The National Archives. Microfilm.
L.T and W.	Little Turtle and William Wells Files. Fort Wayne Public Library. Newspaper clippings.
MACKINAC	Williams, Meade C. *Early Mackinac.* 1898.
MCDONALD	McDonald, John. *Biographical Sketches of General Nathaniel Massie, General Duncan McArthur, Captain William Wells and General Simon Kenton.* . . . 1852 (original edition, 1838).
MCFARLAND	McFarland, R. W. "Forts Loramie and Pickawillany." *Ohio Archaeological and Historical Society Publications,* 8 (1899), 479–88.
MCMASTER	McMaster, John Bach. *A History of the People of the United States.* 8 vols. 1885–1913. vol. 1.
MEEK	Meek, Basil. "Harmar's Expedition." *Ohio State Archaeological and Historical Quarterly,* 20 (1911), 74–108.
MIAMI	Callender, Charles. "Miami." In: W. C. Sturtevant, ed., *Handbook of North American Indians.* vol. 15. 1978.
MICHIGAN	*Michigan Pioneer and Historical Collections,* 10 (1886); 19 (1891); 20 (1892); 23 (1893).
MOHICAN	Brasser, T. J. "Mohican." In: W. C. Sturtevant, ed., *Handbook of North American Indians.* vol. 15. 1978.
MORRIS (1)	"The Journal of Captain Thomas Morris 1764." *Old Fort News,* 6, no. 1. 1941.
MORRIS (2)	"Journal of Captain Thomas Morris." In: Reuben Gold Thwaites, ed., *Early Western Travels.* 32 vols. 1904–7. vol. 1, 293–328.
NILES	*Niles' Weekly Register* (1811–49). vol. 3. 1812.
NORTHWEST	Northwest Territory Collection. Indiana Historical Society Library.
OUIATENON	Kellar, James H. "The Search For Ouiatenon." *Indiana History Bulletin,* 47 (1970), 123–33.
PARKMAN	Parkman, Francis. *La Salle and the Discovery of the Great West.* 1911 (original edition, 1869).
PAXSON	Paxson, Frederic Logan. *History of the American Frontier, 1763–1893.* 1924.

259

PECKHAM (1)   Peckham, Howard H. *Captured by Indians.* 1954.
PECKHAM (2)   Peckham, Howard H. *Pontiac and the Indian Uprising.* 1947.
PECKHAM (3)   Peckham, Howard H. "Josiah Harmar and his Indian Expedi-
                tion." *Ohio Archaeological and Historical Quarterly,* 55 (1946),
                227–41.
PENNSYLVANIA   *Pennsylvania Colonial Records: Minutes of the Provincial Coun-
                cil of Pennsylvania.* 16 vols. 1861. vol. 5.
PHILBRICK   Philbrick, Francis S. *The Rise of the West, 1754–1830.* 1965.
PHILLIPS   Phillips, Paul C. "Vincennes in Its Relation to French Colonial
                Policy." *Indiana Magazine of History,* 17 (1921), 311–18.
PIRTLE   Pirtle, Alfred. *The Battle of Tippecanoe.* 1900.
POPE   Pope, Clifford. *Turtles of the United States and Canada.* 1939.
PRUCHA   Prucha, Francis Paul. *American Indian Policy in the Formative
                Years: The Indian Trade and Intercourse Acts, 1790-1834.* 1962.
QUAIFE (1)   Quaife, Milo M. *Chicago and the Old Northwest.* 1913.
QUAIFE (2)   Quaife, Milo M., ed. *The Indian Captivity of O. M. Spencer.*
                1968.
QUIMBY   Quimby, George Irving. *Indian Life in the Upper Great Lakes.*
                1960.
ROOSEVELT   Roosevelt, Theodore. *The Winning of the West.* 6 vols. 1889.
                vol. 5.
ROBERTS   Roberts, Bessie Keeran. "William Wells: A Legend in the Coun-
                cils of Two Nations." *Old Fort News,* 17, nos. 3 and 4. 1954.
ROBERTSON   Robertson, J. Ross, ed. *The Diary of Mrs. John Graves Simcoe,
                1792–96.* 1911.
ROY   Roy, Pierre-Georges. "Sieur de Vincennes Identified." *Indiana
                Historical Society Publications,* 7, no. 1. 1923.
SABREVOIS   Mémoire donné par M. de Sabrevois sur les Sauvages du Canada
                jusqu'a la rivière du Mississippi, sur les moeurs et le négoce des
                ces Sauvages (1718). MGI, Series C "A," vol. 39, fol. 354–61v.
                Public Archives of Canada. Photocopy.
SAGAMORE   Guthrie, James M. *Sesquicentennial Scrapbook* [of Indiana]. 1966.
ST. CLAIR   Smith, William H. *The St. Clair Papers.* 2 vols. 1882.
SARGENT   Sargent, Charles. "Winthrop Sargent's Diary While with General
                Arthur St. Clair's Expedition Against the Indians." *Ohio State
                Archaeological and Historical Society Publications,* 33 (1924),
                237–73.
SCHOOLCRAFT   Schoolcraft, Henry Rowe. *Personal Memoirs of a Residence of
                Thirty Years with the Indian Tribes of the American Frontiers.*
                1851.
SHEEHAN (1)   Sheehan, Bernard W. *Seeds of Extinction: Jeffersonian Philan-
                thropy and the American Indian.* 1973.
SHEEHAN (2)   Sheehan, Bernard W. "The Famous Hair Buyer General: Henry
                Hamilton, George Rogers Clark and the American Indian." *In-
                diana Magazine of History,* 79 (1983), 1–28.
SHEER   Sheer, Luke J. *The Ouiatenon Miami Before 1717.* 1979.

SLOCUM   Slocum, Charles Elihu. *A History of the Maumee River Basin.* 1905.

SMITH (1)   Smith, Dwight L., ed. "From Greene Ville to Fallen Timbers: A Journal of the Wayne Campaign." *Indiana Historical Society Publications,* 16, no. 3. 1952.

SMITH (2)   Smith, Dwight L. "Notes on the Wabash River, 1795." *Indiana Magazine of History,* 50 (1954), 277–91.

SMITH (3)   Smith, Dwight L. "William Wells and the Indian Council of 1793." *Indiana Magazine of History,* 56 (1960), 217–26.

STONE   Stone, William L. *The Life of Joseph Brant—Thayendanegea.* 2 vols. 1838.

SYMPOSIUM (1)   "The French, the Indians, and George Rogers Clark in the Illinois Country." *Proceedings of an Indiana American Revolution Bicentennial Symposium.* 1977.

SYMPOSIUM (2)   "This Land of Ours: The Acquisiton and Disposition of the Public Domain." *Papers Presented at an Indiana American Revolution Symposium.* 1978.

TANNER   Tanner, Helen Hornbeck. "The Glaize in 1792: A Composite Indian Community." *Ethnohistory,* 25 (Winter 1978), 15–39.

TECUMSEH   Eggleston, Edward, and Seelye, Lillie Eggleston. *Tecumseh and the Shawnee Prophet.* 1878.

THORNBROUGH (1) Thornbrough, Gayle, ed. "Letter Book of the Indian Agency at Fort Wayne, 1809–15." *Indiana Historical Society Publications,* 21. 1961.

THORNBROUGH (2) Thornbrough, Gayle, ed. "The Correspondence of John Badollet and Albert Gallatin, 1804–36." *Indiana Historical Society Publications,* 22. 1963.

THORNBROUGH (3) Thornbrough, Gayle, ed. "Outpost on the Wabash, 1789–91." *Indiana Historical Society Publications,* 19. 1957.

THORNTON   Vocabulary of the Miami Language taken at the City of Washington, 11 Jan.y 1802 in part from Little Turtle, but principally from Capt. Wells, the Interpreter By William Thornton. Communicated by Mr. Jefferson. American Philosophical Society Library. Photocopy.

THWAITES (1)   Thwaites, Reuben Gold, ed. "The French Regime in Wisconsin." *Wisconsin Historical Society Collections,* vols. 16, 17, 18. 1904–6.

THWAITES (2)   Thwaites, Reuben Gold, ed. *The Jesuit Relations and Allied Documents, 1610–71.* 73 vols. 1896–1901. vol. 54.

TROWBRIDGE   Trowbridge, C. C. *Meearmeear Traditions.* 1824. (Vernon Kineitz, ed., 1938).

TURNER   A Discription of the Emigration, Habits, etc. of the N. Western Indians. as received from the most Intelligent and Ancient Indians. By William Turner of Welsington for his Friend, Major Francis S. Bretton of Detroit. 1817. Ayer Ms. 589. The Newberry Library. Transcript.

261

UNDERWOOD — Shepard, Lee, ed. *Journal, Thomas Taylor Underwood, March 26, 1792 to March 18, 1800: An Old Soldier in Wayne's Army.* 1945.

VAN EVERY — Van Every, Dale. *Ark of Empire: The American Frontier, 1784–1803.* 1963.

VOLNEY — Volney, Constantin F. *A View of the Soil and Climate of the United States of America.* 1968 (original edition, 1804).

WALAM OLUM — *Walam Olum or Red Score. The Migration Legend of the Lenni Lenape or Delaware Indians.* 1954.

WATCH — "Little Turtle's Watch." *Northwest Ohio Quarterly,* 38 (1965), 17–32.

WENTWORTH — Wentworth, John. *Early Chicago: Fort Dearborn, an Address delivered at the Unveiling of the Memorial Tablet . . . May 21, 1881. . . .* 1881.

WESLAGER — Weslager, C. A. *The Delaware Indians: A History.* 1972.

WHITLEY — *Bulletin of the Whitley County* [Indiana] *Historical Society.* February 1967; April 1970; June 1970; August 1971; June 1973; February 1974; December 1976; October 1980.

WHITSETT — Whitsett, Robert B., Jr. "Snake-Fish Town, the Eighteenth Century Metropolis of Little Turtle's Eel River Miami." *Indiana History Bulletin,* 15 (1938), 72–82.

WILKINSON — Wilkinson, James. *Memoirs of My Own Times.* 3 vols. 1816.

WILL — Jefferson County [Kentucky] Will Book. vols. 1, 2, 3.

WILLIAMS — Williams, Mentor L. "John Kinzie's Narrative of the Fort Dearborn Massacre." *Journal of the Illinois State Historical Society,* 46 (1953), 343–52.

WILSON — Wilson, Frazer E., ed. *Journal of Captain Daniel Bradley.* 1935.

WINGER (1) — Winger, Otho. *Little Turtle: The Great Chief of Eel River.* 1942.

WINGER (2) — Winger, Otho. *The Last of the Miamis.* 1935.

WINTER — *The Journals and Indian Paintings of George Winter.* 1948.

WOEHRMANN — Woehrmann, Paul W. "At the Headwaters of the Maumee. A History of the Forts at Fort Wayne." *Indiana Historical Society Publications,* 24. 1971.

WRIGHT — Wright, Muriel H. *A Guide to the Indian Tribes of Oklahoma.* 1951.

WUNDERLICH — Wunderlich, S. H. *Map of Whitley County, Indiana compiled from surveys and old records.* 1862.

YOUNG (1) — Young, Calvin D. *Little Turtle (Me-she-kin-no-quah), The Great Chief of the Miami Indian Nation.* 1917.

YOUNG (2) — Young, Calvin D. "The Birthplace of Little Turtle." *Ohio Archaeological and Historical Publications,* 23 (1914), 105–49.

Index

A Note on the Author

HARVEY LEWIS CARTER is emeritus professor of history at Colorado College. A Hoosier by birth, he was educated at Wabash College and the University of Wisconsin, from which he received a Ph.D. in 1938. The author of numerous articles and reviews in various history journals, he has also written *"Dear Old Kit": The Historical Christopher Carson* (1968) and most recently (with Thelma Guild) *Kit Carson: A Pattern for Heroes* (1984). An honorary life membership was conferred on him by the Western History Association in 1975 and an honorary L.H.D. degree by Wabash College in 1978. In 1986 Gov. Robert D. Orr of Indiana named Harvey Carter a Sagamore of the Wabash.